Private Equity Demystified

This book deals with risk capital provided for established firms outside the stock market, private equity, which has grown rapidly over the last three decades, yet is largely poorly understood. Although it has often been criticized in the public mind as being short-termist and having adverse consequences for employment, in reality this is far from the case. Here, John Gilligan and Mike Wright dispel some of the biggest myths and misconceptions about private equity. This book provides a unique and authoritative source from a leading practitioner and academic for practitioners, policymakers, and researchers that explains in detail what private equity involves and reviews systematic evidence of what the impact of private equity has been. Written in a highly accessible style, the book takes the reader through what private equity means, the different actors involved, and issues concerning sourcing, checking out, valuing, and structuring deals. The various themes from the extensive systematic academic evidence are highlighted in numerous summary vignettes placed alongside the text relating to the practical aspects. The main part of the work concludes with an up-to-date discussion by the authors, informed commentators on the key issues in the lively debate about private equity. The book contains further summary tables of the academic research carried out over the past three decades across the private equity landscape including the returns to investors, economic performance, impact on R&D and employees, and the longevity and life-cycle of private equity backed deals.

John Gilligan is the Director of the Oxford Saïd Finance Lab at Saïd Business School, University of Oxford, Visiting Professor at Imperial College Business School, and a non-executive director and Investment Committee member of Big Issue Invest.

Mike Wright founded the Centre for Management Buy-out Research, CMBOR, in 1986, and was Professor of Entrepreneurship at Imperial College Business School and Chair of the Society for the Advancement of Management Studies.

Private Equity Demystified

An explanatory guide

Fourth Edition

JOHN GILLIGAN AND MIKE WRIGHT

OXFORD
UNIVERSITY PRESS

Great Clarendon Street, Oxford, OX2 6DP,
United Kingdom

Oxford University Press is a department of the University of Oxford.
It furthers the University's objective of excellence in research, scholarship,
and education by publishing worldwide. Oxford is a registered trade mark of
Oxford University Press in the UK and in certain other countries

This edition first published in 2020
Previous editions published in 2008, 2010, and 2014 by the
Institute of Chartered Accountants in England and Wales

Published in the United States of America by Oxford University Press
198 Madison Avenue, New York, NY 10016, United States of America

British Library Cataloguing in Publication Data
Data available

Library of Congress Control Number: 2020935590

ISBN 978-0-19-886696-1 (hbk.)
ISBN 978-0-19-886699-2 (pbk.)

Printed and bound by
CPI Group (UK) Ltd, Croydon, CR0 4YY

Mike died in November 2019, a few weeks after this edition of
Private Equity Demystified *was submitted to the publishers.*
He was a great researcher, teacher, and friend. Many academics, institutions, students,
and friends owe him a debt of gratitude. My life would have been different, and worse, if
I hadn't known him. I owe him a great deal and will miss him.
He will be remembered for his enduring contribution to academic research and his
generous contribution to life and the lives of others.

John Gilligan
27 November 2019

Praise for Private Equity Demystified

'Mike Wright was one of the towering figures in the field of private equity. He pioneered rigorous data analysis of buyouts and private equity a long time before it became fashionable to do so and stimulated a vast body of research on the subject as a consequence. This book exemplifies the major contribution that Mike made to the field.'

Colin Mayer CBE FBA, Peter Moores Professor of Management Studies at the Saïd Business School, University of Oxford

'As private equity's influence continues to swell all of our lives are now inextricably linked to the asset class. It has never been more important to remove the barriers and complexities private equity often seeks to hide behind. *Private Equity Demystified* is therefore essential reading for each and every one of us to ensure this asset class is kept in check.'

Alice Murray, Editor, The Drawdown

'Demystifying the private equity industry - specifically leveraged buyouts - is no small feat, requiring exceptional expertise, powerful insight and great depths of knowledge. Gilligan and Wright display it all, as they take the reader through what is a thorough explanatory guide that Invest Europe recommends most highly.'

Eric de Montgolfier, Chief Executive Officer, Invest Europe

'Much is written about private equity and a lot of it, even the articles in certain major newspapers, can be extremely superficial or ill informed. This publication is the antithesis of such coverage of the subject. The book is thorough, considered and balanced. John Gilligan's experience as a practitioner and the huge body of data compiled by CMBOR under the leadership of the late Mike Wright are blended together to make it very readable despite tackling quite complex concepts. This book should be a must-read for people aspiring to either work in private equity or cover private equity news.'

Neil Macdougall, Chair of Silverfleet Capital and Chair of BVCA

'If you are looking for a book that provides you with a full picture of the structure and economics of private equity there is no finer source. The text covers the history of the field, its economic role, a balanced view of its merits and results, and a great deal of vital information on how deals are done and investments made to prosper. Its bang up to date with lots of new content especially on the recent explosion of the use of fund leverage. Simply excellent.'

Jon Moulton, Chair of finnCap and of The International Stock Exchange, member of the board of the ICAEW Corporate Finance Faculty

'This book is an outstanding effort to describe a complex topic by a practitioner and a special scholar. It is Mike Wright's last piece of published work. He was an exceptionally kind man, whose body of work is one of the most extensive contributions to the field of private equity. He will be missed.'

Ludovic Phalippou, Professor of Financial Economics at Saïd Business School, University of Oxford

'The new edition of *Private Equity Demystified* addresses critical questions about the role of private equity at a crucial time for global economic and social recovery. Well-directed capital should support a sustainable recovery and allow businesses around the world to build back better.'

Michael Izza, Chief Executive, ICAEW

'*Private Equity Demystified* is an extraordinarily comprehensive compendium of information on private equity. It provides a detailed analysis of how private equity funds operate, how and why they are structured the way they are, and how they can provide value for investors and society. The book is an important resource for investors and other market participants, and a useful handbook for academic scholars that study private equity.'

Wayne Landsman, KPMG Distinguished Professor of Accounting, Kenan-Flagler Business School, University of North Carolina at Chapel Hill

'I only wish all commentators had such an informed and balanced view of a complicated area. I gave it to my sons to explain what I do for a living – I can think of no higher praise.'

Philip Rattle, Managing Partner, August Equity

Preface to the Fourth Edition

For over two decades, from the early 1980s, the developing private equity industry largely flew below the radar of public scrutiny. In 2007 the private equity industry came under intense public scrutiny including a House of Commons Select Committee inquiry and a Senate inquiry in the US. The first edition of *Private Equity Demystified* was published with the ICAEW in August 2008. There followed a period of unprecedented financial turmoil.

The second edition built on the first edition to reflect the effects of the recession, and examined the way in which the banking market changed its approach to private equity investments. It also included more discussion of both mid-market buyouts and the dynamics of the restructuring industry. There was an update to the second edition in 2012 to reflect the developments in private equity as the recession came to an end.

The third edition was published against a backdrop of new regulation on both sides of the Atlantic. The European Commission's Alternative Investment Fund Managers Directive covering private equity funds was implemented.

A burgeoning body of academic evidence also continues to provide systematic insights as to the impact of private equity.

In this fourth edition we have taken the opportunity to make a thorough revision of earlier editions and to write extensively on the changes to both the private equity and the private debt markets.

The financial crisis rewrote the book on debt markets, on both sides of the Atlantic. Over a decade on from that crisis the implications of sustained low interest rates and new debt market participants are profound. We discuss this is in an extensive new section.

The levels of debt we see in the market today are as high as they have ever been. With low interest rates this may be sustainable. If interest rates return to market-driven levels in the developed economies interest cover will fall and the cost of capital will rise. A rise in the cost of capital will cause a fall in financial asset prices and an increase in interest costs will stress cash flows. This is the scenario that many are trying to assess in terms of likelihood, timing, and severity.

As we forecast in the very first edition, the liquidity needs of various market participants have had major impacts on the old simple model of long-term commitments and tightly aligned returns. To reflect this, we have expanded and deepened our look into the often opaque world of fund management agreements.

Over the years we have made these points repeatedly:

– private equity before fees has been a winner, but who got those gains varies greatly. We expand extensively on this in a new section looking at the proliferation of measures trying to assess private equity performance;

– long-term commitments with no liquidity mismatches stopped the spread of financial contagion in the crisis.

These conclusions are not as firm as they were, but the evidence that we have to date has not yet overturned them. We remain of the view that the success of private equity as an industry is based on sound ideas and sound historic data. We acknowledge that in any rapidly growing and financially lucrative new industry there is the possibility for abuses, and we highlight areas where they have been identified.

We remain of the view that it is the role of regulators to constrain behaviours that society wishes to curtail. These regulators have relentlessly acted to rein in what are characterized as excesses in the private equity sphere (and others), but as the world changes continuously, their work is never ending.

We sent this manuscript to the publishers knowing that we are at the top of a market that has always been cyclical.

John Gilligan and Mike Wright

November 2019

Acknowledgements

Over the twelve years we have been writing the various editions of this book, we have benefited immeasurably from the support, challenge and positive criticism of many people, including reviewers, students and colleagues within both Oxford Saïd Business School and the Centre for Management Buyout Research at Imperial College as well as BDO and many other people. ICAEW and its Corporate Finance Faculty have supported us from the very first edition.

The Corporate Finance Faculty and its members have been instrumental to our work on demystifying private equity. Chris Ward, Chairman of the ICAEW Corporate Finance Faculty from 2004 to 2008, not only saw the need for the first book in 2007, but tirelessly reviewed many early drafts with an eye for both detail and the big picture second to none. Jon Moulton, Chairman, finnCap has reviewed and challenged us on each edition. Both have given far more of their time over the years than we could have expected and they could have anticipated when we first started.

Mark O'Hare, Katherine Whale, and Chris Elvin of Preqin provided data on the private equity and private debt markets to this and earlier editions.

Adam Frais and James Pratt of BDO contributed materially to the sections on taxation aspects in this and earlier editions.

We also thank Chris Lowe (EY), Chris McDermott (Coller Capital), Fenton Burgin (Deloitte), Mo Merali (Grant Thornton), Roger Gregory (BDB Pitmans), Maurice Dwyer, Steve Tudge of ECI, Vijay Gupta (EY), James Ranger (Lloyds Bank), and Jim Strang (Hamilton Lane).

Without David Petrie, Shaun Beaney, and especially Katerina Joannou of ICAEW the report would never have seen the light of day. The support of OUP has been invaluable in taking the book forward and we are grateful for their work and support.

In the absence of any tangible reward we offer our sincere thanks to all of these people and the many others who have helped us over the years.

All errors and omissions are entirely our own responsibility.

Contents

List of Figures

List of Tables

About the Authors

John Gilligan has worked in the private equity and venture capital industry for over thirty years.

He started his career in 1988 at 3i Group plc as a financial analyst. He was a Corporate Finance Partner of Deloitte and latterly BDO for over twenty years. He is the Director of the Oxford Saïd Finance Lab at Saïd Business School, a non-executive director and Investment Committee member of Big Issue Invest, one of the largest social impact investors in the UK.

He is also a visiting professor at Imperial College Business School and has degrees from Southampton University, Nottingham University, and London Business School.

Mike Wright pioneered research into management buyouts and private equity. He founded the Centre for Management Buyout Research, CMBOR, in 1986.

He was Professor of Entrepreneurship at Imperial College Business School and Chair of the Society for the Advancement of Management Studies. He published extensively on entrepreneurial ownership mobility and finance in leading academic journals and has over 81,000 Google Scholar citations. His books include *Accelerators: Successful Venture Creation and Growth* (2018), *The Routledge Companion to Management Buyouts* (2018), *Student Start-Ups: The New Landscape of Academic Entrepreneurship* (2019), and *How to Get Published in the Top Management Journals* (2019). He edited several journals and was an editor of Foundations and Trends in Entrepreneurship. He was a member of the British Venture Capital Association Research Advisory Committee. Mike died in 2019 shortly after this book was finished.

1

The Private Equity Market

In this chapter we set the scene: we clarify some definitions, describe the origins of the private equity market, and examine the data on the size and growth of the private equity industry.

What is Private Equity?

'Private'

Private equity (PE) is risk capital provided outside the public markets. It is worth emphasizing at this early stage that the word 'private' has nothing to do with secrecy. It simply contrasts with the 'public' quoted markets. Public markets offer shares to institutions and individuals and are accordingly regulated.

Private transactions are not unregulated, but they are regulated differently. The idea is that public markets provide protections appropriate to individuals whereas the regulation of private markets is appropriate to the parties to those transactions, who are usually, but not always, sophisticated institutions and high net worth individuals.

'Equity'

Equity is the umbrella term under which you find an array of financial instruments that equitably share in the profits and losses of a business. Traditionally equity has been defined as a residual claim on the profits and assets of a business after all other claims have been settled. It has usually been seen as being synonymous with 'ordinary shares' or 'common stock'. It is still the convention to refer to an equity percentage meaning the percentage of ordinary shares or common stock held. However, as we will expand upon, equity has a broader meaning when used in the phrase 'private equity'. It means the total amount of capital that is both put at risk of loss in a transaction and that, as a financial package, has a share in any capital gain earned. As we shall elaborate in Chapters 5 and 6, a private equity investment will often be in the form of both ordinary shares and loans and may well include a variety of exotic financial instruments.

The key idea to focus on is that the 'equity' in private equity is a package of financial instruments.

Private Equity Demystified: An explanatory guide. Fourth Edition. John Gilligan and Mike Wright, Oxford University Press (2020).
© John Gilligan & Mike Wright. DOI: 10.1093/oso/9780198866961.003.0001

What Is the Difference between Venture Capital, Growth Capital, and Private Equity?

The businesses invested in by private equity range from early-stage ventures, usually termed venture capital investments, through businesses requiring growth or development capital to the purchase of an established business in a management buyout or buy-in. In this sense private equity is a generic term that incorporates venture, growth, and buyout capital (see Figure 1.1). However, while all of these cases involve private equity, the term is now often used to refer to both later-stage development capital and, predominantly, buyouts of established businesses. These are generally the focus of our commentary, although we will also comment on the resurgent growth capital sector when relevant. Private equity usually contrasts with Venture Capital which is used to describe early-stage investments.

The term therefore has a confusingly loose definition, being both a generic term for 'not quoted equity' and a more precise definition referring specifically to the market for institutional private equity funds that target buyouts and growth capital. Care is needed to be clear which definition is being used when discussing or researching private equity.

Each of these categories is known as an 'investment strategy'. Buyouts constitute the largest of the investment strategies by value. They account for the majority of primary deal value and, when secondary strategies are included, they represent some 40 per cent of the private equity market value (Figure 1.2).

The evolution of the term is perhaps best illustrated by the naming of the various trade bodies: the British Private Equity and Venture Capital Association (originally, the British Venture Capital Association), BVCA, is the UK trade association; EVCA, which is the European trade body, renamed itself 'Invest Europe' in 2015.

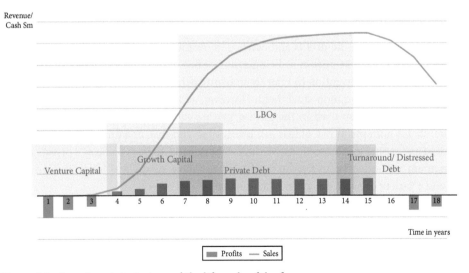

Figure 1.1. Investment strategies and the life cycle of the firm

AGGREGATED CAPITAL RAISED IN 2018 BY FUND STRATEGY

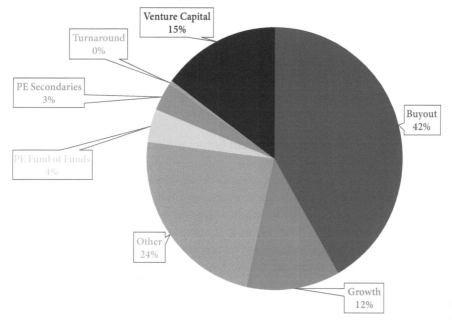

Figure 1.2. Relative size of different private equity investment strategies
Source: Preqin

What Do Private Equity Fund Managers Do?

Private equity fund managers have five principal roles.

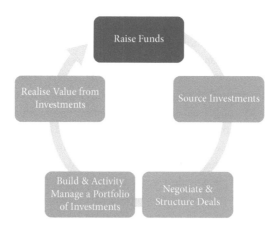

Raise Funds from Investors

These funds are used to make investments, principally in businesses which are, or will become, private companies. Funds are raised from investors, often internationally, such as pension funds, insurance funds, foundations, family offices, banks, and insurance companies. There are collective ways for individuals to invest in private equity in some countries, but generally most money comes from institutions. These investors will generally invest via a limited partnership, as will the private equity fund managers themselves. In Chapter 2 we expand on the fund management roles of private equity. Increasingly, as discussed later, some large fund managers are becoming multi-asset managers with contracts to manage a variety of fund types including, but not exclusively, private equity.

Source Investment Opportunities

A private equity fund must source and complete successful transactions to generate profit and support the raising of further funds. A significant amount of effort and resource is invested in prospecting for transactions and relationship management with individuals who may give access to deals. In addition to potential investee companies, these relationships include investment bankers, lawyers, accountants, and other advisers and senior figures in industry.

Increasingly, investment teams are focusing on particular sectors of the economy. Historically most funds were geographically constrained to their local market. Today we see global private equity funds.

The holy grail of private equity is to have a strong source of so-called proprietary deal flow. This is a rich seam of transactions that can be completed without a competitive process being run on behalf of the vendor. An increasing amount of effort is going into direct targeting of businesses, meeting them ahead of any potential transaction to build knowledge and relationships and, potentially, investments outside of full-blown intermediary-led processes.

Negotiate, Structure, and Make Investments

Having found investment opportunities, private equity fund managers have to negotiate the acquisition and structure the finances of the transaction to achieve the multiple objectives of the various parties. Fund managers therefore need skilled financial engineers and negotiators in their team to create the desired blend of incentives and returns while managing the associated risks. In the early days of private equity, fund managers were usually financial experts rather than sector or operational management specialists. This has changed over the years. It is argued by advocates of private equity that this trend has contributed to the development of more effective management techniques within its investments. In Chapter 5 we explain the basics of deal structuring and we provide a worked illustration in Chapter 6.

Private equity uses third-party debt to amplify investment returns (see Chapter 2). Fund managers therefore need to be skilled in creating financial packages that generate the required blend of incentives without creating excessive risk.

Actively Manage a Portfolio of Investments

Private equity fund managers have become hands-on managers of their investments. While they do not generally exercise day-to-day control, they are actively involved in selecting management teams and setting and monitoring the implementation of strategy.

This is the basis of the argument that private equity has become an alternative model of corporate governance. The growth in the operating partner groups who focus purely on the performance of portfolio companies is indicative of the growing importance of active management of PE investments.

Realize Returns

Fund managers realize returns primarily through capital gains by selling or floating private equity investments, but also from income and dividend recapitalizations, which we examine in Chapter 3. The vast majority of PE exits are to trade buyers or other PE funds. The industry generally now talks of a four- to six-year exit horizon, meaning that the investment will be made with the explicit assumption that it will be sold or floated within that timeframe. This exit horizon is the source of the criticism that private equity is a short-term investment strategy. Private equity managers often work out their likely exit routes before they make any investment.

There are pressures to vary the length of fund lives, either shortening (by providing liquidity in the secondary market) or extending the life of the fund. These create new issues that we discuss in Chapter 3. Much of the change in private equity investment over the past few years has been in fund management strategies, both by PE fund managers and by their investors.

What Is a Private Equity Fund?

Much, but not all, of the investing done in the private equity market is by private equity funds. A PE fund is a form of 'investment club' in which the principal investors are institutional investors such as pension funds, investment funds, endowment funds, insurance companies, banks, family offices, high net worth individuals, or funds of funds, as well as the private equity fund managers themselves. The objective of a PE fund is to invest equity or risk capital in a portfolio of private companies which are identified and researched by the PE fund managers. Private equity funds are generally designed to generate capital profits from the sale of investments rather than income from dividends, fees, and interest payments, although this has changed over the years as new forms of PE vehicles have emerged. We discuss this further in Chapter 2.

A Private equity fund may take minority or majority stakes in its investments, though generally it will be the latter in the larger buyouts. At the same time that a Private equity fund makes an investment in a private company, there is usually some bank debt or other debt capital raised to meet part of the capital required to fund the acquisition. This debt is the 'leverage' of a leveraged buyout.

What Are the Objectives of Private Equity Investment?

An alternative definition views private equity as institutional investors who buy businesses with the explicit intention of selling them when the business is acquired.[1] This definition

---

[1] Jeremy Coller, founder of Coller Capital, 2019.

provides a useful way of thinking of the industry and has the advantage of capturing all types of fund structures.

Obviously, all purely financial investors wish to make a return. This can be either an income, from fees, interest, or dividends, or a capital gain by selling a particular investment when it has become more valuable. Private equity is predominantly about generating capital gains. The idea is to buy equity stakes in businesses, actively managing those businesses and then realizing the value created by selling or floating the whole business on a public market. The appetite and incentives of most private equity investors are firmly focused on achieving capital gains. They generally aim to achieve capital growth, not income. The objective of private equity is therefore clearly focused on increasing shareholder value.

This contrasts with other investors who buy businesses aiming to own them forever and generate their return by taking out cash in dividends.

Are There Any Theoretical Ideas behind the Private Equity Investment Model?

Private equity has been widely studied for many years. If you went to Google Scholar and typed in 'private equity' you would find around 215,000 references, of which about 20,000 were added in the last two years. Volume is no measure of quality, but it does point to interest. A Google Ngram search on the same term shows the rising levels of interest in books in English since the term emerged in the late 1980s (Figure 1.3).

The Paradox of Private Equity Performance

Historically the returns in private equity have been consistently reported as being higher than those in public markets. The assertion of outperformance is itself controversial, but it is certainly true that outperformance is widely claimed and demonstrated, using a variety of methods. Some of these methods are disingenuous, some questionable, but the data are consistent, if surprising. We discuss this in Chapter 3.

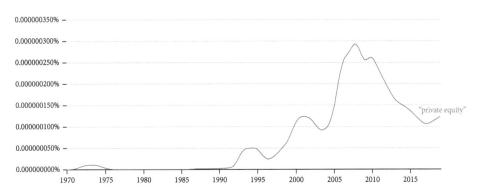

Figure 1.3. Google Ngram on 'private equity', 1970–2010
Source: Google

A second surprising thing about private equity is that this outperformance is found in funds that are highly active in the mergers and acquisitions (M&A) market. The majority of academic evidence, with some recent exceptions, has shown that businesses that are active in the M&A market destroy shareholder value. How is it then, that PE funds, whose core competence is in M&A, seem able to buck that trend?

Furthermore, most private equity funds are buying control of a business in a competitive auction, and the evidence on auctions is again clear: there is usually a 'winner's curse' in any competitive auction because the most optimistic bidder with funds, always wins.[2]

There have been a number of arguments put forward to explain the apparent success of the private equity model of investing.

Seekers of Market Failure

The first and simplest is that private equity seeks out and takes advantage of market failures that create mispricing opportunities. This argument encompasses both a trading strategy, taking advantage of periodic mispricing, and an active search for financial gain by taking advantage of so-called 'loopholes'.

One particular version of this argument that is widely discussed is the question of what impact the tax deductibility of interest has on investment returns. It is worth saying at this early stage that not all interest is deductible against tax and that there are no special exemptions for private equity of any kind. On the contrary, there are in many countries special provisions designed to disallow the deductibility of interest on connected party loans of the type used by PE firms. We revisit the critics' version of this argument in more detail below.

Solving the Principal–Agent Problem

The second and more widely accepted economic theory in the academic literature argues that there is a principal–agent problem in many companies.[3] The shareholders are the principals (i.e. owners) of any corporation. Managers act as agents of shareholders. Managers are incentivized by whatever their employment contracts motivate. They are not generally incentivized to maximize the realizable value to the shareholders. Furthermore, there is no clear way to hold management to account for their actions. In consequence shareholders do not try to hold managers to account. If they do not believe the managers are maximizing value, in publicly traded companies, investors simply sell the shares and move on. Shareholders in private companies that are managed by agents on their behalf will, under this hypothesis, receive lower returns than they otherwise might have received. It is argued that this lack of accountability of senior managers allows them to pursue projects that are either excessively risky or, conversely, excessively conservative. This represents an inefficiency of the market.

[2] Richard H. Thaler (1988), 'Anomalies: The winner's curse', *Journal of Economic Perspectives* 2(1): 191–202.
[3] Michael C. Jensen and William H. Meckling (October 1976), 'Theory of the firm: Managerial behavior, agency costs and ownership structure', *Journal of Financial Economics* 3(4): 305–60.

Private equity seeks to address this principal–agent problem by tightly aligning the interests of managers and shareholders to achieve economic efficiencies over a defined time period. This idea of alignment is central to all the economic structures observed in the private equity market. We expand upon how this alignment is created throughout the main body of the book.

Private equity therefore seeks to address one of the central problems facing what is known as corporate governance: how do shareholders incentivize managers to maximize value and make them accountable for the outcome of their decisions?

Some argue that private equity is an alternative long-term form of corporate governance to traditional public companies. Others see PE as a type of transitional 'shock therapy' for underperforming companies.

The Discipline of Debt

Corporate finance valuation theory is based on the idea that you maximize the value of any financial asset by maximizing the present value of its future cashflows. It is argued that the poor corporate governance created by the principal–agent problem allows managers to hold on to free cash generated by businesses and use it either to reduce their personal risk or to follow projects that would not otherwise be invested in: in businesses with high borrowings, with the need to repay borrowing and service the interest payments, the debt obligation itself creates a discipline that reduces or eliminates the wasteful use of cashflow. In simple terms, those who have to repay loans don't waste money. This argument is a subset of the principal–agent hypothesis, but crucially does not rely on active management by the fund manager to achieve efficiency. The financial corset of high borrowing realigns the incentives of managers to encourage economic efficiency. As we will see, the changes in the banking market over the years have eaten away at this as a credible explanation of the industry's performance.

Using Debt to Reduce Taxation

One of the longest standing and most commonly voiced criticisms of private equity is that it uses 'debt shields' to reduce corporation tax. The argument relies on the assumption that most or all interest charged in a company's profit and loss account is deductible against taxable profit when calculating a company's corporation tax liability. In contrast, dividend payments made to shareholders are not deductible against corporation tax. The critics argue that countries should disallow interest payments, equalizing the tax incentives to companies to use equity and debt, as illustrated in Table 1.1.

This is a very simplistic argument. Firstly, interest is paid to lenders, who will be taxed on their profits. Secondly dividends are payments to equity holders out of post-tax profits. It is in many ways more accurate to think of corporation tax as a 'preferred dividend to the state' rather than a cost of the business. Shareholders who receive dividends are taxed on them as income. We enlarge on this in Chapter 2 on taxation generally.

Disallowing interest costs that are then taxed in the hands of the lenders is a global increase in corporate taxation. This is especially politically attractive if people have been led to think interest has some tax advantage.

Table 1.1. Effects of tax deductibility of interest on post-tax profit

No Debt	No Debt	Interest Deducted	Interest Disallowed
Net Profit	250	250	250
Interest		−100	−100
Pre-Tax Profit	250	150	150
Disallowed Interest			100
Taxable Profit	250	150	250
Tax	−50	−30	−50
Post Tax Profit	200	120	100
Effective Corp Tax Rate	20%	20%	33%

Skilled Acquirers of Unquoted Equity

Private equity firms are generally very process-driven. They all tend to follow very similar, rigorous and prescriptive acquisition and due diligence processes that are the result of the experience of many thousands of transactions over the years. PE funds are very heavy users of external professional advisers to provide a suite of due diligence reports. An entire industry of accountants, lawyers, and consultants exists to support this transactional activity.

Post the acquisition there are often 100-day plans to start to implement changes to any matters identified in the pre-acquisition due diligence. According to McKinsey[4] the top twenty-five PE fund managers all also have in-house operational management teams whose role it is to support and accelerate the implementation of the business plan underlying the investment. PE funds now follow processes and methodologies that are the result of four decades of private equity investing and investment management.

When a PE fund manager decides it is the right time to sell, they outsource the management of the sale process to investment banks, corporate finance houses, and M&A boutiques. The exit process is again very well defined and, while it continues to evolve, it remains a familiar and predictable process based on years of accumulated knowledge.

Very few corporations operate in this rigorous, but expensive, way in the M&A market.

Sacrificing Liquidity to Solve Information Asymmetries

You can reduce risk by holding assets that are easier to sell (which gives you more liquidity) or by maximizing the information you have before and during the period you hold an investment (enabling you to manage risk effectively). If you can do both, you can achieve consistently superior returns with lower risks than any other market participants. That is one major reason why insider dealing in quoted shares is illegal. In reality you often have to trade liquidity for information rights (see Figure 1.4).

Similarly, you can adopt an active investment stance and seek to influence the management of the company or a passive one and simply sell out if you perceive management to be weak or taking the business in the wrong direction. If you have decided to trade

---

[4] https://www.mckinsey.com/industries/private-equity-and-principal-investors/our-insights/private-equity-operating-groups-and-the-pursuit-of-portfolio-alpha.

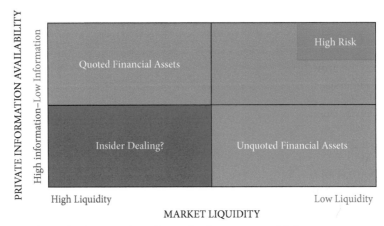

Figure 1.4. Relationship between liquidity and information availability

liquidity for information you severely limit the option to rapidly trade out of investments that are not going in the direction you anticipated.

Private equity is not about trading on public markets, or trading in currencies, bonds or any other publicly quoted security or derivatives. These are the realm of managers of other funds, including hedge funds.

Private equity investments are illiquid and generally traded only on acquisition or exit (although this has significantly changed since the last edition of this work, as we discuss in the chapter on secondary transactions). Generally—but not always—PE managers have good information prior to making their investment, through their due diligence processes. During the investment this level of access to information continues, both through contractual rights to receive information and through close involvement with the investee company at board level.

In contrast, investors in public companies buy liquid assets (shares, bonds, and options) and generally use a trading strategy to try and make exceptional returns. Insider dealing laws are designed to prevent anybody from making exceptional returns from private information not available to other participants in the public markets. These types of investors sell out of companies when they think that they are no longer likely to generate good returns. In summary, they have high liquidity and trade on the basis of publicly available information.

There are instances where companies are publicly traded but have low volumes of trades making them effectively illiquid. These types of business have often been the focus of both active management funds and PE funds looking to complete public-to-private (P2P) transactions.

One of the hardest decisions for holders of publicly traded assets is when to sell, especially if the investor holds a significant stake that could move the market price. In private Equity the investors delegate that decision to the PE fund manager who has access to excellent information and sells the whole business using a well-worn and rigorous process.

Information and Private Equity

The theme that runs through most of these hypotheses is information as a source of improved corporate governance and information availability facilitating both better management and enabling and creating liquidity. We argue that the key to understanding private equity is the collection, management, and use of information, alongside the effects of exaggerated incentives encouraging managers to take difficult decisions and have a clear focus on the growth in the value of the business.

This encompasses the information search processes of due diligence prior to and when making an investment. These expensive processes should enable better investment decisions. The post-investment imposition of both controls and systems provides the shareholder with timely information with which to judge management performance. The exaggerated rewards strongly encourage management to act decisively. The similarly exaggerated rewards to fund managers make them intolerant of management who do not deliver performance. Private equity does not sell shares in badly managed businesses; it changes the management.

Thus, the availability of information, prior to and once the investment has been made, enables better corporate governance.

We therefore suggest that the private equity investment model is able to achieve both economic gains from the more efficient use of resources, and to magnify and realize these gains by using this high-quality information to both change corporate behaviours and to take on greater financial risk via leverage.

In this explanation, timely information, not simple incentive alignment or financial engineering, drives the industry. In the (somewhat simplistic) diagram in Figure 1.5, we argue that private equity has sought to operate in areas where the purchasers have more accessible information than the vendors by aligning with incumbent management. Vendors have reacted by creating processes to extract value from a corporate sale by maximizing competitive tension. In this model, information enables private equity to make sustainable

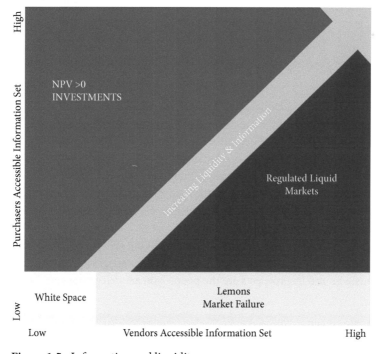

Figure 1.5. Information and liquidity

above-market returns by exploiting information asymmetries. Where information is inaccessible, there is no liquidity and new products and services emerge in the white space. Where information is highly skewed towards the vendor, there is a so-called 'market for lemons', where trade fails even if buyers would want to buy the goods or services if they had better information.[5]

In support of this conjecture we would expect to see private equity funds spending significantly more than most other acquirers on gathering and managing information using specialist third party providers, and relatively more on information systems investments. This is indeed what the industry looks like. There are many thousands of lawyers, accountants, and consultants of all shapes and sizes who target the private equity fund managers as a key source of work. There are also 100-day plans dealing with the professionalization of management that usually start with good information systems.

Against this idea we might expect public-to-private transactions (where information is less accessible) to perform less well than purely private transactions. This is a complicated test to undertake rigorously. The rules around information for public companies have changed in many jurisdictions over the years, in part in response to perceptions of insider conflicts in public company deals. Today's leveraged buyouts of public companies are very different to those of the 1980s. This may explain their decline in popularity.

In summary, we argue that there has been an underemphasis on information as the lifeblood of the market. Very roughly, you might think of liquidity and trusted information as being, to some approximation, the same thing.

What Risks Do Investors in Private Equity Funds Take?

In any equity investment, whether public or private, there is the risk of losing the capital invested. In private equity, investments are long-term, irrevocable commitments to fund unknown, future investment opportunities. An investor commits to these risks and delegates the investment decision to the fund manager.

The unknown investment risk is so-called 'blind risk': investors, and the fund managers themselves, do not know what companies they are going to invest in when a fund is established. This risk is unusually high in the early stage of a PE fund when compared to most other established investment vehicles.

'Selection risk' is how we characterize the stock-picking skills of the fund manager. It is an area of long-standing research in public market fund managers. How good a judge of a particular business and its prospects are the people you are delegating your selection to?

---

[5] George A. Akerlof (1970), 'The market for "lemons": Quality uncertainty and the market mechanism', *Quarterly Journal of Economics* **84**(3): 488–500.

Once invested in a particular company, the external 'market risks' of any investment are, in principle, the same whether the company is owned by a PE fund or by any other ownership structure. What differs is the 'bankruptcy risk' created and amplified by using leverage, as we discuss extensively. This is one of the defining risks of PE investment.

The second defining risk of PE is liquidity risk. This reflects the fact that the commitments both to the underlying investments in the fund and to the fund itself are long-term—although, as we will discuss, this is changing.

Committed versus Drawn-Down Funds

When a PE fund is said to have raised $1bn they do not receive $1bn in cash from investors on day one. Investors only advance cash to the PE fund on an 'as needed' basis. What they have is access to a facility of up to $1bn that they can draw down as and when required to fund investments. It is a crucial distinction between quoted fund managers, who hold assets including from time-to-time cash on behalf of investors, and PE fund managers who only draw down cash on an as needed basis and repay any cash that the fund receives from its investment.

Traditionally these commitments were not tradable, but this has changed significantly as the PE industry has matured. The market is evolving to allow some of these risks and rewards to be traded between investors. (See Chapter 2.)

Furthermore, many funds now use the commitments of their investors to guarantee bank facilities that they use for the immediate drawdown of the funds. This means that the investors do not make a cash commitment when the fund invests, although they are guaranteeing the bank facility, resulting in the same risk. These loan facilities, or so-called subscription lines, have been a much-discussed feature in the past decade. We will return to the matter later in this book.

What Risks Do Private Equity Fund Managers Take Themselves?

To align the interests of investors and fund managers, the fund managers typically invest alongside the investors, on the same terms, in any fund. If a fund loses money, the fund managers will make the same loss on their investment, offset by any income earned from fund management fees not spent on the costs of the fund. To assess the level of alignment created by this structure you need to know how much is invested in the fund by the managers and how this amount compares to the guaranteed income that they will earn and to their net worth.

It is common for managers to borrow against future fees to fund their investment in the fund. This changes the timing of the investment by the fund managers, but not its risk. It can be argued that the commitment of the managers would not be possible without the fees to underpin the loan that pays for it. If you accept this line of reasoning, the idea of alignment between the manager and the other investors is significantly weakened.

What Rewards Do Private Equity Managers Earn?

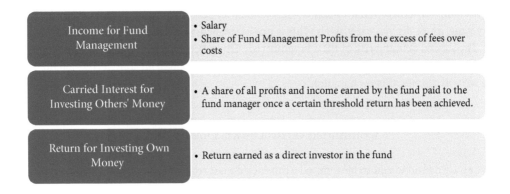

The partners of the fund manager have four sources of reward.

Salary: They receive a salary from the fund management company at a normal market rate.

Partnership profit share: The partners own the fund management company and they therefore receive a share in the profits of that company. This represents the difference between the costs of the fund manager and the fees received from investors in the fund and, potentially, some fees from the companies that the fund has invested in. This income and its impact on incentives has become a focus of attention in the past decade. We expand on this in Chapter 3.

Carried interest: They may receive something called 'carried interest' which is triggered once a minimum threshold return is achieved.

Investor return: They receive a return as an investor in the fund in the same way as any other investor in the fund.

The salary and partnership profit share are independent of the performance of the underlying investments. The investor return and carried interest are directly aligned and proportional to the returns earned by the investors. We look at the relationship between these two streams of return in more detail in Chapter 2.

What is Carried Interest?

If the fund achieves returns above a minimum threshold, the fund manager takes a preferential share of the return in the form of so-called 'carried interest' (or 'carry'). Traditionally the threshold, or hurdle rate, has been 8 per cent per annum over the life of the fund and the share has been 20 per cent of all the fund profits, although this is again changing.

This is a major discussion point when considering taxation in PE (which we return to in Chapter 2). Carried interest is a share of capital gains and income paid to the fund manager. It can be thought of as a success payment for exceeding the objectives of the fund investors. There is much debate as to whether this is a fee (which would be taxed as income) or a share of capital gains which would be taxed accordingly.

What Are the Incentives of the Private Equity
Fund Manager within the Fund?

As we noted above, fund managers are rewarded with salaries partnership profits and carried interest. Carried interest has traditionally been 20 per cent of the profits once the investors have received an annual return (IRR) of 8 per cent. This means that there is a clear incentive to maximize the return to investors as measured by a discounted cashflow calculation, usually IRR, as this is the trigger to pay carry. Detailed calculation of carried interest is complicated, as illustrated in Chapter 2.

This encourages the maximum use of debt and minimal use of equity in any investment. This is in a sense obvious: debt is cheaper and equity more expensive. The constraint on how much third-party debt can prudently be borrowed is the limiting factor. This is discussed in Chapter 3.

Within a fund the incentives of the fund manager are to:

- minimize the use of investors' cash;
- maximize leverage in each investment, subject to risk;
- act quickly to reduce the value needed to exceed the hurdle rate;

and to increase the value of the equity by:

- repaying debt; and/or
- increasing enterprise value;
- negotiating a low hurdle rate.

What Are the Incentives of the Private Equity
Fund Manager when Fund Raising?

In fund raising the incentives are very different. People are motivated by nominal returns: you cannot spend rates of return; you can only spend cash. Large funds not only generate higher fees and therefore proportionately higher revenues but, as they do bigger deals, the successful ones generate more pounds or dollars of carried interest.

A 1.0 per cent fee on a fund of $10bn generates fees of $100m per annum. A 2.0 per cent fee on a £300m fund generates £6m per annum. These are guaranteed incomes to the fund management business. Anything not spent on the costs of those businesses are shared by the partners.

There are very big incentives to be big in all fund management businesses. In private equity fees are high, so the incentives are stronger. This has led to the growth of giant private market funds that have multiple investment funds following multiple investment strategies. The economies of scale in these large fund managers are not currently reflected in the fees charged by their individual funds, which are broadly the same as similar sized funds operating in a defined niche.

When fees become the largest part of a manager's income, the idea of alignment at the heart of private equity is challenged. Arguably there is a point at which a new principal–agent issue is created between the investors in the fund. Investors want prudent investments in a diversified portfolio generating capital gains. The manager wants to maximize assets under management (AUM) to generate a certain fee income.

Furthermore, fee profits are earned early in the life of the funds whereas carried interest is earned much later, after the fund's performance has been realized.

We return to this tension in the chapter on the contract that governs the relationship between investors and managers: the Limited Partnership Agreement (LPA).

What Is Leverage and What Role Does It Play in Private Equity?

Using borrowed money alongside your own reduces the amount you have to invest and so amplifies the returns on any particular investment. This amplification has various names: in the US it is called leverage, in the UK it was traditionally called gearing. They are the same idea. In economic theory it has been shown that under certain assumptions the capital structure of a company cannot change the fundamental economics of a business. The Modigliani–Miller hypothesis[6] is a central idea in corporate finance theory. For our purposes we only need to understand that it suggests that in a perfect market a business cannot achieve enduring competitive advantage through changes in its capital structure: that is, you cannot make above-market returns by changing your debt/equity ratio.

The mechanics of leverage are not complicated. Debt is a prior claim on the cash flows and assets of a business. Equity is a residual claim on the profits and net assets. Therefore, when you use only your own money as equity in an investment, the return on the investment is the same as the return on your equity (Figure 1.6).

If external debt (which has a fixed return) is used to fund the investment, the prospective returns are increased because the equity is reduced and yet it still captures all of the capital gain (Figure 1.7). It is just like the effect of a mortgage on a house.

With no Debt, Equity Return = Total return

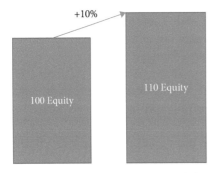

		Buy	Sell	%Return
Asset Value		100	110	10%
Funded By				
Debt		0	0	0%
Equity		100	110	10%
Total		100	110	10%
Debt %		0%	0%	
Equity %		100%	100%	

Figure 1.6. Effects of leverage—no debt
Source: The authors

[6] F. Modigliani and M. Miller (1958), 'The cost of capital, corporation finance and the theory of investment', *American Economic Review* **48**(3): 261–97.
F. Modigliani and M. Miller (1963), 'Corporate income taxes and the cost of capital: a correction', *American Economic Review* **53**(3): 433–43.

With 50% Debt, Equity Return = 2 ×Total return

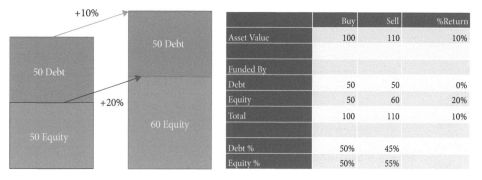

		Buy	Sell	%Return
Asset Value		100	110	10%
Funded By				
Debt		50	50	0%
Equity		50	60	20%
Total		100	110	10%
Debt %		50%	45%	
Equity %		50%	55%	

Figure 1.7. Effects of leverage—50 per cent debt
Source: The authors

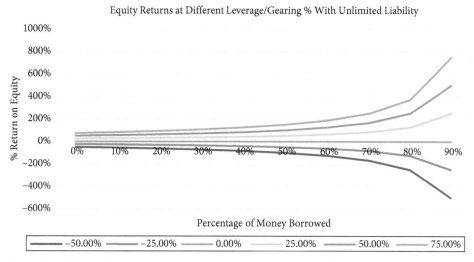

Figure 1.8. Effect of leverage on return on equity at various overall investment returns with unlimited liability

We can easily expand on this simple example and look (Figure 1.8) at what happens at any particular ratio of equity to debt (X axis) and different growth rates to the returns on equity (Y axis). We can also examine what happens at negative growth rates.

What we find is that when we have high levels of borrowing, returns are amplified. Notice that the amplification goes in both directions. Bad deals are really bad and good deals are really good, and for a partnership with unlimited liabilities this would be the case in reality. However, there is a cap on the amount you can lose in a limited company or a limited liability partnership. The most any shareholder or partner can lose is all their investment. This means that the amplification is asymmetrical: you can make a return of up to infinity, but you can only lose your initial investment. The graph therefore should look like the one in Figure 1.9.

Either way, what you can see is that the effect of borrowing is to amplify returns, NOT increase them, as it works in both directions, up and down.

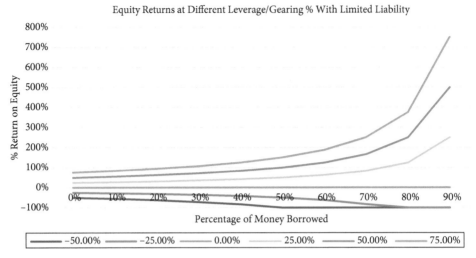

Figure 1.9. Effect of leverage on return on equity at various overall investment returns with limited liability

A colleague of one of us[7] has made the following observation. If assets trade at their net present value, leverage cannot amplify the returns earned. This follows from the work by Modigliani and Miller in the 1950s. Both were awarded Nobel Prizes: Modigliani in 1985, Miller in 1990. The argument in essence is that if markets are efficiently driving transaction values to their net present value, leverage cannot increase the returns, as the returns are competed away by the sale process.

This lies at the very heart of all debates about private equity returns. If you believe that, on the whole, markets are efficient and that the buyers must pay a fair price that equates to the net present value of the investment, you cannot make consistently higher returns by financial engineering. If, on the other hand, you think that the market for corporate control is imperfect, or systematically inefficient, you can hypothesize constantly higher returns, but have to explain why the market is failing.

It is also possible to hypothesize that markets move between states of efficiency and inefficiency creating investment opportunities from time to time.

Much work has been undertaken by academics and others to try and establish what proportion of the return from a private equity investment comes from:

(1) increases in total investment value, or
(2) the effect of leverage on equity returns.

This so-called 'attribution analysis' is a hot topic in both academic studies and the discussions of returns achieved by funds. We return to it later.

What Impact Does Leverage Have on Bankruptcy Risk?

The other side of this amplification of return is increased financial risk. We can characterize risk as being crystallized at the point that the value of the project is less than the value

[7] Ludovic Phalippou (2018), *Private Equity Laid Bare*.

of the debt. Equivalently, the project has negative net worth when the equity value has been consumed. As there is less equity in a geared/levered structure, the probability of becoming insolvent is higher than an ungeared/unlevered structure. As gearing/leverage increases, other things being equal, the probability of becoming insolvent rises. This risk of failure by becoming insolvent is generally termed bankruptcy risk.

Private equity investors use debt to consciously create financial risk in order to amplify the return on equity. We return to this idea frequently. It is vital to appreciate that risk and reward are two sides of the same coin. It is always possible to generate risk without reward, but if you can generate rewards without risk, you have created the economic equivalent of a perpetual motion machine, which is generally impossible.

Leverage in Funds versus Leverage in Investments

It is crucially important to understand that leverage can be found at different levels of many financial structures, and its impact differs.

Private equity funds traditionally use debt in each individual investment, but have traditionally had none within the fund, although as we will discuss, this has changed. The investments stood or fell on their own two feet, with no recourse to the fund. Therefore, while there is bankruptcy risk in each investee company, there was generally none in the fund. This is changing.

In contrast many other types of fund manager have always used leverage within the fund to amplify returns.

In a similar way a trading company may have some borrowings on its or its subsidiaries' balance sheets, often cross-guaranteed by the other companies in the trading group.

The risks of leverage are most threatening when they are compounded: where a geared fund owns geared investments, returns can appear spectacular, but will be at greater risk. There is therefore a mix of incentives leaning towards the use of gearing to amplify returns within any type of fund. The market pressure is to increase borrowings and give investors more liquidity, which if unfettered will lead to increases in risk within the fund structures.

Over the past few years the use of debt within private equity funds has started to become a standard feature. This creates an increase in the risks in the market and distorts comparisons of returns. We discuss this change and its implications below and more fully in Chapter 2.

What Market Risks Does Private Equity Create?

We believe that this distinction between leverage in a fund and in its investments is important in understanding the market risks created by hedge funds and private equity funds, as well as for informing regulatory responses to the systemic failures seen in the past.

We have argued that the traditional private equity fund structure has operated to limit systemic risk by offering long-term, illiquid, unleveraged investment assets mostly to institutional investors with large diversified portfolios. However, pressure to increase leverage within funds and to provide liquidity to investors not matched to the liquidity of the underlying assets is creating increased risk. Whether this is systemic is debatable. Unlike banks, private equity funds do not hold customer deposits or have any important role in the facilitation of trade in the wider economy. They do however take investments from institutions that are important to the wider society, such as pension funds and insurance funds. Increased risk in private equity funds is therefore an increase in risk to the investors. Whether this is compensated for by superior returns is one key question to consider. The second important consideration is the impact on the liquidity of investors as private equity allocations increase. You cannot easily sell a position in a private equity fund, although the markets are developing. We discuss this in the chapter on secondary transactions.

The debt-free structure of a private equity fund was, in most European jurisdictions, a market-driven norm, not a regulatory requirement. We return to this when we discuss regulation in Chapter 2.

A Financial Canary in the Coal Mine?

One might characterize the private equity industry as a group of early adopters of financial innovation, rather than the creators of that innovation. Because of the amplification caused by the use of leverage, coupled with the early adoption of new techniques and practices, if private equity is suffering or booming it may be a sign of things to come in the wider financial markets and economy. Certainly, the rise of mega-buyouts and the loosening of bank terms leading up to the financial crisis was symptomatic of structural issues that heralded problems elsewhere. As such, private equity is potentially an early warning system; a financial canary in the coal mine.

As we write, leverage is high and debt is cheap, and transaction prices are accordingly also high. Many of the graphs we will use in this book suggest that we are at the top of a cycle, but we, along with almost all other commentators, have no way of forecasting when the downturn will start or how sharp and protracted it will be.[8]

How Do Private Equity Funds Control Their Investments?

The ability to act decisively comes from the fact that a private equity fund manager actively manages and controls each company using:

- board representation;
- contracts which require, or limit without the consent of the investors, certain actions of management;
- voting control over all material matters;
- full access to company information and board minutes; and
- a culture and incentive system that rewards success highly and penalizes failure.

These rights are widely spread in the contracts that bind any transaction together. We discuss these later when we walk through a typical private equity investment term sheet.

---

[8] This was written before covid19. See the addendum for an update written as the pandemic broke.

A Summary of the Core Ideas: The 4 As—Amplification, Alignment, Active Management, and Attention to Detail

Private equity firms are strategic investors generally seeking to create and realize value. To achieve this, they follow a series of strategies that can be crudely characterized under the following alliterative headings.

Amplification: Private equity uses debt to consciously create a level of financial risk that exaggerates the returns on equity.

Alignment: Equity incentives are used to create potentially unlimited incentives to motivate people to generate (predominantly) capital gains.

Active management: The body of research on investment performance generally shows that a passive trading strategy of 'stock picking' does not generate materially higher long-run returns than simply choosing to buy indices of stock markets. This has been reinforced by the imposition of insider-trading laws that prohibit the use of private information to achieve superior returns. Those who have generated long-term outperformance since the imposition of the insider trading laws are those who have actively intervened to improve the performance and management of businesses. This appears to be as true of a few public investors, such as Berkshire Hathaway, as it is of private investors, such as the private equity firms. The form of this active management has evolved over the years, but it remains a key feature in explaining the performance of private equity investments.

Attention to detail: Private equity is transactional, whole companies are bought and sold. In consequence a great deal of due diligence is done on each deal and the transaction structure. Great emphasis is placed on measuring and managing every relevant aspect of a business's performance, including, for example, tax structuring. Private equity is very process driven in the way it transacts.

They do all of this while benefiting from excellent information on the businesses they own and control.

We expand on each of these themes throughout this work.

A Brief History of Private Equity

While there have always been equity investments made outside the public markets, private equity as we understand the term today emerged in the 1980s from, broadly, two pre-existing pools of funds: venture capital and development capital. Venture capital (VC) provides equity capital to early and emerging businesses. Development capital provides equity capital to expand existing businesses. The term private equity was adopted from the late 1980s. Before then it was more common to hear institutions refer to themselves as venture capitalists in the UK and leveraged buyout (LBO) firms in the US.

1960/70s: Asset Stripping and Financial Assistance

In the 1970s in many developed countries it became illegal to use the assets of a target company to give security to a lender to a bidder for that company. Essentially you could not promise to give security on assets you did not own. This was specifically designed to stop the asset stripping that had been seen in the late 1960s. In the 1960s corporate raiders sought out companies with undervalued assets, bought the businesses and then closed the business down and sold the assets. This left the unsecured creditors and employees to suffer a loss. The financial assistance prohibition aimed to prevent this by making it a criminal offence to asset-strip in most countries.

However, an unintended consequence of this legislation was that it prevented the rescue of viable companies many of which were subsidiaries of larger failing businesses. These subsidiaries could not provide security to a purchaser's bank that wished to lend money to help acquire and rescue a business. To reverse this unintended prohibition, and to encourage the rescue of viable businesses, a change was made to the law in a number of countries. In the UK, the Companies Act 1981 allowed UK companies to give financial assistance under certain tightly controlled circumstances. The law on financial assistance broadly required the directors to make a statutory declaration that as far as they knew at the completion date of the transaction, the company would be solvent for the next twelve months. If they made the declaration knowing it to be untrue, it was a criminal offence.

1980s: First Buyout Boom

Following the legal change on financial assistance in most jurisdictions, the number of buyouts grew rapidly. Initially growth was seen in the US whereas in Europe the market was overwhelmingly dominated by the UK. By the mid-1980s, 3i, which at that time was jointly owned by the Bank of England and the major clearing banks, had an overwhelmingly strong position in Britain. Other early UK participants were subsidiaries of banks and other financial institutions that had historically focused on development capital and other financial investors with a background in venture capital.

1980s: 'Hands-Off, Eyes-On'

Virtually all early UK funds were generalist investors who had skills in financial engineering and transactions but had little hands-on management input. Investors closely monitored their investments, but the underlying philosophy was passively to back management to manage.

Mid-1980s: New Entrants

The returns earned by the early buyout investors were very good. This led to a growth in the funds committed by existing investors and to the emergence of new funds raised by groups of investors who wished to enter the market. In the UK many of these funds' founder managers were from the relatively small pool of experienced investors (often they were ex-3i executives). In the US they tended to be from consultancy and investment banking backgrounds.

1989: Junk Bonds and Mega-Deals V1.0

In the US two factors enabled the market to expand rapidly. First, a market for subprime 'junk' bonds was created. This enabled investors to issue high yield debt to fund acquisitions. Secondly, the early funds generated returns that were widely held to be outperforming the market. This led to ever-larger funds, capable of doing ever-larger deals. The peak of the market was the iconic buyout of RJR Nabisco in 1988 for approximately $23bn.

Due to the relatively small size of the European funds, the capacity of the European buyout market was severely limited and in consequence many transactions were syndicated between equity investors. To put the scale of the industry in context, a large European buyout during this period was generally defined as one in excess of £10m; in the current market it might be defined as perhaps £0.5bn–£1bn or thereabouts. At the end of the 1980s the largest deal in Europe was the 1989 Isosceles buyout of Gateway Supermarkets for £2.2bn.

Captives versus Independents

By the end of the first wave of buyouts in the 1980s the industry was characterized by a split between so-called 'captive funds', owned by a large corporate parent, and independent firms having the partnership form that we see as the commonest structure today, plus, in Europe, 3i.

Yield versus Capital Gain

Some smaller captive funds and 3i tended to be longer-term holders of an investment (compared to current structures—see Chapter 2) without an explicit exit policy. They demanded a higher yield from their investments. Independent firms were generally structured as 10-year funds (as we see today) and therefore were more focused on generating capital gains with a defined exit policy and had lower yield requirements.

1990s: Blow-Up and Buyouts of Captive Funds

Following the impact of the recession of the early 1990s, and high interest rates, many leveraged investments struggled or failed. Appetite to support in-house private equity declined leading many of the captive funds themselves to be bought out from their parent companies by their partners. Virtually all rebranded themselves as private equity or buyout firms and abandoned any pretension to venture capital activities (Table 1.2). In this limited sense the partners of many private equity fund managers have taken the risks and earned the rewards of a manager in a buyout.

2000s: Early Secondary Transactions

One of the other consequences of the end of most captive private equity funds was the emergence of portfolios of assets that were no longer wanted by their investors. A small

Table 1.2. Predecessors of selected UK private equity firms

Name of firm	Predecessor firm	Type of predecessor
Permira	Schroder Ventures	UK parent captive / employees
Apax Partners	Alan Patricoff Associates (Europe)	US affiliate independent
CVC Capital Partners	Citicorp Venture Capital (Europe)	US parent captive
Cinven	Coal Board Investment Managers Venture Capital	Public sector pension fund manager
3i Group	Industrial and Commercial Finance Corporation	Clearing banks and Bank of England
Terra Firma	Nomura Principal Finance Group	Japanese parent captive
Charterhouse Capital	Charterhouse Development Capital	UK parent captive

group of secondary funds emerged that specialized in structuring transactions to buy these assets, often at a discount to their net asset values. The largest of these transactions was the £1bn purchase of the private equity portfolio of NatWest Bank as part of its defence against a hostile takeover by RBS. Early secondary transactions were often seen as a sign of a failure by the private equity manager to achieve satisfactory returns. They were rarely openly discussed.

Hands-on Investors and Sector Specialization

As competition for transactions increased, the need to generate value in individual investments increased. This led to a variety of strategies aimed at increasing the success rate and the value of each success to funds. Investors generally became much more active in the management of each individual investment. Many investors began to focus on specific industries and sectors to gain an advantage over generalist investors. Today most firms have a sector bias and an active investment style.

Globalization and the Growth of Global Mega-Funds

In the late 1990s and after the turn of the century the market split in two: the largest private equity funds have become increasingly international in their outlook, while in the mid-market the businesses have become more focused on specific sectors or types of business. The trend in globalization has led to a growth in the number of non-UK investors based in London seeking UK and European transactions.

2005–7: Boom

The prolonged period of economic growth with low inflation from the mid-1990s to the 2008 financial crisis was characterized by ever larger funds, larger deals, greater complexity in structures, greater leverage, and an explosion in the size of private equity as a global industry. It was still a poorly understood, little reported industry and operated from a number of unregulated jurisdictions.

The debt markets also metamorphosed and banks that had previously held loans on their own balance sheets sold them into the wholesale market. They ceased to earn the majority of their income from net interest payments and became fee-earning businesses that parcelled up loans to be sold on to other financial institutions.

Innovation in the debt markets led to the emergence of markets in new forms of derivatives. Most of these instruments were designed to allow risk to be traded. This has always been one of the functions of derivatives, but when they were stripped from their underlying loans, they became tradable assets creating some perverse, unintended incentives (see Chapter 2).

New businesses, such as the Icelandic firm Baugur, emerged that mimicked the use of leverage seen in private equity financial structures in individual investments but without certain controls that operate in the traditional fund structures: they created leveraged funds to make leveraged investments, doubling up the risks and apparent rewards.

2007–8: Bust

By 2007 the wholesale debt markets were opaque and poorly understood by most. There was an implicit assumption that there was an available appetite for debt in the global market which was effectively infinite or unlimited. This allowed banking institutions to fund themselves using facilities that were renewed continuously in the highly liquid debt markets. When the default rates on US mortgages turned out to be higher than expected, it was unclear who was holding the associated risk. In the absence of any clear information about who was going to be making losses, banks and institutions started to hold on to all the cash that was available to them and reduced or stopped lending to the wholesale markets. This meant that wholesale credit dried up and banks reliant on renewing facilities were unable to refinance and became insolvent. Initially, smaller banks struggled and failed, but as the scale of the confusion spread, the world's largest institutions turned to governments to provide capital and guarantees. In the case of Lehman Brothers, the US government declined to rescue them and the investment bank failed.

The impact on the private equity market was abrupt and precipitous. Banks needed to hold cash rather than to generate lending. Deal volumes, which are reliant on leverage, collapsed. The largest deals were the worst affected. Those who had used debt within their fund structures rapidly faced insolvency as there was a mismatch between the dates they were expecting to realize their investments and the date that their borrowings were repayable.

2009–12: Hangover

The aftermath of the financial crisis showed both the strengths and weaknesses in the private equity model. On the positive side of the balance, the traditional 'ten plus two' fund (see Chapter 2) was bankrupt remote: it could not spread risk because the whole risk fell on its partners. This is an important and little publicized fact: private equity fund structures in a limited way stopped the creation of systemic risk.

However, perverse situations arose between fund managers and their partners. Many funds had raised billions of dollars prior to the crash on the assumption that leverage would be available to support deals. They found themselves charging fees on capital that would be unlikely to be deployed. Investors were understandably unhappy.

The period of extremely low interest rates that has followed the crisis has prevented the feared collapse of many companies with high levels of borrowings, including buyouts and other private equity investments. Had the recession been accompanied by high interest rates, the failure rate would certainly have been materially higher, in all types of business.

In the US, buyouts have been funded by bonds and debt funds for many years. In the UK, prior to the financial crisis it was much more common that banks funded buyouts. Among the leaders in the UK market were RBS and HBOS and therefore, when they themselves required rescuing, debt funding to buyouts contracted sharply.

Furthermore, the regulations that govern banks' requirement to maintain a strong balance sheet were altered after the crisis. The amount of capital that a bank had to hold against long-term loans was significantly increased. Long-term in this context was (broadly speaking) defined as five years or more. In consequence the amount of capital a bank had to put aside to support buyout loans over five years increased, and the price of loans increased sharply to generate the return on capital that banks required. As a rough rule of thumb, loan margins increased from around 2.25 per cent over LIBOR to 4.5 per cent over LIBOR. LIBOR is a benchmark rate of interest at which banks lend to each other. It is closely correlated to the Bank of England base rate. LIBOR will be replaced in 2021, but the principle will remain the same.

Bank arrangement fees also shot up from around 1.0 per cent of the amount borrowed to 3.0 per cent. The cost impact was not immediately felt because the Bank of England base rate (and all other global interest rates) were reduced to all-time lows by the central banking authorities. In effect base rates fell more than margins increased, so borrowers paid similar overall costs.

2012–19: Debt Innovation in Europe

The increase in margins and fees and the vacuum left by the collapse of lending by the European banks attracted new entrants and start-ups in the buyout debt market. These are debt funds rather than banks. They operate a very similar model to the PE fund. They raise institutional commitments in a limited life fund and earn fees and carried interest if they are successful. These funds have long operated in the US market. In essence the European market was slowly transformed. It started as a market led by banks and bank syndicates in the lower-mid market with investment banks underwriting and placing high-yield bonds in larger deals.

First the depth of the syndication market reduced as banks withdrew from risky lending. Those who remained saw the opportunity to put up prices, and this attracted new entrants who largely displaced the banks from the leveraged finance market (Figure 1.10). We discuss these changes in Chapter 4.

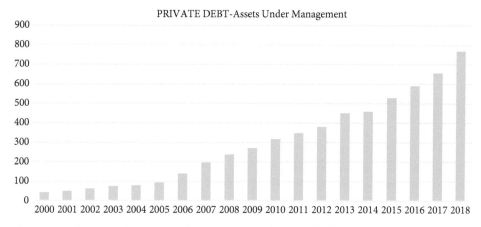

Figure 1.10. Private debt: assets under management by year ($bn)
Source: Preqin

2012–19: Innovation in Secondary Trading

The secondary markets for private equity funds are the place where limited partners (LPs) buy and sell their investments in PE funds. They are by some measures larger than the primary markets. It is important to be clear on terminology when talking about secondary PE. There are companies that undergo more than one buyout: these are secondary (or tertiary, or whatever) buyouts. There are also completely unrelated and different sales of commitments and investments within a fund that are called secondary trades. There has been a growth in both, but here we are referring specifically and exclusively to trades in fund positions, not buyouts.

Large LPs may hold investments and commitments to many PE funds at any particular time. At the date of writing, for example, the European Investment Fund (EIF) has commitments to some 532 PE funds and CalPERS, a large US public pension fund, reported live investments in 258 PE and VC funds. Monitoring and managing such large portfolios is a significant task. Many investors have sought to simplify their portfolios and to actively manage their exposure to the life cycles of funds. For example, managers who are comfortable with blind risk in new funds may wish to sell their mature unquoted fund positions to invest in more new funds. This allows those who do not wish to have blind risk to buy into the unquoted market after the investments have been substantially made.

This enables investors to 'manage the J curve', which we will explain in the next chapter.

2012–19: Managed Accounts, Co-Invest and the Canadian Model

One of the features of the market that has grown significantly over the past decade has been the prevalence of new fund management arrangements and investment strategies. These include the so-called Canadian Model, Managed Funds and co-invest arrangements. We deal with these more extensively in Chapter 2, but in summary these are structures that reduce the cost and in some versions places controls on the discretion of the PE fund manager to invest.

Multi-Asset Managers and the Search for Yield

Most large PE fund managers are no longer focused exclusively on private equity and some are themselves now listed entities. They manage multiple different types of funds ranging from LBO funds to real estate and private debt. The market is separating into large global asset managers raising funds in multiple private markets and small focused equity funds, typically geographically constrained and sector-focused. In 2019 both the equity and debt markets were separating into the large and the niche, with few in between.

2019–20 The Top of The Cycle?

Most seasoned commentators and practitioners in Europe are confident that we are writing at a point near to the top of the market. Interest rates have been artificially low for a decade and this has inflated asset prices. Lenders therefore see good security and good interest cover (see Chapter 4) and have been aggressively lending to leveraged transactions. The amount of debt is often expressed at a 'multiple of EBITDA' (earnings before interest, tax, depreciation, and amortization—we explain this is in Chapter 3). EBITDA multiples are, as we write in 2019, near all-time highs.

How Big Is the Private Equity Market?

There are three important measures of the size of the buyout market: the amount invested in private equity (Figure 1.11), the amount of new funds raised or committed (Figure 1.12), and the amount of assets under management (AUM) (Figure 1.13).

The figures illustrate both the overall growth in the private equity market and its cyclicality. Following the dot.com boom there was a decline in the level of new funds raised. From 2005 onwards fund raisings grew dramatically, peaking in 2008.

After the financial crisis the volume of deals and funds raised fell sharply: global transaction volumes fell in value by approaching 50 per cent. This reflected two key factors. First, even if there had been deals to do, the banking market was severely affected by the crash and there was therefore no debt availability to fund leveraged deals. As there were fewer larger deals, the existing capital commitments were not drawn down as rapidly as had been expected. Existing capital was not deployed. As a result 'dry powder' (the term for undrawn commitments) continued to rise during the crisis, before naturally declining as funds ended their investment period.

Secondly the financial crisis damaged the balance sheets of all investors and in consequence there was less ability to invest in alternative assets.

Looking at the buyout data for Europe over a longer period gives a clearer picture of the cyclicality of the market and the importance of private equity in the overall market for control of corporations.

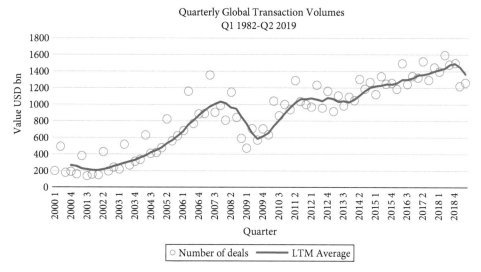

Figure 1.11. Global private equity investments, global aggregate value of private equity-backed buyout deals

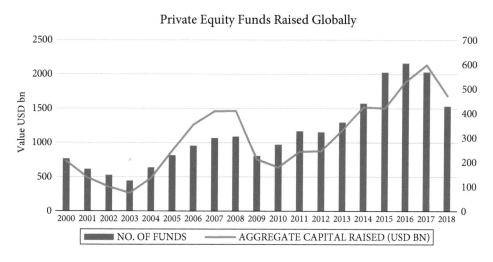

Figure 1.12. Global private equity funds raised ($bn) 2000–18
Source: Preqin

As illustrated in Figure 1.14, the market for buyouts was rising in a cyclical trend up to the 2004–8 boom. During and following the financial crisis the market fell back to levels not seen since the mid-1990s. The lack of availability of debt caused the value of the market to crash by around 90 per cent as large buyouts disappeared. The recovery began in late 2009 and by 2018 numbers and values were at approximately 2005 pre-crash levels (Figure 1.15).

How Significant Are Larger Deals in the Private Equity Market?

Most public interest and much academic research has been focused on the large buyout market. However, the data shows that buyouts with a deal value of £100m or more

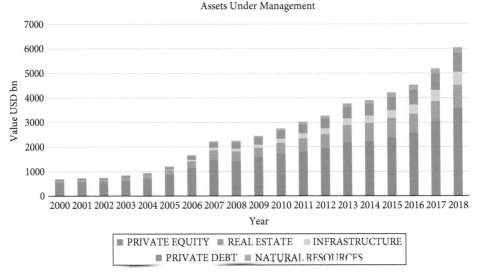

Figure 1.13. Private equity assets under management by strategy

Source: Preqin

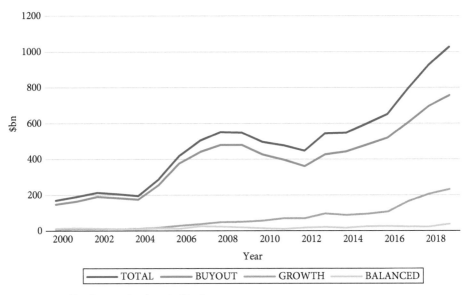

Figure 1.14. Total committed capital by investment strategy

Source: Preqin

represented only a tenth of total buyouts by number, despite representing almost nine-tenths by value (Figure 1.16). Buyouts are therefore a very important feature of the UK mid-market but large buyouts are a small fraction of the UK private equity market by number.

This bias towards discussion of larger transactions is a feature of both media commentary and academic research. In part it reflects data availability (smaller transactions are harder to monitor and analyse) and in part a natural interest in blockbuster deals. Nevertheless, it is of fundamental importance when discussing, reporting on, or regulating private equity to have regard for the vast majority of transactions which are smaller than £100m.

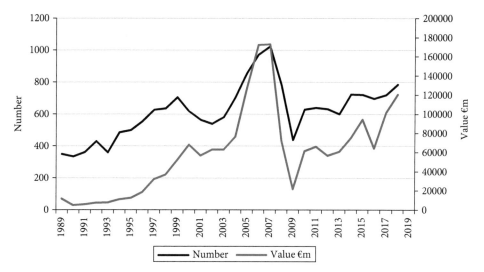

Figure 1.15. Value of European buyouts (€m) 1985–2018
Source: CMBOR/Investec/Equistone Partners Europe

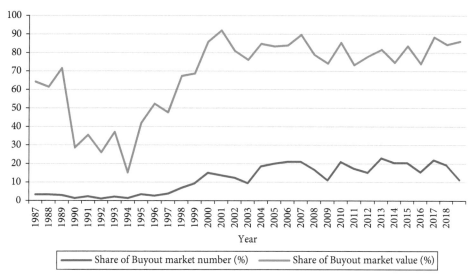

Figure 1.16. £100m buyouts as a percentage of the market by number and value (UK) 1985–2018
Source: CMBOR/Investec/Equistone Partners Europe

The Death of the Management Buyout?

Buyouts come in a variety of flavours, but the two simple definitions used relate to where the management team are prior to the deal. If the management are incumbent in the company, it is a management buyout or MBO. If they are a new team brought into the company as part of the deal, it is a management buy-in or MBI. In the data below, institutionally led transactions where management changes are classified as MBIs, although they are often also called IBOs, or Institutional Buyouts.

Breaking the data down by MBO and MBI reveals a clear trend (Figure 1.17).

Management buyouts have been declining in importance for around twenty years. The days when management decided to attempt to acquire businesses that they worked for, backed by PE funds, are largely in the past. By value the trend is starker (Figure 1.18).

Figure 1.17. Buy-in versus buyout by number (Europe) 1985–2019

Source: CMBOR/Investec/Equistone Partners Europe

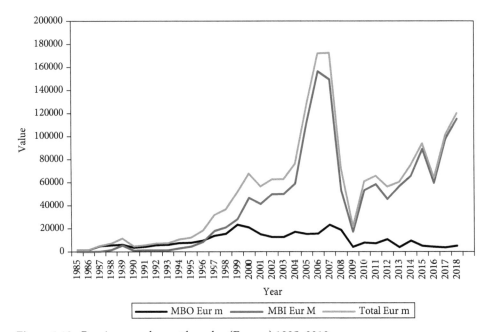

Figure 1.18. Buy-in versus buyout by value (Europe) 1995–2018

Source: CMBOR/Investec/Equistone Partners Europe

It is arguable that the distinction between MBOs and MBIs is now essentially obsolete. In today's market, PE firms are the buyers of businesses, not the management. Whether they choose to keep or change the incumbent management is their decision, often taken post investment.

This is a complete change from the origins of the PE industry when management were at the centre of initiating a transaction.

The Company Auction Process and Compressed Investment Returns

The reasons for this shift relate substantially to changes in the way vendors manage the process of selling companies.

We give more detail on auctions in Chapter 3, but briefly, in the early days of the buyout industry, management often expected to lead a transaction. They would appoint advisers who would raise funds to acquire a business from the vendors. In this process vendors had to attempt to manage a process that could lead to a trade sale or a management buyout. The potential trade purchasers were understandably concerned about the impact on the business if the management team were the losing under-bidders: how motivated would the losing management team be? Similarly the vendors had to manage the potential conflicts of interest with their own management teams who were both running the business and trying to buy it. The problems created by a potential management buyout were therefore twofold: firstly the risks of a deal to other potential buyers increased and secondly there were real conflicts of interest for managers upon whom all parties were relying for information. These conflicts and risks reduced the number of bidders willing to partake in any sale process. Much research on management buyouts focused upon whether the sale process itself appropriated value to successful buyouts. The idea is that since managers could use inside information only available to them, a potential buyout would drive away competing bidders, and so the value of the business would be reduced. This fall in value would be a transfer from the seller to the buyer. Therefore management buyouts would start with an advantage: they could buy the business cheaper.

The solution to this was the wresting of control of the process from management teams, the creation of the company auction process by corporate financiers, and the introduction of disclosure and governance rules for quoted company transactions.

In an auction a sales document is prepared and circulated to potential interested parties including both private equity and trade buyers. The level playing field should reduce conflicts for management and capture more of the value for the vendor. It also encourages private equity houses to team up with external managers in an attempt to gain a sector advantage, giving a boost to the MBI/IBO numbers at the expense of the MBO numbers. Auction processes are virtually ubiquitous both in larger transactions and in disposals by private equity firms (secondary buyouts).

If auctions generally increase the price paid for buyouts by acquirers, there is a transfer of value from the purchasers to vendors. If prices are not higher as a result of the process, there is a leakage of value due to transaction costs. Other things being equal we would expect either of these to reduce returns when compared to past performance. In addition to paying an increased price, there is a further downside as purchasers with poorer access to management in any auction process take on more risk (as they lose access to management's inside view). This again might be expected to reduce returns in private equity overall.

There has been considerable research on returns to private equity investors, which we discuss at length. Within this research is a consistent trend towards so-called compression of returns. It is widely observed that returns to private equity are no longer as dispersed as they were. The difference between the best and worst groups of funds is falling. This compression is consistent with greater maturity and competition in the market. More specifically the compression may be due to the creation of more controlled and managed sale processes around businesses. It is our conjecture that the company auction process has been instrumental in leading to this maturity in what is called by academics the market for corporate control.

Deal Initiation and Proprietary Deal Flow

Private equity funds predictably do not like competitive auctions. They receive poorer access to the company than in an unfettered private process and have to bid against other interested parties, which forces up the price. They therefore invest heavily in 'deal initiation' (or 'deal origination') in order to pre-empt these competitive processes. The transactions that a firm initiates itself are so-called 'off-market' deals. When fund raising, much play is made of these proprietary deals—that is, those 'owned' by the fund in some undefined sense. More proprietary deal flow should in principle mean less competition, lower prices, better access to information, and therefore the holy grail of both higher returns and lower risks.

This is what drives a large proportion of especially mid-market deal initiation activity. A 'good eye for a deal' is one of the key skills for a successful investor.

What Have Been the Biggest UK Deals?

By far the largest European transaction was the 2007 £11bn public-to-private buyout of Boots plc, led by KKR, to create Alliance Boots.

As Figure 1.19 illustrates, from around the turn of the century the frequency of £1bn buyouts sharply increased in the UK. As we described earlier, this stopped in the wake of the financial crisis and re-emerged from 2014 onwards. A list of the deals included in Figure 1.19 is at Appendix 1.

Of the largest transactions shown in Figure 1.19 none failed in the formal insolvency sense, but a number delivered no equity value to their original investors. More information can be found on these and other larger transactions by looking at the Walker Guidelines Monitoring Group website.[9]

Figure 1.20 shows the largest failed buyouts by the year the deal completed against the year of failure. (A list of the deals included in this figure is at Appendix 2.) The number of years to failure is given by the diagonal lines. There is no clear failure pattern and it is

---

[9] http://privateequityreportinggroup.co.uk/.

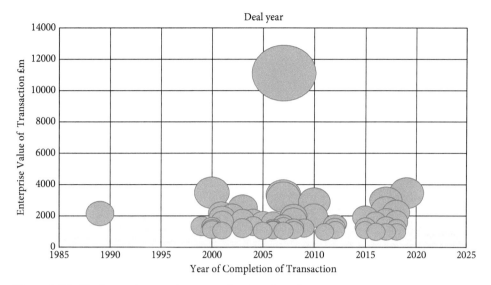

Figure 1.19. The largest buyouts by year and enterprise value
Source: CMBOR/Investec/Equistone Partners Europe

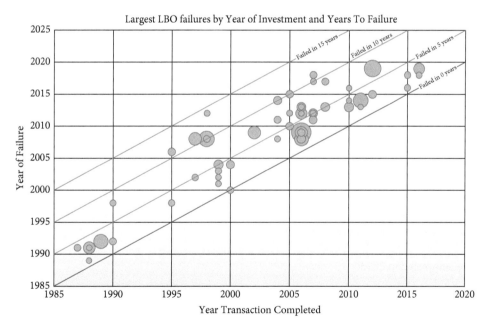

Figure 1.20. Large buyout failures by year of investment, year of failure and original enterprise value
Source: CMBOR/Investec/Equistone Partners Europe

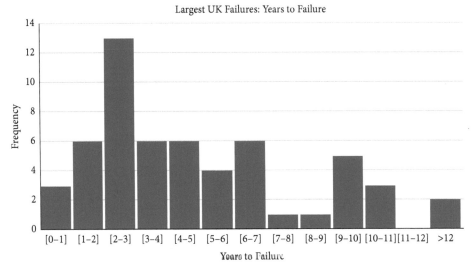

Figure 1.21. Largest UK private equity failures: time to failure
Source: CMBOR/Investec/Equistone Partners Europe

certainly not the case that most fail quickly. To the extent that there are patches of failure in the late 1980s, 1999, and around 2005/6, they cannot be easily distinguished from simple volume-related increases: if you see more deals, you will see more that will fail. What is perhaps most revealing is the very long time it takes for some deals to finally expire (see Figure 1.21).

The clear modal year of failure in these large deals is year two to three, but there is a long tail that stretches out beyond the life of the original fund that made the investment.

What Have Been the Biggest Deals in the World?

Of the largest LBO bids ever made, nearly all took place at the height of the private equity boom that ended around July 2007 (Table 1.3). It is also notable that two of these bids did not complete. Another, Clear Channel, was only completed some two years after the initial agreement, following a legal dispute as the private equity backers placed pressure on the lenders to keep to their agreement to provide debt and negotiations to reduce the purchase price in the wake of the credit crisis. It is also interesting that two of the largest deals were completed in 2013.

What Are the Largest Private Equity Funds in the World and Where Are They Based?

An indication of the largest private equity funds in the world that lead new investments is given in Table 1.4.

The table again illustrates the dominance of US and UK fund managers and the concentration of European private equity funds originating from the UK. Since the last edition of this book, the giant Japanese-managed tech fund Softbank and large state-owned investment funds in China have emerged.

Table 1.3. The world's largest buyouts

Firm	Deal date	Deal size ($m)	Investors	Primary industry
Energy Future Holdings Corporation	2007	45,000	California Public Employees' Retirement System (CalPERS), Citigroup, Energy Capital Partners, Goldman Sachs Merchant Banking Division, Kohlberg Kravis Roberts, Lehman Brothers, Morgan Stanley, Quintana Capital Group, TPG	Energy
Equity Office Properties Trust	2006	39,000	Blackstone Group	Property
HCA Holdings Inc.	2006	33,000	Bain Capital, Citigroup, Kohlberg Kravis Roberts, Merrill Lynch Global Private Equity, Ridgemont Equity Partners	Healthcare
First Data	2007	29,000	Citi Private Equity, Goldman Sachs Merchant Banking Division, Kohlberg Kravis Roberts	Financial services
H.J. Heinz Company	2013	28,000	3G Capital, Berkshire Hathaway	Food
Caesars Entertainment Corporation	2006	27,800	Apollo Global Management, Blackstone Group, California Public Employees' Retirement System (CalPERS), TPG	Leisure
Alltel Corporation	2007	27,500	Goldman Sachs Merchant Banking Division, TPG	Telecommunications, media
Hilton Worldwide	2007	26,000	Blackstone Group	Leisure
Dell Inc.	2013	24,900	MSD Capital, Silver Lake	Hardware
Clear Channel	2006	24,000	Bain Capital, Thomas H Lee Partners	Advertising

Source: Preqin.

How Significant Are Public-to-Private Transactions in the UK's Private Equity Market?

Public company acquisitions by private equity funds ('public-to-privates', or 'P2Ps') have attracted much scrutiny and comment. We suggest that there is an overemphasis on P2Ps in the press and academic literature, due in no small part to a greater availability of data on public companies. Questions of insider dealing and the failure of corporate governance have been examined by a number of authorities in the UK and US. As seen above, around half of the largest UK buyouts by value have been P2Ps. A sustained period of activity, beginning around 1998, accelerated from 2004 culminating in the UK's largest

Table 1.4. Estimate of the world's largest private equity funds by value

Fund	Value (m)	Vintage	Strategy	Fund manager	Fund manager location
SoftBank Vision Fund	$98,583	2017	Hybrid	SB Investment Advisers	Japan
China Integrated Circuit Industry Investment Fund II	¥200,000	2019	Growth	SINO-IC Capital	China
Apollo Investment Fund IX	$24,714	2018	Buyout	Apollo Global Management	US
China Integrated Circuit Industry Investment Fund	¥138,700	2014	Growth	SINO-IC Capital	China
Blackstone Capital Partners V	$20,365	2006	Buyout	Blackstone Group	US
GS Capital Partners VI	$20,300	2007	Buyout	Goldman Sachs Merchant Banking Division	US
China Structural Reform Fund	¥131,000	2016	Growth	CCT Fund Management	China
TPG Partners VI	$18,873	2008	Buyout	TPG	US
Carlyle Partners VII	$18,500	2018	Buyout	Carlyle Group	US
CVC Capital Partners Fund VII	€16,400	2018	Buyout	CVC Capital Partners	UK
Apollo Investment Fund VIII	$18,380	2014	Buyout	Apollo Global Management	US
Blackstone Capital Partners VII	$18,000	2016	Buyout	Blackstone Group	US
Apax Europe VII	€11,204	2007	Buyout	Apax Partners	UK
Advent Global Private Equity IX	$17,500	2019	Buyout	Advent International	US
KKR Fund 2006	$17,267	2006	Buyout	KKR	US
Hellman & Friedman Capital Partners IX	$16,000	2018	Buyout	Hellman & Friedman	US
TPG Partners V	$15,372	2006	Buyout	TPG	US
Blackstone Capital Partners VI	$15,114	2011	Buyout	Blackstone Group	US
Warburg Pincus Private Equity X	$15,107	2007	Balanced	Warburg Pincus	US
Warburg Pincus Global Growth	$14,800	2018	Balanced	Warburg Pincus	US
China State-Owned Capital Venture Fund I	¥102,000	2016	Venture	China Reform Fund	China
Apollo Investment Fund VII	$14,676	2008	Buyout	Apollo Global Management	US
Silver Lake Partners V	$14,500	2017	Buyout	Silver Lake	US
CVC European Equity Partners V	€10,750	2008	Buyout	CVC Capital Partners	UK
Permira IV	€11,100	2006	Buyout	Permira	UK

Source: Preqin.

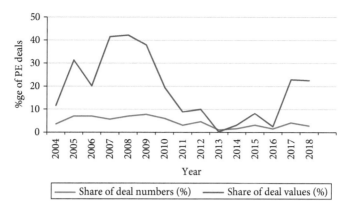

Figure 1.22. Percentage share of public to private buyouts by number and value (UK) 2004–13
Source: CMBOR/Investec/Equistone Partners Europe

P2P transaction to date, Alliance Boots plc in 2007. However, as illustrated in Figure 1.22, P2Ps represent a relatively small proportion (by number) of the overall private equity market.

At time of writing P2Ps have started to re-emerge after nearly a decade when they were less than 10 per cent of the market by value. They continue to be a small fraction of the number of transactions: this reflects changes to rules relating to public companies that increased the difficulty of executing such transactions. The rise in P2P transactions coincided with the top of the last cycle. Similar trends are seen in the USA.

2

The Private Equity Fund

This chapter looks at the typical fund structures and who invests in private equity, and compares and contrasts alternative investment options. We examine the universe of advisers surrounding PE and look at the incentives that exist in their markets. In the section on taxation we try to blow away some myths and explain why certain structures were created, In what we are calling a 'deep dive section', we take a closer look at what is actually in a typical Limited Partners Agreement (LPA) and examine why some of the structures are what they are.

What Is a Private Equity Fund?

As we noted in Chapter 1, much, but not all, of the investing in the private equity market is by PE funds. A private equity fund is a form of 'investment club' in which the principal investors are institutional investors such as pension funds, investment funds, endowment funds, insurance companies, banks, sovereign wealth funds, family offices, high net worth individuals, and funds of funds, as well as the PE fund managers themselves.

How Are Private Equity Funds Structured? 'Ten plus Two' Funds

The fund manager manages one or more funds. These are invested in by a variety of institutions and other bodies. The funds have a limited life, meaning that there is a pre-agreed date on which they will stop making new investments and subsequently be wound up. Typically, a fund invests in new projects for six years and is wound up in ten years. There is a standard extension period of two years in most fund agreements, hence they are generally known as 'ten plus two' limited life funds. This is discussed more extensively below.

In the past few years some longer-term funds have started to be raised by some fund managers. These are typically targeting growth capital.

While the structure of a PE fund does not change over time, we separate out the features of the initial commitment phase and the investment and realization phase of a fund's life in the diagrams and description below.

In the set-up phase of the fund (see Figure 2.1), the investors establish a limited life fund. External investors—known as limited partners (LPs)—and the partners of the fund manager invest directly in the fund. In addition, the general partner (GP) is set up and invested in by the fund manager. All investors arc typically invested on the same economic terms, although this is changing due to co-invest and feeder funds, which are discussed later.

Private Equity Demystified: An explanatory guide. Fourth Edition. John Gilligan and Mike Wright, Oxford University Press (2020).
© John Gilligan & Mike Wright. DOI: 10.1093/oso/9780198866961.003.0002

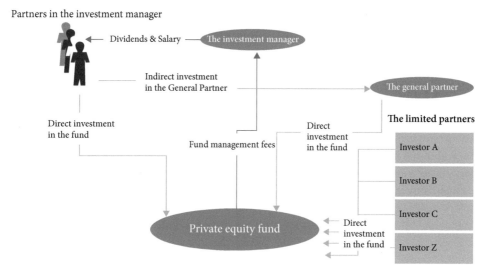

Figure 2.1. Structure of a typical private equity fund: **investment phase**

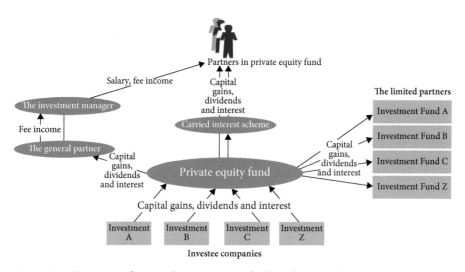

Figure 2.2. Structure of a typical private equity fund: **realization phase**

In the investment and realization phases (Figure 2.2), the portfolio of investments is acquired, drawing down on the fund commitments as the deals are done. These investments may pay fees, interest, and dividends to the fund which will distribute them to the investors and fund manager in accordance with the agreements between them. As investments mature, they will be realized, and capital gains earned and losses made. Gains are also distributed back to investors in accordance with the agreements. We discuss this further below.

Why Are Private Equity Funds Partnerships and Why Are Some Offshore?

The fund manager itself may or may not be a partnership. However, each fund is usually a separate limited-life partnership. There is much misrepresentation and confusion about why these structures exist. In essence the problem that needed to be solved was: how can a group of institutions and individuals create a limited liability structure that would bind them together as investors for a finite period without creating multiple tax charges?

Note that the starting point is not to avoid tax, it is to avoid duplicating tax charges whilst maintaining limited liability. Each investor should be taxed according to their individual tax position. The problem was to avoid creating a vehicle that would also be taxed before the investors were paid out. If a limited company had been formed, for example, it would have had a corporation tax liability and would have had to be solvently liquidated at the end of the investment period. This creates double taxation: once when the company pays corporation tax and again when the distribution is made. As the investors are often exempt from capital gains tax, this would mean that private equity paid corporation tax before distributing any gain, whereas buying and selling shares in quoted companies would not. This would make private equity pay more tax than investing in public equity if you were a tax-exempt investor, and would therefore fundamentally undermine the Private Equity industry.

Similarly, in a traditional partnership (at that time) all the partners in the partnership jointly and severally guaranteed each other's obligations—in other words, each partner would be jointly liable for the other partners' liabilities. Clearly this is not a vehicle that would be appropriate to a mutual investment fund with multiple disparate investors. No investor would join a scheme where they guaranteed other investors' risks.

In the UK, to solve these types of problems, structures created by an obscure piece of early twentieth-century legislation were revived. These are called limited life partnerships. They allow partners to come together to cooperate for a finite period without creating a new layer of taxable income or requiring the partners to jointly and severally guarantee each other's liabilities.

Similar vehicles exist in other jurisdictions. Where they do not, investors will create the fund in a legal jurisdiction that can allow the creation of fixed-term, shared investment funds without creating extra tax liabilities. One way to do this is to create a limited liability company, which does pay tax, in a jurisdiction with zero corporation tax—you pay tax, but at zero per cent. This is a major reason why you see offshore funds in Private Equity. It is usually due to a combination of controlling liabilities and eliminating double tax or corporation tax that would not be paid on a similar quoted investment. It has a number of other added features, including lower disclosure requirements which has attraction for those seeking secrecy, but also creates widespread suspicion.

In funds with multinational investors, some may not wish to invest directly in the jurisdiction of the fund but may instead invest in feeder funds (which can be offshore limited liability corporations created for the purpose) that then invest in the main fund. As it is a zero-tax jurisdiction, double taxation is eliminated. There are therefore legitimate reasons why investors use offshore vehicles to invest in businesses, including PE funds. There are also opportunities to use the veil of secrecy to avoid disclosing activities for any reason.

What Are LPs and GPs?

The external investors are called limited partners (LPs) because their total liability is limited to the amount they invest. The manager is often called the general partner (GP). The general partner has potentially unlimited liability for the actions of the fund. To put a

cap on this potentially unlimited liability many GPs are in fact limited companies or partnerships. Technically, the fund manager invests in the general partner; however, in common (technically incorrect) usage, LPs are investors and GPs are PE fund managers. We
will usually use this common parlance.

Limited Liability and Management Control: An Important Caveat

One of the most important things to understand about limited-life partnerships is the way
liability works. The LPs are only exposed to losing a maximum of their own investment *if
they are not acting as managers* of the fund's activities. If they do act as managers, they risk
becoming General Partners and having unlimited liability. This sharply constrains the
ability of LPs to intervene in the day-to-day running and investment decisions of the fund.
As soon as an LP starts to act as a manager, limited liability is in question. This acts to
effectively prevent LPs from being involved in active management and assigns them to a
permanently passive role. Many of the issues surrounding LP–GP relations stem from this
historic split between passive investor with limited liability and active manager with wider
responsibilities and liabilities.

Alternative Fund Structures

Several alternative fund structures have been used, including:

Deal by Deal
Some private equity investors operate on a deal-by-deal basis. Each investment is funded
by a panel of investors who exercise discretion over their own funds. Carried interest is
also therefore on a deal-by-deal basis. This is a much more ephemeral hand-to-mouth
existence than a traditional fund, but examples of successful teams following this strategy
do exist, both as new entrants to the industry and as successors to former fund managers
who did not raise a follow-on fund.

Rolling Commitments
Rolling funds that provide an ability to trade in and out of the manager have been established. Alchemy Partners was a high-profile early UK fund that initially took 12-month
commitments from its investors. It subsequently reverted to a more traditional fund
structure.

Captives and the Canadian Model
While most captive PE teams were spun out in the 1990s as we described in Chapter 1,
there were a few exceptions. The largest in the UK is Lloyds Development Capital, which
remains a subsidiary of Lloyds Bank as we write.

There has also been a re-emergence of captive teams, led by the Canadian public pension funds. The motivation for establishing these teams seem to have been a desire to
reduce fees and a strategy that seeks to hold investments for much longer than a traditional fund would. These teams not only compete for primary transactions, but also co-
invest and invest in PE funds as LPs.

Some commentators predict that these in-house teams are the future of private equity.

Investment Trusts

There are a few quoted investment trusts that have invested in primary PE deals. 3i in the UK is still probably the largest, being a member of the FTSE 100 as we write. It invests from its own balance sheet and from funds that are broadly traditionally structured. Others are legacy structures from earlier strategies that now largely co-invest alongside funds.

Fund Raising and Investors in Private Equity Funds

It is of course a necessary condition of being a private equity investor to have funds to invest. In Chapter 1 we described the move away from captive funds and the emergence of the old 'standard model': the 'ten plus two' limited-life fund. Usually these funds make investments for around six years then the fund moves into a period where no new investments are made, other than further capital committed to existing companies.

Competition for Funds by Private Equity Managers

When funds are being raised, investors are offered the opportunity to commit an amount of capital to the fund. As the fund has no underlying assets, other than the goodwill of the manager, there is no pricing mechanism in the cost of fund units to ration demand. There is, however, generally a minimum amount which can be committed. If a fund is oversubscribed, by agreement with LPs the Private Equity fund managers may enlarge the fund, or may scale back investors' applications.

GPs have created innovative ways to capitalize on the rise in demand for allocations of private equity assets. One tactic that has emerged is the so-called GP-led secondary. We discuss this in greater detail below, but essentially the GP uses the demand for new fund allocations to create liquidity in old funds. The GP ties together an offer to invest in the new fund, with either a purchase or a restructuring of old funds. The potential for conflicts of interest to arise is material.

The demand for investing in a fund will, to a large extent, depend on the perceived investment track record of the private equity fund managers. However, an investment decision by an LP will also be influenced by the way it is proposed to share investment returns between the LPs and the manager. There is, therefore, competition between funds based upon the management fees charged, the hurdle rate of return, and the priority of the returns between LPs and the GP and the carry percentage (see below).

Where Is the Private Equity Industry?

We can examine the industry by where funds are raised, where they are managed, or where they are ultimately deployed in transactions.

Figure 2.3 shows funds raised by the location of the fund manager's business. For these purposes it is the 'home' region of the fund manager that is being presented. A large US fund with global offices is therefore still counted as North America in the data.

An alternative is to track deal locations—the head office or major location of the companies where the money is invested rather than where it is managed from (Figure 2.4).

Using either metric, the US has been the historic home of large-scale private equity, and while it has been seen as an Anglo-Saxon form of investment and governance, the asset class is present in all major economies of the world.

The emergence of China and the growth of Germany have been key features over the past five years. The UK has declined in relative importance over the period, but this reflects growth elsewhere rather than contraction in the UK.

If we examine the top ten countries in the world (excluding the US) by value of investments we can see the general global growth that has occurred (Figure 2.5).

This dominance of US private equity by value has implications for any general investigation or conversation about PE. The overwhelming majority of research has been done on US funds, either by choice or because the historic data is saturated in US funds.

The UK and European research base of CMBOR[1] is predominantly at the company level. It is important to understand this distinction when looking at research findings. Fund level research has less to say on deal level matters.

Who Are the Investors in Private Equity Funds?

While the situation is very different around the world, in the UK anyone can find out who are the investors or nominees in a UK limited partnership by looking up the fund and

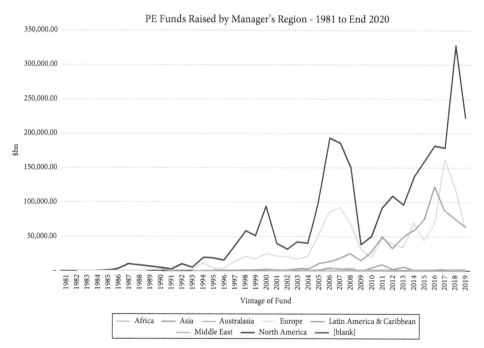

Figure 2.3. Private equity funds raised by manager's region—1981 to end 2020
Source: Preqin

---

[1] The Centre for Management Buyout Research was founded by Mike Wright in 1986.

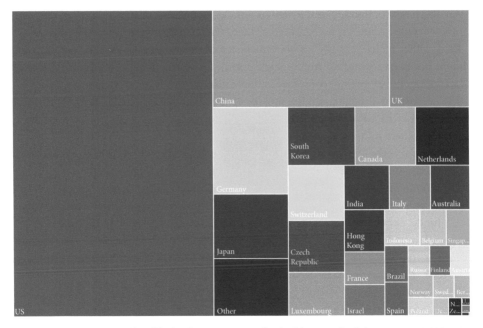

Figure 2.4. Aggregate value ($bn) of private equity-backed buyout deals by country, 2009–18
Source: Preqin

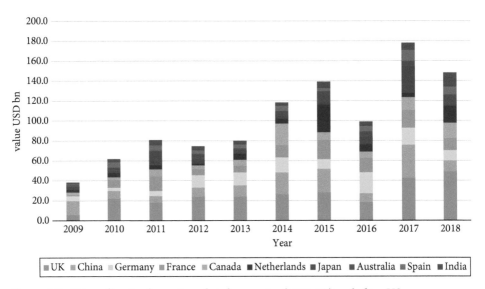

Figure 2.5. Value of top ten buyout markets by country (2009–18) excluding US
Source: Preqin

finding the so-called LP6 Form on Companies House records, which are available free online. In most of the world this is not the case.

The data that we can access suggests that pension funds constitute the largest category of investors in private equity funds and that the largest proportion of funds raised are buyout funds (Figure 2.6). The largest investors are the largest pension funds, which are generally public sector schemes around the world. Ultimately many of the investors are members of the wider public who contribute to pension schemes and collective saving funds and who purchase pension products.

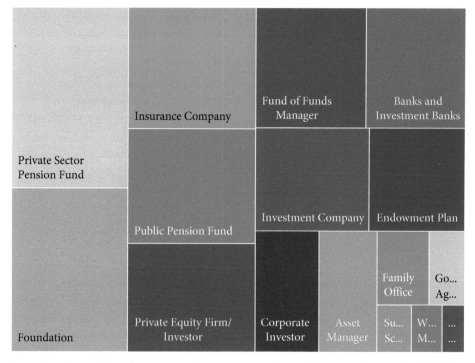

Figure 2.6. Proportion of investors with known commitments in buyout funds 2019 YTD: by firm type

Source: Preqin. (As public pensions are required to disclose more data than non-public investors, the results will be weighted towards the more transparent institutions that provide this information.)

Note that many of these investors are pension funds and charities which are typically not liable to tax. Therefore, any structure that imposed a tax at the level of the investment vehicle (a limited company, for example) would be a unique tax on private equity. These investors pay no tax on investing in public shares, and some of the complex structures seen are how a similar position is reached in private equity.

The three largest investor categories—pension schemes, foundations, and insurance companies—all have long-term liabilities that they need to invest to fund. The long-term nature of private equity funds makes them appropriate for investors with a long-term horizon. If the investors are likely to require their money back in the short term, private equity is an inappropriate asset class to invest in. The market for secondary PE transactions, which we discuss later in this chapter, is an emerging solution to provide liquidity to those seeking to trade out of PE fund illiquid positions.

Many LPs will have a broad PE investing programme covering a range of different territories, fund sizes, and fund strategies—large buyout, venture, country specific, mid-market, etc.

What are Funds of Funds?

A fund of funds is a collective investment vehicle established to invest in primary private equity funds. It allows groups who would not be able to access PE funds to collaborate in a collective investment vehicle that is managed on their behalf. The advantage is that the investors gain access to opportunities that they otherwise would not see. The

Table 2.1. Top ten fund-of-funds investors in global private equity (2019)

Firm name	Private equity assets under management ($bn)	Firm country
Partners Group	45	Switzerland
Pathway Capital Management	45	US
AlpInvest Partners	44.2	Netherlands
Pantheon	36.8	UK
Bpifrance Investissement	35.5	France
Adams Street Partners	35.4	US
StepStone	30	US
SVB Capital	28.8	US
Portfolio Advisers	21.3	US
Horsley Bridge Partners	15	US

Source: Preqin

disadvantage is the extra layer of costs and fees that fund-of-funds managers charge. Some of the historical funds-of-funds have changed their business models to both provide bespoke portfolio management to LPs and start direct and co-investment teams at the opposite end of the spectrum.

Later we also summarize the findings on investment performance by private equity funds. We are not aware of any research that similarly analyses fund-of-funds managers, the largest of which are shown in Table 2.1.

What Are Sovereign Wealth Funds?

Sovereign wealth funds have become increasingly large investors in private equity, both directly and in funds. They are mostly investment programmes run on behalf of governments with accumulating budget surpluses that are not used to fund government programmes. The largest of these funds are those associated with countries that are resource rich (such as oil states).

How Can Individual Investors Invest in Equity Funds?

There are retail funds and venture capital trusts that invest in smaller private equity transactions. There are also quoted investment trusts that invest in PE funds and transactions including larger deals: as commented on above, KKR, Blackstone, EQT, and Carlyle, among others, have all offered interests in the fund manager to the public. The flotation of certain fund managers has altered the ability of retail investors to access private equity, but this is not explored in this publication as we are focused on the PE market, not the shares in publicly listed PE fund managers.

It is worth noting that in the US a number of the quoted PE fund managers have changed their organizational form from partnerships to corporations to attract investors.

In general, larger private equity funds have a minimum investment amount per fund that precludes most private investors, and managing the drawdown from private investors would be a significant burden. (The minimum investment varies from fund to fund but a threshold of $10m is not uncommon.) Furthermore, due to the regulatory protections afforded to retail investors in most markets, the costs and regulatory burdens of raising retail funds mean that no large private equity fund markets to a retail investment audience.

In order to provide wider access to PE funds a number of fund-of-funds and specialist fund managers emerged. These allow smaller institutional investors, who cannot justify the costs of an in-house team making private equity fund investments, to collectively invest in the larger PE funds. However, the fund-of-funds manager will charge a fee (and take a share of any profit) before the investor earns a return, and for similar reasons to those above, few are open to retail investors.

In any reasonable sense, other than a few exceptions (such as indirect investment and specialist venture capital trusts), the private equity market should therefore be viewed as a wholesale market available only to institutional investors and regulated accordingly.

The Economics of Private Equity

Committed versus Invested Capital

It is important to understand that private equity funds do not generally draw down funds until they are needed. An investor makes a commitment to invest in the opportunities that a fund manager selects for the fund. They do not deposit the cash with the fund manager. The GP fund manager has certainty of funds, but the LP investor in the fund has an uncertain cash commitment to any particular fund, both in terms of timing of drawdown and the total amount that will be drawn down.

This makes private equity funds particularly difficult to forecast from a cash perspective. GP fund managers protect themselves from the risk of an LP being unable to fund their commitments by putting in place a mechanism whereby if an LP funder cannot invest then the other LPs take up that investment (up to their maximum commitment). LPs failing to fulfil their commitment then substantially lose their rights and returns under the investment agreement.

Figure 2.7 shows an illustrative life cycle of a fund (at cost). In the early years there are large undrawn commitments (so-called 'dry powder'). As cash is invested (gross investment) dry powder diminishes and the portfolio (at cost) is built. As loans made to investee companies are repaid and realizations made as investments are sold ('return flow') the cash flows reverse and become positive for the investors, typically from around the end of year six or seven.

The graph above illustrates a typical investment cycle and the planned return flow from the portfolio (excluding realizations and refinancings). As investments are often geared with shareholder loans, there is a frequently a redeemable element that is repayable, usually in years 5, 6, 7, 8 depending on the particular deal terms.

Gross Investment

Gross investment is the cash invested in each company. It can be a first investment into a new company to the portfolio, or a further investment into an existing portfolio company. Traditionally a fund could make first investments up to the end of year 6 and thereafter it could only make supporting further investments in companies already in the portfolio. Therefore, in order to be able to make ongoing new investments a private equity fund

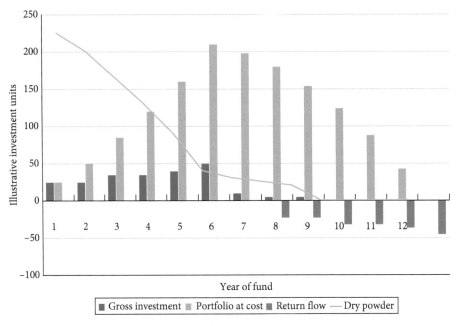

Figure 2.7. Private equity investment cycle

manager had to raise new funds before the end of the existing fund's five–six-year investment window.

Return Flow

This is the name given to cash receipts from the underlying investments. These consist of
income in the form of interest, dividends and (sometimes) fees, plus any capital repaid,
from for example loans made as part of an investment. In addition, any capital gains will
be received as they are realized.

A second key feature of most private equity funds is that they do not generally recycle
capital. Repayments are typically paid back to the investors as they are received, not reused
by the fund. Therefore, a fund is limited to gross investment up to its committed capital,
but not beyond, irrespective of how much cash is returned through return flow and capital
gains. Private equity investors are not 'flush with cash' after a realization: it all goes back to
the investors.

There are circumstances when capital recycling is permitted, usually to allow for reuse
of capital that returns much more quickly than expected. The most usual category for
recycling is where part of an initial commitment is re-financed early in the investment life
(usually within a year) rather than a rapid sale of the whole investment. The partnership
agreement may allow the fund manager to reuse that capital on another investment.

As a commercial matter, most funds rarely invest all of their capital as they usually hold
back some ability to make further investments in assets that they own. It would be impru-
dent to find that a business needed a financial injection but the fund had no capacity
to invest.

As we will see when we come to discuss the way that private equity managers earn their
returns, it is important that funds do get invested and managing this balance between getting cash invested and leaving a prudent uninvested buffer is important.

Investor Cash Flows: The J Curve (at Cost)

As a result of the investment and realization profile of any fund, an investor will generally see a highly uncertain pattern of cash flows, but one that will tend to have net cash out in the early years and net cash inflow in later years.

In practice private equity is characterized by very lumpy cash flows, in terms of both new investments and realizations. The stylized example in Figure 2.8 does not assume any early realizations from successful investments.

When private equity funds represented relatively small commitments by very large institutions, the fact that the LP investors had volatile cash flows was comparatively unimportant. In the scheme of a large institutional investor these volatilities were not a material management problem. As fund sizes and the number of funds grew, these volatilities started to present significant cash flow management issues to some investors, in particular those with borrowings predicated on cash flows from existing investments and those with high levels of commitment relative to their overall business. This is one of the factors that has encouraged the emergence of debt products to smooth the investors' cash flows, and large secondary markets that allow investors to trade both the assets that they have invested in and the undrawn commitments to funds as a package.

Subscription Line Funding

One of the structures that has become almost ubiquitous since we first wrote this guide to private equity are so-called subscription line funding facilities. These are working capital facilities that allow a PE fund to allow them to draw down funds from a bank facility rather than directly from the LP investors. They are secured against the undrawn commitments to the fund and usually subsequently repaid from drawdowns from LPs.

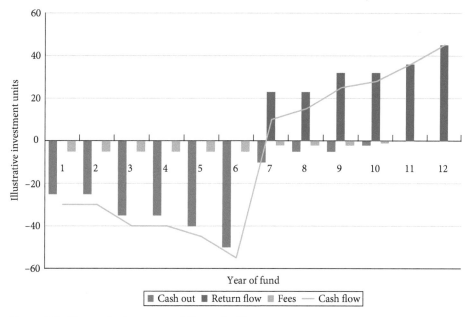

Figure 2.8. Illustrative investor cashflows: the 'J' curve

Subscription line funding emerged as a means to manage the volatility that LPs experienced when large cash calls came at very short notice. This gave rise to two big operational problems:

- First, an LP had to have large facilities or hold large amounts of liquid assets just in case the fund made a large investment, and also needed to have in place people and processes that could rapidly respond to a cash call. This was easy when private equity funds were small, but as they grew in size the uncertainty became a material management issue, compounded by the risk of drawing down capital only to have to return it. In an auction (see Chapter 41) the buyer will have to prove certain availability of funds, especially if bidding for a public company. If you need a few days to draw down you risk having a series of draw-and-repay situations if you lose out in the auction. This can be resolved by allowing recycling, but it is a major headache in calculating carried interest and in managing the cash flows of the fund and its investors.
- Secondly, as private equity deal doing became more competitive, it was highly advantageous to be able to move rapidly to complete a deal. Vendors and their advisers in any deal always have concerns about the transaction risks, including certainty of funds. In the original limited partnership agreements an LP might be given a few days' notice to transmit cash. In the modern auction that can mean the difference between doing a deal and losing out to another bidder. As speed of execution is a key private equity advantage in any large transaction, having funds available at all times is a major advantage.

Subscription lines were therefore introduced to manage working capital for LPs. They have subsequently become tools to massage returns. We return to the mechanics of this below as part of a more detailed discussion on limited partners agreements.

How are Private Equity Fund Managers Rewarded?

As we discussed in Chapter 1, in addition to a salary and the returns as an investor, GPs receive two other income sources.

Fee Income

Fund managers (GPs) receive management fees that are expressed as a percentage of the funds committed. The larger the fund, the greater the absolute amount of fee income, although the percentage generally declines from around 2.00 per cent in smaller funds to 1.00–1.25 per cent in larger funds. The management fee was originally intended to pay for the operating costs of employing staff and other expenses associated with the fund manager's business, plus the reasonable salaries of the partners. Any excess over these costs is retained by the management company (the manager) and may be paid to its partners/shareholders. Fund managers have to balance the use of fee income to reinvest in growing the personnel, infrastructure, and assets of the business with the requirement to recruit and retain their best partners by offering industry-competitive remuneration.

Fees are generally charged on committed capital during the investment phase and then on invested capital after the fund closes to new investments. This is different to other fund managers who charge fees on assets under management in the public markets and on invested capital in private debt markets. It reflects the fact that the usual definition of assets under management (AUM) in private equity is the sum of capital invested plus undrawn commitments.

The way that PE funds draw down cash impacts fee comparisons between asset classes. A hedge fund might charge 2.0 per cent per annum on invested cash. A PE fund charging 2.0 per cent on the same amount of committed capital will charge higher fees as a percentage of the amount of cash invested, because fees are charged on the undrawn portion. However, the LPs earn a return on the undrawn capital, and the interest earned on the undrawn commitment may be greater than the fee. In reality, as we shall see, it is much more complex than this simple comparison.

It has been argued that the growth in fund size has resulted in the creation of a new principal–agent problem within private equity funds. As illustrated in Figure 2.9, the larger funds often generate fees that may result in substantial profits to their partners. These profits accrue whether or not the fund itself is successful. This challenges the central idea of alignment of interest driving value creation. Partners are receiving a risk-free return if they can raise a large fund. The evidence regarding historical sustained outperformance by the best funds has prevented new entrants from competing away the profit from fee income.

This is made more complex by the fact that even managers who only have a single strategy will after a few years have more than one fund vintage under management. A single strategy fund (say, UK mid-market buyouts) will have a clause within the LPA stating that until (typically) 70 per cent of the fund is invested, no new fund following that strategy can be raised.

Private equity investing is a largely fixed-cost business because the variable costs are charged to the investments made (we will explain much more of this later). This means that if the fees on fund I cover the fixed and variable costs of the manager, the contribution from fund II will be almost all profit as long as both funds are in the investment period. Even when the first fund is closed to new investments after around five years, the manager receives fees from both funds.

Imagine a fund manager who raised three funds that are rapidly 70 per cent invested (or follow different strategies), the first in year 0, then the others in years 3 and 6 respectively (Figure 2.10). Each fund is bigger than the last, with fixed costs largely being personnel, marketing, and premises. (In fact, for many PE funds in the UK, one of their biggest costs is irrecoverable VAT on advisers' fees, but that is outside our scope here.) The variable costs of deal doing are largely charged to the individual transactions. Variable costs are therefore a relatively small proportion of assets under management.

If fees on fund I cover fixed and variable costs, there will be no profit or loss. Fund II is raised and the manager receives 'double' fees for years 4 and 5, and by year 6 the fee income jumps again as the last and largest fund is raised. If the fund manager stops raising funds and keeps the same cost base, they will have falling fees as the funds wind down. However, in reality, any manager who stops investing will adjust their costs to the fee income and will not have the decline we have shown in our simple illustration above. In single strategy funds it is likely that the overlap of full fees will be small, but there will still be multiple, but lower fees, from any funds not fully realized.

The important general point is that the more funds are being managed, the greater the fee income. Because making investments is a largely fixed-cost business, having multiple

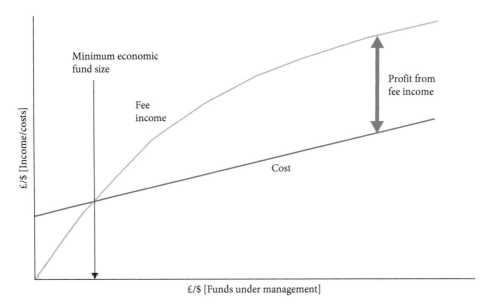

Figure 2.9. Relationship between fee income and fund manager profit

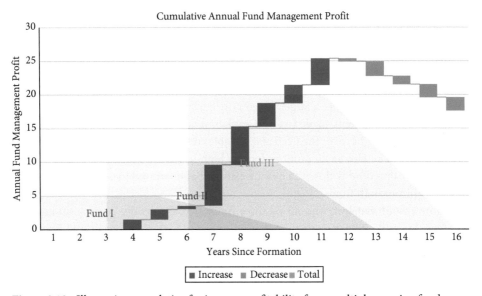

Figure 2.10. Illustrative cumulative fee income profitability from multiple growing funds

overlapping funds creates years with high profits from fund management irrespective of the performance of the funds. This breaks the alignment model between the LP investors and the fund manager at the level of the fund manager, even if the structure of each fund tightly aligns the LPs and manager in that particular fund.

Therefore, to really understand the alignment in the fund manager an investor needs to understand both the fund that they are looking to invest in, and, crucially, the economics of the existing funds that the manager has already raised and is managing. If you cannot see the terms of the old funds, you cannot reasonably understand how the incremental fee income will change the incentives of the manager.

Carried Interest

The second source of reward for private equity fund managers is a share in the profits of the fund; this is generally known as carried interest (or carry). Once the investors have achieved the hurdle rate, the fund managers will share in the profits made. Usually this was 20 per cent of any profits. The hurdle rate (historically around 8 per cent per annum but variable from fund to fund) is calculated on the amounts invested. Note that the manager receives 20 per cent of all of the cash flows as long as the return is more than 8.0 per cent, not 20.0 per cent of the excess above the hurdle. To do this there is a mechanism called a catch up.

The mechanics of the calculation are intricate (Figure 2.11). Over the life of the fund, net income and capital distributions will be made in the following order:

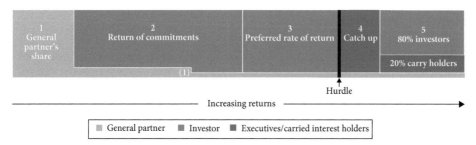

Figure 2.11. The mechanics of carried interest

(1) The GP receives a priority share of partnership returns each year.
(2) The investors then receive a 100 per cent return of commitments advanced and a preferred rate of return (8 per cent).
(3) The carried interest holders receive 100 per cent of all distributions until such time that they have received 25 per cent of the investors' preferred return (2 above). This is referred to as 'catch up'.
(4) Thereafter the remaining distributions are split as follows:
   • 80 per cent to investors
   • 20 per cent to carried interest holders.

The fund can go 'into carry' if all called commitments and the hurdle rate have been paid and then go 'out of carry' if a further draw down is made.

As the market has matured there has been a constant refinement of industry practice to attempt to ensure that the carried interest calculation tightly aligns the interests of investors and fund managers. However, in a long-term, illiquid investment business with low levels of transparency to new entrants, this process of realigning interests may take longer than in other industries.

There are two basic carried interest models:

• **The American style** model, where carry is paid on a deal-by-deal basis, which may require a clawback of carry if later investments underperform, and

- **European style** carry which is paid on the whole portfolio. Both systems can result in the same absolute amount being paid, but the American system significantly increases the speed with which carry is paid out.

These funds are known as 'two-twenty' funds: i.e. 2 per cent fee and 20 per cent carried interest. The origin of this model has been the source of some academic investigation. It seems to be no more than a 'sticky' industry norm. Its resilience is underlined by the fact that it appears to stem from medieval Venetian trading contracts between ship owners and merchants.

Other Fees

In addition to these fees and profit share that are common to most funds, other fees may be receivable by the fund managers.

- Monitoring and/or non-executive director fees are widely payable by individual investee companies to defray some of the costs of employees and partners of private equity managers monitoring the investment. These fees may be payable to the PE fund or to the manager, or more likely are split between them in a predetermined proportion.
- The growth of operating partners who only work on portfolio companies can lead to consultancy arrangements between the investee company and the fund manager or connected parties. In the US this has led to a number of SEC investigations and fines. We discuss this further later when examining the details of funds.
- Transaction costs incurred by the private equity fund in making an investment are usually payable by the new company established to affect the buyout (Newco) and not by the PE fund. Abort costs of transactions which fail to complete may be borne by the fund or the manager or more likely shared in a pre-agreed ratio.
- Private equity fund managers may charge an arrangement fee to the investee company expressed as a proportion of the amount of money invested in a deal. These fees may be up to 3 per cent of the equity invested. Usually they are credited to the fund but they may be split on a pre-agreed basis with the manager.

Typically, but not always, the net of all these fees would be included in the calculation of the management fee and would not increase the overall rewards of the private equity fund managers.

All of these individually negotiated arrangements within a fund manager's business impact the individual returns of investors over the long term.

Moreover, the economic impact of the array of fees charged is unclear. If a newco borrows from its lenders to pay fees to its lenders, what profit has been made and when? The allocation and levying of transaction fees gives rise to further potential principal–agent issues between LPs and GPs.

LPs and management need to be aware of the impact of the proliferation of fees to funders on both returns and, importantly, incentives.

What is Co-Investment?

First, we need to distinguish between the past and the present use of the term.

Co-investment used to be used in some funds instead of, or alongside, carried interest. In these arrangements, managers (and sometimes other founder investors) were permitted to invest directly in each individual investment as well as, or instead of, in the whole fund. This practice was called co-investment.

For fund managers this is increasingly uncommon as it can create misalignment between the fund investors and the fund managers where the gains in one investment are disproportionate to the value of the overall portfolio.

However, co-investment has re-emerged in a new guise. Investors who have significant amounts of capital and wish to negotiate bespoke terms are increasingly turning to co-investment arrangements. Co-investment in this sense gives the investor the right, but not the obligation, to invest alongside the fund on the same terms. The question of who gets offered co-investment rights and on what terms is often wholly opaque and bespoke to each situation. It may be that any transaction over a certain size is offered to co-investors or it can be totally at the discretion of the manager.

Cash invested outside the fund is not subject to management fees. LPs therefore see co-investment as a cheaper way to invest in private equity. However, the process of making a co-investment decision requires resources to be available to make a decision at whatever time the co-investment opportunity arises. Typically, the process involves the receipt of the fund's investment papers and due diligence reports and a short period to say 'Yes' or 'No' to the opportunity. The period may be as short as a few days in an accelerated transaction. There are few organizations able to employ a suitably qualified team to make these decisions in a timely manner. You need significant transaction volumes to justify the cost of the co-invest team.

Separate Managed Funds

One solution is to create separate managed funds. These are partnerships that mimic the main fund vehicle but have only the fund manager and the investor as partners within them. They may, sometimes at the discretion of the investor as well as the fund manager, co-invest alongside other funds managed by the fund manager. There are also co-invest arrangements with some investors that allow them to invest directly alongside the fund on a case-by-case basis.

These are dilutions to the traditional long-term commitment to a fund with discretion purely in the fund managers' hands. They have grown in popularity in both direct private equity funds and in funds of funds.

A second solution is to use a professional manager to handle your co investment rights on your behalf. Several large investors now provide these types of services to smaller investors. There are even funds that only managed pooled co-investment rights.

Fund Extensions

If by the tenth anniversary of closing the fund the investments have not been realized, the manager can seek a fund extension. Seeking an extension used to be seen as a sign of poor performance; however, increasingly it is the case that holding a portfolio of investments for longer has been the desired outcome and 'positive' extensions now occur. The differing appetites of LPs to stay invested or realize their investments is one of the key drivers of the secondary market that we discuss later.

An extension of the investment period earlier in a fund's life is typically a sign that the manager has not been able to deploy the capital commitments as planned. This was common in the funds raised in the period immediately prior to the 2008 crash. In a number of these cases the LP investors took the opportunity to amend the terms of the original agreement by reducing fees and promoting tighter alignment of objectives.

Comparing Private Equity Funds

What Are the Walker Guidelines?

The Walker Guidelines were first published in 2007, following a request of the BVCA, with the intention to bring greater transparency to the private equity industry's largest investments and investors. The guidelines are a voluntary code of practice. They are monitored by the Private Equity Reporting Group (PERG) consisting of a chairman, two independent representatives from industry and/or the trade unions, and two representatives from the private equity industry.

From the end of 2010, adjustments to the criteria were introduced to apply to portfolio investee companies:

- with an enterprise value of £350m at acquisition (previously £500m) or £210m in the case of companies that were quoted prior to acquisition (previously £300m); and
- having 50 per cent or more of their business in the UK; and
- employing over 1,000 people in the UK.

From 2016 the guidelines were expanded to include a sample-based approach to assessing the level of compliance with a broader set of criteria.

Any private equity firm that has invested in a business covered by the guidelines is then required to make disclosures about itself. This represents a relatively small proportion, by number, of the total population of companies that have been invested in by the private equity industry but accounts for a significant proportion of the total amount invested by private equity firms (Table 2.2). A number of funds and firms that are no longer considered private equity-like have been removed from the scope of the guidelines.

The guidelines have four main components:

(1) portfolio companies should prepare disclosures as stipulated in the guidelines in their audited annual report and financial statements and prepare a mid-year update;
(2) portfolio companies are required to publish their annual report and a mid-year update in a timely and accessible manner on their company website;
(3) private equity firms should publish certain disclosures on their own website;
(4) portfolio companies are required to share certain data, presented in an aggregated performance report to illustrate the contribution of large private equity-backed companies to the UK economy.

Table 2.2. Compliance with the Walker guidelines

	2008	2009	2010	2011	2012	2013	2014	2015	2016	2017	2018
Portfolio companies required to conform	27	45	43	78	73	72	71	62	60	52	55
Portfolio companies voluntarily conforming	27	15	12	9	7	17	5	4	3	2	1
Total number of portfolio companies covered by the code	54	60	55	87	80	89	76	66	63	54	56
Total number of private equity companies covered by the code	32	34	35	43	47	53	59	65	74	59	51

Source: Authors' analysis of Private Equity Research Group data

The guidelines broadly require that companies provide the same kind of information to the public that would be provided if the companies were publicly traded. The guidelines operate on a 'comply or explain' basis so that non-compliance can be explained. The information required is included in an annual review published on the private equity fund's website. It is not required to (and generally does not) contain accounting or investment performance data. It seeks to identify who the individuals are within the private equity fund and what investments they hold. Limited information on intended investment duration and limited partner type (but not identity) is also given. The PERG issued a guide providing practical assistance to companies to help improve levels of transparency and disclosure, and which included examples of portfolio company reporting reviewed by the group.

Further data provision to the BVCA for their annual report is also required that does include high-level financial data including the amount of capital raised, number and value of investments made, and fees paid to advisers. Data that analyses the source of investment performance in exited investments is also sought to enable the annual review to be completed.

At the time they were introduced, there was some scepticism about the likely extent of compliance with the Walker Guidelines. In the event, compliance increased over time and remains generally high. However, there is some variability in the quality of disclosures. While the large majority of portfolio companies make the audited report and accounts available on their website as required by the guidelines, not all do so. In the latest report at the time of writing, which related to 2018, good-quality disclosures produced by portfolio companies were noted in relation to details on board composition, analysis of development and performance during the year, and position at year-end and financial key performance indicators. However, several areas were noted where standards of disclosure required improvement, notably in relation to identification and analysis of financial risks, gender diversity, and human rights issues. The report 'names and shames' firms that do not comply with the guidelines. The PERG has had some success in persuading firms that are non-compliant to become compliant but notes that oftentimes compliance is basic and not in line with good FT350 firm reporting. All BVCA members are committed to complying with the guidelines, with any non-compliance tending to be by non-BVCA members. The PERG continues to enhance the provisions of the guidelines to ensure that all companies covered report to a level comparable to current good practice in the FTSE 350.

How Does a Private Equity Fund Differ from a Quoted Equity Fund?

Funds that invest in public companies operate using different business models. The strategic intent of the investors may be similar, to make money from investing, but the methods are totally different.

Some quoted funds are specifically designed as income funds that seek to pay to investors a running yield generated from dividend income from shares and interest on bonds.

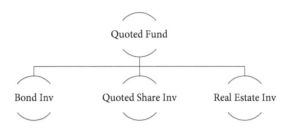

As noted above, private equity funds do not generally aim to generate yield. They are comparable to capital growth quoted funds that seek to generate the majority of their return from increased value in their investments. Key differences between the funds are set out in Table 2.3.

In essence, private equity fund managers seek to control the businesses they invest in and to choose an optimum capital structure for each of their investee companies. Thus, PE funds operate with much better information and stronger controls and influence over management than funds holding quoted equities. To achieve this, they forgo liquidity in the individual investments.

A very important differentiating factor is the 10-year fixed-term fund structure. This structure is a key determinant of the behaviours of the industry. Unlike permanent funds, limited life funds do not generally reinvest proceeds received from investments. They distribute proceeds to their investors. These investors then may, or may not, choose to reinvest the money in a subsequent fund. It is this long-term commitment to the fund, coupled with the way funds are distributed, that has been the defining feature of private equity investment to date.

Table 2.3. Key differences between private equity and quoted equity funds

Private equity funds	Quoted equity funds
Control and influence	
Private equity funds usually own a substantial or controlling stake in the business.	Funds investing in quoted companies usually acquire small minority stakes, which offer no control and no special rights.
Individual Private Equity investments are controlled using a detailed legally binding shareholder's agreement that establishes the contractual rights and obligations of the company, its management and the investors.	Institutional shareholders may be influential, but usually have no contractual control over day-to-day management decisions or strategy.

Financial structure of individual investments

Private equity transactions are financed using a combination of the private equity fund's own capital, and third-party debt provided on a deal-by-deal basis; thus there is usually a degree of debt within a private equity fund's individual investments.

The financing structure of a private equity investment usually requires the business managers to personally invest in the company they manage. They share the risks and rewards of the business.

Funds that invest in quoted shares do not increase the borrowings of the company that they invest in. They may have borrowings within their fund structure, but they do not introduce debt to the company as part of their investments.

The rewards for management in quoted companies are a matter for the remuneration committee, not the shareholders. Managers are not generally required to buy shares in their company although they may benefit from capital growth through option schemes.

Private equity funds	Quoted equity funds

Information prior to investment

Private equity funds will undertake substantial financial, commercial, and legal due diligence prior to making an investment.

Quoted company funds have access to and rely on only publicly available information on the companies they invest in.

Information and monitoring while invested

Private equity fund managers receive wide-ranging commercially sensitive information including detailed monthly management information and board minutes from each company the fund is invested in, and also often have board representation.

Investors in private equity funds receive regular detailed information and commentary on each of the private equity fund's investments from the fund managers, including opinions on future prospects. The guidance for this communication is summarized in the International Private Equity and Venture Capital Investor Reporting Guidelines.[2]

Quoted fund managers predominantly rely on analysts' reports, company announcements, management presentations and analysts' research to monitor their investments.

Investors in quoted funds receive no unpublished or preferential information on the operations or management of the individual investments.

Private equity funds	Quoted equity funds

Liquidity in underlying investments

Private equity investments are illiquid: private equity funds cannot generally sell a portion of their investments and therefore rely on a sale of the whole company to achieve a capital gain (but see sections on secondary transactions).

Quoted shares are freely tradable, albeit in small 'parcels', on whatever stock exchange they are quoted. Quoted funds can therefore readily vary the proportion of their investment in any company by trading up or down.

Rewards to fund managers

Private equity fund managers receive management fees from each fund they manage. They also invest directly in the funds they manage and further share in any aggregate realized profits of the fund over its whole life through 'carried interest'. As carried interest can take many years to build up and be paid, it has

Quoted fund investment managers receive fee income from the funds they manage and are often rewarded for the quarterly increase in the value (realized and unrealized) of the portfolio they manage.

Continued

---

[2]   http://www.privateequityvaluation.com/Valuation-Guidelines.

Table 2.3. Continued

Private equity funds	Quoted equity funds
been argued that private equity fund managers are in effect tied into their funds for a longer period than equivalent quoted fund managers.	

Rewards to the managers of the company acquired/invested in

Private equity funds	Quoted equity funds
Management are incentivised primarily to achieve a capital gain. They invest in the financial instrument with the highest risk/reward profile in the capital structure. The private equity investor negotiates the senior managers' employment terms directly with the managers.	Managers are incentivised to achieve whatever their employment contracts reward and whatever the board agrees. In many cases this is not explicit, but may be a combination of increasing the share price, increasing profits, or growing the scale of the business. Public shareholders have little direct control of employment terms which are usually agreed at a remuneration committee of non-executive directors

Fund structure and fund liquidity

Private equity funds	Quoted equity funds
Generally, private equity funds have a limited life of ten years. Investors in private equity funds make commitments to invest in the fund and pay in their capital when required to do so to fund investments recommended by the private equity fund managers. When realizations occur, the fund will repay capital to investors. An investor cannot withdraw their investment and future commitment from a fund. If they wish to change their commitment, they require the fund manager's approval of an alternate investor. There cannot therefore be a 'run' on a PE fund.	A quoted equity fund has permanent capital in the form of share capital or units in a unit trust, and investors in such a fund commit all their investment to the fund when they invest but can sell their shares or units when they choose to. Funds are provided by new investors and retained earnings. Some also use borrowings at the fund level to increase returns.
Earnings are distributed not retained. Historically PE funds had no leverage in the funds. This is no longer true. PE funds use both subscription lines to fund drawdowns and other loans to repay investors. (See Chapter 3.)	

How Does a Private Equity Fund Differ from a Group of Companies?

Periodically you will hear commentators talk of PE funds and managers as a new form of conglomerate. We believe that this is fundamentally wrong. Private equity funds and trading groups of companies are compared and contrasted in Table 2.4.

The key difference is the strategic intent of all the parties. Most corporations act as if they will own their subsidiaries effectively forever.

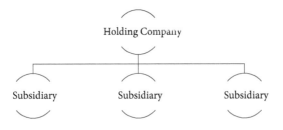

Private equity is diametrically opposed to this view. When Private Equity buys a business, it assumes it will sell it in around three to five years.

A group structure, therefore, shares a number of the features of a private equity fund. In particular the information asymmetries seen between PE and quoted funds do not generally exist. However, there are significant differences including tax advantages for corporate entities (for example with respect to the ability to offset losses in one subsidiary against profits in others) that are not available to investment partnerships.

The key differences are in the incentives that private equity funds provide. PE funds and managers of investee companies are tightly aligned to generate capital gains on a sale/flotation of each individual investment, whereas trading groups may have to seek a wider range of goals that are articulated by the trading strategy of the overall group, rather than the individual company within the group. Managers in corporations are rewarded (typically annually) with a relatively small proportion tied to medium/long-term realized value growth.

The differences in the risks of the traditional private equity fund model when compared to a highly geared corporate acquirer were seen in the rapidity of the failure of Baugur, an acquisitive Icelandic corporate. Baugur acquired a number of UK companies, with a particular focus on retailers, using debt within each of its investments and further debt within its own balance sheet to generate high levels of risk and potential reward. Furthermore, it was a major shareholder in a number of its lending banks. Following the collapse of the Icelandic banks in the financial crisis, Baugur was declared bankrupt on Friday 13 March 2009. It failed due to the use of excessive levels of debt in each layer of its business creating systemic risk. Private equity structures used to explicitly eliminate this type of risk. Today, the emergence of leverage within funds brings risk to the asset class.

A number of the bankers and executives involved in Baugur were prosecuted and jailed in Iceland after the crisis.

Table 2.4. Key differences between private equity and trading groups of companies

Private equity funds	Trading groups
Control and influence	
In principle, similar but in reality, often very different. Public company boards operate as providers of corporate governance, overseeing the executive management on behalf of all stakeholders. Private equity boards are smaller and more akin to an executive committee, focused on the strategy and execution of the business's management. The shareholders are in the boardroom in a PE investment.	
Financial structure of individual investments	
Borrowings are ring-fenced within each investment without recourse to the private equity fund. Profits and losses in each investment are taxed separately from other investments and therefore interest cannot be offset against profits in other investments.	Any borrowings are often cross-guaranteed by all companies in a trading group. Profits and losses within a group can be offset against each other. This allows interest to be offset against profits in a group wherever profits occur.
Information prior to investment	
In principle similar, but private equity firms, as professional acquirers often with less sector knowledge, use more external advisers than a corporate acquirer during due diligence. PE funds are very process driven and all have a suite of formal due diligence providers who work alongside them on all deals.	

Continued

Table 2.4. Continued

Private equity funds	Trading groups
Information and monitoring while invested	
In principle similar, although private equity firms are known for their tight monitoring of cash flow and performance against budget. This is reinforced by the so-called 'discipline of debt' if the leverage in the business has significant cash requirements.	
Rewards to the managers of the company acquired/invested in	
Management are shareholders and are incentivised primarily to achieve a capital gain. They invest in the financial instrument with the highest risk/reward profile in the capital structure. The private equity investor negotiates terms of employment directly with the senior management.	Managers are employees whose rewards are a function of their employment contracts and parent company policy. In a quoted group, managers are likely to own shares possibly through a share option scheme or other share incentive scheme.
Liquidity in underlying investments	
Similar: both must sell/float an investment to realize value although value created may be reflected in the share price of the holding company in a quoted group of companies.	
Rewards to fund managers/corporate managers	
Fund managers share in the net performance of the investment portfolio over the life of the fund and are incentivised to realize capital gains.	Parent company management are incentivised as managers, not investors. There is no explicit assumption that companies are bought with a view to a subsequent sale to realize a capital gain.
Fund structure and fund liquidity	
Usually private equity funds have a limited life of ten years. Investors cannot generally withdraw their investment and future commitment from a fund. If they do wish to do so, they require the private equity fund manager's approval of an alternate investor. There cannot therefore be a 'run' on a PE fund. Earnings are distributed not retained. Historically PE funds had no leverage in the funds. This is no longer true. PE funds use both subscription lines to fund drawdowns and other loans to repay investors. (See Chapter 3.)	If quoted, the shareholders (and option holders when options are exercised) can sell their shares in 'parcels' in the market. The organization will fund itself by a mix of debt, equity, and retained earnings.

What are Hedge Funds and How Do They Differ from Private Equity Funds?

Hedge funds emerged to invest in shares and in derivative assets used by corporations to hedge their risks. The original hedge fund investment proposition is that the fund manager can make a superior return by making a series of trades in these derivatives and the underlying assets. The original hedge funds often sought arbitrage

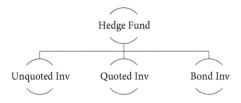

opportunities arising from the misalignment in the price of derivatives and/or the assets underlying the derivatives.

In order to generate these returns the hedge fund manager will tend to use both financial leverage, in the form of borrowings in the fund itself, and leveraged trading positions (derivatives). This generates increased risk, matched by increased returns when successful.

The key difference therefore used to be that private equity funds are long-term commitments by the investors, and historically used little debt within the fund structure itself to generate returns. This distinction is dissolving, as we suggested that it would in earlier editions of this work. We return to this change frequently in this edition.

As markets become more globally integrated and liquid, the returns earned from pure arbitrage by hedge funds have diminished. These funds therefore have sought to widen their trading strategies to achieve returns, and some have turned to investing in private equity transactions as debt and/or equity providers.

Hedge funds, in their private equity activities, therefore, generally sit between the private equity fund model based on low liquidity, financial engineering, high control and information on the one hand and, on the other, the quoted fund model based upon a trading strategy in highly liquid stocks. The key differences between private equity and hedge funds are listed in Table 2.5.

Hedge funds with different mandates and a focus on private equity investments may exaggerate market risks in the PE market, for example:

- hedge funds, which themselves are often leveraged, investing in investments using debt, would increase gearing and thus compound the risks associated with leverage; and
- funds that offer investor liquidity investing in illiquid investments create a mismatch of assets with liabilities. Since we first made this observation in the first edition of this publication in 2008, a large number of hedge funds have indeed failed or been required to restructure due to the liquidity provided to their investors.

The term 'hedge fund' does not have a precise definition and covers a wide variety of fund models, which makes drawing general differences difficult. We have tried above to characterize fairly the key differences in the general business model and structures utilized. In reality there is overlap between the various fund types at the margins: some private equity funds invest in alternative assets and quoted assets, and some hedge funds have long-term capital commitments. However, the general principles of fund management remain that the fund must match the term of its assets and liabilities and that competitive pressure can lead institutions to a mismatch that only becomes apparent when liquidity tightens.

Table 2.5. Key differences between private equity and hedge funds

Private equity funds	Hedge funds
Investment strategy	
Private equity funds are skilled in using transactions and active management to generate profits outside the quoted markets.	Traditionally hedge funds make returns from a series of related trading positions, rather than single investment decisions. They are generally skilled in using markets and market inefficiencies to generate profits.

Continued

Table 2.5. Continued

Private equity funds	Hedge funds
Control and influence	
Private equity funds usually own a substantial or controlling stake in the business. Individual Private Equity investments are controlled using a detailed legally binding shareholder's agreement that establishes the contractual rights and obligations of the company, its management, and the investors.	Hedge funds generally invest in quoted companies and may acquire large minority stakes, which offer no control and no special rights, but may have some influence over the company's board. Trading strategies differ: some are 'active funds' that seek to change management or strategy; some are pure trading funds seeking to benefit from market price movements.
Financial structure of individual investments	
Private equity investments have borrowings within the investee, but generally low levels of borrowings in the private equity fund.	Hedge funds may create financial risk and reward by using derivatives (options, swaps, etc.) rather than debt. It is common for larger hedge funds to have borrowings within the fund, using financial leverage to increase risks and rewards.
Information prior to investment	
Private equity funds will undertake substantial financial, commercial, and legal due diligence prior to making an investment. In a management buyout, the knowledge of the incumbent management is extremely valuable in assessing risk and reward.	Investors in quoted assets, such as many hedge funds, have access to and rely only on publicly available information on the companies they invest in. However, hedge funds use similar due diligence methods to private equity funds when investing in unquoted assets.
Information and monitoring while invested	
Private equity fund managers receive wide-ranging commercially sensitive information including detailed monthly management information and board minutes from each company the fund is invested in, and also often have board representation.	Where assets are quoted, hedge funds rely on public information to monitor their investments. The active funds' investment thesis is that they will use their stake to positively influence the direction of the businesses in which they invest. Pure trading hedge funds may simply take a 'position' in a company in the anticipation that the company's value will change to their benefit.
Liquidity in underlying investments	
Private equity investments are illiquid: private equity funds cannot generally sell a portion of their investments; they rely on a sale of the whole company to achieve a capital gain.	Quoted assets are freely tradable, albeit in small 'parcels', on whatever stock exchange they are quoted. Large stakes are less easy to place (sell) than smaller ones. Therefore, broadly, the greater the influence sought, the less liquidity is available.
Rewards to fund managers	
Private equity fund managers invest in the fund they manage and share in any aggregate realized profits of the fund over its whole life through 'carried interest'. As carried interest can take many years to build up and be paid, it has been argued that private equity fund managers are in effect tied into their funds for a longer period than equivalent quoted fund managers. Fee income is also paid by each fund.	Hedge fund managers are often rewarded for the quarterly increase in the value (realized and unrealized) of the portfolio they manage. In addition, they receive fee income from the funds. There is not usually a hurdle rate of return to exceed.

Private equity funds	Hedge funds
Fund structure and fund liquidity	
Private equity funds are usually long-term illiquid commitments for a finite period, and they cannot suffer a 'run' on the fund. There is a low level of borrowing within the fund and therefore there is generally low bankruptcy risk. Private equity funds usually have a defined narrow investment focus, although this is becoming broader and less defined in successful funds. Historically PE funds had no leverage in the funds. This is no longer true. PE funds use both subscription lines to fund drawdowns and other loans to repay investors. (See Chapter 3.)	Hedge funds are open-ended investment commitments that allow their investors to sell their units of investment (subject to various lock-up clauses), typically in a public market or a periodic private market. They also often have borrowings within the fund. They therefore carry a risk of bankruptcy and can have a 'run' on the fund. Hedge funds can and do fail. Hedge funds often combine wide-ranging investment strategies seeking superior returns.

Emerging and Converging Alternative Asset Investors

The analysis above draws distinctions between different types of fund structures. As funds have grown, many of the largest private equity fund managers have diversified into areas outside the traditional PE model. Similarly, investors in hedge funds, investment banks, and other institutions have moved into private equity investing. Essentially, we have seen the emergence of 'alternative asset' fund managers and advisers.

We can illustrate this by looking at the evolution of some of the large PE funds. We use as examples KKR and CVC, for no reasons other than the fact that theirs are relatively long histories and the data availability is good (but not perfect).

Preqin have data on thirty-eight of the fifty funds KKR have raised, or are raising, at the time of writing. The chart shows the evolution of the size of the funds raised over time. First, we note that in their early days KKR raised a new fund approximately every two years, with each fund bigger than the last. Each of these was a buyout fund. When the first buyout bust happened in the late 1980s, there was a large gap when the data suggests that they did not raise any funds. In the late 1990s the sequence restarts but with a marked difference. KKR began raising non-US buyout funds and also debt funds. Between 2006 and 2008 they raised three large buyout funds targeting the US, Europe, and Asia separately. The largest was $18bn.

Following the crisis in 2008, they continued to raise smaller funds across a range of niche strategies in debt, equity, and mezzanine. Today they are no longer only a private equity fund manager. They manage an array of private and quoted assets around the world. This is a very typical trajectory for many of the largest global private equity firms.

A similar analysis of CVC, Europe's largest PE fund, shows a similar evolution from a sequence of equity funds to a series of parallel funds in multiple investment strategies. CVC was bought out from Citicorp by its partners in 1993 and raised its first fully independent fund in 1996.

We suggest that an examination of the hedge fund industry may similarly find that the largest hedge funds have started to become active in the private equity market, whether as equity investors or as providers of debt and mezzanine to support buyouts.

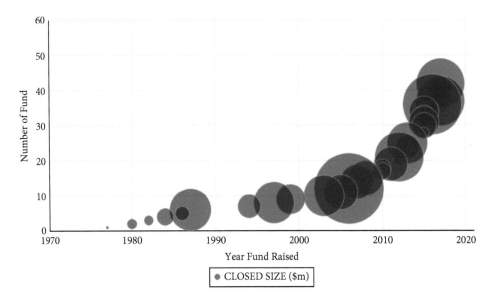

Figure 2.12. Evolution of KKR as a fund manager: year fund raised, number of funds, and size of fund (bubble size)

Source: Authors' analysis of Preqin data

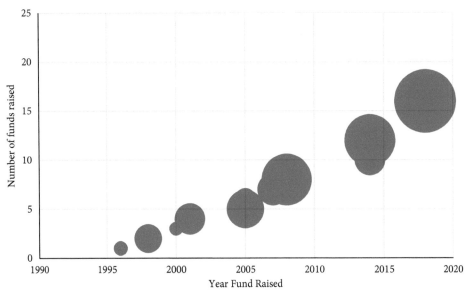

Figure 2.13. Evolution of CVC as a fund manager: year fund raised, number of funds, and bubble size of fund ($m)

Source: Author's analysis of Preqin data

It is clear that the boundaries of the various alternative investors are now blurred and porous: there are private asset managers, quoted asset managers, and everything in between. The days of a discrete private equity market are in the past. Today, there are a myriad of overlapping funds all chasing the returns that were reported by the PE pioneers.

Can a Private Equity Fund or a Private Equity Manager Fail?

As explained in Chapter 1, private equity funds were not traditionally structured using third-party debt and therefore did not generally carry significant bankruptcy risk. A private equity fund may lose all the investors' capital, but, unless they use debt in the fund or create liabilities by mismanagement (e.g. guaranteeing obligations of investee companies), they are unlikely to become formally insolvent.

Today there *is* borrowing in funds and therefore there is bankruptcy risk. However, the levels of debt at the fund level are usually backed by commitments from LPs or by assets, making them relatively secure loans. The major risks are default by an LP guaranteeing a working capital line, or incorrect or overvaluing of an asset provided as security for a so-called NAV loan. We discuss these in detail later.

As we have said in every edition of this publication since 2008, there is a risk that borrowing in funds will rise and create systemic risk. This is a major change in the market since the last edition in 2014. Currently, despite the fact that the absolute risk of bankruptcy of a fund is remote, it is clear that some funds perform badly and investors do lose some or all of their committed capital. We return to this again in the 'deep dive' later in this chapter and look at the effect on fund returns.

An unusual circumstance arose in the case of UK investor Candover. Established in the 1980s, Candover grew to become one of the world's large private equity funds. It had a slightly unusual structure that led to its demise. Its general partner (also confusingly named Candover) was itself a quoted company on the London Stock Exchange. In the financial crisis it became clear that the quoted general partner (which had debt within it) could not be certain of being able to finance its commitments to the latest Candover fund. In consequence the other investing LPs were able to renegotiate a cancellation of the fund commitments, leaving Candover without a new fund to invest from. This arose because it was the general partner which could not commit to the fund, rather than any of the limited partners.

In the case of Permira, its founder investor, SVG Capital, also a quoted company, found itself with similar capital constraints. However, because SVG is an LP in Permira, not the GP like Candover, the renegotiation that ensued simply scaled back the size of the fund.

As we have emphasized above, it is important to understand that the failure of a fund does not mean that its investments will also fail, unlike in most corporate structures. There is no guarantee from the investments to the fund. There may be adverse impacts, for example due to a lack of follow-on funding, but the private equity fund structures have, to date, acted to contain, not disseminate, risk.

In extremis the investment agreement usually has a 'divorce clause' that allows investors to terminate the agreement if (typically) 75 per cent by value of the committed investors agree to do so.

There is virtually no evidence or research in academic studies regarding the failure rates of private equity fund managers, in part due to the rarity of its occurrence.

Where do Private Equity Fund Managers Operate?

Since the mid-1980s many of the larger private equity fund managers have opened overseas offices in order to source deals internationally. In the 1990s, US private equity funds

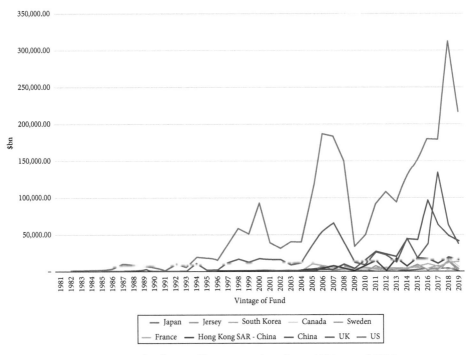

Figure 2.14. Private equity funds raised by manager's region—1981 to end 2020

began to establish European offices, predominantly in London. Today the largest PE funds operate in a market funded by international investors as private equity markets have developed worldwide. The US private equity market dwarfs all others, but the UK's is the second largest in the world after the US. Again, we can look by funds raised (Figure 2.14) or by deals (Figure 2.15).

Note that Jersey is a jurisdiction that attracts European funds for a host of regulatory, disclosure, and tax reasons which we discuss later.

Why Were European Private Equity Funds Predominantly in the UK?

Private equity fund managers require four necessary conditions to operate:

- availability of funds to invest;
- opportunities to make investments ('deal flow');
- people with the necessary skills to source, negotiate, structure, and manage investments; and
- the availability of exit opportunities (stock market, active M&A market).

Each of these necessary conditions was met in the UK. However, the number of alternative locations worldwide where they are also met is increasing due to the globalization of

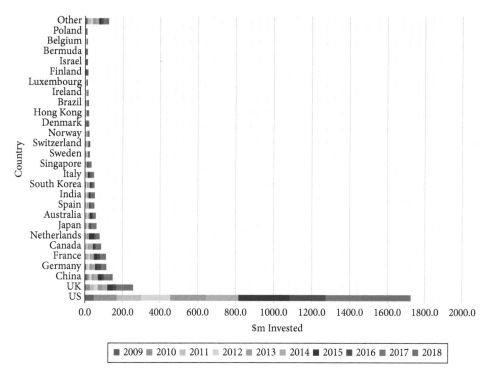

Figure 2.15. Aggregate Value ($bn) of private equity backed buyout deals by country, 2009–19 YTD (at least $10bn invested)

Source: Preqin

both financial markets and professional service firms. The UK leaving the EU materially complicates the picture. The choice of the UK is therefore increasingly dependent on a complex interrelation of other economic, legal, and cultural factors, including:

- **Economic environment:** local costs and benefits and the overall economic infrastructure of the location are very important. Private equity funds are heavily reliant on third-party advisers both for the provision of services (legal, accounting, corporate finance etc) and for deal flow. Similarly, the reliance on leverage requires a banking infrastructure able to provide efficient support for leveraged acquisitions. There is an increasingly symbiotic relationship between the private equity industry and the various providers of professional services and leveraged capital. The latter are heavily dependent on transaction-driven fees; the former are reliant on external technical advice and sources of deals. Similarly, the availability of exit opportunities in a location is a further factor favouring the UK. The London stock markets historically provided both deal flow and exit opportunities.
- **Regulatory environment:** at the margin, regulatory risk impacts both the availability of funds and the cost of funds. This in turn flows directly to managers' personal rewards. The UK's regulatory environment imposes costs, but nevertheless confers benefits, on fund managers that are generally regarded as being at best favourable or at worst, not unacceptable. There has been growing national and international pressure to increase

the regulation of private equity in, for example, both the EU and the US. The impact of this on the London market is as yet unclear.

- **BREXIT:** The withdrawal of the UK from the EU may radically alter the regulatory environment in the UK. The reaction of many fund managers in London has been to open offices within EU countries to have the option of moving management out of the UK if it becomes necessary. The 'nationality' of funds is now something of a moot point. One of the largest PE funds has its largest office in London but calls itself a Luxembourg-based investor. Others have opened offices in Dublin and Frankfurt to remain within the EU.
- **Taxation environment:** the objective of any fund manager is to maximize the returns to its investors. The funds are structured to attempt to manage the tax burden from the investee company to the ultimate fund investors in such a way as to avoid double taxation and legitimately to minimize the overall tax burden. In principle this is no different from any other investment business.
- **Legal environment:** the efficient enforcement of contract law is important where there are potential default risks and the stated objective is to sell or float the investment in a given period. There are also particular legal structures such as the limited partnership available in the UK (and indeed in other jurisdictions) which allow for the management of liabilities without causing double taxation.
- **Cultural environment:** Private equity funds are becoming increasingly multicultural as they expand their activities internationally outside Anglo-Saxon economies. They are, however, by ancestry largely an Anglo-Saxon phenomenon, and while this may be less important in the future due to the changing mix of new recruits, they were until recently still largely run by senior partners from the UK and North America.

In summary, the necessary infrastructure and services to support private equity are found in the UK, together with a strong capital market. As the industry developed, the UK had a wide range of competitive advantages over other potential locations. However, the scale of the industry and its increasing international outlook have weakened the cultural and historical ties to the UK. BREXIT may force funds to have an EU presence as AIFMD, the regulations that govern alternative asset fund managers, including PE funds, broadly assume that funds raising capital in Europe are in EU countries or will comply with EU regulation. It is important to note that being located in the UK does not preclude any business from having significant offshore activities.

Why are Funds Located in Jersey?

In Figure 2.14 you may have noticed that the island of Jersey features among the top ten locations for PE fund managers. Given its size and location, this may have been somewhat surprising. Jersey benefits from many of the advantages listed for the UK above. In addition it has made regulatory changes under the Limited Partnerships (Jersey) Law 1994, the Separate Limited Partnerships (Jersey) Law 2011, and the Incorporated Limited Partnerships (Jersey) Law 2011, that are designed to facilitate private fund managers' operations.

Jersey has three types of limited partnership. Broadly they are designed to allow sophisticated investors to come together with high levels of confidentiality and to avoid double taxation, while public investors are separately regulated and protected. It is a manifestation of the old idea that sophisticated investors should be allowed to make whatever decisions they see fit, while public investors require more stringent regulatory protection.

In addition to the general reasons above, the specific reasons for residing in Jersey (and similar places) typically fall under three broad headings:

(1) Taxation: each form of limited partnership is exempt from tax in Jersey. The investors will be taxed where they are, not where the fund is.
(2) Confidentiality: Unlike the UK there are no requirements to disclose who the investors are to the public. They are disclosed to the regulators.
(3) Regulation: Jersey is not in the EU and never was. It is therefore outside the regulatory environment that was developed after the financial crisis.

This regulatory arbitrage, where funds base themselves in low regulation jurisdictions attracts huge public and regulatory attention.

What is a First/Second etc Close?

A manager is usually seeking to build a broad investor base within the fund. The involves extensive marketing of the fund and its manager to potential global investors. You can think of the process as book-building for new investors. There will be a minimum size for the fund and a larger target size. It may also have a hard cap beyond which the fund will not go. During the fundraising process there may come a point where the manager has firm commitments that exceed the minimum fund size, but is not yet at the target or hard cap. They may then decide to formally sign up the commitments to the LPA with the right to admit more investors later. They may do this a number of times. These are the so-called first close, second close, and so on. We describe some of the complexities this creates in the next section.

Fund Advisers and Other Service Providers to Private Equity

Private equity funds outsource many functions. Unlike larger banks, few PE funds have departments of in-house accountants and lawyers, and most outsource as much as possible. These outsourced service and advisory relationships fall into three broad categories— services, transactions advisers, and fundraising advisers. Here we consider the typical funds advisers (see Figure 2.16). In Chapter 4 we discuss the advisers around the transaction process (acquisition and sale) and during the assets' ownership.

What are Outsourced Reporting Services to Funds?

These are outsourced suppliers to the fund management business providing day-to-day support to management and reporting of the fund's business. As regulation of private equity and other so-called alternative asset classes has increased, the requirement to report

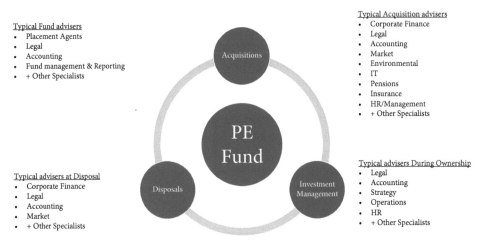

Figure 2.16. Advisers and other service providers to private equity

and demonstrate management control has also increased. What were once small partner-ships managing small portfolios of tightly held businesses are now in a minority of cases large multinational fund managers.

Regulation brings standards and this drives reporting. An industry of businesses has grown up to service the reporting requirements of private equity businesses. Many of these businesses are themselves funded by private equity.

What are Placement Agents?

Placement agents are used by many funds. These are specialist advisers who provide assist-ance in raising funds as well as advice and access to potential investors in private equity funds globally. As the market for private equity has matured, the role of placement agents has migrated from being one that primarily consisted of broking investments by potential limited partners, to both broking and project managing the process of fundraising.

Potential investors are naturally keen to have comprehensive information on the track record of general partners and to have access to the key people behind whom they are potentially investing. These key individuals also have to manage the portfolio and new business activities of their funds. As funds have grown in size a fundraising specialism has emerged both within the funds themselves and outside the funds to efficiently manage the time-consuming process of fundraising.

Placement Agents and the Placement Fees Scandal

As funds grew, and the investing community became increasingly international, it became common for private equity managers to retain placement agents to assist in the arranging of new funds. These agents were rewarded with commissions if they brought new investors to the funds being raised. They were especially important if funds were being raised in coun-tries where the fund managers themselves were not known, for example European fund managers seeking US investors for European-focused funds. In the US in a series of scandals and criminal cases it became apparent that some placement agents had been lavishly entertaining representatives of some of the large investors in private equity. Subsequently it was found that in at least one case, commissions were being shared with the investor's representatives illegally. The SEC acted swiftly and closed down this risk of corruption by banning many commissions to placement agents in US states. The cases highlight the need for regulation and legislation even in the market for sophisticated institutional investors.

A Deeper Dive into a Limited Partners Agreement

In this new section we walk you through the details of a representative Limited Partners Agreement. Our aim is to go a bit further into the detail. Readers looking to understand the basics might want to move on to Chapter 3 and return here later if they want more detail.

What is in a Limited Partners Agreement?

The contract that governs each individual limited life partnership is the Limited Partners Agreement or LPA. It is a contract between all the partners of the fund, both the general (GP) and limited (LP) partners.

There is not, as yet, a standard Limited Partners Agreement, although there is a strong tendency towards standardization. There is an industry body, ILPA,[3] that is working on a draft of a standard document, but it has not been finished or released as we write. As there is no global standard, we therefore analyse a publicly available version of a widely used English LPA to draw out the general themes, rather than linger on the specific details.

The contract follows the standard form for legal agreements by having a list of all the parties who are bound by the contract at the start. This is usually followed by sections broadly under the following headings. We briefly describe each section below, but again remind you that there is no standard form.

Definitions and Interpretation
A large part of any contract will be taken up by the definitions used in the body of the agreement. It is common for defined terms to be capitalized and listed in alphabetical order. You can often get a good sense of the details of the contract by reading just the definitions.

Purpose of the Partnership
This section lays out the investment mandate of the fund. It may be very broad or have tight limitations. You might find geographic restrictions or sector restrictions in this section. This is a key section to protect limited partners and to restrain the manager. We described earlier the way that a limited partnership controls the liability of the partners. To recap, any partner involved in the management of the fund will have *unlimited* liability for the fund's activities (in an English partnership; the situation in the US and elsewhere is

---

[3] Institutional Limited Partners Association, https://ilpa.org/.

comparable). Limited partners will not want to take positions that could be seen to be managing the fund. Restrictions therefore need to be embodied in the section governing the purpose of the partnership, before the fund starts investing, if the limited partners want to avoid or encourage any particular investment strategy.

Other matters covered in this section will include:

(1) the length of the partnership;
(2) the amount and currency of each partner's commitments;
(3) a reference to the representations and warranties that each partner has given and relied on when joining the partnership.

Procedures to Admit New Partners

We need to be careful that we understand and appreciate the difference between partners in a particular fund and the people who are called partners who are managing the funds. If an individual is called a partner of a PE business this will usually (but not always) mean that they are a partner in the fund management business that manages all the funds. This is totally different to a general partner or limited partner, which usually refers to an institutional investor in the specific fund (see Figure 2.17).

This clause refers to the procedures used to admit new limited partners who invest in this particular fund. There are intricate calculations that will be described that are designed to ensure that all partners are treated equally, even if they join the partnership at different times. For example, if a fund has a first close and then makes an investment, any new limited partner joining at the second, or any subsequent close, will need to 'buy' its share of the investment already made and pay its share of any fees that were accrued or paid before they joined. Much of this section of the contract is about how to do these calculations.

Capital Contributions and Partnership Loans

The partners in the investment fund do not invest all of their money as permanent capital. This is nothing to do with taxation as it is sometimes mistakenly characterized. The partnership is, as we have previously described, transparent to the tax authorities, meaning the partners are taxed individually based on their own circumstances, not collectively.

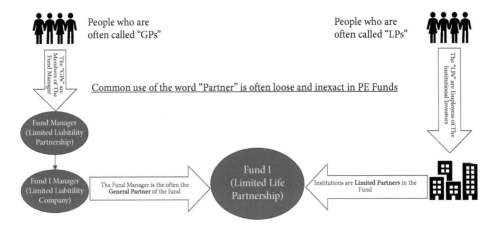

Figure 2.17. Partners in private equity funds

The loan capital is a way of reducing long-term risk. The limited partners are liable for the fund's liabilities up to their capital contribution. This liability lasts, even after the capital has been repaid. The general partner has unlimited liability. Therefore, if you can minimize the capital contribution, the limited partners can sharply reduce their maximum potential liability in the long run. They do this by using loans to fund the majority of the investment alongside a small nominal amount of permanent capital. You will therefore usually see the investment in the vehicle expressed as, say, 10p or 10c alongside £990.90 or $990.90 of loan contribution.

The loans are usually interest free and are drawn down as the manager requires to make investments. There will be a date after which funds are no longer available which will coincide with the end of the investment period of the fund. It will usually be staged to allow follow on investments in the existing portfolio before ceasing when the fund agreement ends or extends.

US investors have been the most significant in private equity funds to date. There are therefore standard terms that are designed to accommodate US investors in most agreements. These usually cover specific US taxation and sanctions related matters and require the fund to avoid creating a liability to the LP for any action of the fund.

What Happens if a Partner Does not Pay Its Share?

It is a widely held belief that no limited partners have ever declined to meet a capital call. This is not true: there have been circumstances where partners have declined to meet their commitments, but they are rare.

The reason it is rare is that firstly the courts have found that it is a clear breach of contract. Partnerships are not companies, they are collections of people cooperating together based on a contract, in this case the LPA. In a company, the shareholders' liabilities are limited to the subscription cost of the shares they hold. In a partnership the courts (in the US, but the situation is broadly the same elsewhere) have found that there are subtly different obligations both to other partners and to external creditors. In essence, the courts have found that partners in limited liability partnerships ought to be liable for the amount of capital that they committed.

Secondly, the commercial impact of not meeting a capital call are intended to be draconian. The partner will be sued for breach of contract by the other partners and case law is clear that they will almost always lose. If a limited partner does not fulfil their obligations under the LPA, the general partner will probably have the right to sell the assets at a large discount (usually 50 per cent or more) to other investors. The consequences of not meeting obligations are therefore the certainty of being sued and the loss of most benefits. It would therefore almost always be a better outcome to pay another party to take on any outstanding obligations, even if the assets of the fund were worthless. Therefore, a secondary transaction is a better alternative to a default on the obligations.

So-called *overcall provisions* also exist in many partnership agreements that require other partners to fill the shoes of any partner who defaults. This has implications for the detailed operation of subscription line funding discussed later.

The structures therefore provide legal protections to make the investor pay and commercial remedies to very strongly incentivise them to do so. Furthermore, even if these incentives do not force payment, there is a proportional guarantee, limited to their commitment, from the other partners that will cover the shortfall.

Management of the Partnership

As we described above, one of the important guiding principles in the relationship between LPs and the fund is the rule that LPs are passive investors without management control. If limited partners have day-to-day management oversight and decision-making powers, they lose the valuable benefit of limited liability for the fund's activities. It is therefore crucial that the limitations, expectations, and processes used in the management role taken by the fund manager are fully documented.

The Fund Manager Role

In ordinary conversation about private equity you will routinely hear even the most seasoned professionals talk about LPs and GPs as if the LP was the investor and the GP the fund manager (we have done so ourselves in this publication). In fact, the fund manager is almost never the general partner. It is usually a separate legal entity controlled and appointed by the general partner as we described above.

The fund manager has particular legal and regulatory responsibilities and requirements in most markets. In the EU regulation is delegated by the European Securities and Markets Association (ESMA) to relevant competent national authorities, which in the UK is currently the Financial Conduct Authority. In the US, the SEC is the regulator. Therefore, although all the personalities may often be broadly the same people and will usually, but not always, be owned by the same group, the fund manager is in fact a separate legal entity.

Terminating the Management Contract

Having a legally distinct and separate manager from the GP has the advantage of making it possible to put in place conditions under which the management of the fund can be transferred to a new fund manager. Exercising this option is very rare, but the contract will stipulate the circumstances when it can be done.

Other LP Protections

There will usually be a raft of obligations designed to protect all the LPs from abuses by the GP or the manager. These are constantly evolving but in general fall in to two categories: financial protections and information rights.

What is the Role of the Investor Committee (LPAC)?

As described, day-to-day management rests with the general partner and fund manager. There are however circumstances where the wider partners do have rights to be consulted usually via the Investor Committee or Limited Partner Advisory Committee (LPAC). The function of the Investor Committee is to be a consultation body for the manager on:

- general policies and guidelines;
- prospective investment sectors;
- conflicts of interest in respect of the partnership;
- whether a proposed investment falls within the investment policy; and
- key man issues.

The members of the Investor Committee do not take part in the management of the partnership's business, nor do they sit on the Investment Committee, or IC, which is the approval body for any new investment.

Financial Protections

These include a formal limitation on the liability of the LPs to their committed capital plus the loans at any date. In addition, there will be controls on borrowing and giving guarantees and rules about the management of the LPs account. There are also rules clarifying the principles of who owns what monies and when they are to be paid.

Fees and Fee Offset

Because PE funds control the boards of their investments, there is a risk of their abusing this power to extract value in ways that conflict with their investors. PE funds often charge investee companies negotiation fees and non-executive director and other monitoring fees.

They also may receive abort fees in certain, relatively rare, circumstances—an example might be a break fee. Occasionally when a deal goes into exclusivity, the potential buyer negotiates the protection of a break fee that is paid if the business is subsequently acquired by a higher bidder. The fee acts as an incentive to commit to the costs of completing the deal while allowing the vendor to keep open the option of accepting a higher bid if one emerges.

In the early PE funds, you would find an array of different ways of allocating these fees between the manager and/or the fund. This became even more opaque as PE funds began providing, among other things, consulting and corporate finance advice to the underlying investment companies. The concern is that the fund manager can establish consulting businesses that earn all of their income from investments controlled by the parent fund manager. This takes value away from the LPs. As we shall see in the section on deal structuring, it is usual to see PE funds present adjusted profit numbers that add back any costs that are purely associated with their ownership. They therefore added back these fees when exiting the investments and expected the buyer to use underlying adjusted profit as the start point for their valuation.

Nevertheless, even if you add back the fees charged in starting a valuation calculation, the net debt of the business is higher due to these external costs. This gives rise to potential conflicts with the LPs. Many GPs manage this by not charging for the support services of operating partners.

Use of Proceeds from Investments

To address this an offset mechanism was created. It is driven by the desire to eliminate conflicts. The mechanism is simple: if a GP or fund manager earns fees from the investment portfolio these are shared with the investors. Sometimes this is 100 per cent shared with the investors, sometimes a proportion is specified. Often this reflects the carried interest split, so you will often see fees shared 80:20 between the LP and GP.

If the fees were simply paid to the LPs, they might be seen by the tax authorities to be receiving income that they had not earned. In the US this is called Unrelated Business Taxable Income (UBTI). Unlike all the other interest, dividends, and capital gains earned, this income is not tax exempt if the LPs receive it, even if they are themselves tax exempt.

Therefore, rather than passing a taxable revenue to the LPs, the fund offsets the fees against the management fees that the LPs must pay (i.e. they reduce the management fee by the amount of the other fees earned). This allows the LPs to share in the benefit of any income earned by fees without creating any UBTI (or similar) taxable charge in their accounts.

Table 2.6. Fees as percentage of commitment (LP/GP) or equity investment (portfolio company) under differing fee offset conventions

Summary fees (paid)/received before tax		Cost to LP	Fee to GP	Portfolio company
No Pass-through or offset	%ge	2.00%	3.55%	3.00%
Fees passed through 100%	%ge	0.45%	2.00%	3.00%
Fees offset 80:20	%ge	0.76%	2.31%	3.00%

For example, consider three different ways you could share the fee income:

i. 100 per cent offset fee income by reducing management fees;
ii. pass the fee income to the LPs as a taxable UBTI;
iii. allow the Manager/GP to keep the fee income.

The consequences of each treatment are expanded upon in a hypothetical example in Appendix 3 and summarized in Table 2.6.

If 20 per cent of the fees go to the manager, their income simply increases as they charge the fees, so they are incentivised to maximize the fees charged to the portfolio company. If the offset were 100 per cent, there would be little point in charging the fees to the company. All that would happen is that the management fees would be reduced by the offset with no gain to the manager.

In the limit the management fee could appear to be reduced to zero if the fund deploys its capital rapidly and charges high fees to the portfolio companies.

This has implications for the way that data is presented by LPs to their ultimate investors. If they show the management fees after the offset, they are misleading when compared to other fund management fees being charged.[4]

In the case of any transaction fees, the fund must invest more cash to pay the fees. You are therefore just moving cash from one pocket of the investors to the other. They lend to pay the negotiation fees and reduce their management fees by the same amount. In fact, once the fees being offset are greater than the management fee, there is a tax disadvantage to the investors. They are in effect lending money to a company to pay it back to themselves as taxable income, which is a very strange thing to do indeed.

Distributions: European and American Waterfalls

The waterfall is the way that cash is distributed between each of the partners. The metaphor relates to the way that each claimant's pool needs to be filled before cash flows to the next claimant's pool.

In a European waterfall, distributions are made to the carried interest scheme after the fund has generated returns higher than the hurdle rate on the total commitment.

In an American waterfall the distributions are made in advance when the fund exceeds the hurdle on the investments that are fully realized. If the fund subsequently falls below

---

[4] Phalippou, L., Rauch, C., and Umber, M. P. Private equity portfolio company fees (April 5, 2016). Saïd Business School WP 2015–22. http://dx.doi.org/10.2139/ssrn.2703354.

the hurdle rate overall, there will need to be a clawback of carried interest in an American-style waterfall. There are various mechanisms that can help alleviate this problem. It is not uncommon to see a percentage of amounts paid under American waterfalls held in a separate account in case there is a clawback.

If 100 per cent is held in these accounts the two waterfalls are essentially the same (except for interest earned). If there is no amount held on account, the American water-fall effectively lends the carried interest amounts to the carried interest scheme until the final amount is calculated at the end of the fund. The difference in cash flows can be very material.

Distributions in Specie

A distribution in specie occurs when a fund manager (or anyone else) does not sell an asset and distribute the cash, but instead distributes the assets themselves. For private equity funds, this usually means distributing shares in the company that the fund has invested in. This can occur in a number of situations, but the two most common are after a flotation of an investment, and when a fund is wound up.

Flotations

If an investment is floated the fund often continues to hold shares in the business. The asset is however no longer in any meaningful sense a private equity investment, as it is quoted on a public market. The fund could therefore distribute the quoted shares to their investors who could hold or sell them as they saw fit. This distribution rarely happens. Most PE funds continue to manage the quoted shareholding on behalf of the investors. A number of explanations have been put forward for this. It might be that the manager wishes to continue to earn fees from the investment. It could be due to lock-up agreements made as part of the flotation.

We prefer to conjecture that this again reflects information advantages rather than fee extraction. Immediately prior to the flotation the PE fund has unfettered information rights. This is a valuable insight into both the past performance and the business's prospects. Furthermore, the fund has relationships with the management and may still have board representation in some cases. It therefore seems entirely rational that the investors seek to capitalize on this enhanced information prior to flotation, by delegating their trading decisions to the fund manager and paying a fee to do so.

Liquidations

The second situation is clearer cut. If a fund passes out of its agreed term and still has assets within it that are not sold, the LPs could receive those assets in specie. In reality, most LPs have no facility to manage or administer a portfolio of residual unquoted shares in a small group of businesses. Furthermore, the requirement to coordinate a large group of LPs who control a business means that some central manager is always needed, even if the shares were distributed. Therefore, it is vanishingly rare that any portfolio is wound up by distribution in specie. It is far more likely that the fund's residual assets will be sold in a secondary transaction to a specialist manager who can work out the assets.

Information Rights

Information rights for LPs in private equity funds are usually extensive. LPs are almost always far better informed about the underlying portfolio of investments than they would be in an equivalent fund managing quoted investments. It could be argued that since LPs cannot influence the buy/sell decisions made by the manager, there is not much use for the information that they receive. This however misses two important issues: corporate governance and secondary trading in PE fund commitments.

Good governance relies on good data. Peter Drucker, one of the founders of management theory, is credited with saying 'what gets measured gets managed'. This idea is at the heart of the private equity governance regime.

Moreover, the quality of this data has become vitally important as the market to trade positions in funds has grown. The market is discussed in Chapter 1, and the rights of LPs to trade are covered below in the discussion of the secondary market.

Should There Be a Standard LP Agreement?

It is reasonable to ask whether there even ought to be a standard document. The arguments for standardizing the template of an LP agreement rest on two foundations:

(1) While GPs and original LPs will always wish to negotiate terms, a standardized template significantly reduces transaction costs. The more a set of terms is standardized, the easier it is for the parties to concentrate on the substance of the relationship.

(2) The greater the standardization, the easier it is to create a secondary market to buy and sell the investment positions in the partnership. Standardizing terms in loan documents led by the Loan Markets Association (LMA) and Loan Syndications and Trading Association (LSTA) on either side of the Atlantic facilitated the growth of the leveraged loan market. Increased standardization in the LP agreements would be similarly advantageous to the market for LP positions.

The problems of non-standardization are both the ongoing cost of checking each contract when a party wants to trade and, more subtly and importantly, the information problems that can build up that can cause markets to freeze and fail. It has long been understood that where there are sharp information asymmetries, the market pricing mechanism can fail. George Akerlof won the Nobel prize for economics in 2001 for his paper first pointing this out in the early 1970s.[5]

When markets are perturbed or shocked, there are often forced sellers seeking to generate cash quickly. The price ought to fall to allow these people to sell. If there are large amounts of hidden information, or dispersed, difficult to access information, the pricing mechanism can fail. Trading complex non-standard products, like individually tailored LP positions in private equity funds, have all the characteristics of markets that can freeze.

---

[5] Akerlof, G. A., 1970. The market for 'lemons': Quality uncertainty and the market mechanism, *Quarterly Journal of Economics* **84**(3): 488–500.

What Is Most Favoured Nation Status and How Does It Impact Investors?

One way in which investors have sought to guarantee that they are getting the best terms possible has been to insert a so-called 'most favoured nation' or 'MFN' clause into the contract. This will require the general partner to confirm that no investors have received terms that are better than those on offer to the limited partner in question. The idea is to ensure that if any one LP gains better terms, then all LPs benefit equally.

There are however usually caveats and exemptions around most favoured nation clauses. First, GPs may wish to have tiered terms to encourage larger investors in preference to smaller ones. It is entirely normal for large funds to offer better terms to the largest investors. To do this while maintaining the most favoured nation clause they add a caveat. The caveat says that no investors who have made commitments of the same amount or less than the particular LP in question have received better terms. Sometimes there will be a clearly tiered structure with breaks at certain values—say $1m, $10m, $100m, or whatever—below which all LPs are treated equally. This means that an LP is assured that all investors of their size or smaller are receiving terms no better than they are.

There are also MFN exemptions based on the breadth of an LP's relationship across the funds that the manager has raised. In large multi-asset funds, there will often be a clause saying that most favoured nation does not apply to investors who have an aggregate investment in funds of £/$m or who have a so-called managed funds relationship.

The conclusion is that there are differences between the terms that partners receive and that they are generally based on the size of the commitment. They are also difficult to verify for any individual LP.

What Are Side Letter Rights?

In addition to the matters that are in the LPA, there may be an array of side agreements between the manager and certain limited partners. These may often include co-investment rights and rights to invest in subsequent funds.

These create the potential for conflicts of interest and should be a focus for any investor. The general way that the contract seeks to sweep up these potential conflicts is by inserting representations and warranties from the general partner to the limited partners that give explicit comfort that the conflicts are managed appropriately. As co-invest has grown in importance in recent years, the focus on managing these potential conflicts has risen.

How Does Subscription Line/Credit Financing Work?

As we have stated, investments in private equity are usually commitments to invest in the future, not hard cash placed on deposit with a fund manager. Funds are called down as they are needed. Subscription line financing is the name given to an overdraft facility guaranteed by the investors that is used by PE funds to make investments without immediately calling for capital from the investors. It has three functions:

(1) When a fund is fund raising and has multiple closes to the investment round, the facility simplifies the way that later investors compensate earlier investors for any

investments (and fees) paid. In simple terms, early investors at the first close of the fund need to transfer a share of any assets bought to investors who come into the fund later. One way to simplify this is to use bridge finance between the first and final close of the fund. This has the added benefit to the manager of boosting the returns to earlier investors who do not have to commit capital until the final close (although they are fully at risk of losing that capital if the investments fail).

(2) Because private equity is about buying and selling generally illiquid assets in negotiated transactions, PE fund managers generally cannot accurately predict or decide when they buy a particular asset. Completions happen when the deal is agreed and signed (often late at night). Therefore, to avoid having to draw down from multiple investors in a short time period prior to the completion of any investment, many funds use essentially the same facility structure after the final close of the fundraising.

(3) For the LP investors, the facility reduces the volatility of the cashflows required to invest in PE funds. This enables them to reduce the amount of cash that they hold available to fund periodic PE investments. This reduces the costs and risks of being a large-scale PE investor.

This facility makes it significantly easier for LPs to manage their relationship with the fund. Prior to the emergence of subscription lines a manager might find themselves in a large competitive auction with multiple bidders, racing to completion in a so-called contract race. In this scenario they need certainty of funds to complete the deal, but have no certainty that they will be the 'winners' of the contract race. They therefore had a risk of issuing a notice to call down capital from their LPs that they would have to return to them if they 'lost' the race. In this scenario, which is not uncommon in larger deals, the LPs have significant treasury issues to manage that are costly and inefficient. The solution is an overdraft facility provided by a bank collectively guaranteed by the investors to bridge any uncertainty. The LPs then know that the fund will draw down on a particular day in the year (usually quarterly or half-yearly) and the fund manager can give them clear guidance as to how much they need to pay into the fund. There are clear benefits to returns of using this type of guarantee of a bank facility.

One of the defining features of a subscription line is that the facility is secured on the undrawn commitments of the LPs, not the assets of the fund. The creditworthiness of each investor will therefore need to be individually assessed. A good credit might be allowed a high advance rate against their total commitment; a poor credit may not be eligible at all. Once these individual assessments are made, a facility will be made available to the manager based on the analysis of the individual credits. Typically, there will be a tiered structure with different rates of advance and costs associated. In the stylized example shown in Table 2.7 we use credit ratings to aid understanding and to illustrate the concepts. In reality, each advance rate is individually assessed, not credit rated.

The borrowing base is the total value of all the commitments included in the subscription line. The manager can borrow up to a percentage of the borrowing base. In our stylized example the borrowing base is $5bn out of commitments of $7bn, 71 per cent of the fund's total commitments. Due to the various advance rates, the manager can borrow $3bn or 60 per cent of the borrowing base, which is 43 per cent of the total commitments.

Note how this structure incentivises the manager to seek out highly rated investors to maximize the advance rate. Given the choice between $1bn from a low-rated investor or $1bn

Table 2.7. Illustrative calculation of subscription line advance

	Investor group	Credit rating	Commitment ($m)	Advance rate %	Borrowing base ($m)	Advance ($m)
Included	A	AAA/Aaa	1,000	80.0%	1,000	800
Investors	B	AA/Aa2	1,000	70.0%	1,000	700
	C	A	1,000	60.0%	1,000	600
	D	BBB/Baa2	1,000	50.0%	1,000	500
	E	BB/Ba2	1,000	40.0%	1,000	400
	F	B/B2	1,000	0.0%	-	0
	G	CCC	1,000	0.0%	-	0
		Total	7,000	43%	5000	3000
	% commitment		100%		71%	43%
	% borrowing base		140%		100%	60%

from an investment grade investor, the fund manager will have an incentive to take the higher credit rated investor because this will increase the advance rate of the subscription line.

Normally a subscription line is a short-term working capital facility. The LP will draw down quarterly, half-yearly, or annually to repay their share of the commitment. In some funds the facility is longer term. There is usually an annual clean-down clause in the agreement to protect LPs from having to treat the guarantee as a long-term commitment requiring more tier one capital from regulated investors. Unregulated investors have no such concerns.

To give an entirely illustrative example:

Imagine a fund investing for five years using the borrowing base and commitments of Table 2.7. Let's assume a gross investment profile as shown in Figure 2.18, with 90 per cent of commitments invested in five years. The insight we are trying to give from our analysis is about changing the cash flows of the LPs. It therefore isn't material to that analysis what the shape of this investment profile is. It would change the shape of the graphs and the magnitude of the effects, but we are trying to draw your attention to the timing differences created, not the specific return impacts. The fund would draw down on the subscription line until the total drawdown reaches the limit of 71 per cent of commitments in the table. (We have assumed that there is no 'clean down' at the year ends.)

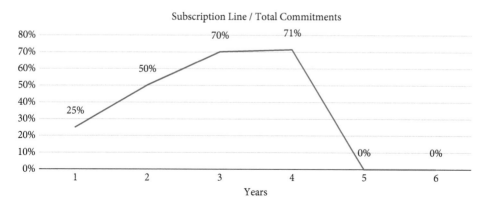

Subscription Line / Total Commitments

Figure 2.18. Illustrative drawdown of five-year subscription line

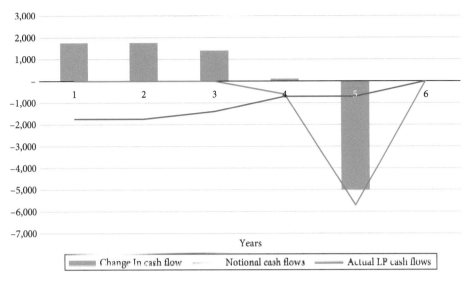

Figure 2.19. Illustrative effect of subscription line funding on cash drawdowns

After the investment period ended, the LPs would repay the facility in a single payment in our stylized example.

The availability of the subscription line declines as the commitments are matched to drawn-down investments.

The effect on the cash flows of the LPs is to eliminate the need to pay into the fund in the early years and to create a known large cash flow at the tail end of the investment cycle.

What Effect Do Subscription Lines Have on Returns?

Because you have delayed the cash drawdown you have almost certainly increased the present value (and IRR) of the fund's net cash returns.

We can illustrate this by comparing the same investment with and without a subscription line in place. To emphasize the effect, we illustrate using both a traditional one-year facility and then a stretched facility at the upper end of the range of possibilities.

First, we will look at the traditional short-term, annual subscription line. These are seen in most funds. If you imagine an investment made on 1 January funded by a subscription line, we can see the effect on reported IRRs (there are of course no money multiple effects other than a reduction due to interest costs). For simplicity, let's assume that the investment doubles in value by 31 December of the year then never changes in value again.

In the long run there is not much impact, but in the short term the reported IRRs are materially flattered by any delay of the cash drawdown.

Secondly, we look at the effect of longer-term facilities. These are much rarer. When a subscription line is available, it is possible to use the facility to pay management fees and interest. The cashflows of the same investment with a one-year/five-year/whole of life subscription line would then be as shown in Table 2.8.

We again see that a one-year facility is not materially changing DPI but provides a modest boost to returns over the longer term. A longer-term facility, five years in our example,

Table 2.8. Illustrative effect of subscription lines of varying lengths on returns, cash flows, and profits

Year	No Subscription Line	1 Year Subscription Line	5 Year Subscription Line	Whole Life Subscription Line
	−102.00	0.00	0.00	0.00
1	−2.00	−104.25	0.00	0.00
2	−2.00	−2.00	0.00	0.00
3	−2.00	−2.00	0.00	0.00
4	−2.00	−2.00	0.00	0.00
5	−2.00	−2.00	−121.25	0.00
6	−2.00	−2.00	−2.00	0.00
7	−2.00	−2.00	−2.00	0.00
8	−2.00	−2.00	−2.00	0.00
9	298.00	298.00	298.00	161.75
IRR	11.47%	12.87%	24.21%	nm
NPV @ 8%	32.9	39.7	58.4	74.9
Net DPI	1.80	1.80	1.71	nm
Profit	180.00	179.75	170.75	161.75

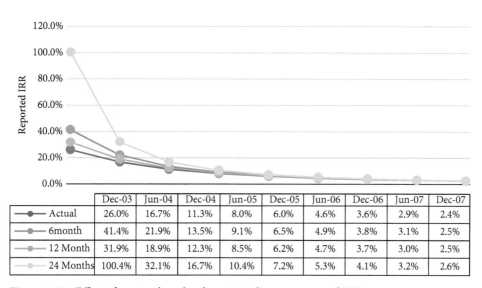

	Dec-03	Jun-04	Dec-04	Jun-05	Dec-05	Jun-06	Dec-06	Jun-07	Dec-07
● Actual	26.0%	16.7%	11.3%	8.0%	6.0%	4.6%	3.6%	2.9%	2.4%
● 6month	41.4%	21.9%	13.5%	9.1%	6.5%	4.9%	3.8%	3.1%	2.5%
● 12 Month	31.9%	18.9%	12.3%	8.5%	6.2%	4.7%	3.7%	3.0%	2.5%
● 24 Months	100.4%	32.1%	16.7%	10.4%	7.2%	5.3%	4.1%	3.2%	2.6%

Figure 2.20. Effect of varying length subscription lines on reported IRR

materially boosts IRR and reduces DPI. In the limit a full-life facility would have infinite returns calculated as an IRR and a further material reduction in accounting profit (DPI).

Note however that if you are calculating a return on capital at risk (as opposed to cash invested), as an accountant might, there is a no positive effect on returns. The LP always carries the full liability for the investment. The LP is providing a 100 per cent guarantee of the cash drawdown on the subscription line and therefore has exactly the same risk as if it had paid the cash over.

Ignoring the potential benefit of using the cash elsewhere, the subscription line merely creates a timing difference, not a real increase in risk adjusted returns. Indeed, the reported profit (and DPI) will be lowered by the interest cost of the subscription line.

Subscription lines therefore highlight the distinction between accounting profits and economists' and investors' measures of rates of return. The former is a prudent measure of returns taking no account of opportunity cost. The latter is a measure that incorporates, somewhat imperfectly, the idea of opportunity cost. We return to this when discussing returns.

Why Draw Down Capital at All?

The obvious question to ask is: if banks will lend based on the guarantees of investors, why do funds ever draw down the cash from the investors? Why not just use the overdraft facility at all times? Indeed, there is anecdotal evidence of funds that have long term subscription structures of up to ten years.

There are both practical constraints and knotty regulatory and tax implications.

On a purely practical level, because the borrowing base is smaller than the total commitments of the fund and returned capital is not (usually) recycled, if the fund invests more than the borrowing base you must draw down cash from the LPs at some point. If you don't, the overdraft limit on the subscription line will be reached.

You could only fully rely on a subscription line if you had all commitments in the borrowing base and invested less than the advance rate on that borrowing base. So, if you had 70 per cent advance rate overall, you could only invest 70 per cent of a fund with all the commitments in the facility.

A second reason is the taxation of certain US investors. In the US, if the investor is a tax-exempt organization (such as a state pension fund) they are only exempted from tax as long as they use their own capital to make investments. If they use third-party capital, they may, under certain circumstances, lose their tax exemption. This is a powerful incentive for some LPs not to borrow to fund investments.

The full details are beyond our scope, but this is an important constraint on gearing in private equity funds with US tax-exempt investors. It also helps to explain some of the complex feeder structures you may see in PE funds. One way to isolate LPs from specific risks like this one is to create a series of separate funds that have their own bespoke arrangements that then invest in the main fund.

Finally, as mentioned above, there are regulatory capital implications if the subscription line extends over a year for some investors.

How Do Subscription Lines Cope with Default Risk?

If there is a financial return, there is usually a related financial risk lurking in the vicinity. In this structure the risk can be intricate.

If an investor defaults, we have seen that the LPA will trigger the clause for other funders to overfund and fill the resulting gap. However, if the fund is using a subscription line, the investor will not receive a capital call and cannot therefore default. The subscription line lender will advance funds before the investor can default. Unless the manager knows and draws the matter to the attention of the bank, the first that the lender will know of the default will probably come when repayment of the subscription line is due, potentially several months or even years later.

If the defaulting investor is one of those in the borrowing base, the lender will be advancing a higher percentage of the borrowing base than planned against a potentially narrower base of investors. This is an increase in risk to the bank. To limit and try to avoid this situation, there will usually be a limit on the amount that can be drawn down on a subscription line to fund a defaulting investor. This is known as the overcall limitation. The impact is to push risk onto investors outside the borrowing base.

The detailed intricacies of the flow down of risk are beyond our scope. We draw this to the reader's attention so that you can begin to understand the fine detail of the structures that are usually painted with broad brush strokes.

What Are NAV Loans?

Subscription lines are secured on undrawn capital commitments of funds. As the capital is committed, the facility ceases to be available for further investments. Once the fund has invested the borrowing base, there is no facility left to drawdown.

A net asset value (NAV) loan is structured to provide debt to a mature investment port-folio. It takes security not on the undrawn commitments of the LPs, but on the underlying assets of the portfolio (or in some cases the covenant of the fund derived from those assets). It can be thought of much like a mortgage on a domestic property or any other fully secured, asset-based loan. There are certain eligible assets, or eligible investments in this case. The bank will assess these and offer to lend a percentage of the NAV of these assets. There will be various controls to prevent risk being overly concentrated in any par-ticular asset. Because these are loans secured on illiquid equity assets, advance rates are low. This type of lending is at the risky end of the spectrum.

The loan will have criteria for eligibility of the assets advanced against. These might typically include a clause stating that the asset concerned is not itself in default of any of its own lending obligations.

There are many technical legal and tax complications with NAV loans, but one of the most obvious is the problem of valuation. The lender needs to have comfort that the assets they are lending against are worth what the borrower says they are. In a private equity fund they are illiquid, unquoted shares in geared businesses. They are therefore potentially uncertain and volatile.

Implications of Leverage within a Private Equity Fund

These are important innovations for buyout funds because it changes one of the central features of the private equity model.

This has substantially changed since we last wrote (or perhaps our assessment has changed). For many years in each version of this book we have argued that private equity does not create a risk of systemic contagion because PE funds are not themselves geared. In 2014 we wrote:

In the future, pressure to increase leverage within funds and to provide liquidity to invest-ors may lead to geared private equity funds which would lead to increased systemic risk.

The (admittedly very tentative) forecast was correct and we stand by the implications of that analysis.

Today PE funds, and indeed other funds, are using debt facilities at the fund level. This creates a risk of bankruptcy that did not historically exist. We have no way of sensibly quantifying this risk. It may be entirely inconsequential or not—we do not know. This is an area where regulators are looking closely, and data and research is urgently required.

Secondary Sale Rights

The LPA will set out the process and rights of the partners in the event that one of them wishes to sell their interests in the secondary market. The GP cannot sell its rights without receiving the consent of the investors.

The GP and other LPs will be concerned that any proposed alternate LP is able to fund any undrawn commitments and that the information any new partner receives does not commercially damage the fund or its manager. Furthermore, there are usually regulatory requirements on the partnership under anti-money laundering legislation that the manager will need to comply with. Therefore, there is almost always a process whereby the fund manager has to approve any new LPs. The manager therefore has significant ability to control the secondary market transactions in most funds.

Extending the Agreement

We saw in Chapter 1 that the life of a private equity partnership is often much longer than the ten-year period originally planned. There will be a mechanism to agree that extension and to set the economics of the arrangement going forward. In some partnerships the carried interest scheme will be recalibrated to reduce the amount of carry that the general partner receives. Fees may also reduce. The original intention when designing the fund structures was to penalize extensions. Over the years it has become clear that in some cases an extension is a perfectly reasonable way to continue to hold the underlying assets and the balance has shifted.

Removal of the General Partner

It is very rare that a general partner is removed from a fund, but there are always provisions to do so. There are two broad types of removal. The first is a 'for cause' removal, which covers the GP breaching a term of the agreement. These usually cover criminality, fraud, and misconduct as well as materially breaching the partnership agreement itself.

The second is a 'without fault' clause which allows the LPs to simply decide to change the GP for any reason. The latter usually require a very high number of LPs (75 per cent or more) whereas 'for cause' has a lower threshold, typically 50 per cent. Market practice has historically differed in the US and Europe. The US has not traditionally had without fault clauses, whereas Europe has included them. This again highlights the heterogeneity of private equity market practices.

If the GP is removed there will be provisions to reset the carried interest and fees so that a replacement GP can be found and incentivised.

Exclusivity and New Funds

There will usually be a clause that stops the fund manager from raising a new fund using the same investment strategy until around 70 per cent of the fund's capital has been deployed. The exclusivity clause commits the manager to the fund even if it is not performing well and therefore will not generate carry. The idea is to close down the option to raise a new fund if an existing fund is not performing well. It has a secondary, and potentially unwanted, incentive impact. If a fund is close to being drawn to the threshold that allows a new fund to be raised, there is a strong economic incentive to do a deal to push the fund over the threshold so that a new, fee-generating fund can be raised and double fees on commitments be earned as we described earlier in this chapter.

There are also significant implications for multi-asset managers who have funds that are in adjacent or similar markets. Many funds have both large and SME buyout funds where the investment size thresholds can be unclear. You can easily envisage conflicts between funds. For example, is a particular transaction a large investment for the small fund or a small investment for the large fund? Is a deal a growth capital transaction or a secondary buyout? There will be an overarching requirement for the manager to ensure that these potential conflicts are managed appropriately.

Confidentiality and Secrecy

Prior to the 2000s, private equity funds revealed very little data about their investors. It was common for Managers and GPs to require LPs to sign tight confidentiality agreements. This relaxed over the years due to freedom of information rights in Europe and the requirement to disclose the investment activities of US public sector pension funds. Much of what we know about the PE industry came to light as a result of the disclosures by public bodies who were forced to disclose information under freedom of information legislation.

Summary

The LPA is a necessarily large contract. They are typically not standardized or public and this impedes the efficiency of the growing secondary market.

The Institutional Limited Partners Association (ILPA) which represents the LPs' interests issued a suggested standard LPA template in late 2019. As it coincides with our finishing this edition, it is far too early to say whether it will be adopted by the market. It is a contract that assumes a Delaware partnership and is drafted to be governed under the laws of the state of Delaware: there are therefore some obvious limitations outside the US. It is possible that a parallel non-US template could emerge in the same way as the LMA debt templates we discuss below emerged after the LTSA created the first drafts of templates for leveraged loans.

Within any LPA there are both explicit processes and broader warranties, representations and duties of care that are designed to try to ensure that the GP and the manager are aligned with, and act in, the interests of the LPs. There are however many possible areas where interests can diverge, and any investor requires professional advice to assess and manage these risks before committing to any investment. Once invested there are control mechanisms, but they are rarely invoked unless there is a serious cause for concern about the fidelity, liquidity, or competence of the GP.

Taxation

The structuring of a fund will have a direct impact on the tax position of the various stakeholders involved. It is therefore important that a fund is structured to be attractive based on each stakeholder's relationship with the fund.

Below we consider the tax position of three classes of stakeholder:

- investors in a private equity fund;
- private equity executives who will manage the fund; and
- investee portfolio companies.

Investors in a Private Equity Fund

Any fund must present an attractive investment opportunity for an investor. The way in which returns to an investor are taxed will directly affect the quantum of the return received. It is therefore important that a fund's profits can be distributed in a tax-efficient manner. As an overarching principle of structuring private equity funds, an investor should not be worse off from making an investment through a fund than if they had made that investment/those investments directly.

As a general rule, it is usually the investor who pays taxation on any investment activity, not the investment vehicle. The country in which an investor pays tax will be determined by where they are resident for taxation purposes and the country in which the investment itself is located. As illustrated above, many investors in private equity funds are not based in the country of the fund. They are located in a wide variety of tax jurisdictions. Many are themselves collective investment vehicles, such as pension funds, insurance companies, or funds of funds. Taxation will therefore generally be paid by the ultimate investors in those funds, wherever they happen to be resident for tax purposes.

Any fund manager will need to consider the tax paid by investors.

What is Double Taxation?

The investments made by private equity funds are often in companies that are located in a wide variety of countries. The funds are therefore structured to allow the returns to be earned without creating 'double taxation'. Double taxation occurs when a government taxes profits in one country and these profits are taxed a second time (without offset of the initial tax paid) when they are received by the ultimate investor.

Most private equity funds are structured as limited partnerships. These are treated as being 'transparent' for tax purposes in the majority of jurisdictions, meaning that the partners are taxed, not the partnership itself. Profits made by the fund will be taxed directly on the partners. Dividends or interest received by the fund will be taxed as dividends or interest in the hands of the investors. Gains made by the fund will be taxed on the investors as chargeable gains.

Why Are Partnerships Offshore?

The transparent nature of limited partnerships means the location of the partnership itself should not affect the tax position of the investors. Accordingly, the decision as to whether a partnership is located onshore or offshore will typically be driven by commercial factors, rather than for tax reasons.

Historically in the UK limited partnerships also reduced the level of disclosure as, in certain circumstances, formal accounts did not need to be filed at Companies House. Similarly, details of the investors in a fund did not appear on public record until recently. Today there is a form LP6 filed at Companies House that discloses the identity of the immediate investors.

What Are Non-Doms and How Are They Taxed?

There exists in common law a concept of being domiciled in a particular country. It may be different to a person's nationality or the country in which he or she lives. The concept broadly encompasses the idea of where an individual is 'actually from' and is confusingly different from either where they are resident or where they are resident for tax purposes. There are a series of tests that establish whether a person is UK domiciled, relating to where they were born, where they live and the domicile of their parents.

There has been continual refinement and change in the taxation of non-doms that is out of the scope of this analysis. It is highly complex and requires specialist analysis.

What Is Withholding Tax?

Withholding tax on dividends, interest and capital gains is often the key tax issue that will impact the returns to an investor. Withholding tax is a prepayment of tax to the government by the fund. It is conceptually equivalent to PAYE taxation of an employee's income, where the employer prepays the employee's tax liability. Withholding tax is used to reduce tax avoidance.

Depending on the residence of the investor, it may be possible to make use of double-tax treaties to lower the rate of withholding tax or even reduce the rate to nil.

In the UK, an exemption from the obligation to withhold tax on interest exists for quoted Eurobonds. Debt provided by funds to UK-resident portfolio companies can often be listed on an appropriate stock exchange, such as the International Stock Exchange (TISE)—formerly Channel Islands Securities Exchange (CISE)—before interest is paid to benefit from this exemption.

The extensive network of double-tax treaties that the UK has with other jurisdictions, and exemptions such as the quoted Eurobond exemption, make it an attractive jurisdiction for investment. The UK also does not withhold tax on dividends.

Private Equity Funds and Executives

As noted earlier, fund managers will take a stake in the fund directly, via an interest in the fund directly or through a separate team vehicle and via a 'carried interest'. They will therefore benefit in the success of a fund and are incentivised to maximize performance (Figure 2.21).

The general partner will often take the form of another transparent entity, either another limited partnership or a limited liability partnership. Again, the partners are taxed, and not the partnership, which eliminates any double taxation.

However, most of the profits attributable to a general partner will be paid out to the investment manager. It is therefore not unusual to see general partners which are companies.

Why Are Scottish Partnerships Used as Carried Interest Vehicles?

As mentioned above, fund managers will usually have a carried interest vehicle (normally a Scottish limited partnership).

A Scottish limited partnership has a separate legal identity whereas an English limited partnership does not. A Scottish partnership is therefore capable of owning assets in its own name and of being a partner of a limited partnership, such as the main fund vehicle.

UK 'Standard' mid/lower mid market fund structure

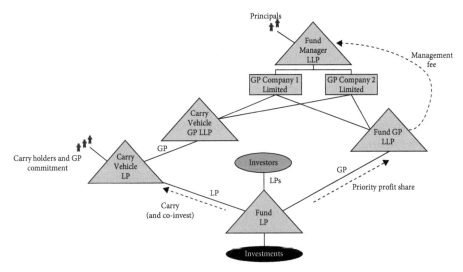

Figure 2.21. Detailed structures in a typical private equity fund
Source: BDO

Allocations of Income and Gains and Applicable Tax Rates

Many investors in a fund are typically non-taxable entities (pension funds, foundations, endowments, or sovereign wealth funds). They are likely to be indifferent as to the nature of the underlying profits allocated to them.

Fund managers who are individuals investing directly or via a carried interest partnership will, however, be subject to a variety of tax rates dependent on the nature of the allocated profits. At current rates (and assuming that none of the anti-avoidance rules discussed below apply), a taxpayer paying tax at the higher rates will pay UK tax at:

- 45 per cent on interest;
- an effective rate of 38.1 per cent on dividends; and
- 20 per cent on capital gains (28 per cent if they are carried interest).

How are Private Equity Executives Taxed?

As set out above, profits arising to participants in a fund are, prima facie, taxed according to the underlying nature of the fund's profits. This was a stable position resulting from an HMRC statement of practice in 1978 and a specific memorandum of understanding between HMRC and the BVCA from 1987, with an additional MoU in 2003.

This treatment is based upon the principle that the partners invest in the capital of the business and only achieve a gain if the fund increases in value. In many cases, returns on carried interest will be taxed as a capital gain (see above). In other cases, some of the carried interest may be received as dividend, fees, and interest and taxed as income. These memoranda also confirmed that, providing certain conditions are met, the fund executives will be treated as having paid market value for their carry, meaning they should not be exposed to income tax on the acquisition of carry.

Beginning in 2014, a series of anti-avoidance measures were brought in which have significantly changed the rules governing the taxation of amounts received by private equity executives. These measures included:

- disguised employment rules to tax at higher employment rates executives purporting to be self-employed who do not meet certain tests of self-employment;
- 'mixed member' rules to prevent perceived abuse which took advantage of the flexibility of partnerships, particularly planning using corporate members of LLPs;
- disguised investment management fee (DIMF) provisions which addressed, amongst other things, perceived abuse whereby executives lowered their effective tax rate by participating in the general partner's share of the fund's profits;
- capital gains changes to eliminate the so-called 'base cost shift' (see below);
- the introduction of the concept of 'income based carried interest' originally aimed at hedge funds and similar trading (rather than investment) funds which were seeking to bring their performance fee arrangements within the tax treatment of carried interest.

Base Cost Shift

Base cost shift historically provided a benefit to private equity executives' effective tax rate as set out below. It arose as a natural consequence of the 1987 MoU between the BVCA and HMRC mentioned above.

Initially, a carried interest partnership will have a limited interest in the fund. All profits will be allocated to either the general partner or the investors. However, once the fund has achieved its hurdle rate of return, the carried interest partnership will generally receive an enhanced share of future returns (normally 20 per cent).

At this time the members of the carried interest partnership will 'acquire' a right to 20 per cent of any proceeds arising to the fund on any future disposal. They will also be deemed to have 20 per cent of the base cost of any assets held by the fund under partnership tax rules (the 'base cost shift'). As the carried interest partners have contributed minimal capital to acquire the assets in the first place, they effectively receive an additional 20 per cent deduction on their share of any gains.

Following the base cost shift, the other investors will have a reduced base cost. Accordingly they will make a larger taxable gain on any subsequent disposal. There are therefore intricate arrangements between the partners to adjust for the base cost shift.

Broad View of Current Private Equity Executive Taxation

The DIMF rules introduced in 2015 set the default position for all amounts received from a fund, 'disguised investment management fees', as being trading income (taxed at an effective rate of 47 per cent including tax and national insurance) apart from two exclusions. Those exclusions are: (1) amounts invested on reasonably comparable terms to external investors (ie GP commitment/team co-investment) and (2) carried interest. This change sought to counteract schemes through which executives were in part remunerated by the receipt of loans (non-taxed) or other lower taxed receipts from the general partners of funds. Such receipts are now taxed at the highest marginal income tax rates under the DIMF rules.

Carried interest (which is not treated as incomebased carried interest—see below) is taxed at a 'floor rate' of 28 per cent of the amounts arising to the executives. There is no longer any relief for the base cost shift. Where carried interest is comprised of dividends or interest then the higher rates applying to these income sources will apply.

The income-based carried interest rules recharacterize carried interest amounts as a disguised investment management fee (taxable at an effective rate of 47 per cent), broadly where the weighted average holding period of investments is less than thirty-six months. A graduated recharacterization applies with a weighted average holding period between thirty-six and forty months. Where the weighted average holding period of investments is forty months or more, the income-based carried interest rules do not apply. Accordingly, the rates discussed above—i.e. 28 per cent to 45 per cent—would apply, depending on the nature of the underlying profits comprised in the carried interest.

Further complexity is introduced when considering the interaction of these rules and the tax position of non-UK resident executives who perform some of their services in the

UK. Still further complexities arise when considering the interaction of these rules with the rules governing the position of non-UK domiciled individuals.

Do Private Equity Fund Managers 'Pay Less Tax than Their Cleaners'?

In 2007 Nicholas Ferguson, then Chairman of SVG, a quoted fund of funds that invests in Permira and other private equity funds, made an oft quoted (and, as it is rarely the same quote, misquoted) remark comparing the tax paid by private equity fund managers and those of 'the cleaning lady'. It was picked up widely in the media that private equity fund managers paid less tax than 'their cleaners' and that therefore there must be something untoward going on. In fact the comment referred not to the amount of tax paid, but the tax rate that was being paid at that time.

Because private equity funds target capital gains, most of the profit is taxed at capital gains tax rates, as described above. Both the way capital gains tax (CGT) is calculated and the rate of CGT were progressively changed and reduced from 2000 onwards. As a result CGT rates fell to below the basic rate of income tax. Therefore, if you assumed that all private equity fund managers earned was capital gains (which is incorrect), they might pay a lower rate of tax than basic rate taxpayers, who might (or might not) include people who clean for a living. They would however, still pay more tax as an absolute amount of money.

The issue was resolved by the introduction of the anti-avoidance provisions described above. Save for amounts invested on terms reasonably comparable to external investors, all amounts received by private equity executives are now generally subject to a minimum tax rate of 28 per cent.

Investee Companies

A new entity, Bidco, will normally be incorporated by the fund to effect the acquisition of a target entity. Bidco will usually be part of a two- or three-tier structure, as shown in Figure 2.22.

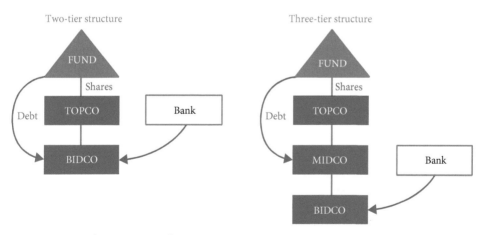

Figure 2.22. Different common buyout structures
Source: BDO

Senior lenders (i.e. banks) may wish to ensure that their debt is structurally subordinated (giving them a prior claim to the underlying assets) ahead of that of the investors, and therefore a three-tier acquisition may be used with the bank financing being provided to Bidco and the investor debt in Midco.

Tax Deductibility of Interest

The deductibility of interest arising on any debt in the acquisition structure and the utilization of those deductions in a tax-efficient manner will be the key issue for any company.

There are many different provisions which can restrict the tax deduction available for interest. The complexity in this area has been greatly increased by the introduction of further measures (anti-hybrids rules and the 'corporate interest restriction') as a response to the OECD's BEPS (base erosion and profit shifting) project. The BEPS project consists of countries 'collaborating to put an end to tax avoidance strategies that exploit gaps and mismatches in tax rules to avoid paying tax'.[6] As a result of the action points issued by the OECD, many jurisdictions have introduced new anti-avoidance rules in a number of areas, including interest deductibility.

As well as these newer rules, the tax deduction for interest on the loan notes and other debt issued by a portfolio entity in the UK is restricted to the amount of interest that corresponds to arm's-length terms (those equivalent to an unconnected, non-shareholder, lender).

Any restriction of the interest deduction arising on the debt provided by the fund under this arm's-length rule can affect the way interest received is taxed on the investors who are UK tax resident.

In Chapter 1 we briefly talked about interest deductibility and gave the example shown in Table 2.9.

If we reflect these payments in our very simplified example, we can see that disallowing interest increases taxes in the overall economy. For simplicity we assume corporation tax and income tax rates are the same (they are not), all overheads are wages to the public (they are not), all profit is paid as dividends to the public (it isn't), and that the lenders have no costs of funds or overheads (they do). There are also obviously many timing and other issues in the real world, but we are trying to draw attention to only one effect.

The effect of disallowing interest costs is to increase gross taxation and increase the proportion of value added in the economy that is taken by the state in taxation to more than it would have been if all businesses were wholly equity funded. In principle, in a closed economy, allowing the deduction of interest does not reduce taxation revenues; it simply moves the taxable profit from trading companies to banks and other lenders. Disallowing interest is an increase in corporate taxation.

Since the 1980s many countries have tightened up the regulation of interest deductibility for corporation tax. Many now have thin capitalization rules that only allow interest on a certain proportion of debt, and some have arm's-length tests that stop shareholders lending to the companies they own and taking interest instead of dividends. Furthermore, there has been international cooperation via the OECD BEPS programme to reduce the ability to arbitrage international tax differences. The general point that

---

[6] https://www.oecd.org/tax/beps/.

Table 2.9. Stylized example showing effects of tax deductibility (in any currency)

Trading Companies	No Debt	Interest Allowed	Interest Disallowed
Sales	1,000	1,000	1,000
CogS	−500	−500	−500
Gross Profit	500	500	500
Overheads	−250	−250	−250
Net Profit	250	250	250
Interest		−100	−100
Pre Tax Profit	250	150	150
Disallowed Interest			100
Taxable Profit	250	150	250
Tax	-50	−30	−50
Post Tax Profit	200	120	100
Dividends	−200	−120	−100
Retained Profit	0	0	0
Corporation Tax Rate	20.0%	20.0%	20.0%

Lenders	No Debt	Interest Allowed	Interest Disallowed
Pre Tax Profit (Interest)	0	100	100
Tax	0	−20	−20
Post Tax Profit	0	80	80
Dividends	0	−80	−80
Retained Profit	0	0	0
Corporation Tax Rate	20.0%	20.0%	20.0%

Public	No Debt	Interest Allowed	Interest Disallowed
Income	250	250	250
Dividends	200	200	180
Total Income	450	450	430
Tax	−90	−90	−86
Post Tax Income	360	360	344
Income Tax Rate	20.0%	20.0%	20.0%

Tax Receipts	No Debt	Interest Allowed	Interest Disallowed
Corporate	−50	−50	−70
Individuals	−90	−90	−86
Total Tax Paid	−140	−140	−156

observers need to appreciate is that not all interest is deductible against corporation tax and that the rules and their interpretation materially change over time, invariably (to date) in ways that do not favour highly geared companies, like PE-backed buyouts.

The subtle points that need to be understood are that interest is taxable in the accounts of lenders and dividends are paid out of after-tax profits, so have already been taxed.

Disallowing interest costs that are then taxed in the hands of the lenders is a global increase in corporate taxation. This is especially politically attractive if people are led to think that interest has some tax advantage.

Abolition of 'Tax Free' Income

In the past, where interest was not deductible against corporation tax, a UK resident investor might receive that interest tax free. The argument was that the interest had in effect already been taxed, because it had not been deducted from profits, so it should not be taxed again when received by the investors. These rules were perceived to allow interest to be paid to UK investors free of tax. The rules changed with effect from October 2013 to stop this. The new rules largely bring the UK into line with other jurisdictions. As a result, in certain circumstances such non-deductible interest is now treated as a dividend when received by individual UK investors. UK corporate investors may continue to benefit from a corresponding adjustment.

Interest disallowed under the more recently introduced anti-avoidance provisions is not typically recharacterized in this way. It would remain taxed as interest in the hands of investors despite not being deductible in the portfolio company.

Accrued versus Paid Interest Timing Differences

Interest can be deducted either when it is actually paid in cash, or when it is charged to the company's accounts (i,e. when it is accrued). Generally, tax deductions for interest on shareholder debt will only be allowed on a paid basis. However, it can be allowed when it is paid within twelve months of the end of the period in which it accrued. This twelve-month window creates limited opportunities to time interest payments to ensure that tax deduction can be utilized in full. It avoids tax relief becoming 'stranded' in the company.

The 'paid basis' was originally introduced as an anti-avoidance measure. It was to deny claims for tax deductions on interest that might not actually be paid until sometime in the future.

There are other provisions that can restrict the tax deductions available for interest. These include the worldwide debt cap and other measures that can reclassify interest as a non-deductible distribution. These other measures generally apply where there is a particular tax avoidance motive or purpose for the debt or where the debt exhibits similar characteristics to equity (e.g. the rate of interest varies based on factors including performance of the company and its size).

Summary

The general points to appreciate are that there are no special deals for private equity. The tax environment is necessarily complex because businesses are multinational and complex. When any corporate transaction occurs, there will be consideration to the tax implications of the deal. Private equity is a transformatory process for the target business. That transformation includes changing the balance sheet structure and reviewing the tax structure of the target.

Box 2.1 Findings: What Are the Effects of Taxation on Private Equity? The Academic Evidence

---

Using debt rather than equity to fund a business may reduce the corporation tax bill of any company because some interest is deducted from profits before tax is calculated, whereas dividends are not. Since 2005 the rules in the UK (and elsewhere) have been tightened so that if debt is provided by a shareholder on a 'non-arm's-length basis' then the interest is not allowed to be deducted against corporation tax. In LBOs, a great deal of effort is applied to creating a structure that is tax efficient. This is generally the case for almost any company but comes into sharp relief when a company changes the way that it is funded, as in a buyout. It has been argued that the returns earned by leveraged buyouts can be explained by the effect of interest payments on corporation tax, and there is extensive academic research investigating this hypothesis. Early studies in the US showed some support for the argument, but since these studies were completed there have been many changes in the taxation of leveraged buyouts in many countries, including the UK (Appendix 9). At the time of writing, the most recent studies around the world have found no evidence to suggest that taxation is an adequate explanation for the performance gains seen in successful buyouts.

It is the role of states and their tax authorities to decide the legal framework within which any organization operates. It is the responsibility of the funds to obey those laws.

The Secondary Fund Market

What Is the Secondary Fund Market?

As we have seen, investors in private equity funds typically make a ten-year commitment to each fund. Compared to many other investment fund types, this is a long-term commitment. However, as we have also made clear above, a commitment is not the same as an investment. Investors only invest cash as the fund is drawn down.

For investors seeking to exit from these investment and commitments there is a growing market in private equity fund positions, the secondary fund market, and a number of specialist funds now exist to acquire secondary positions. With the private equity fund manager's consent, the investor can sell to another party both their share of the actual investments in the fund and their obligation to fund future investments. Historically, the early secondary purchases were generally only of actual investments rather than future commitments and were usually sold at a discount to their carrying value. Today these may be at a premium or discount and will include the acquisition of the obligation to future funding commitments.

Although the secondary fund market has existed for some time it was given added impetus by tight liquidity conditions in the global financial crisis. In some cases, stock market falls meant that some LPs were over-allocated to private equity in relation to their statutory target limits (the so called 'denominator effect').

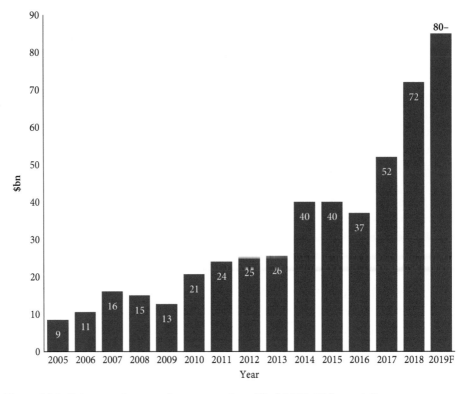

Figure 2.23. Private equity secondary transactions ($bn) 2005–19 forecast £bn
Source: Evercore, Greenhill, Coller Capital

How Big Is the Secondary Fund Market?

Because secondary sales were associated with poor performance or urgent liquidity needs, very few were publicized in the early years of the market. It was opaque even by the standards of private equity. Today data on the secondary market is still not complete and not widely available. The best estimates from some of the major participants in the market are shown in Figure 2.23.

If these are correct, the secondary market is larger than the primary market and growing more rapidly.

If the data is broadly correct, exits by way of secondary portfolio transactions represent around 20–25 per cent of the value of total exits by way of sale of the individual companies by the funds. This is up from 5 per cent in the period 2005–6, just before the global financial crisis. The increase therefore reflects not only the growing scale of the global private equity market, but also the emergence of a new trading strategy for limited partners invested in the global market.

How Does a Secondary Fund Market Transaction Differ from a Secondary Buyout?

Terminology here is confusingly similar for totally different concepts. In a secondary (or tertiary or whatever) buyout the company is sold to a new private equity fund in a discrete stand-alone transaction. Secondary buyouts are just buyouts of companies that have already been subject to an earlier buyout.

In the secondary fund market, whole portfolios, bundles of assets within portfolios, or strips of portfolios are bought and sold at the fund level. The secondary market has exploded over the past two decades. Somewhat unusually for private equity, it is more mature in Europe than in the US. We normally observe innovations in the larger US market before they emerge in Europe.

Structures differ but broadly there are two basic deal structures:

Direct Secondary Deal

In a direct transaction the secondary fund (or any other purchaser) simply purchases the interest of another LP and steps into their obligations under the existing Limited Partners Agreement. There is no reset of the relationships embodied in the partnership and everything remains essentially the same. This process benefits the LPs wishing to sell and may allow the fund manager more time to realize value from the portfolio of assets if the new LP group allows a fund extension. We can think of these deals as trading LPs with limited scope for conflicts to arise.

The structure works well to create liquidity for specific LPs seeking to exit the fund for either liquidity or investment strategy reasons.

Secondary Asset Sales

There is more flexibility in a wholesale secondary asset sale. In this structure a new entity is established (Newco above) funded by the secondary fund. This entity buys all of the assets of the existing fund either for cash, or for those who prefer to remain invested, for a share in the new entity (Figure 2.25).

The fund manager usually stays the same and they negotiate a new LPA contract with the secondary fund going forward. This essentially entails the termination of the old fund and the creation of a new one. It is the traditional structure to exit funds with zombie assets in them.

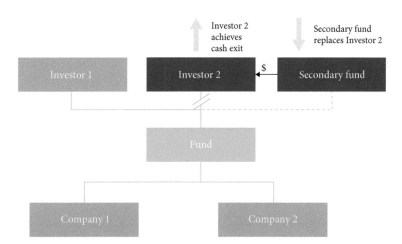

Figure 2.24. Structure of a direct secondary deal
Source: Coller Capital

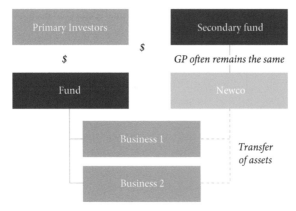

Figure 2.25. Structure of a direct secondary asset sale
Source: Coller Capital

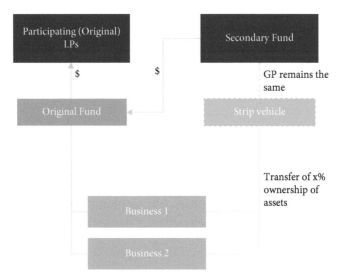

Figure 2.26. Structure of a strip asset sale
Source: Coller Capital

More complexity and flexibility can be added by creating a hybrid of the asset/direct sale models.

Strip Asset Sales
In a strip sale the fund sells portions of some or all the underlying assets to a new fund (Figure 2.26). The new fund has the potential for new terms to be negotiated with the manager. The possibility of conflicts of interest increases as the two funds terms diverge.

Top-Up Funds
In situations where more investment is desired, but an exit is not, a top-up fund can be created. To meet the ongoing needs of the portfolio a new fund is created with new terms, and may make new investments in new companies. LPs in the existing fund can either

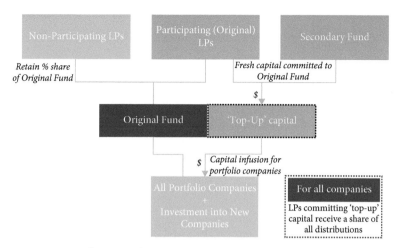

Figure 2.27. Structure of a top-up fund deal

commit to the new fund or simply retain their shares in the old fund. This structure works well for portfolios that require more capital than anticipated but are still seeking to achieve an exit within the timescales of the original fund. This can be due to, for example, a change in strategy in a big portfolio company (perhaps a big acquisition) that would breach the concentration limits of the original fund, or to a large rescue funding requirement for a business in the original fund.

What Drives Secondary Market Transactions?

When the market started to emerge, it was usually the case that secondary transactions reflected limited partners' selling. They were usually offering the rump end of poor performing assets (zombie funds) or had an acute need to create liquidity. The earliest large transaction for example was the sale by NatWest bank of its entire private equity portfolio to Coller Capital as part of its failed attempt to defend itself from a hostile takeover bid by RBS in early 2000.

As the market matured, LPs who were seeking to tactically manage their cash flows began to use a trading strategy. They would sell some or all of their mature PE investments (and associated undrawn commitments) to alter the shape of their portfolio.

What Are GP-Led Secondary Transactions?

The most recent iteration of the model has been the GP-led secondary transaction. In these transactions the fund manager initiates an offer to the LPs to buy out their investments in a fund that they are managing on their behalf. They will raise funds from a secondary fund and banks to set up a new fund that will acquire the existing LPs' interests. If sufficient LPs agree to proceed with the deal under the limited partnership agreement, each LP will have a choice of either taking the cash offered or rolling over into the new

---

Box 2.2 Findings: Secondary Fund Market—The Academic Evidence

---

There is limited academic evidence on the secondary funds market. Available evidence (Appendix 8) indicates that private equity fund interest is more liquid if the fund is larger, has a buyout-focused strategy, has less undrawn capital, has made fewer distributions, and is managed by a manager whose funds were previously sold in the secondary fund market. Private equity funds' liquidity improves if more non-traditional buyers, as opposed to dedicated secondary funds, provide bids and overall market conditions are favourable.

---

fund structure. In a transaction initiated by the fund manager to buy out the LPs in a fund (that they manage) with a new group of LPs who have invested in a separate fund (that they also manage), there are significant potential conflicts of interest.

What Impact Does the Secondary Fund Market Have on Incentives?

Earlier we talked about the alignment created by the long-term relationship between all the investors in the private equity partnership. We argued that in this sense, private equity is a very long-term, illiquid investment vehicle. The secondary fund market weakens all those relationships by allowing membership of investment partnerships to evolve and change over time. This allows investors to come into private equity after investments have largely been made, but before they have been exited, eliminating so-called 'blind risk' (the risk of not knowing what the fund's assets will be). Conversely investors who prefer the risks and rewards associated with a new fund with no investments can realize their investments independently of the fund manager's ultimate decision to sell any particular company.

It has been hugely important in the post-crash environment for LPs to be able to trade their fund positions. Investors found that they had to change their asset allocations for a host of regulatory and financial reasons. Large secondary firms have emerged able to acquire multi-billion-dollar portfolios and positions in private equity funds.

Had these secondary fund markets not been created, it is likely that limited partners having commitments to private equity funds that they could not meet might have defaulted and a crisis in confidence in the PE model would have ensued.

3

Measuring Private Equity Performance

Private equity funds provide a great deal of information to their investors in various forms. They have not generally provided the same level of information to third parties. They have had no obligation and little incentive to do so. This made early academic studies difficult due to data shortages.

Early academic studies employing the then available commercial data bases, usually only of large public-to-private buyouts, were impaired when it was found that the data providers stopped updating after ten years. This resulted in a need to reappraise some early studies and a process of replication that altered some conclusions.

Over the years this data scarcity has been alleviated by a number of factors. One of the most important is the fact that public bodies are large investors in private equity funds, and they have a duty to disclose various matters if requested to do so. In the US, public pension schemes have become a key source of data. This transparency followed a series of scandals in the late 2000s when it was found that at least one large public pensions scheme manager at CalPERS was accepting bribes to assist a placement agent.

Since around 2000, there have emerged commercial data suppliers such as Preqin and Pitchbook who collate and aggregate the various disparate sources of data on private equity that are scattered in the public arena.

Furthermore, there are data sources, such as Burgiss, made available to researchers through the Private Equity Research Consortium, and the Centre for Management Buy-Out Research founded by Mike over thirty years ago.

Gross versus Net Data

One of the key distinctions to be focused on is the gross vs net performance of a fund or investor:

- gross returns are the returns earned by the fund before fees are paid to the manager;
- net returns are the returns earned by the investors in the fund after the fees of the manager have been deducted.

The gross returns can be compared to other asset classes before fees are charged to assess whether or not the investor is adding any value by creating and managing the port-folio. However, the net return is the one that should concern investors, since this is the return they would have actually earned if they had invested.

A high gross return that is paid to the manager may yield a low net return to the LPs. Furthermore, as we have seen, not all LPs are equal in any LPA and therefore there may be dispersion in net fees amongst LPs.

Private Equity Demystified: An explanatory guide. Fourth Edition. John Gilligan and Mike Wright, Oxford University Press (2020).
© John Gilligan & Mike Wright. DOI: 10.1093/oso/9780198866961.003.0003

One of the biggest debates surrounding private equity is how to measure net returns and whether or not, all things considered, net returns exceed those that could be earned elsewhere.

Committed versus Paid-In Capital

The first problem with measuring returns is to decide what investment an LP has made in the private equity fund. In quoted funds or hedge funds this is straight forward: you pay in cash, you receive returns. In PE it is more complicated because you make an irrevocable commitment to pay in cash, but only actually pay the cash later (see Figure 3.1). The LPs therefore have a contingent liability to pay money later.

If you just measure the cash flows into and out of the fund you are ignoring the cost and risk of the undrawn contingent liability. If I commit all my wealth to a particular fund, I can't also commit it all to another fund: I need to hold the undrawn commitment in some form of liquid assets. This is particularly important in private equity funds because, unlike quoted funds, there is no ability to easily rebalance a portfolio of PE investments because they are, to a first approximation, illiquid.

This cost of undrawn funds is rarely considered in any performance analysis, but it is real. We return to this below when discussing the effect on returns of subscription line funding.

In the harshest test, you could calculate returns based on the total commitment on the date it was made against the cash flows that were received back over the life of the fund. This would measure returns on the contingent risk.

More reasonable would be to use some version of the public market equivalent test discussed below. In this you would notionally hold the commitment in liquid assets and transfer them to the fund as drawn down. You would then calculate the return based on both the actual and the notional returns from the undrawn liquid assets. You would compare this to the return you would have received if you had just held the liquid assets to assess the benefit of investing in private equity. This would give a return that reflected the opportunity cost of illiquid investments not made due to the effect of the commitment.

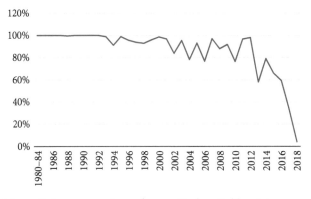

Figure 3.1. Paid-in capital as a percentage of committed capital by vintage

Source: BVCA/PWC

This is a similar, but not identical approach to Kaplan-Schoar PME (Public Market Equivalence) that we discuss later.

What are DPI and TVPI as Measures of Return?

Various measures are applied to monitor and adjust for the timing differences between total return and receipt of cash flows. We describe and illustrate the most commonly used measure, the internal rate of return (IRR), in Chapter 5.

One of the simplest trend measures is the value per £1.00 invested at valuation and including realizations as illustrated in Figure 3.2. This measure captures the trends in value appreciation in the portfolio as it matures.

In the jargon of the industry,

- DPI measures distribution as a percentage of paid-in capital;
- TVPI measures total value as a percentage of paid-in capital.

Both are measures of value per £ or other currency.

The two are equal in fully liquidated funds, but diverge when funds are holding valuable undistributed assets.

Cash Flow versus Valuation

Since private equity funds own assets that are not quoted, there is no market price with which to value investments. This creates both accounting and wider commercial issues that are relevant to the debate on disclosure by PE fund managers. As a number of commentators have remarked, the only value that ultimately matters to a limited partner (or the fund manager) is the difference between the total cash invested in the fund and the

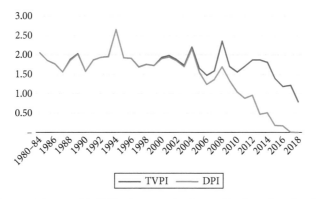

Figure 3.2. Value per £ invested in UK private equity firms: distributed and undistributed value by fund vintage as at 31 December 2017

Source: BVCA/PWC 2017, https://www.bvca.co.uk/Portals/0/Documents/Research/Industry%20Performance/ BVCA-Perfomance-Measurement-Survey-2017.pdf

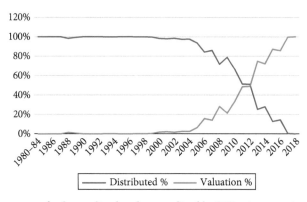

Figure 3.3. Percentage of value realized and not realized by UK private equity firms by vintage of funds (as at 2017)

Source: BVCA/PWC 2017

total received back once the fund has closed, and so the theoretical values attributed to an investment prior to its ultimate exit were once considered to be of limited practical use.

However, since funds are ten-year commitments with a five-year investment horizon, new funds are always being raised before existing funds are fully realized. This is clearly illustrated in Figure 3.3. It shows that in funds that were six to eight years old in 2018, between 40 per cent and 60 per cent of the total return in funds is attributable to unrealized investments. Equivalently, only 40 per cent–60 per cent of total return has been received in cash from funds six to eight years old.

Therefore, the valuation of recent unrealized investments is a material piece of information to both the fund manager and potential investors in any new fund being raised.

The second reason that valuation matters is the emergence of secondary market transactions. We discussed these in Chapter 2. Their emergence is a sign that portfolio rebalancing is emerging. Most trades are expressed as discounts or premia to net asset value (NAV), which is the current value of the portfolio.

It is common practice for managers to carry out quarterly valuations as part of the reporting process to investors. This ongoing valuation is therefore particularly important in private equity.

How Do Private Equity Funds Value Unrealized Investments?

Detailed guidelines intended to represent current best practice on the valuation of private equity investments are published in the *International Private Equity and Venture Capital Valuation Guidelines*[1] (IPEV Guidelines). In summary the IPEV Guidelines identify six different 'most widely used' methods available to value an investment. Within each method there are a number of variables that require a decision on the part of the valuer.

(1)   **Price of a recent investment:** when a recent investment has been made in a company, the implied market value of the company in that investment round may be used to value any instrument. In first investments, this means that they are valued at cost. In

---

[1] http://www.privateequityvaluation.com/Valuation-Guidelines.

further investments (for example a development capital or a rescue) the total investment (including any earlier rounds) might be valued at the price of the latest investment.

(2)   **Earning multiple valuations:** these are commonly used for profitable investments.

There is an array of alternative methods including:

a) P/E ratios: equity value/profit after tax;
b) EBIT multiples: enterprise value/earnings before interest and tax;
c) EBITDA multiples: enterprise value/earnings before interest, tax, depreciation, and amortization.

Each calculation can be performed using historical, current, 'sustainable', or projected data. It is usual to use comparable ratios derived from the quoted markets and/or relevant recent transactions. Having decided which of the potential comparable market ratios to use, it is normal to apply a discount to the quoted market ratio to reflect a liquidity discount. This discount may be reduced if a fund manager believes a sale or flotation to be imminent.

(3)   **Net asset valuation (NAV):** where a business is not profitable or carries out an activity that is essentially involved with purchase and management of assets (such as a property investment company) they may be valued by reference to their net tangible assets. Goodwill created by the acquisition should normally be excluded along with certain other intangible assets. As in an earnings valuation based on market comparables, a discount is typically applied to the tangible asset valuation.

(4)   **Discounted cash flows (DCFs) in the company:** economic theory tells us that the present value of any asset is the value of its future cash flows discounted to reflect the time until the cash is received and the risk that the cash flow will vary. DCFs, therefore, have the strongest theoretical underpinning. However, in practical use they are extremely sensitive to the assumptions made regarding discount rates and timing of cash receipts. Furthermore, there is a requirement to estimate the value of the business at the end of the discrete period for which cash-flow estimates are available. This is itself a valuation estimate.

(5)   **Discounted cash flows from the investment:** where an investment generates most or all of its returns from reasonably predictable cash payments and relatively little (or none) of its return from a terminal payment on sale, DCFs may be an appropriate valuation method. Loan stock, mezzanine and preference share investments are more suitable to this approach than most equity instruments.

(6)   **Industry benchmarks:** some industries have commonly quoted metrics that are not based on cash generation or profitability. Multiples of sales are often quoted for companies that are either loss making or where profits are not disclosed. Similarly, the growth of new subscriber businesses was characterized by the use of 'value per subscriber'. All of these methods are proxies for the future cash generation that will accrue from the business. In general, the further the valuation metric moves away from being based upon future cash generation, the greater the likelihood that it will be proved to be inaccurate.

Where the selected methodology results in an estimate of the enterprise value (EV) of the underlying business (for example EBIT/EBITDA multiples or DCF), the EV is apportioned between the holders of debt and equity instruments in accordance with the respective claims of those instrument holders (having due regard to the impact of any ratchet arrangements and/or outstanding options) assuming a sale of the business at its estimated EV.

Understanding Private Equity Portfolio Valuation Movements

When looking at the movement in the valuation of a private equity portfolio, there are four classes of variable that contribute to the change in the equity value:

- changes in valuation method;
- changes in company performance;
- change in external market comparators
- change in net debt.

The first element (changes in valuation method) is almost always relevant to funds in their early stages. All first investments in any fund are normally initially valued at cost. Once the first accounts after the investment are received, the fund manager will generally revalue based on the investment performance. Note that the audited accounts relate to the prior period and may therefore have a limited relevance to current trading. This creates significant timing lags if only audited accounts are used. If unaudited management accounts are used to adjust for this timing lag, a lack of external verification of the data used to underpin valuations arises.

The basis of valuation therefore fundamentally changes from one based on the actual price paid to some proxy for an external market value.

Many private equity investments are based on an investment thesis that a business requires restructuring or realignment: 'one step backwards to take two steps forwards'. In such cases the actual performance of the business, and its lagged valuation, may fall before the benefits of any repositioning emerge.

Valuations therefore move for a mix of reasons, some related to the performance of the business, some the external market, and some purely due to a change in valuation method.

Furthermore, the significant costs and transaction taxes paid in completing a deal must be recovered before any value accrues to the equity holders. Other things being equal, it might therefore be expected that the value of an investment would fall after completion (by at least the amount of the costs) before recovering as a result of the planned restructuring or realignment.

This timing effect is compounded by the widespread belief that 'lemons ripen faster than plums': failures (lemons) emerge quickly whereas successes (plums) take longer to fully emerge.

What you probably should not expect to see is a predictable steady accretion of value in the early years of an investment's life or that of a portfolio. Once the fund moves out of the investment phase its volatility might start to decrease as major transformational transactions cease. However, if the portfolio contains platform investments that are acquisitive, the number of deals may not decrease at all.

Valuation of Limited Partner Holdings: The J Curve Revisited

In addition to the change in the valuation of the portfolio of investments, the value of a limited partner's holding will be further impacted by the timing differences between fees paid to the manager and any value growth, realizations, and yield from the investment portfolio. Management fees are higher during the investment phase of any fund and generally decline when the fund closes to new investments and is concentrated on realizing the investments made. Therefore, with investments valued at cost, the investors will generally see a decline in the return of their investment due to fees in the early years of any particular fund.

When accounting for the total return from an investment portfolio the effects of all revenues including fees, valuation movements, and realizations are brought together and the movement in the portfolio at value calculated.

Total return = revenue profit/(loss) + realized profit/(loss) over valuation + valuation increase/(decrease)

The cash flows of the fund are initially negative as investments are made, and will become positive once the investments generate yield and are realized. Coupled with the fees noted above, this results in the cash flow profile known as the J curve, as discussed earlier.

The difference between the total return and the cumulative cash flow will, in all probability, be further exaggerated as the total return statement should include a discount for non-marketability, whereas the realized cash flows include the actual realized value of the investments, which, other things being equal, should be higher.

Only by the close of the fund do the cumulative cash flows equal the cumulative total return.

Measures

The second problem with performance has been to agree appropriate measures of performance. We have explained the calculation of the measures we discuss here in Chapters 5 and 6. Here we want to illustrate portfolio measurement issues, not focus on the financial arithmetic.

A Closer Look at Internal Rates of Return

The industry has used Internal Rates of Return (IRRs) to assess potential and past investments for many years.[2]
Definition: The annualized discount rate that makes the Net Present Value of a series of cashflows equal to zero.

---

[2] This section owes a debt of gratitude to my colleague Ludovic Phalippou's teaching and research, although the argument is ours.

$$NPV=\sum_{n=0}^{n}\frac{C_{n}}{(1+r)^{n}}=0$$

Where:

NPV = Net Present value

n = the number of years from 1,…, N

C = cash flow

r = the IRR or discount rate that makes NPV = 0.

There are a number of serious limitations to IRR as a stand-alone performance measure. Most importantly, maximizing IRR does not maximize the return to investors.

IRR is a cash flow measure that allows for the timing of cash flows. It therefore contains an assumption about the opportunity cost of any investment. The problem arises when you start to compare IRRs across different time horizons or when you get very large cash flows early in a series that swamp any later cash flows due to discounting.

For example, consider the two track records shown in Figure 3.4.

The first fund invested £100 and received a quick win of £300 followed by losses of £5 every year thereafter. The second fund also invested £100 and received £50 per annum each year for seven years. The returns are shown in Table 3.1.

What you can clearly see is that IRR is strongly suggesting that track record 1 was the better investment, whereas the profit from track record 2 is materially higher in absolute terms (and looks much more repeatable).

At the 8 per cent discount rate there is actually not much to choose between the two cash flow series (*ex post*) with the net present values very similar, but marginally favouring the second series.

There are two ways of looking at the IRR problem. First, and most intuitively, you can say that cash flows received early in the series are disproportionately important in determining the IRR. We can see this by looking at a simple cash flow series and seeing how

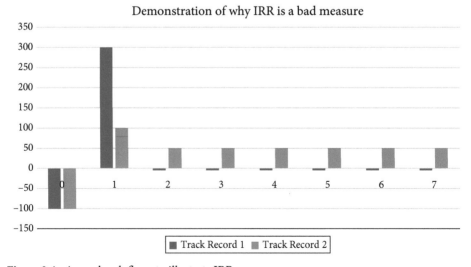

Figure 3.4. Annual cash flows to illustrate IRR

Table 3.1. IRR, TVPI, and NPV of cash flows

Track record	IRR	TVPI/ Money multiple	NPV @ 8%
A	197%	2.7X	145
B	47%	3.0X	148
Max	A	B	B

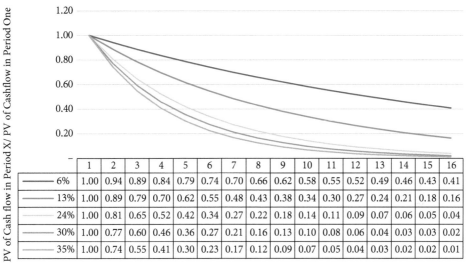

	1	2	3	4	5	6	7	8	9	10	11	12	13	14	15	16
6%	1.00	0.94	0.89	0.84	0.79	0.74	0.70	0.66	0.62	0.58	0.55	0.52	0.49	0.46	0.43	0.41
13%	1.00	0.89	0.79	0.70	0.62	0.55	0.48	0.43	0.38	0.34	0.30	0.27	0.24	0.21	0.18	0.16
24%	1.00	0.81	0.65	0.52	0.42	0.34	0.27	0.22	0.18	0.14	0.11	0.09	0.07	0.06	0.05	0.04
30%	1.00	0.77	0.60	0.46	0.36	0.27	0.21	0.16	0.13	0.10	0.08	0.06	0.04	0.03	0.03	0.02
35%	1.00	0.74	0.55	0.41	0.30	0.23	0.17	0.12	0.09	0.07	0.05	0.04	0.03	0.02	0.02	0.01

Period X of cash flow

Figure 3.5. As IRR increases, the importance of later cash flows decreases

much is contributed to the present value of the series by each year's cash flow (which will of course be £0 in total, because IRR is the solution that solves to make the total £0). We do this in Figure 3.5. You see that if the IRR is over 25 per cent the value contributed by the latest cashflows is effectively £nil.

The second way of looking at the issue is to look at the calculation more deeply. The IRR formula works out the discount rate for all cash flows in a series that makes the NPV equal to zero. This means that it implicitly assumes that cash flows in year 1 are reinvested each year until the end of the series earning the IRR.

Tables 3.2 and 3.3 contrast two methods of calculation of an NPV at 8.0 per cent discount rate. Table 3.2 uses the traditional method of discounting using the discount factor raised to the power of the number of periods $(1/(1+r)^n)$. Table 3.3 illustrates the year on year contribution from compounding internally. Each cash flow is growing at the rate of return of the whole series, as Table 3.3 shows.

What this means is that if we have a cash flow series with a large positive inflow early in the series, it becomes disproportionately important in determining the IRR. At high IRRs, later cash flows are effectively, in the limit, irrelevant.

'So what?' would be a good question at this point. What does all this detail actually mean?

Table 3.2. NPV calculations using traditional discounted cash flows method

Period	0.00	1.00	2.00	3.00	4.00	5.00	Present value
0.00	−100.00	0.00	0.00	0.00	0.00	0.00	−100.00
1.00	0.00	25.00	0.00	0.00	0.00	0.00	23.16
2.00	0.00	0.00	25.00	0.00	0.00	0.00	21.46
3.00	0.00	0.00	0.00	25.00	0.00	0.00	19.88
4.00	0.00	0.00	0.00	0.00	25.00	0.00	18.42
5.00	0.00	0.00	0.00	0.00	0.00	25.00	17.07
Total	−100.00	25.00	25.00	25.00	25.00	25.00	0.00

Table 3.3. NPV calculations using internally compounded method

Period	0.00	1.00	2.00	3.00	4.00	5.00
0.00	−100.00	−107.93	−116.49	−125.73	−135.70	−146.46
1.00		25.00	26.98	29.12	31.43	33.93
2.00			25.00	26.98	29.12	31.43
3.00				25.00	26.98	29.12
4.00					25.00	26.98
5.00						25.00
Total	−100.00	−82.93	−64.51	−44.62	−23.16	0.00

The point of this detour is to highlight how important time is in IRR calculations that are at high rates. By high rates, we are really talking about anything that an investor in risky financial products might deem acceptable. This means that any IRR-based decision system is strongly encouraging haste. This is a good thing if you are issuing a call to action and need to make changes to achieve your objective. There is often no benefit in waiting to start treating an acute problem. However, if you use IRR to judge success you are in grave danger of choosing only those who achieve big results quickly and ignoring the slow-burn winners. If you do this, you will not maximize the return to your investors.

Nevertheless, as long as carried interest is calculated using an IRR hurdle rate, IRRs will be a powerful incentive in the private equity universe.

Public Market Equivalents (PMEs)

One solution proposed on a number of independent occasions has been to change the way that the IRR is calculated. Instead of assuming that the cash flows compound at the rate of the whole series, you assume that they are invested in some liquid market. The logic is that you can either hold some liquid assets (usually an equity index) or the investment you bought. When you invest cash in a private equity asset, you should reduce your invest-ment in the index and vice versa.

At the end of the investment you compare what you earned by making the investment to what you would have earned by just sticking with the index. If you have more cash, the investment is a winner; if you have less, you would have been better off not making it. You

Table 3.4. Major PME calculations

Methodology metric	Metric	Outperformance if:	Description of calculation strengths and weaknesses
KS PME (Kaplan-Schoar)	Ratio Value	> 1	Calculated by discounting the private equity fund cash flows by the public market index value.
			The discounted distributions plus the current remaining value are divided by the discounted contributions to obtain the ratio.
			The calculation looks at the ratio of outflows versus inflows as opposed to generating an IRR, which is time-dependent and is easily manipulated.
			Easy to interpret.
			Ignores the timings of cash flows.
LN PME (Long-Nickels)	Annualized rate	Estimated PME IRR < PE fund IRR	Contributions to PE fund are converted to an equal purchase of shares in the public index. Distributions represent liquidation of share in public index.
			IRR calculation uses same contributions and distributions as PE fund, but with a different final period remaining value.
			LN PME IRR is directly comparable to the PE Fund IRR, allowing an apples-to-apples comparison.
			IRR sensitive to early distributions. Large distributions could cause a negative PME final period remaining value, making PME IRR calculation computationally impossible.
Capital Dynamics PME+	Annualized rate	Estimated PME IRR < PE fund IRR	Uses a fixed scaling factor (lambda) to modify each distribution to ensure the PME final period remaining value is the same as the PE fund remaining value. IRR calculation uses modified contributions and distributions but same final period remaining value.
			As for LN PME, with the added benefit of avoiding a final period negative remaining value, making PME IRR calculation possible in more cases.
			PME+ does not match the cash flows perfectly.

Source: Preqin Special Report PME July 2011.

turn this into an index by dividing the value of the cash you earned by the value of the cash you would have earned by holding the liquid assets.

There are, currently, at least, three different approaches.

The question now becomes what index to use as the base to compare to?

The PMEs available in Preqin's database in 2019 give a sense of the complexity that this causes (Table 3.5).

Even without absorbing all the detail in the tables, you can readily see that we have gone from a problem of having a familiar measure of performance that can lead us to make poor decisions, to having a proliferation of potential measures that create complexity and potential confusion.

Table 3.5. PMEs calculated in the Preqin database (where data is available)

Index	Type of PME	Index	Description	Potential uses
S&P 500 LN-PME	Long Nickels	S&P 500	Largest 500 US quoted companies	US PE
S&P 500 KS-PME	Kaplan Schoar	S&P 500	Largest 500 US quoted companies	US PE
S&P 500 PME+	PME+	S&P 500	Largest 500 US quoted companies	US PE
RUSSELL 2000 LN-PME	Long Nickels	Russell 2000	2000 Smallest companies in Russell 3000	US PE
RUSSELL 2000 KS-PME	Kaplan Schoar	Russell 2000	2000 Smallest companies in Russell 3000	US PE
RUSSELL 2000 PME+	PME+	Russell 2000	2000 Smallest companies in Russell 3000	US PE
RUSSELL 3000 LN-PME	Long Nickels	Russell 3000	Largest 3000 US quoted companies	US PE
RUSSELL 3000 KS-PME	Kaplan Schoar	Russell 3000	Largest 3000 US quoted companies	US PE
RUSSELL 3000 PME+	PME+	Russell 3000	Largest 3000 US quoted companies	US PE
MSCI EMERGING MARKETS LN-PME	Long Nickels	MSCI Emerging markets	Mid and large cap from 26 emerging economies	Emerging markets PE
MSCI EMERGING MARKETS KS-PME	Kaplan Schoar	MSCI Emerging Markets	Mid and Large cap from 26 emerging economies	Emerging markets PE
MSCI EMERGING MARKETS PME+	PME+	MSCI Emerging Markets	Mid and large cap from 26 emerging economies	Emerging markets PE
MSCI EUROPE STANDARD LN-PME	Long Nickels	MSCI Europe	Mid and large cap from 15 developed European economies	European PE
MSCI EUROPE STANDARD KS-PME	Kaplan Schoar	MSCI Europe	Mid and large cap from 15 developed European economies	European PE
MSCI EUROPE STANDARD PME+	PME+	MSCI Europe	Mid and large cap from 15 developed European economies	European PE
MSCI US REIT LN-PME	Long Nickels	MSCI REIT	US equity real estate investment trusts (REITs)	US property
MSCI US REIT KS-PME	Kaplan Schoar	MSCI REIT	US equity real estate investment trusts (REITs)	US property
MSCI US REIT PME+	PME+	MSCI REIT	US equity real estate investment trusts (REITs)	US property
MSCI WORLD LN-PME	Long Nickels	MSCI World	Mid and large cap from 23 developed European economies	Global PE
MSCI WORLD KS-PME	Kaplan Schoar	MSCI World	Mid and large cap from 23 developed European economies	Global PE
MSCI WORLD PME+	PME+	MSCI World	Mid and Large cap from 23 developed European economies	Global PE

Source: Authors' analysis of Preqin data

Net Present Value

We could use Net Present Value at some discount rate to assess each investment. This has the advantage of being the theoretically correct way to measure the value of cash flows over time. If you maximize NPV you do maximize shareholder value. It has the disadvantage of being very sensitive to whatever assumption you make about the discount rate, which also may vary for each investor.

The hurdle rate for carried interest might be an appropriate rate to use as the discount factor were it not for the fact that some funds no longer have a hurdle rate. The old market norm of 8.0 per cent also has arguments in its favour, or the long-term return on one of the equity indices above, which brings back all of the complexity of PME.

Whichever route you choose to go down you are faced with complexity—and almost certainly a lack of raw data to calculate the measures yourself. If it is calculated by the manager themselves you are open to the risk of gaming the various measures.

Money Multiples: TVPI and DPI

We showed above when discussing valuation how money multiples can be reflective of both cash received and current (but changeable) valuations. There has been a great deal of analysis done using these money multiples and increasingly you will see them quoted by commentators, academics, and investors. They suffer from two serious drawbacks.

First, as they are simple money multiples, they do not reflect opportunity cost, or the time value of money. Doubling your money in twenty years is a return you could get without taking any material risk by buying a 3.5 per cent long term AAA-rated bond (if such a thing existed). Doubling your money in twelve months is obviously a more attractive investment and a very different opportunity indeed.

Secondly, and more subtly, the inclusion of valuations introduces an array of potential misaligned incentives and risks. Fund managers may overstate values to attract new investors, or simply systematically make valuation errors that lead to poor decisions by LPs about further investments or selling their interests in the secondary market.

Only when you are seeing complete liquidated cash flows are money multiples—or indeed any valuation method—giving the full picture of any particular investment's performance. Unfortunately, there no circumstances when that luxury is available before you invest. Once committed the data will become available, but by then you are in a long-term investment that it can be costly to exit.

What Is the Range of Returns for Investors?

It is important to understand both the overall industry returns and their variance and volatility over time. The variation in returns between the most successful and least successful fund managers is a key statistic in understanding the performance and risks of the industry. Data on the performance of mature funds is presented annually by the BVCA. This is an industry body whose interests are therefore in favouring the industry in the UK.

The latest data was published in December 2019, covering periods up to 31 December 2013, and is summarized in figures 3.6 to 3.8. These illustrate the average (median) return

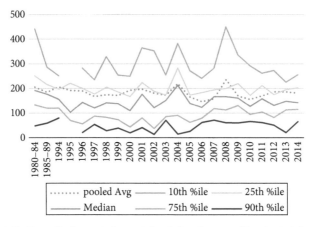

Figure 3.6. Distribution of returns to buyout funds by vintage of fund—total value per £ invested (funds over six years old)

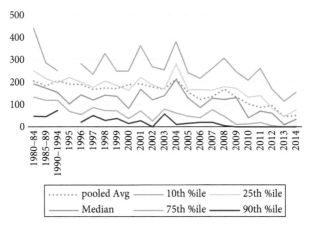

Figure 3.7. Distribution of returns to buyout funds by vintage of fund—paid out value per £ invested (funds over six years old)

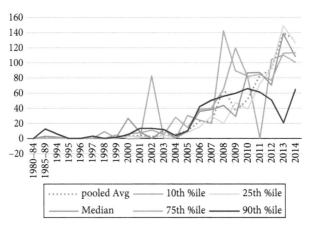

Figure 3.8. Distribution of returns to buyout funds by vintage of fund—residual value per £ invested (funds over six years old)

Source: BVCA/PWC

responding private equity funds, and give data on the distribution of the returns of the various funds. Later returns are not published because of the J curve effect distorting the returns.

We present this data in figures 3.9 to 3.13. In these graphs,

DPI = total cash distributed per $ invested by vintage of fund;
RPI = residual undistributed value per $ invested by vintage of fund;

so

$$TVPI = DPI + RPI$$

where TVPI = total value per $ invested by vintage of fund.
Or, in words, the total value per dollar invested is the sum of the distributions plus the residual value per dollar invested.

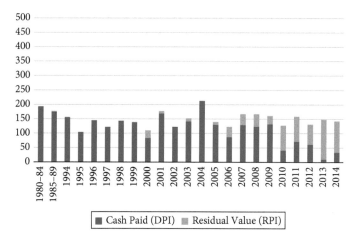

Figure 3.9. Median money multiples (TVPI, DPI, value)
Source: Author's analysis of BVCA/PWC data

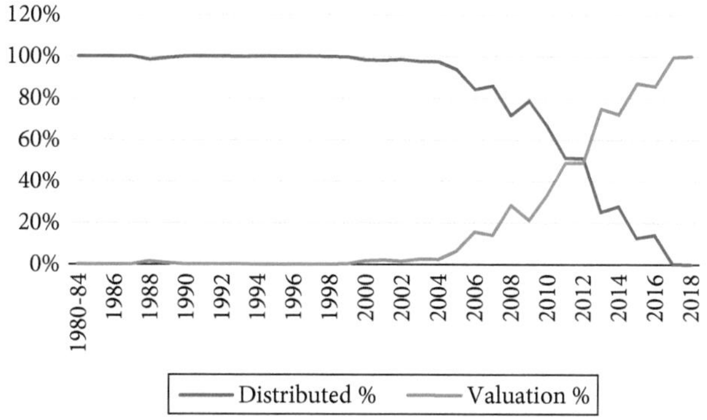

Figure 3.10. Distributed cash vs valuation: whole sample
Source: Author's analysis of BVCA/PWC data

The industry often talks of 'upper quartile' funds. This is the rule-of-thumb target for most investors. The BVCA data suggests that upper quartile net returns have generally been in the range 1.5–2.0 times the capital invested.

The data suggest that the median return has always generated cash distributions of less than twice the amount invested (200 TVPI), and since 2010 has generated less than the amount invested in distributed cash (100 DPI).

The top performing fund boundary is the tenth decile. This boundary shows that the top funds have comfortably generated more than two times cash distribution in every vintage to 2011 (see Figure 3.11).

The data covers the period up to 2018. Therefore, the vintage 2008 funds will have reached the end of their original planned life of ten years. As we saw earlier, there remains significant value in funds from pre-2008 vintages (see also Figure 3.12). This arises due to fund extensions. As we discussed in Chapter 2 in relation to the secondary fund market, the market for funds and the emergence of so-called GP-led restructurings has changed the clarity of this data. A secondary transaction may repay the original investors (paid DPI). It may also simultaneously create a new the fund in a new vintage year. That fund will have value already embedded within it. The effect is to shift DPI to the old fund and RPI to the new extension. When looking at the data, we need to be aware that it is not as pure as it used to be and the fund returns do not map directly onto the individual investors' returns (due to secondary trading, subscription lines, and NAV loans).

The worst-performing funds below the ninetieth decile boundary complete the picture. Figure 3.13 shows that other than for the 1994 vintage, the poorest funds do not return the cash of investors and do not look likely to do so.

The picture given by the data collated and published by the UK Private Equity Trade Association is one of widely dispersed returns. Thus, while the median outcome in funds has favourably compared with many other investment categories, the variance of outcomes is wide. As these are measures of funds, not of fund managers, it is difficult to extrapolate these conclusions further. However, it is clear that there are very material variations in performance between funds, and averages are no great use in understanding the industry.

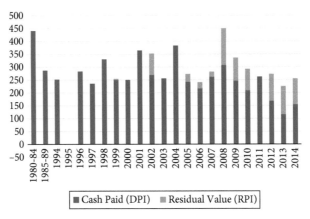

Figure 3.11. Top decile (10 per cent) fund TVPI, DPI, and value
Source: Authors' analysis of BVCA/PWC data

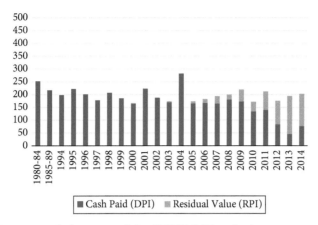

Figure 3.12. Upper quartile (25 per cent) fund TVPI, DPI, and value

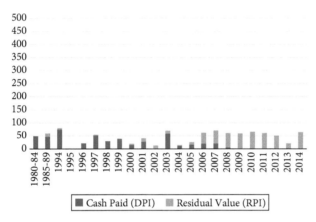

Figure 3.13. Bottom decile (10 per cent) fund TVPI, DPI, and value
Source: Author's analysis of BVCA/PWC data

According to the BVCA Performance Measurement Survey and Report on Investment Activity (for 2018) over a thirty-five-year horizon in a dataset containing 454 separate funds:

- nearly half of all private equity funds pay no carried interest;
- one in four funds loses around one-eighth of its capital;
- one in ten funds loses around half of its capital.

Combining Money Multiples and IRR: 'IRR/DPI Space'

So far we have looked at IRRs and money multiples in isolation. One method to attempt to address the weaknesses of the two key measures is to combine them by looking at the position of the fund or investment in what we might call 'IRR/DPI Space'.[3]

---

[3] This discussion owes a debt a gratitude to Jim Strang of Hamilton Lane, but the argument is the authors' alone.

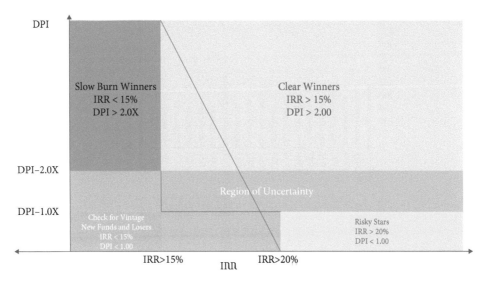

Figure 3.14. IRR/DPI space

IRRs (which include assets at valuation) capture opportunity cost and DPI captures cash money multiples excluding valuations.

IRRs that are being driven by high valuations have low DPIs. These are potential stars but any investor needs to closely examine the valuation basis that underpins the calculations. Conversely high IRRs with high DPIs are clear winners with little residual risk of underperformance.

Where IRRs are low but cash flow multiples are high, you are looking at slow burning successes where time has reduced the IRR despite the strong cash multiple.

If funds are mature and have low DPI and low IRRs they are probably, but not certainly, underperformers. A significant turnaround in valuation that delivers cash flow is needed to move to the right in the diagram.

The difficult areas to evaluate are where funds are young, DPI is below ~2.0 and IRRs are not exceptional. This is the region where both judgement and luck are needed.

To give a sense of what the universe of funds looks like, we present below an analysis of funds in the Preqin database.

Figure 3.15 shows IRR (X axis) vs total value per $ invested or TVPI (Y axis) for all 954 buyout funds in the database at 31 March 2019. (We have cut off the axes at 10 × TVPI and 100 per cent IRR.) The first thing to draw your attention to is the cluster of data along each axis where we have data on only one of the variables. This is an important characteristic of the private equity market for LPs today: incomplete information. It is impossible to have an IRR of 0 per cent and a TVPI> 0. Some of this is because new funds that have not made many investments do not have meaningful data to report on distributions or IRRs. Nevertheless, we still see funds publicly reporting high TVPI but not reporting net IRRs.

If instead of using valuations in TVPI we instead use just cashflows (DPI) we see a slightly different pattern in the data (Figure 3.16).

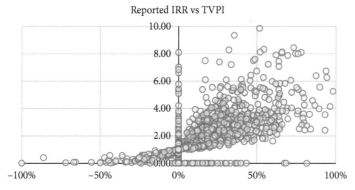

Figure 3.15. IRR (X axis) v TVPI (Y axis): 954 buyout funds at 31 March 2019
Source: Author's analysis of Preqin data

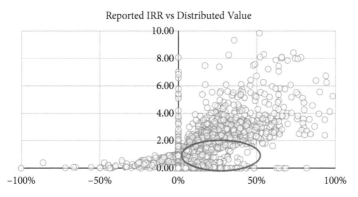

Figure 3.16. Reported IRR (X axis) vs cash distributed per $ invested (DPI) 954 buyout funds at 31 March 2019
Source: Author's analysis of Preqin data

Note the highlighted group of funds where DPI < 1.00 but IRR is greater than 0. These IRRs are dependent on valuation (RPI), not cash flow (DPI). We might pause for a second to contemplate what it means to use an illiquid valuation in an IRR calculation. IRR is a cashflow measure. RPI is a non-cash accounting value. We are assuming that we could, should the manager choose, sell the residual fund assets and distribute them as cash (or sell the LP position at value). This is not always the case and can have material impacts on actual returns.

Another potential explanation is that the fund has used either subscription lines, which as we have seen boost IRRs, but reduce DPI or other bridging loans secured on the (illiquid) assets of the fund.

The general point remains: only where cash underpins IRR is the IRR a solid measure of performance.

We can therefore categorize funds by their position in the IRR/DPI space, confident in the reported IRRs of those underpinned by historic cash flows but needing to examine the valuation of the underlying undistributed assets and funding structures in funds where the DPI does not support the IRR. It is far easier to explain this graphically.

Assume DPI = 2.0 is a satisfactory cash return, and 20 per cent IRR a very good return. We can now define some broad categories (see Figure 3.17):

(1) Clear winners: funds that have both DPI > 2 and IRR > 20 per cent are clearly successes.
(2) Slow-burn winners: funds with IRRs up to 20 per cent and DPI ≅ 2 are funds that have returned cash more slowly.
(3) Risky stars: funds with IRRs over 20 per cent but DPI < 1 still contain significant valuation risk.
(4) Losers: funds with negative DPI and IRR are probably losers.
(5) There is a grey area with DPI between 1.0 and 2.0 and IRRs under 20 per cent, and it is unclear where some of the funds will ultimately land.
(6) Unknown: where the data makes no sense—e.g. if DPI > 0 and IRR = 0.

The stage of the fund—whether or not it is investing, realizing, or liquidated—also needs to be considered. We return to this later.

The dispersion allows us to see the number of funds with high IRRs but moderate to low DPIs—these are likely quick flips that are flattered by the IRR measure.

In Table 3.6 we add a further category of funds exceeding 8.0 per cent IRR (i.e. the historic hurdle rate of funds). We can now quickly look at the population to see the proportion of winners, losers, and those that we cannot yet assess, as well as a measure of data completeness.

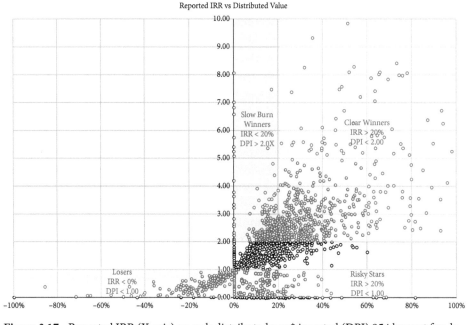

Figure 3.17. Reported IRR (X axis) vs cash distributed per $ invested (DPI) 954 buyout funds at 31 March 2019, categorized

Source: Author's analysis of Preqin data

Table 3.6. Distribution of returns of 954 LBO funds

DPI	IRR				
	Under 8%	8%–20%	Over 20%	Not known	Total
Less than 1.00	90 (9%)	28 (3%)	18 (2%)	48 (5%)	184 (19%)
1.00–2.00	123 (13%)	198 (21%)	62 (6%)	23 (2%)	406 (43%)
Greater than 2.00	1 (0.1%)	73 (8%)	253 (27%)	11 (1%)	338 (35%)
Not known	5 (0.5%)	11 (1%)	10 (1%)	0 (0%)	26 (3%)
Grand total	219 (23%)	310 (32%)	343 (36%)	82 (9%)	954 (100%)

Source: Authors' analysis of Preqin data

Across the whole data set,

- 68 per cent of funds report beating the 8.0 per cent hurdle rate of return, and
- of these, 27 per cent of all funds also report 2.0 cash return or better;
- 9 per cent report an IRR over 20 per cent with either no data on cash or DPI less than 2.0. Valuation of the unrealized investments is therefore the key issue in any assessment of these apparently high-performing funds.

We can drill into the data to look at liquidated versus non-liquidated funds. This enables us to be less ambiguous about the performance of the liquidated funds, as they do not rely on valuation to support a reported return. The unliquidated funds still contain assets held at valuation that support the reported IRRs. If the asset values fell, the IRRs would also decline.

Let's define success as achieving both an IRR over 8.0 per cent and more than 1.0 cash-on-cash return (which to a first approximation is what the majority of liquidated buyout funds need to achieve to pay carried interest). This data suggests that the majority of funds ought to pay carry.

If we use also the significantly higher hurdle of 20 per cent IRR and DPI >1, the historic data still shows a majority of funds succeeding. The historic data on liquidated funds is therefore strong.

The unliquidated funds highlight that data incompleteness and uncertainty grow as funds become more recent, which is to be expected. It also highlights the large number of funds that are reported as in a grey area, neither clearly successful nor unsuccessful. This data is much less supportive. This is also what drives an active secondary market.

We can continue the analysis, noting that we lose certainty as we slice the data thinner, and look at each decade's broad performance.

First, the data completeness declines. Figure 3.19 shows that for the last decade up to 30 per cent of the data isn't publicly available. This is an important issue if we are to properly assess a market.

Secondly, we see that the proportion of clear winners declined over the decades. In the current decade this is to be expected, as many of these funds are still in the investment phase and therefore their returns are yet to unfold, but the data is also consistent with the prevailing narrative of falling numbers of clear winners due to increasing competition.

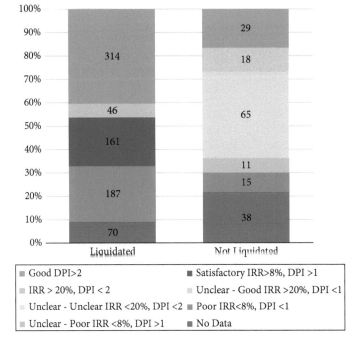

Figure 3.18. Broad assessment of buyout fund performance liquidated n= 778 vs unliquidated n=176 based on IRR and DPI

Source: Author's analysis of Preqin data

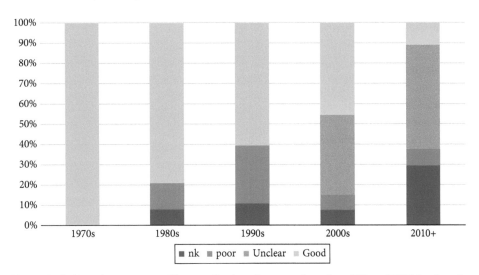

Figure 3.19. Broad assessment of buyout fund performance based on IRR and DPI, by decade

Source: Author's analysis of Preqin data

Thirdly, we see that the ability to accurately assess the outcome of the fund population declines as we move forward in time. The more recent funds have less data availability, and the data that is available shows IRRs more dependent on valuations rather than distributed cash. This is again not surprising, Private equity is a long-term investment commitment, but it is important in the context of understanding the data.

Box 3.1 Findings: Performance of Private Equity Funds—The Academic Evidence

Private equity funds provide extensive information to their investors, but hitherto they have provided very little information to any external parties, which has made it difficult independently to assess the performance of funds.

The available data is contradictory (Appendix 7). Evidence sponsored by the private equity industry trade associations indicates that private equity funds outperform alternative forms of investment such as quoted shares, although the variation between the top-performing funds and the others is very wide.

Academic evidence attempts to adjust for risk and fees, as well as whether investments are realized or not.

However, considerable debate has now emerged from a plethora of academic studies about the performance of buyout funds.

Much of this debate centres on the problem that apparent over- or underperformance may be down to the database being used.

While proprietary databases—such as those held by funds of funds—provide access to performance data that is not publicly available, they may potentially be biased, depending on the scope of the funds that are covered.

Initial US evidence showed LBO fund returns (gross of fees) exceed those of the S&P 500 but that net of fees they are slightly less than the S&P 500.

After correcting for sample bias and overstated accounting values for non-exited investments, separate evidence shows that average fund performance changes from slight overperformance to underperformance of 3 per cent per annum with respect to S&P 500.

There is also quite strong evidence that some buyout fund managers generate more from fees than from carried interest. Buyout fund managers earn lower revenue per managed dollar than managers of VC funds.

More recent studies have cast doubt on the underperformance, with several finding over-performance using various stock market comparator benchmarks and more robust data sources. One study finds a zero-alpha gross of fees, meaning that the funds had no overperformance relative to the market.

However, it is important to adopt the appropriate benchmark given that buyout funds typically invest in smaller deals than the S&P 500. Adjusting for the size premium, there is some evidence that the over-performance disappears.

The timing of fundraising may also be important: private equity returns on buyout funds appear to be higher for those funds raised in the 1980s than those raised in the 1990s and 2000s, suggesting a declining trend over time.

Funds raised in boom times (which generally correspond to the second halves of the past three decades) seem less likely to raise follow-on funds and thus appear to perform less well. These studies also find that the top-performing funds had enduring outperformance, notably top decile rather than top quartile funds.

More Recent Leveraged Funds and Returns: Comparing Apples and Pears

We discussed the used of subscription line funding above. You can think of a subscription line as being an overdraft guaranteed by the LPs and the GP that makes the business of the fund manager easier to operate. It also has an impact on any cash flow measure using a discount factor.

As subscription lines become more prevalent and longer, the comparability of past data erodes. It is important to look through the effects of these facilities to understand what is going on in the market.

Net Asset Value (NAV) loans are also becoming available, both to LPs directly and to funds. These allow either the LP or the fund to borrow a proportion of the fund's NAV. This is repaid to the LPs as an advance against future cash that will be received when the assets are sold. This again can flatter returns significantly, but carries with it risk.

The assets in PE funds are usually illiquid. The loan's repayment date may therefore not coincide with the liquidity of the asset, creating a timing mismatch that the borrower will need to finance. This is a classic mismatch of the term of an asset and a liability that creates insolvency risk for the borrower. If this is the LP, there is no change in overall risks. If it is structural leverage within the fund, the fund bears the insolvency risk.

Co-Investment and Direct Investments by LPs

Private equity firms market themselves as specialist intermediaries with the expertise to select and add value to portfolio companies. However, high fees and the poor performance by some PE firms has been behind an increase in direct investments by LPs. For example, a number of Canadian pension funds have established direct investment businesses. In principle, direct investment in portfolio companies, either as sole investor or as a co-investor with a private equity firm, provides greater control for the LP in the selection of particularly attractive investments while saving on fees.

As private equity fund performance is highly cyclical, direct investment may also enable LPs to better time the market and manage their risk exposure if LPs are under less pressure to invest at peak times than are GPs.

Box 3.2 Findings: Direct Investments by LPs—The Academic Evidence

There is limited academic evidence on the returns to direct investments by LPs.

The main available study (Appendix 8) shows that solo investments by LPs outperform co-investments. Where there is outperformance this appears to be driven by deals where informational problems are not severe, such as where the deals are late stage so that the investee company has a track record, or are located close to the investor and when deals are undertaken in peak years. The poor performance of co-investment deals appears to be due to selective offering by private equity fund managers to LPs of large deals.

On the other hand, LPs may be less skilled in picking attractive investments. They need to recruit and reward professionals with investment expertise, which may be difficult within the traditional structures of LPs.

In Chapter 1 we talked about the history of private equity and described how captive managers bought themselves out or left to start new firms to create the landscape we see today. Today we see a re-emergence of captive funds as a reaction to high costs and market growth.

Fees, Again

As we have described, fees are paid on committed capital in the investment phase and drawn capital once the investment phase ends. In a typical quoted investment fund, all capital is drawn down when the investment is made and investors can periodically withdraw their investment, paying fees on the amount invested.

Comparing these arrangements can result in strange results. First, consider fees as a percentage of the cash 'at work' on behalf of the investors. To avoid some unnecessarily complex algebra that generalizes the system, we will again use an example to illustrate the more general point.

Consider two funds, a PE fund and a quoted investment fund, both of £1bn. They are invested in equities at the same rate (£100m per annum); assume neither fund makes any profit or loss, to allow us to focus just on fees. The portfolio at cost therefore grows from £0 to £1bn at £100m per annum.

We will also assume interest rates are zero, so we can ignore interest earned by the investors and fund managers.

The quoted fund draws down £1bn and invests £100m per annum in quoted shares and holds the balance in cash or some other liquid asset. It charges 2.0 per cent per annum on the £1bn, all of which is 'at work'.

The PE fund only draws down £100m per annum, but charges 2.0 per cent on the full £1bn, whether it is drawn or not. It therefore charges significantly higher fees as a percentage of invested capital in the early years. Even after the fee steps down after the investment period, it is not materially lower than a quoted fund modelled with the same investment profile (see Figure 3.20).

As we discussed on the first page of this book, private equity investments often include loans or similar instruments that are repaid before the investment is sold. You get some money back from the loans whether the shares are sold or not.

We can look also at fees annually in relation to committed capital, invested capital, or outstanding capital at risk (invested + undrawn committed capital). This gives a very different perspective (Figure 3.21), with fees stepping down as the portfolio is sold or repaid.

Critics will quote the data in the first graph, showing fees as a percentage of invested capital are much higher in PE funds on a like-for-like basis.

Proponents will quote the second analysis to show that fees are similar or lower on the same like-for-like basis.

A reasonable view can be obtained by comparing cumulative fees paid in both investment strategies over the same period and by measuring it against the capital invested. The

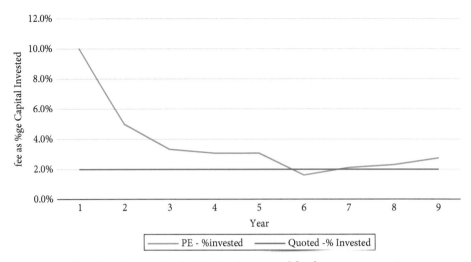

Figure 3.20. Fees In private equity fund vs tees in a quoted fund as percentage of invested capital

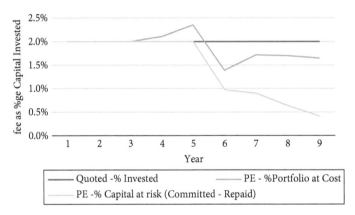

Figure 3.21. Fees in private equity fund vs fees in a quoted fund as percentage of invested capital

analysis shows that the cash paid is lower in a PE fund with no profits or losses in actual cash terms (due to the step down after the end of the investment period), but higher as a percentage of capital invested cumulatively because of the delay in drawdown (Figure 3.22).

Generalizing this simple example requires many more assumptions that cloud the analysis. For example, in loss-making quoted funds fees reduce; in profitable quoted funds fees increase, as they are charged on the value of the fund, not its cost. This cost of success is paid in carried interest in PE funds once it is realized and the hurdle is passed.

If you had the entire population of funds and compared all fees paid you would begin to see the relative price of the two investment strategies. This cannot yet be done: first, the data is not completely public; secondly, as we have seen, fee offset clouds data comparability. However, when it has been attempted the data does suggest that, on average, private equity fees are higher than those of quoted funds.

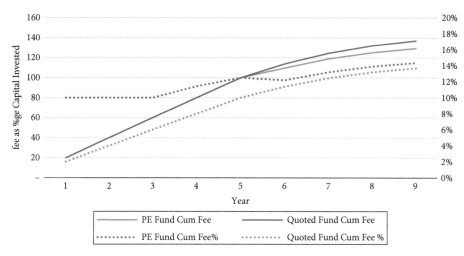

Figure 3.22. Cumulative fees as a percentage of cumulative investment

Summary

Performance is the most contentious issue in any investment class. The evidence in private equity remains patchy but is improving fast. Regulation on disclosure has revealed much, and commercial data providers have done a great deal to bring together the data in ways that provide a lens into the market.

As observers we are constantly receiving information and commentary from market participants and critics that is loaded with vested interest, and sometimes reveals more about the commentator than the market.

At a research level we are faced with the challenge of many papers based on proprietary data that makes replication of findings difficult. What has been found consistently in the peer-reviewed studies is that on the whole, private equity funds have performance before fees that supports the industry's assertion that these funds did outperform other investment strategies. However, because PE funds are long-term investments, this conclusion is always at least five years out of date and needs constant review.

Once fees are taken into consideration we cast another veil of uncertainty over the findings, but the evidence, such as it is, suggests that much (but not all) of the outperformance has, on average, been captured by the fund managers.

Very few empirical studies have demonstrated underperformance, although some have deduced that it exists.

The large research databases suggest that results are compressing and on average declining, but still beating other markets; however, the measure you choose as your proxy for opportunity cost can change your conclusions from outperform to underperform.

Success has been well rewarded. However, performance is very varied, and the public data remains weak. Most studies make little attempt to tease apart different regions and investment strategies in ways that would make sense to market participants. Private equity is a heterogeneous world. It ranges across strategies and geographies and therefore it is a legitimate question to ask whether the average performance of the 'industry' has any meaning at all. The performance of Softbank, for example, has little to add to an analysis of a regional growth capital investor in, say, France or India. Similarly, a buy-and-build specialist's results shed little light on the prospects of a business seeking to manage turnarounds.

What we do know is that the private market is growing faster than the public one. That requires explanation, as well as thought about how regulation will protect what is good about private equity and catch and eliminate what is bad.

4

Doing A Deal

The Process of a Private Equity Transaction

In this chapter we turn our attention away from the funds and look in more detail at the participants in a private equity deal. We walk through the array of advisers in the private equity universe, then examine the auction process that lies at the heart of many PE deals.

In a new section, we look at the key terms that will be in most PE deals and consider why they are there and what they are seeking to control or incentivise. In Chapter 5 we turn to financial structuring and financial engineering.

Who's Who in a Private Equity Transaction

There are two sides to every corporate transaction: those acting with or for the purchaser (the buy side) and those acting with or for the owners of the target company, the shareholders (the sell side) (Figure 4.1).

In a buyout the key parties on the purchaser's side are the private equity fund that will invest in the transaction, the bankers or other lenders who will lend in support of the deal, and their respective advisers. They must negotiate between them a funding package to support the bid.

The bid will be made by a newly formed company, 'Newco', which will be funded by the bank and the private equity fund. The debt will be lent to a subsidiary of Newco, often called 'Debtco' or 'Midco', for reasons to do with the security of the loans that we will cover in Chapter 5.

On the target's side are the shareholders, who are generally seeking to maximize the value they receive from any sale. They will be represented by the management of the business or by independent advisers (or both) who will negotiate with the private equity fund acting on behalf of Newco. If the target has a pension fund, the trustees of the fund may also negotiate with the private equity fund regarding future funding of the existing and future pension fund liabilities.

The role of the incumbent management of the business in any buyout varies. They may be part of the group seeking to purchase the business and therefore be aligned with the private equity fund (as illustrated in Figure 4.1). This is often termed an insider buyout, or more often simply a management buyout or MBO. Pure MBOs are increasingly rare as vendors have taken control of the sale process as we describe later in this chapter.

The private equity fund may be seeking to introduce new management if they successfully acquire the business. This is an outsider buyout, or management buy-in or MBI. In some circumstances management find themselves acting as both vendor and purchaser. For example, in a buyout by a private equity fund of a company that is already owned by another

Private Equity Demystified: An explanatory guide. Fourth Edition. John Gilligan and Mike Wright, Oxford University Press (2020).
© John Gilligan & Mike Wright. DOI: 10.1093/oso/9780198866961.003.0004

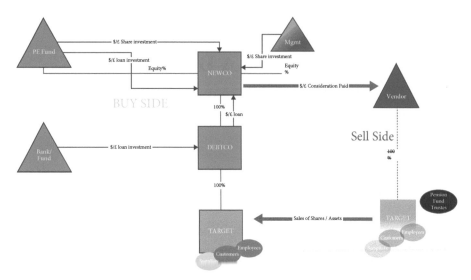

Figure 4.1. Participants in a leveraged buyout

PE fund, a so-called secondary buyout, management may on the one hand be vendors of their current shares but also be purchasers of shares in the company set up to acquire the target. We look at the mechanics of rolling over investments like this in Chapter 5.

Where management have a conflict of interest, the shareholders' interests are typically represented by independent financial advisers and, in a quoted company buyout, by the independent non-executive directors of the target.

The role and rewards of management are a key difference between a corporate takeover and a management buyout. In a management buyout, management will be expected to invest their own money in the business acquiring the target and expect to have the risks and rewards of a shareholder, not an employee, of that business. Most of the rewards to management therefore take the form of capital gains payable on successful exit, not salary and bonuses paid during the life of the investment. This tightly aligns the interests of management and investors.

What Are the Roles of the Target's Wider Stakeholders?

In general, the wider stakeholders have certain statutory protections against asset stripping and similar practices, but have only commercial influence at the time of, and subsequent to, any transaction.

In Figure 4.1 there are no negotiations highlighted between the wider stakeholders and the acquiring or vending groups. In reality their position varies from deal to deal. If the assets of the target are being sold there are various rights created under TUPE legislation as discussed below. These rights were the source of much discussion in the UK and even led to a brief attempt to change legislation around employment rights. For this reason, we take a short detour to discuss TUPE. In summary TUPE rights are not additional to any rights under employment law, they protect them.

Readers who do not care for such details can skip forward without any loss of continuity.

What Is TUPE and When Is It Applied?

TUPE legislation is designed to protect UK (and EU) employees from being adversely impacted by the sale of businesses' assets rather than a sale of the shares in a company. TUPE was established in 1981, revised in 2006 to incorporate the EU Directive on Acquired Employment Rights and amended by the Collective Redundancies and Transfer of Undertakings (Protection of Employment) (Amendment) Regulations 2014.

Employees have a legal contractual relationship with the company that employs them. This is embodied in their employment contract and is supplemented by protections guaranteed by employment law. When shares are sold and the ownership of the company transfers to new owners, this has no impact on the contractual relationship between the employee and the company being sold: the legal relationship remains unchanged and is legally identical before and after a sale. If a purchaser subsequently wishes to change any employment conditions it must do so in exactly the same way as if no sale had occurred.

If the assets or the business undertaking are sold, rather than shares, the employees will have a new contractual relationship with the acquiring company. They will cease to be employed by their former employer and become employees of the company that bought the assets or undertaking.

TUPE is designed to protect employees from employers who seek to use the change of legal employer to vary the employment terms or to use the sale to dismiss workers. TUPE gives employees an automatic right to be employed on the same terms (with the exception of certain specific occupational pension rights which are outside the scope of this report) by the new employer. These rights include the right to be represented by a trade union where the employees transferred remain distinct from the employees of the acquiring company. This is almost always the case in a primary private equity transaction because Newco has no business prior to the transaction, and therefore has no employees other than those acquired as part of the transaction. The regulations apply to all companies and public bodies without exception.

The regulations require that representatives of the affected employees be consulted about the transfer by the employers. They have a right to know:

- that the transfer is to take place, when and why;
- the implications for the employees legally, socially, and economically; and
- whether the new employer intends taking any action that will have a legal, social, or economic impact on the employees.

TUPE also places obligations on the selling employer to inform the acquirer about various employment matters.

Advisers and Other Service Providers to Private Equity

As we have stated, private equity funds outsource many functions. We discussed the in-house adviser in Chapter 2. Here we are focused on the advisory relationships at three stages of an asset's ownership cycle: acquisition of the target company, during the ownership life, and finally at disposal (Figure 4.2). We focus both on what the advisers are doing

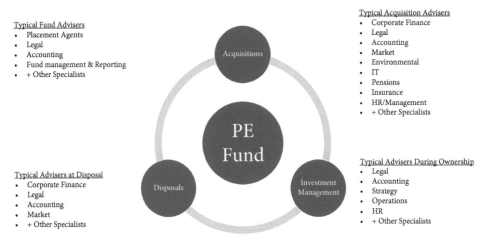

Figure 4.2. Advisers and other service providers to private equity

and at the incentives that this creates in the broader private equity market, particularly in regard to reciprocity.

Who Are Transactions Advisers?

Private equity funds are transactional businesses that are always involved in, or preparing for, deals of one sort or another. This makes them prolific users of the advisory services that surround transactions. Transaction advisers generally include investment bankers, accountants and lawyers, and an array of consultants and experts working on the target company and its markets.

Investment Bankers/Corporate Finance Advisers

As we describe in the section on the M&A auction process below, the M&A teams of banks and other advisers run most M&A processes. This makes them both a source of deals for the private equity fund, when the investment bank is advising the vendor of a business, and a provider of advisory and distribution services (syndication) when advising the private equity funds.

Thus, an investment bank may be providing advisory services to the newco and private equity fund at the same time as underwriting the banking and arranging the syndication of the transaction debt (Figure 4.3). This creates a complex series of incentives: the corporate finance and syndication fees are, on the whole, payable only if a transaction completes. However, if a transaction that is not attractive to the market is arranged, the underwriting arm of the bank will be left holding the majority of the transaction debt. The incentives are therefore to maximize the transaction flow subject to the limitation of the appetite of the syndication market for debt. The bubble of the late 2000s in the secondary banking market released the normal action of this constraint and allowed the almost unrestrained growth in the size and scale of buyouts prior to the credit crunch. Furthermore the significant fees for advising and arranging the subsequent sale or flotation of the business will depend to some degree on the reputation for quality that an organization or individual builds up.

Further complications arise around the notion of reciprocity. Private equity funds are a valuable source of a regular flow of sales and refinancing mandates that drive M&A fees.

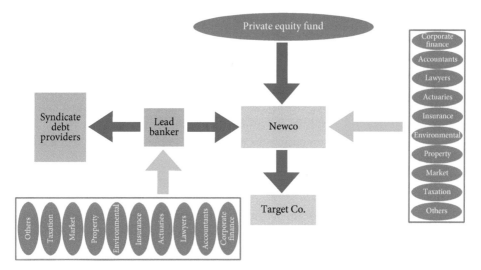

Figure 4.3. Illustrative advisers to a typical transaction

They are also potential buyers of many of the businesses that the advisers are retained to sell by other clients. As the scarcest thing in private equity is a good deal opportunity, there are powerful incentives to use reciprocity to try and ensure that the PE fund gets to 'see' every opportunity in their field of interest. Most advisers and funds activity measure and monitor reciprocity—i.e. who introduced what to whom.

One increasingly common way to feed the reciprocity loop is to use buy-side advisers paid on a no-deal, no-fee basis. Given that the market developed for many years without these buy-side advisory relationships, it is natural to ask why they have emerged in the market. Whilst they fit with the outsourced model of private equity firms, there is also a suspicion that they are disguised reciprocity payments to advisers who may bring future deals.

The vendor's advisers' role is described more fully in the later section on transaction process.

Accountants

Accountants provide due diligence and taxation advice on transactions and ongoing audit and tax advice to acquired companies. The corporate finance advisory businesses of the accountants also provide similar advisory services to those of the investment banks in the mid-market in many countries, but less so in the US.

The accountancy firms (and other M&A boutiques) argue that they provide advice independent of the debt and equity distribution capacity that is provided by the investment banks. However, the accountancy firms sometimes provide both advisory and due diligence services to the same transaction. Where this is the case the relative size and contingency of the fees for these services needs to be considered to avoid a conflict of interest.

Many private equity funds have sought to maximize the incentive of their due diligence advisers to be objective by forging long-term relationships with one or two providers. In these arrangements it is argued that the volume of transactions that any active private equity fund pursues will compensate the due diligence providers for the losses associated with those that do not complete successfully.

Lawyers

Lawyers are providers of legal and tax advice on transactions, fund-raising and structures. Every party to each contract in a transaction will generally have a legal adviser. The legal contract is the deal. If there is any dispute about what was agreed, the signed contracts will be used to resolve or frame any disagreement.

Lawyers provide both due diligence services, reviewing data on the target, and negotiation and documentation services in the production of the final legal agreements. The vendor's lawyers will often be responsible for managing the online dataroom that houses much of the company data provided to the purchaser.

Commercial Due Diligence

Most transactions will have some form of market due diligence provided by a sector expert from a third-party consultancy. In the early days of private equity many of these were small independent boutiques focused on specialist niches servicing businesses already in those sectors. Larger deals would attract the global consulting businesses, but private equity was not a core sector for most global consultancies. Today many of the niche practices have been acquired and consolidated by larger firms and PE is a major sector for all global consultancies.

Reciprocity and Conflicts of Interest

The volume and value of all private equity M&A transactions which we described in Chapter 1 amply explains the market opportunity for transactional advisers. Private equity is a consistent and predictable source of transactions, and transactions are the source of opportunities to all advisers and consultants. The reciprocity loop is common to many businesses where buyers and sellers can be either side of a transaction or relationship from time to time.

However, one of the defining features of private equity has been the sharp incentives created by a desire by PE funds to have contingent success fee arrangements for their advisers. For PE funds this means that fees are largely only incurred when deals are completed. The advisers charge a premium to reflect their risks when faced with contingent fee arrangements. At completion those fees are charged to the acquiring company in a new deal or to the fund's investors in an exit. Contingent fees therefore reduce abort costs on deals that do not go ahead, but increase the costs to deals that do complete. As a result, deal fees reported in private equity transactions tend to be high, but the data does not reflect the abort costs that advisers incurred on deals that did not happen. This can create conflicts of interest between earlier and later funds.

The fact that fees are generally charged to portfolio companies or to the fund's investors potentially creates perverse incentives. The principal–agent hypothesis says that the CEO of a quoted company may spend shareholders' money in the pursuit of schemes that do not maximize shareholder value. The PE fund manager may similarly use the ability to pay high success fees to potential deal sources knowing that these fees will be charged to the fund's investments or investors, not to the fund manager themselves.

These success fees may be paid to advisers who are a source of new transaction opportunities, and may influence which PE funds get to see which transaction opportunities.

In-House Advice and Conflicts of Interest

In some of the large funds, in-house advisory teams have been established to provide some of the functions that typically used to be bought in. These range from consulting teams to M&A teams working on the acquisitions for existing portfolio companies. These in-house service providers sometimes charge fees for their services exclusively to businesses owned by funds managed by their parent company. Not every private equity firm will charge fees for its operational teams, but as the fund managers also control many aspects of the board's decision-making (through the reserved matters that we discuss in the deep-dive into the equity terms later in this chapter), the potential for conflicts is material.

Following the changes in regulation in 2010 when the Dodd–Frank Act in the US brought many PE funds under the regulation of the SEC, there were a large number of instances where fees charged by PE funds were found to be poorly justified, recorded, and accounted for. A number of firms were heavily fined by the SEC for extracting fees from portfolio companies. This is an area of ongoing debate and scrutiny.

In essence the argument of the critics is that PE fund managers control the companies that are owned by the investors in their funds. They also sell services to those companies. They can therefore extract value from the companies by requiring them to use in-house advisers.

This is in principle little different to any corporation using in-house services that could be bought on the open market. A key difference is that the prices observed on the open market reflect the risks of contingent fee arrangements. If a fund charges 'market price' for in-house services, but has control of the contingent risks, they will make extra-ordinary profits in their in-house transaction service businesses.

Company Auctions

Most transactions will go through a process led by a corporate finance adviser. Over the years this process has evolved. We will describe here a typical auction process for a private company (or subsidiary of a public company). The process is not unique to private equity buyers, but it is important to understand. Many of the behaviours of PE funds in auctions are entirely rational and are caused by the process structure imposed by the vendors and their advisers.

Figure 4.4 shows a typical sale process at a high level. We enlarge on the stages below, but what we are seeking to draw to your attention is the intensity of the workflows (signified

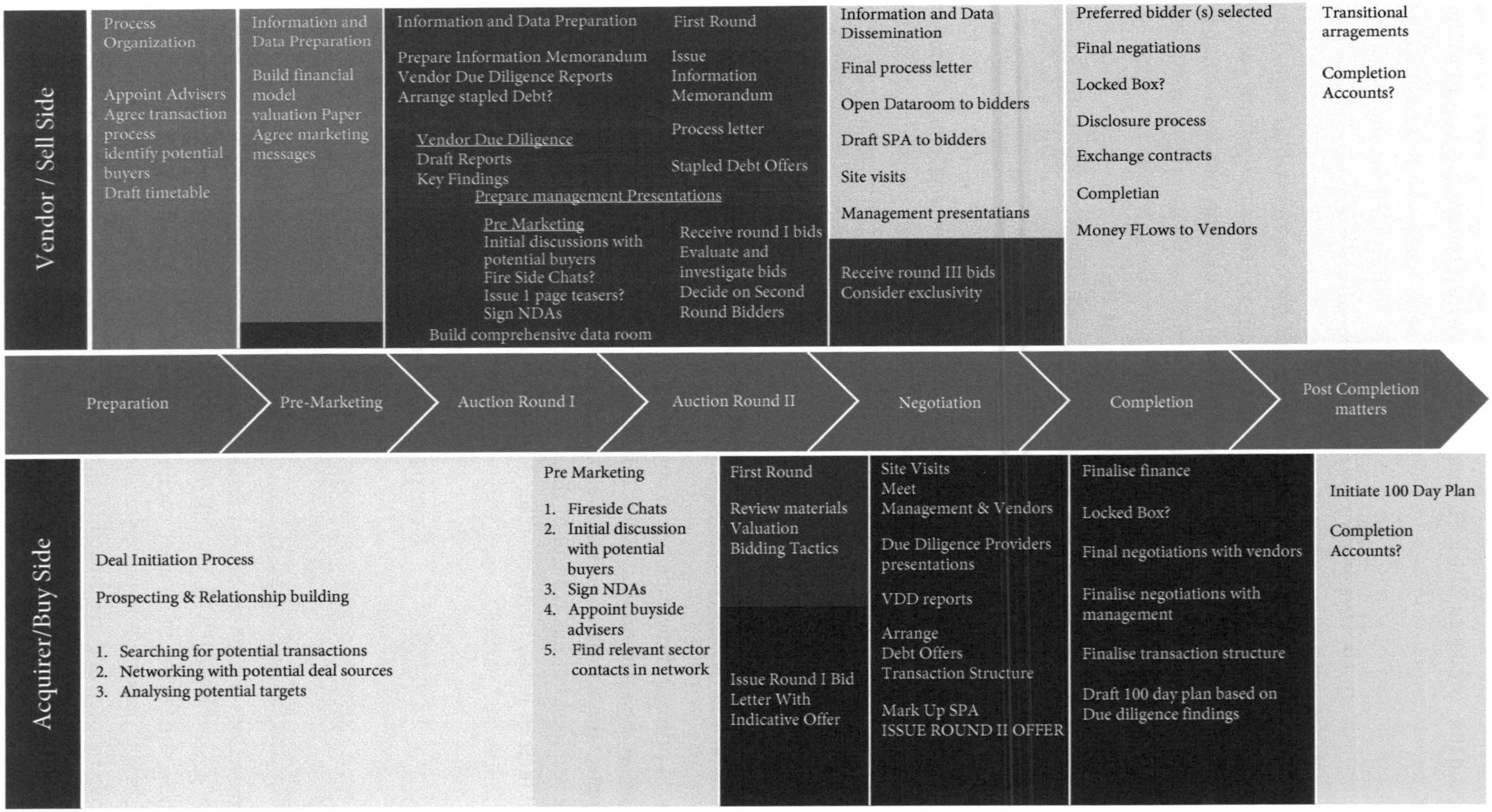

Vendor / Sell Side

Preparation	Pre-Marketing	Auction Round I	Auction Round II	Negotiation	Completion	Post Completion matters
Process Organization	**Information and Data Preparation**	**Information and Data Preparation**	**First Round**	**Information and Data Dissemination**	**Preferred bidder (s) selected**	**Transitional arragements**
Appoint Advisers	Build financial model	Prepare Information Memorandum	Issue Information Memorandum	Final process letter	Final negatiations	Completion Accounts?
Agree transaction process	Agree valuation Paper	Vendor Due Diligence Reports	Process letter	Open Dataroom to bidders	Locked Box?	
identify potential buyers	Agree marketing messages	Arrange stapled Debt?	Stapled Debt Offers	Draft SPA to bidders	Disclosure process	
Draft timetable		**Vendor Due Diligence**		Site visits	Exchange contracts	
		Draft Reports	**Prepare management Presentations**	Management presentatians	Completian	
		Key Findings	Receive round I bids		Money FLows to Vendors	
		Prepare management Presentations	Evaluate and investigate bids	Receive round III bids		
		Pre Marketing	Decide on Second Round Bidders	Consider exclusivity		
		Initial discussions with potential buyers				
		Fire Side Chats?				
		Issue 1 page teasers?				
		Sign NDAs				
		Build comprehensive data room				

Acquirer/Buy Side

Preparation	Pre-Marketing	Auction Round I	Auction Round II	Negotiation	Completion	Post Completion matters
Deal Initiation Process		**Pre Marketing**	**First Round**	Site Visits	Finalise finance	Initiate 100 Day Plan
Prospecting & Relationship building		1. Fireside Chats	Review materials	Meet Management & Vendors	Locked Box?	Completion Accounts?
1. Searching for potential transactions		2. Initial discussion with potential buyers	Valuation	Due Diligence Providers presentations	Final negotiations with vendors	
2. Networking with potential deal sources		3. Sign NDAs	Bidding Tactics	VDD reports	Finalise negotiations with management	
3. Analysing potential targets		4. Appoint buyside advisers	Issue Round I Bid Letter With Indicative Offer	Arrange Debt Offers	Finalise transaction structure	
		5. Find relevant sector contacts in network		Transaction Structure	Draft 100 day plan based on Due diligence findings	
				Mark Up SPA ISSUE ROUND II OFFER		

Figure 4.4. A typical auction sale process

by the darkness of the colour scheme) and the relative amount of preparation by a vendor and compressed time for a putative purchaser.

The vendor side has intense work leading up to the launch of the process, and becomes more reactive as the process unfolds. The potential purchaser, including a private equity house, benefits materially if they have researched and identified the potential acquisition before the process starts. This explains why so much of the time of the senior partners in PE houses are spent networking with people who may give valuable insights into transactions, and why so much junior resource is invested in searching out and analysing potential acquisitions long before they come to market.

Once in the transaction process, the vendor will want a swift route to completion at the highest valuation. The purchaser may well want the maximum amount of time to assess the business. Time is often the best form of due diligence. The attractiveness of the target and the competitiveness of the process will usually determine who wins this debate.

What Are the Objectives of the Sale Process?

The sale process seeks to efficiently and confidentially explore the universe of potential buyers. Corporate sales are transactions involving large amounts of public and private information, some of which is commercially very valuable. The process attempts to make a market by carefully transmitting and receiving information from potential seller to potential buyer.

If the buyer does not have sufficient information to value the business, the process will fail. It is a classic 'lemons' problem of the type described by George Akerlof (as mentioned before in the context of syndication).

If the seller reveals too much information, potentially including the fact that the sale is being contemplated, the commercial damage to the business can be extensive.

The skilled adviser manages this information dynamic whilst building a competitive market to attempt to deliver an optimal mix of risk and return to the seller's shareholders and other interested parties.

The adviser will prepare and communicate an initial information package to enable potential buyers to make an indicative offer for the business. Based on these offers and their own insights, a limited number of potential purchasers will be given more extensive information to make a final offer, subject to contract. The contract negotiations will lead to an exchange of the contract and finally a completion of the deal.

We expand upon the nuances of this broad process below.

Confidentiality: What Is an NDA?

An NDA is a non-disclosure agreement or confidentiality agreement. It defines the obligations of the parties when they share private information and the remedies if that information is leaked or misused. Litigation under NDAs in private equity is surprisingly rare in Europe. It is however the first legally binding contract between potential vendors and buyers and the negotiation of its terms sets the tone of the legal negotiations to come. There have been attempts by various organizations to standardize NDAs in auction processes, but they are still often a bone of contention.

When funds were small generalists it was unlikely that any material commercial advantage was gained by a private equity fund having access to any particular transaction. As PE funds have grown and specialized, the importance of NDAs and confidentiality more broadly has grown. Today most PE funds have sector preferences and are active participants in the M&A landscape in those sectors.

An NDA can be anything from one page to a multi-page contract, but essentially it has a number of parts:

- first, it defines what confidential information is.
- secondly, it limits and defines who has the right to view the information and for what purpose. This will usually include provisions allowing the recipient to reveal information if required by certain laws;
- thirdly, it gives a process to store and recover the information. It then gives the broad basis on which the information is provided and how any remedy will be calculated if the agreement is breached;
- finally, it gives a time limit for the agreement and what legal jurisdiction it is covered by (e.g. US or UK law).

What Are Fireside Chats?

You will notice from Figure 4.4 that on the sell side a great deal of work is preparation for the sale process. These preparations include the identification of potential buyers and may also include extensive pre-marketing to potential key buyers. One of the most valuable pieces of contact that a buyer can have is with the management team of the business. This is sometimes arranged in an informal meeting called a 'fireside chat'. The management, usually chaperoned by the vendor's advisers, meet with potentially interested parties before the launch of the formal process.

Fireside chats are very important ways to signal interest to buyers and sellers and to start to transmit informal and unstructured information to both sides.

What Is an Information Memorandum (IM)?

When selling a business there is a balance to be drawn between revealing sensitive information to competitors and allowing interested buyers to know enough to form a valuation that they can deliver. To ensure a level playing field and bound the information set, information memoranda are usually prepared. These are usually a highly professionally produced financial brochure putting forward the opportunity in its best light. The IM is typically produced by the vendor's corporate finance advisers in collaboration with the vendors.

The IM will contain enough information on the business to allow a bidder to make an informed offer, subject to due diligence and contract, in the first-round bidding auction. Typically, it will include, at a minimum:

(1) Product/service analysis;
(2) Analysis of the market(s) of the business;
(3) Strategic and competitor analysis;
(4) Operational analysis;
(5) Organization structure;
(6) Historical financial performance and projections;
(7) and many more options specific to the business, its circumstances, and those of the potential purchaser.

The IM is a key sales document that will form the basis of negotiations. Amongst the most important figures in the plan are often the historical and forecast EBITDA.

What Is EBITDA?

As EBITDA—Earnings (profit) before Interest, Taxation, Amortization and Depreciation— has become so central to the way that corporate finance is discussed we examine it more fully in Chapter 5. Briefly:

- **depreciation** is the gradual recognition of the costs of fixed assets to reflect their deterioration over time in the company's profit and loss account (earnings statement);
- **amortization** is the recognition of the cost of intangible assets in a company's profit and loss account. It can be thought of as being essentially very similar to depreciation. To a first approximation, amortization is the depreciation of intangibles, although there are differences outside the scope of this work.

EBITDA is intended to show the profitability of a business over a period of time disregarding how the business is financed. EBITDA can therefore be related to enterprise value, which, as we will discuss in Chapter 5, is what private equity is all about.

What Are EBITDA Multiples?

It is important to state clearly that EBITDA does **NOT** cause value. Value is determined by supply and demand. In financial assets (only) value can be estimated by looking at projected cash flows. This is because in financial assets demand is assumed to be a simple function of cash flows. You can almost define financial assets as being those things whose value is solely determined by their cash flows.

EBITDA is a commonly used metric that emerged in the 1990s becoming one of the commonest ratios of profitability quoted in transactional corporate finance (Figure 4.5).

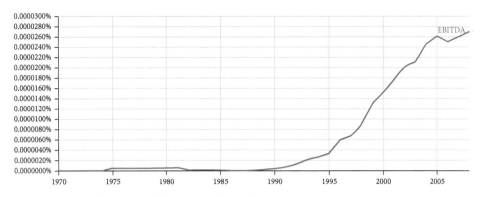

Figure 4.5. Google Ngram of the term EBITDA (1970–2010)

EBITDA multiples compare enterprise value to EBITDA.

EBITDA multiples are measures and descriptors of value, not causes. EBITDA multiples are how we talk about valuation, not how it is created.

You can think of it as a price signal. If we told you that this book cost £10,000 a copy you'd rightly ask—Really! what is so special about this book to justify that price? Similarly, if you see a high EBITDA multiple you ought to ask yourself, what is so special about that company to justify that fancy valuation?

The value of financial assets is determined by future cash flows, a forward-looking concept, so historic EBITDA multiples are questionable on that basis. Projected EBITDA multiples do not capture the complex interaction of volume, timing, volatility, uncertainty, and risk of expected future cash flows that are the causes of the demand for a financial asset. We return to this in Chapter 5.

What Is Vendor Due Diligence (VDD)?

Traditionally a potential buyer would make an offer and then commission advisers to complete due diligence on their behalf. This creates both delay and risks to the vendor. They will not necessarily see the due diligence before the final negotiations.

To mitigate both negative factors, a vendor may commission and underwrite the costs of vendor due diligence (VDD). They arrange for an independent third-party expert to draft reports on the financial, market, and any other area that they deem critical to valuation, usually prior to the release of the information memorandum to buyers. This means that the vendor should be aware of any potential major due diligence issues before sending out the information pack that will form the basis of initial offers and subsequent negotiations. If there are any negative issues highlighted in the VDD, the vendor must decide whether to remedy them (if possible), or how to position the matter in the negotiation.

These VDD reports will only be made available to final-round bidders under a suitable engagement letter from the report's authors. They will usually be updated prior to completion and whoever completes the transaction will have the final reports addressed to them. They will therefore be able to rely on them, meaning that they can potentially sue the authors of the reports if there is a material omission or error.

The disadvantages to the sell side of VDD are cost and a change in the timings of the sale process. If the purchaser already knows the business well and is comfortable with the risk, adding in a VDD process can unnecessarily delay a transaction.

The disadvantages to the buy side are more complex. Having VDD may enable a buyer to rapidly understand a business in a granular way. However, nobody would choose to have their due diligence scope or engagement terms agreed with the provider on their behalf by the vendor. There are clear potential conflicts of interest for the VDD provider, who is instructed by the vendor at the start of the process but will have a duty of care to the purchaser at the end. As a result, for material areas particularly of CDD and FDD, buyers often appoint their own advisers to conduct independent analysis or top-up work.

How Does a Typical Private Company Auction Proceed?

Most auctions have at least two rounds of bidding, but there can be many more. In public companies the regulator may step in to require a limit to the number of rounds of bidding to maintain an orderly market.

Round I

In round I indicative offers are sought from potential bidders. Bidders will receive the IM and very little other information. Preferred bidders may have had a fireside chat.

The process will be governed by the vendor's corporate finance adviser who will issue a process letter explaining the time scales and requirements. Bids will be secret and will usually be non-binding letters of intent. The advisers and vendors will review the bids and decide how, and with whom, to proceed in the second round.

Selection criteria will often be based on some combination of price and non-financial terms and deliverability (e.g. How serious is the bid? Is the bidder credible as a potential buyer? What is the bidder's reputation?)

Round II

Bidders will receive much more information, including the VDD reports and probably presentations by their authors, a full management presentation, and much greater dialogue with the vendor's advisers on any other matters of particular concern.

The vendor's intention is to maintain competitive tension while enabling the purchasers to be in a position to make a final offer, subject only to a minimal number of outstanding matters.

The vendor may issue a draft Sale and Purchase Agreement (SPA) and require the potential purchasers to mark up the draft. This enables the vendor to start to clearly understand the contract that is being created and the areas of contention.

The potential purchasers must decide whether to incur the costs that accrue in these processes. In highly competitive auctions these are significant costs that, as we saw when discussing fees in funds in Chapter 2, are usually recharged to the fund's LPs.

Negotiation and Exclusivity or a Contract Race?

Following Round II bids there will be an intense period of clarification and negotiation. It is important to understand that while price is the key thing that is being assessed, risks are also crucial to any decision.

A high price with an onerous set of warranties from a litigious buyer may presage a long, costly, and ultimately value-destroying post-completion wrangle.

A simple clean price with reasonable risk protections may be preferable. A great deal of the post Round II negotiations will be the interaction between price and transaction risks.

A key decision is therefore whether or not to offer a bidder exclusivity. Exclusivity is a period during which the vendor undertakes to negotiate exclusively with only one party to seek to close the deal. Exclusivity offers the bidder the certainty needed to incur the costs of completing the deal. These include the opportunity costs of devoting management time to the deal as well as the pure financial costs of external advisers.

As we discussed earlier, private equity funds traditionally drew down capital only to complete deals. Furthermore, one of their competitive advantages vis-à-vis trade purchasers is their transactional agility and quick decision-making. The ubiquity of the company auction is one of the changes in process that has led to the emergence of subscription line funding. Being able to offer to complete a deal rapidly in a short period of exclusivity can be a deciding factor in doing the deal.

An alternative to exclusivity is a contract race between a number of potential buyers. This is a parallel negotiation with two (or potentially more) potential buyers that ends when one of them agrees and signs a satisfactory agreement with the vendor.

Vendors maintain competitive tension to completion and should therefore extract most value. However, purchasers understandably hate contract races for both cost and transaction risk reasons. If the PE fund(s) are backing the incumbent management a contract race prevents relationship building that will be crucial post completion. This increases risk to the purchaser and therefore may actually reduce price. In the limit the bidder will simply walk away if the costs and risks are too high.

Contract races also put significant burdens on vendors and advisers. Managing more than one bidder in the final negotiations of a deal is very expensive and time-consuming, as you have to duplicate many processes and negotiations for each bidder.

Completion and Exchange

When all matters are agreed, the SPA and all other contracts involved in the deal will be signed by all the parties and a copy given to each side. This is the point of exchange.

Completion of the contract occurs when any pre-conditions of the contract (conditions precedent, or CPs, in the jargon) are met and the ownership of the business passes to the purchaser. There may be a gap between exchange and completion whilst the CPs are met, but generally all parties will seek to have a simultaneous exchange and completion.

The commonest reason for a split exchange and completion are regulatory approvals required to transfer a business. In transactions that delist a public company (a P2P) there will a gap between the offer being posted and completion. This allows the public shareholders to review and vote on whether or not to accept the offer and to allow the formal process to delist the business.

We expand on completion mechanics below in the deep dive into the heads of terms.

Do Private Equity Funds 'Chip the Price'?

There is no peer-reviewed academic research on private equity bidding in auctions. We can only therefore examine incentives, experience, or hearsay.

A two-stage secret bid auction as described above creates particular incentives when analysed by game theory. First, if only the highest bidders are taken forward, and all bids are non-binding, the most rational bid in Round I is the highest plausible bid. Bidding your true valuation and not being in Round II is not a winning strategy. Therefore, if the bidders are rational, you should expect to see high bids in Round I.

Round II is more serious as all parties are incurring significant costs. In Round II the purchaser will need to balance the costs of an aborted transaction with the risks of exclusion due to underbidding. The incentives are still to bid strongly, but to seek to claw back as much value as possible if exclusivity is granted. This set of incentives has two consequences.

First, it encourages overbidding in the first round, and subsequently in exclusivity following Round II, attempts to claw back value through price reductions. Therefore, 'price chipping' is what vendors and their advisers might expect to see from any rational bidder in a simple two-stage competitive auction.

However, there is also an alternative multi-round game theory analysis. As private equity funds are often transacting with the same adviser community multiple times per year, frequent price chipping (without due cause from new information revealed or discovered after final bids) will create a negative reputation that vendor advisers will start to factor into their consideration of the credibility of future bids. Reputations like this get spread around and can be hard to shake off. This acts as some constraint on gratuitous price chipping for any PE firm that aspires to do multiple deals in a market.

Do Auctions Increase Costs?

The second impact of the auction process is that it encourages private equity funds to seek to use advisers on a contingent fee basis, as we discussed above. Contingent fees are higher than underwritten fees because the adviser concerned bears the risk of their client losing the auction and them not being paid. This therefore pushes up transaction costs to the winning bidder but reduces the abort costs to the losers. Overall, whoever wins the auction process has paid the highest costs, and these are passed on to the fund via the investment. This is in addition to the Winner's Curse that we talked about in Chapter 1.

A Deeper Dive into a Private Equity Investment Agreement

In this section we walk through the key terms that appear in most private equity investments. Our intention is to try to explain why the terms are present, not take any position on whether they should be in an agreement or to prescribe any particular outcome to a negotiation around them. A pro-forma detailed term sheet is at Appendix 4. This is representative of a mid-market UK buyout with management rolling over some of their investment.

Not every transaction will involve a formal heads of terms document: on many occasions the process will skip straight to a formal draft of an investment agreement and a sale and purchase agreement.

What Are the Key Contracts in a Private Equity Deal?

There are many contracts to any deal, but if we simplify the situation to its most basic form, the essence will be clearer.

Articles of association: As described above, a buyout involves setting up a new company (Newco) that will acquire the target and adopt its articles of association. In growth capital investments you may see an investment into a new class of shares in the existing target company. If so, the target company's existing articles of association will be replaced or amended to accommodate the rights of the new private equity investor. In this scenario the negotiation issues are similar, but rather than starting from a clean sheet with a new off-the-shelf company, you rewrite the existing contracts. Note that it is rare that a PE fund simply buys or subscribes for ordinary shares or common stock. One of the defining features of PE investment is the active controls that are embodied in the agreements between the shareholders.

Here we will concentrate on the typical buyout structure, where a newco is established. The issues are fundamentally the same in growth capital and VC deals, but it is simpler to explain in a newco structure.

An **investment agreement** is a contract between the equity investors in the acquiring company about the relationship between them (see Figure 4.6). The company may also accommodate many of the terms of the investment agreement directly into the articles of

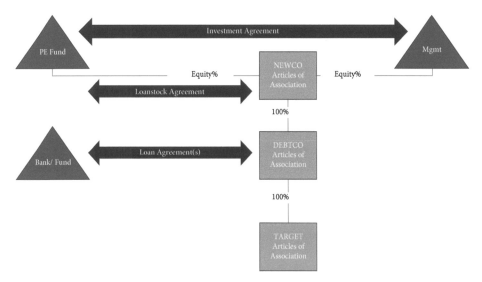

Figure 4.6. Major contracts in a buyout

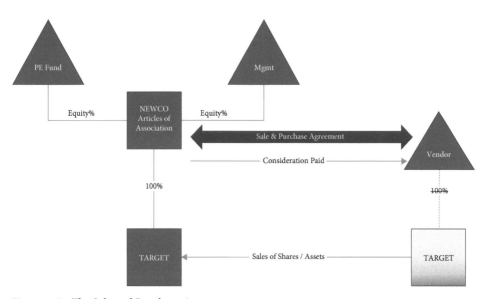

Figure 4.7. The Sale and Purchase Agreement

association of the company. Every company must have articles of association, but an investment agreement is not a required document. For our purposes we can think of the two documents as interchangeable. They key idea to understand is that there is a contract between the shareholders that is enforceable in law.

There will also be a **loan stock agreement** (in Europe) between Newco and the private equity fund, governing the terms of its loans, just as there is between the banks or debt funds that fund the transaction. If the bank or other lenders lent directly to Newco, there would need to be an **inter-creditor agreement** (literally an agreement between creditors), but the way we have presented it above uses a Debtco which eliminates the requirement for that contract. There will be many more contracts, but these are the fundamental building blocks of the deal that might be covered in the heads of terms. We are ignoring the **bank/debt fund loan agreement** in this section; we will return to this in detail later.

The **sale and purchase agreement** (SPA) is the key contract between the sellers and buyers explaining what deal they have done (Figure 4.7). In a sense, this document *is* the deal that is being done, because this is the primary contract the courts will look to if there is any dispute.

Most of the important items in these two/three documents should be addressed in the **heads of terms**, if only to acknowledge that the final position on the matter has not yet been agreed.

The Heads of Terms

A heads of terms is a non-binding agreement that sets out the key terms of the deal prior to starting to draft the formal contracts. The advantage of a formal heads of terms is the clarity it brings to all parties: you know broadly what you are signing up to before you have committed to incurring all the transaction costs.

The disadvantage is that the search for clarity in what is meant to be a high-level summary often causes many unresolved issues to surface before either party is ready to agree them. This can result in a raft of outstanding items at the time when you are trying to create agreement and clarity. There is therefore the risk and tendency for heads of terms to become a prequel to the formal negotiation of the contracts that it is intended to be a short cut towards.

Who Should Draft a Heads of Terms?

There are two basic approaches: Either the principals draft the summary of their agreement between themselves and pass it to the legal teams to document, or the principals work with the lawyers to draft the document.

If drafted by the respective legal advisers, the structure will often anticipate the contracts that will form the transaction. You can view this as a rough draft of the key planks of the emerging agreement. The fine details will follow, but the structure is loosely set.

If it is not drafted in consultation with the legal teams, it will often not follow the structure of the formal documents, and may look much more like an indicative offer than a first draft of the contract.

The Contents of a Typical Heads of Terms

There are undoubtedly many deals that have been done 'on the back of a napkin' by decisive entrepreneurs, but here we are dealing with a typical professional process involving an institutional investor. As we have tried to emphasize throughout, private equity firms have processes that they follow both to manage risks and, equally importantly for fund investors, to demonstrate management and control of risks. Even if a PE firm writes on the back of a napkin, their lawyers and investment committees won't, and the LPs who are funding a deal certainly won't expect them to. You should therefore expect to see rigour and process in any PE-backed transaction.

Essentially a heads of terms answers three questions: who? what? how? Who are the people agreeing? What are they agreeing about? How does the process of implementing the agreement work?

Who Are the Parties to the Deal?

The parties to the sale and purchase agreement are, naturally enough, the buyers and the sellers. If the deal is a simple acquisition, there is nothing different about the SPA from any corporate sale.

However, in buyouts there are often managers and manager/shareholders who are both sellers and buyers. If the business is a founder-owned business, the sale may be a partial sale to a new investor with the founders 'rolling over' some of their proceeds into the new company. Economically you can think of this as simply selling for cash then instantaneously buying an investment in the newco with some portion of the proceeds (Table 4.1). There are knotty tax issues that we will deal with in the section on taxation of rollover in Chapter 5.

What Is the Price? Definition and Consideration

This is obviously a key term. As we have said, price in most private equity deals (except public to privates) is the enterprise value, expressed as the debt free/cash free value of the business with a normalized level of working capital. We explain the normalization later in this section.

Carefully checking the definition of enterprise value is important. Some bidders will exclude corporation tax liabilities, arguing that these relate to past profits and are therefore rightly for the vendor's account. This is no different to any other creditor, and in any case many companies pay corporation tax in advance, but it is an argument that will still be made and needs to be checked.

The price will include cash and any other consideration that is paid to the vendors. In this example we have chosen a relatively intricate deal that involves the receipt of cash, shares, and loan notes. This is common in secondary buyouts and partial sales to private equity funds.

Assume that a PE fund offers to buy a business for £100m, paying £80m in cash and £20m in a mix of loans and shares (see Table 4.1).

Table 4.1. Pro-forma transaction structure with a vendor rollover

Resulting structure	PE fund	Vendor	Total
Shares	8	2	10
Equity %	80%	20%	100%
Loans	72	8	80
Total	−80	20	100
Cash flow	−80	80	

Note that the price is expressed as enterprise value, assuming a cash free/debt free balance sheet and a normal level of working capital.

When Will the Price Be Paid? Exchange and Completion/Closing

There are at least two points in a transaction when you might consider it to have been finalized. The first is when the final contracts are signed and exchanged between all the parties. This is final in the sense that there is nothing left to agree and all that should happen after signing is the execution of whatever the contract agrees will happen. This point is, perhaps unimaginatively, known as exchange.

Completion (or, in America, 'closing') is the other natural end point of a transaction. It is the point at which the parties pay and receive the consideration and deliver the shares or assets to the purchaser.

It is possible that there will be a gap between exchange and completion for an array of technical reasons. You might require an external approval before you can complete the deal. These might include regulatory approval in certain industries or approval by the relevant competition authorities if there are potential concentration issues. In public-to-private transactions there is a formal process required to acquire all the shares in issue that can only take place after exchange of contracts.

There may be other matters covered by the contract that happen after completion. These may be material to the transaction value, especially if there are completion accounts adjustments. This is covered below.

Material Adverse Change Clauses (MACC) and Reverse Termination Fees

If there is a gap between exchange and completion the purchaser will prefer to have the option to withdraw before completion, whereas the vendor will want complete certainty that once any CPs are satisfied completion will happen automatically.

A material adverse change clause (MACC) is a wide-ranging condition that allows the purchaser to pull out of the deal if the has been a material adverse (bad) change in the circumstances of the deal. MACC clauses are common in North America but much rarer in the UK; their use varies across the rest of the world.

Some vendors seek to protect themselves using a 'reverse termination fee' payable by the purchaser if they pull out of the deal.

The full broad-ranging details are beyond our scope, but it is worth drawing attention to what happened in the global financial crisis in the US. In a number of large buyouts including Huntsman, Acxiom, and Sallie Mae, the private equity funds sponsoring the deal chose to pay the termination fee and invoke the MACC clause to withdraw from the deals. They cited the performance of the businesses and their prospects, not the crisis itself. After the crisis it was reported that average reverse termination fees increased from around 3.0 per cent of the equity value to 4.0–8.0 per cent of the equity value.[1]

MACC clauses are not required, and many European vendors will not accept them. The vendor wants certainty and will usually require exchange to be wholly unconditional. In most private deals the issue is avoided entirely by ensuring that exchange and completion happen at the same time: you sign, and you pay the consideration contemporaneously.

What Is the Process for Ensuring that the Seller Has Delivered What They Said They Were Selling?

Having agreed to pay the consideration the purchaser will want a method to verify that they did indeed get what they agreed to acquire. If there is any difference, there will be some process to address the difference (or not as the case may be). In a heads of terms this is a sensitive issue.

---

[1] *New York Times*, 2 May 2012.

EBITDA Multiples and Minimum Net Assets

You will see a variety of ways to define the price. They will almost always state that the price is based on delivering some financial metric—usually EBITDA—in a particular timeframe. This signals clearly that EBITDA is going to be one key number that is under scrutiny in due diligence between the heads of terms and completion.

The rule of thumb is that if EBITDA falls the price will probably fall, usually by the EBITDA multiple that is being paid. If EBITDA rises it is much harder, but far from impossible, to get an acquirer to increase the price.

You may also see an assumed level of net assets as a target metric. If net assets are less than the agreed amount there will be an adjustment to the price to make good the lost assets.

Note that EBITDA results in a much higher reduction in consideration than a net assets target. Also note that you should not pay twice: if EBITDA is reduced it is likely that net assets will also fall.

Mechanisms to Verify the Assets and True-Up the Consideration

Completion mechanics vary markedly between different deal types and different geographies.

Public Company Takeovers (P2P)

In a public company takeover, completion is very straightforward, and there is no process to adjust the consideration after completion. You bid for the shares and if the shareholders accept you get the shares. You must be unconditional in all respects when you make the offer. You cannot have any process to check the assets or profits after you take control.

Private Company Takeovers

Most private equity deals are private company transactions. In a private transaction you will often, but not always, have a mechanism to confirm profitability and net assets either just prior to, or just after completion.

What Are Completion Accounts?

Most contracts for the purchase of private companies (but not public takeovers) will have a mechanism to check that the assets and liabilities acquired are substantially the same as the accounting records say they are.

All accounts involve judgements on the part of the people preparing them. There is therefore often a negotiation around the basis on which the accounts are prepared. This is especially important when the acquirer and the vendor use different sets of accounting principles. If a US acquirer has assumed USGAAP (US Generally Accepted Accounting Principles) but the vendor has based their calculations on their own internal application of IFRS (International Financial Reporting Standards) the possibility for a long technical debate is obvious. The appropriate standards therefore need to be agreed if completion accounts are to be used.

The contract will have a minimum net asset amount that the vendor is to deliver to the purchaser. To check whether this has happened, the accountants of the vendor, or much more usually the acquirer, will prepare a balance sheet at an agreed date. The contract will state a mechanism to adjust for any material discrepancy. This is the so-called £-for-£ net asset adjustment.

Some of the consideration may be held in an escrow account until the completion accounts are agreed. An escrow account is a bank account created by an adviser to hold cash in suspense until any disputes have been agreed. Once they are agreed the amount will be released, less any deductions for the net asset adjustment, to the vendors.

All of this process and the negotiation of it takes place after completion of the transaction.

The advantage of completion accounts lies mainly with the purchaser. Their accountants usually prepare the first draft of the accounts and will therefore tend to favour the buyer. The disadvantages are the protraction of the M&A process beyond completion. This is as important to buyer and seller.

This mechanism is common in the US, but has fallen in use in Europe due to the emergence of the locked box completion mechanism.

What Is a Locked Box Completion Mechanism?

Locked Box Process

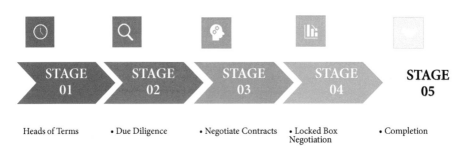

STAGE 01	STAGE 02	STAGE 03	STAGE 04	STAGE 05
Heads of Terms	• Due Diligence	• Negotiate Contracts	• Locked Box Negotiation	• Completion

In Europe (but not in the US) there has been a move away from completion accounts after the deal completes. In their place a date is agreed prior to completion on which the net assets will be verified and valued. This is the locked box date and is usually the month end prior to completion. After the locked box, the vendor warrants not to make any distributions or payments to the shareholders or any other party other than in the ordinary course of trading. All cash generated by trading after the locked box date is for the purchaser's account, although it is customary to have a negotiation about a fixed interest charge to the vendor to cover the period. The impact is to eliminate the post-completion negotiation of completion accounts.

Normalized Working Capital

One of the risks of agreeing a price based on enterprise value is that the vendors are incentivised to minimize debt and maximize cash on the day of completion or the day of the locked box closing. To illustrate the issue by *reductio ad absurdum*, a vendor could stop investing in capital expenditure, stop paying suppliers, and aggressively start to collect outstanding debtors to the extent that customer relationships were damaged. This is an intricate and technical area where lawyers and accountants usually do the detailed work, but the essence is easy to follow.

All businesses have some degree of seasonality, if only reflecting quarterly rent payments or annual or semi-annual tax payments. When bidding for a company a buyer will want to ensure that the business has a normal level of working capital. If it is too low, the purchaser will have to put money into the business to fund the decrease. If it is too high the vendor will have funded the working capital and when it reduces the purchaser will receive a windfall cash inflow, effectively a reduction in the price paid.

To avoid this and avoid having to do full completion accounts, a mechanism is often used that simply compares the working capital balance on the day of the locked box to the average over the full cycle. If the working capital is lower than the agreed average, the price is reduced. Conversely, if the working capital is higher, the price is increased.

This can be very material in businesses like retail where in Western Europe and North America, Christmas accounts for a very large proportion of sales. One of the reasons that failing retailers are often put into insolvency just after Christmas, or on Christmas Eve, is because the working capital is at a minimum and the cash a maximum as stocks are low, sales have been high, and rent and tax payments are due in the new year.

Information and Warranties in the Deal Process

Three economists—George Akerlof, Joseph Steiglitz, and Michael Spence—shared the 2001 Nobel Prize in economics. Their work deals with information asymmetry (the study of the economic consequences on trade of one party having more information than another). The problem arises when you are selling a company in a particularly severe form. Companies are the most complex things that are traded. Selling a business may transfer all the future and historical risks and rewards to the new owner. If you cannot persuade the new owner that the net value of those risks and rewards is quantifiable and positive, you probably won't sell the business. This is one of the commonest areas in which M&A transactions fail.

A corporate sale process needs a comprehensive strategy of managing and transmitting information. If it does not have one, transactions may fall apart later in the process. In the late stages of any deal, purchasers narrow the information asymmetry, usually via due

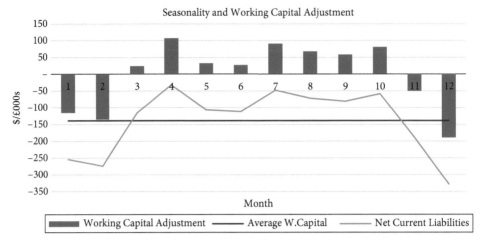

Figure 4.8. Seasonality and average working capital balance

diligence. If the purchaser finds that what they were told at the start of the process is not true and the reality is worse, they will reduce price or pull out.

What Are the Different Negotiating Positions regarding Warranties?

There are a number of ways to deal with information asymmetry.

- No access, no warranties: the simplest and crudest solution is to ignore the issue entirely. A vendor can provide limited data and tell purchasers to rely on their own judgment. In essence, this is what happens in an unsolicited hostile takeover, and may well be the reason that so many hostile approaches subsequently turn out to be failures.
- Transmit information and/or give warranties: to bridge the asymmetry you can either transmit information (under a suitable confidentiality agreement) or agree to take residual risks away from the purchaser by giving warranties.

At the extremes, the negotiating positions are either

- Full access, no warranties: 'We will give you access to do whatever due diligence you like, but we are not warranting anything'; or
- Full warranties, no access: 'We will warrant that the information we give to you is materially correct, but you are not getting any more access than that'.

The trade-off matrix is identical to the one we described for the disclosure/warranty trade-off.

In reality a number of solutions have emerged to alleviate this sharp distinction. Information memoranda, fireside chats, vendor DD, and management presentations

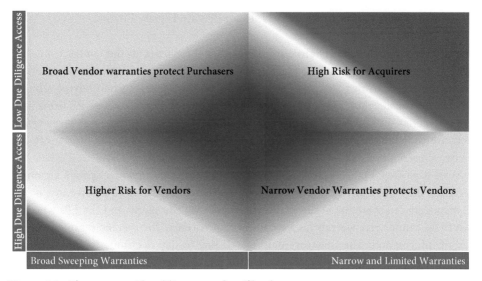

Figure 4.9. The warranty/due diligence trade-off landscape

transmit information and reduce asymmetries. Disclosure letters and warranties also transmit information as they provide comfort to buyers.

The approach to this broad question needs to be decided early on in any sale as it flows through the entire transaction approach and materially influences the form of legal agreement that will emerge at the end of the process.

Each contract will have its own warranties. The SPA will have warranties from seller to buyer (and possibly vice versa). The investment agreement will have warranties from the management team to the investors.

Seller Warranties

The general principle in corporate transactions is *caveat emptor* ('buyer beware'). There are protections against fraud and misrepresentation, but overall the buyer needs to rely on either their due diligence process or warranties to protect them.

Warranties are statements that the purchaser is entitled to rely on when they are buying an asset. They are written into the contract. They can be specific (e.g. 'The company owns all the assets listed in the fixed asset register dated dd/mm/yy') or general (e.g. 'The shareholders do not know of any reason why the vendor should not proceed with the transaction').

The definition of knowledge can also be crucial. It might mean anything from what a reasonable person ought to know, if they had carefully checked each warranty and all the information disclosed, to what a person actually does know, having not had time to do a review of any kind. Agreeing the definition of knowledge is an important detail.

If any of the warranties turns out to be incorrect, the purchaser has a claim under those warranties.

Warranty to Title: A Note on Private Equity Firms

One of the warranties that is always given is that the parties to the contract are the owners of the shares being sold. In fact, this (and the right to enter into the contract) is almost the only warranty that you can guarantee you will receive when buying a business from a private equity firm in Europe. It is different in the US, where PE firms will give warranties. In the past what starts in the US has come to Europe, but as we write there are still significant differences in the warranty positions reported by lawyers on the two sides of the Atlantic.

As we have seen, PE firms are fund managers. They are investing other people's money alongside their own. The ultimate owners of the shares are therefore passive investors. PE managers can therefore argue that they do not own the shares and the LPs who do own them cannot give warranties for commercial reasons. The specific reason given is lack of information. The investors delegate all day-to-day decisions to the PE fund manager. They therefore cannot reasonably warrant matters that they do not necessarily know anything about. They are, in effect, in the same position as if they were holding public company shares, and public company sales routinely complete without warranties worldwide.

Management Warranties

When transactions were initiated and led by managers who wanted to lead a management buyout, it was wholly reasonable to expect the managers to give warranties to the incoming investors. As the market matured and transactions have become auctions where management are no longer in the driving seat, they have become less central to the transaction. As a rule of thumb, the further management are away from controlling the deal, the weaker any warranties will be. If managers do not hold or receive equity in a deal they will generally not be required to give warranties.

It is argued that management warranties are immaterial in the finances of the transaction but crucial in bridging the information asymmetry that exists between buyer and seller. The purpose of the management warranties is therefore usually to encourage disclosure rather than to have any financial recovery in the event of a warranty claim. Financial recovery is usually via the SPA.

How Do Warranty Limits Work?

Jointly or Severally?
The purchaser is concerned to be able to get their money back if there is a warranty claim. They therefore want to be able to have a single lawsuit against all the vendors jointly. The vendors on the other hand will usually wish to deal separately with their own particular warranties and will wish to give the warranties severally (i.e. on their own).

There will therefore be a wrestle over whether any or all warranties are individual and several or are collective (joint and several). By bringing together the vendors there will be a need to discuss how any liability is shared amongst the warrantors. This is particularly important where one warrantor is very wealthy and the others are not, or where some of the warrantors know more about a particular aspect of the business than the others. For example, should the sales director be expected to warrant anything about the way accounting principles are used in the way the management accounts are prepared?

De Minimis/Throwaway Limits

One of the risks of giving any warranties is that it invites claims against them. To stop spurious claims there is always a limit below which any individual claims are ignored. This is the de minimis or throwaway limit. It stops a vexatious acquirer from starting a swathe of spurious claims against a vendor. For example, you cannot sue if it turns out that the number of paper clips or pencils is less than the company records suggest (unless of course it is a paper clip or pencil manufacturer or distributor).

Threshold or Basket Limit

In addition to the de minimis, there will be a basket limit below which any group of claims is considered not material. Only once the basket limit is breached can any claim be made. The vendor therefore wants a high de minimis and a large basket limit, whereas the purchaser will tend towards more caution when agreeing the limits.

There is often a negotiation about whether the basket 'tips over' or 'overflows'. A **tipping basket** gives the claimant the right to the total amount if a claim is made, including the basket. An **overflowing basket** only gives the right for the claimant to claim the excess above the basket limit. The difference can be material.

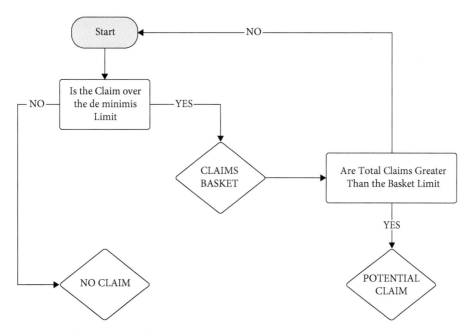

Figure 4.10. The warranty claim process

Limit of Warranty Claim

There will usually be an upper limit on the total value of any warranty claim. The vendors will want it to be low. The purchasers will argue that they should be able to get all their money back if the loss is greater than the amount paid. One complexity is that the vendors will have paid tax on their proceeds and therefore may not have the total amount of consideration even if they simply banked all the consideration in cash. A negotiation ensues.

Time Limits of the Warranties

There will also be a date beyond which claims can no longer be made. This is often made by reference to an anniversary of a time after a certain number of audits have been completed. The idea is to draw a line under the deal but to allow the purchaser a reasonable amount of time to establish if there are any potential claims.

Tax Deed and Tax Indemnity

It is normal for a vendor to give a tax indemnity. This requires the vendor to be responsible for any tax matters relating to the period before completion on a £ for £ basis. The deed simply means that the purchaser does not need to show loss before being recompensed for any historical tax costs not provided for.

Warranty Insurance

Since the early 1990s an array of insurance products has developed that are designed to provide cover against potential warranty claims. Warranty insurance protects the warrantor against the unknown, not against the known. Because insurance contracts are entered into on the basis of full disclosure to the insurer, you cannot achieve a position that insures against false warranties. In the words of Donald Rumsfeld, warranty insurance only covers known unknowns and unknown unknowns (see fig 4.11).

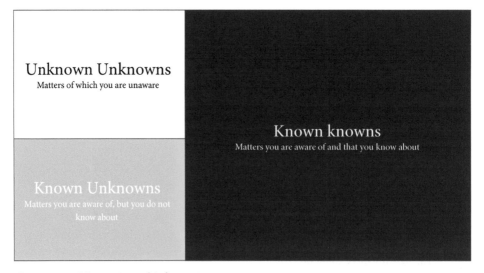

Figure 4.11. Warranties and information

When it was first developed there was some resistance to the idea of reducing the vendors' and management's exposure under the warranties. The argument was that insurance weakened the threat that was being used to force disclosure of all bad news prior to a deal completing.

Warranty insurance is now common. It is usually paid for by the buyer. It benefits the vendors and the management team who are warranting as it reduces the risk and amount of any warranty claim against them. It also benefits the buyer as it makes a claim less politically difficult and reduces the risk of non-recovery (e.g. if the vendor has no money left when the warranty claim arrives).

Disclosure

Prior to completion the vendor will prepare a disclosure bundle to be given to the purchaser. This disclosure letter will include any matters that the vendor wants to bring to the purchaser's attention before completion. Anything in the disclosure bundle is deemed to be known by the purchaser before they entered into the deal. They therefore cannot sue for anything that has been fully and fairly disclosed (see Figure 4.12).

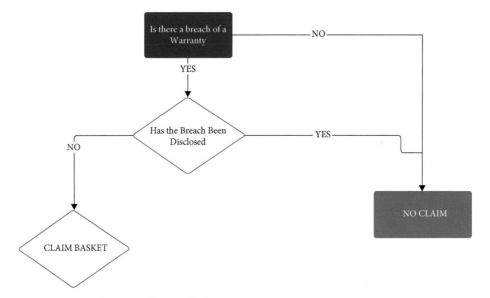

Figure 4.12. Disclosure and warranty claim process

There is therefore a tension and trade-off between the interests of the vendors and purchasers that needs to be reconciled. Vendors and management always wish to disclose widely. They may argue that anything that the purchaser has discovered in their due diligence is deemed to be disclosed and that everything that has been made available to them is also disclosed. Purchasers will not usually accept these sweeping disclosures, in part because they have to be able to analyse the disclosure bundle to ensure there are no bad surprises.

To make disclosure efficient it is crucial that the vendors and their advisers keep meticulous records of what is provided to whom. This is usually done by creating a data room where all documents that are provided to the bidder are indexed and electronically stored.

Attitudes towards disclosure of the contents of data rooms have softened over the years. When they first began to appear in the 1990s, acquirers would vigorously resist disclosure of all the data room contents on the grounds that they could not read them in the time available. They therefore did not know what was being disclosed. As warranties have evolved it has become more common for acquirers to accept wider disclosure.

The timing of disclosure is also important. It usually occurs immediately before completion. This means that the bundle is as up to date as possible but gives the acquirer the issue of absorbing all the information before the contracts are signed. Managing this process is a key thread in the legal process in a well-run acquisition. Planning ahead and agreeing the scope of disclosure early avoids unexpected problems at or near to the completion meeting.

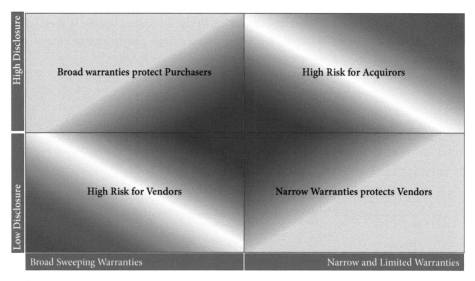

Figure 4.13. Warranty and disclosure landscape

Management Warranties in the Subscription Agreement

As we mentioned, in many private equity investments there are two sets of warranties: those given by the vendors in the SPA and those separately given by the management in the investment agreement in a buyout.

The limitation on management's warranties needs to be understood in the context of the leaver provisions (see below). Dismissal for a material warranty breach would normally make the manager a bad leaver, resulting in them losing any equity upside. It is difficult to envisage a situation where a material warranty breach led to a legal case to make a claim against a manager who was still with the business. The effect of suing employees is only going to increase the risk that at best they are wholly demotivated and at worst will wish ill upon the business. In consequence the limits are usually relatively small: 1 x annual salary is common in Europe.

Governance and Control: How Will Newco Be Owned and Run?

The rest of the heads of terms usually deals with the terms of the investment between the ongoing shareholders. It will state in some detail the financial terms of the investment of all parties.

What Is the Equity Structure of the Group after the Deal?

The newco equity split shows the details of the ordinary share class rights including the financial rights of the shareholders regarding capital distributions, voting, and dividends.
  We cover the other key rights in Chapter 5, but briefly they may include:

- pre-emption rights: these are rights to buy shares that become available after the deal, either because someone needs to sell or because there is a new issue of shares;
- swamping rights: the right for the investor to outvote others in certain situations;
- drag/tag: the right to sell if the investor sells and the obligation to sell if the investor sells.

What is Good Leaver/Bad Leaver?

A contentious issue can arise when shareholders leave the business without there being an exit. As we know, alignment in private equity is achieved primarily by creating large financial rewards for the people responsible for delivering the outcome desired. Leverage is used to magnify equity returns. This means two things:

- first, equity is very valuable and scarce in leveraged transactions; and
- secondly, leakage of equity outside the key people in the business is very undesirable.

As a result of this there is a presumption that anyone who leaves a PE-backed firm will return their shares when they leave. This is justified by the fact that the equity that was allocated to the manager concerned will be required to attract and motivate a replacement.
  The question then becomes at what value does the leaver sell their shares back to the company (or a warehouse facility which holds them)?
  Vesting: In the US the use of options and the concept of vesting partially solves the problem. The shares of managers only gradually pass into unconditional ownership. Leavers whose options haven't vested leave without the options. If they have vested, the leaver may continue to own them.
  The usual approach in Europe is slightly different, in part due to tax differences. European style deals define two classes of leavers:

Good leavers are those leaving for reasons that are accepted as being reasonable and are usually unforeseen or are out of the leaver's control. This results in the darkly comical outcome of people who are too ill to work or die being 'good leavers'. Being a 'Good Leaver' is rarely a 'Good Thing'.

Good Leavers are paid an amount that represents the market value of their equity when they leave. If this can't be agreed, there will be an arbitration process that gets an independent valuation from an expert valuer to calculate a value of the transfer.

Bad Leavers are people who leave either because they are fairly dismissed for poor performance (or some such matter) or who quit to work in another business. These people will usually get a lower value, often the lesser of cost or market value.

There is a larger range of negotiable items in this apparently simple system. For example, are leavers assumed to all be Bad Leavers unless they are Good, or vice versa? What happens if you are unfairly dismissed? How long does the Good/Bad distinction apply? Is it fair that someone who has contributed for many years and then been made redundant through no fault of their own loses their shares? Should there be a sliding time limit, similar to a vesting schedule? If so, how long should it be?

As you can see, this is fertile ground for negotiation, although rules of thumb and common practice have emerged.

What Controls do the Private Equity Investors have?

Investor Consent and Reserved Matters

The major control that investors have is the contractual requirement for management to receive investor consent for certain named things and for other matters to be reserved for investors.

The difference is a nuance in legal terminology.

Consents are things that executive directors propose, and the investors need to agree to before they can be done.

Reserved matters are things that only the investor director, rather than the executive directors, can propose.

In practice the distinction is a moot point unless there has been a fundamental breakdown of relationships.

There will always be a raft of things that management cannot do without explicit investor consent. These include both the making of key decisions and the requirement to run the business using clear processes within the consents. The constitution of the company will require board meetings, the production of management accounts, and annual forecasts and budgets. All of the key blocking controls will be in the hands of the PE manager.

We should not conclude from this that the PE manager is exercising day-to-day management. These contractual limits have evolved over the years to circumscribe the area within which the executive management can act unhindered. The rules create frequent and meaningful communication between the company's managers and owners about all material matters. It is a structure that directly attacks the principal–agent problem by forcing dialogue with the owners.

You might expect to see consents or reserved matters around for example:

- material capital expenditure;
- any acquisitions or disposals;

- employing staff with incomes greater than a certain amount;
- changes to employment contracts of key staff;
- bonuses;
- appointments to boards and key executive committees;
- appointment of certain key advisers;
- entering into or amending any major financial contract, such as debt or hedging.

In addition, the investors will approve plans and budgets, or have a majority on the boards that approve them. If relationships between managers and investors fail for any reason, these constraints give the investors overwhelming influence on the business and its actions.

Equity Covenants and Swamping Rights

Banks and debt funds seek to control their interests by covenants. Private equity investors always want to have the maximum warning of a covenant issue and they therefore sometimes mimic the bank covenants but make the equity covenants tighter. They then insert swamping rights into the voting rules of the business.

These state that if the company breaches an equity covenant, the A Ordinary shares vote enough votes per share to swamp all other shareholders. This gives temporary de facto control to the PE fund. The intention is threefold: first the mechanism gives a clear incentive to avoid breaching an equity covenant; secondly it may give the equity holders a window in which they can act to rectify the problem before breaching a bank covenant, and thirdly it seizes control of the board to allow rapid decision-making if necessary.

What Are the Operational Controls that a Private Equity Investor Will Expect?

The boards of private equity firms are smaller than those of public companies. They operate more like executive committees rather than governance oversight bodies. The non-executive directors on a public company board are responsible for governance and oversight of the executives. On a PE-backed board the shareholders' representatives are sitting at the table and receive the full management information pack each month. This is the biggest single difference in the relationship between managers and owners in the operation of the company.

The investment agreements will contain extensive provisions regarding the constitution of the company including such matters as:

- board composition
- frequency of board meetings
- board information pack
- employment contracts.

Non-Executive Directors

Historically investors did not want to take directors' roles as the position creates certain legal obligations. The rules were tightened over a number of years creating the concept of shadow directors, who are people who are directors of a company in all but name and therefore carry the same, or similar, liabilities as a director. As the distinction between director and shadow director narrowed and private equity firms became more active in the management of their investments, by the 1990s PE funds had started to routinely formally appoint their investment executives to the boards as investor directors.

Once the position of investor director emerged, the ability to assign special powers to the person holding that position was a small step. The way that reserved matters and investor consents are handled is by requiring the consent of the investor director to do those things. This is wholly unlike a normal board where members vote and the chair has a deciding vote in event of a tie. In PE investments certain named matters are treated as if they are the prerogative of the shareholders' representative.

Concerns about liabilities of directors reappear from time to time and when they do the regime reverts to PE funds having observers at the board who do not vote. They exercise control through required investor consents from the fund manager, not an investor director. You can probably sense that the dividing line between the two positions is very thin and easily crossed in practice.

Board appointments are in the control of the PE fund managers and it is rare to see independent non-execs on a board in the way you would in a public company. Sometimes the appointment of a number of new non-execs signals the move towards a flotation where the corporate governance regime is very different.

Non-Executive Chair

In European private equity investments (but less so in the US) the Chair is not usually an employee of the PE fund. They are usually nominally independent and act as both a mentor to the executive directors and as a bridge between investors and management, as in any public company. The difference lies in the equity that often is allocated to the role of the chair. This is in the gift of the PE fund, not the board of directors. Furthermore, the appointment or removal of a chair is almost always either a reserved matter or requires investor consent. The chair rarely has their own deal flow and so is again beholden to their relationships with PE funds to find positions.

The economics and processes around the position of chair make it very difficult to argue that they are in any real sense independent. They may well be independent of thought and action by inclination, but they need the approval of the PE fund manager to get appointed in the first place.

Arrangement Fees

In Chapter 2 we talked about the effect of fees and costs on the returns of the PE fund managers and their investors. We talked about fee set-off and the way fees are paid to the various parties. The equity term sheet shows in detail how this can work.

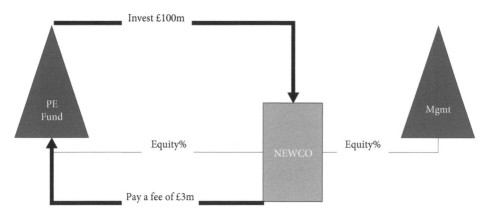

Figure 4.14. Circular flow of arrangement fees

Funds often charge arrangement fees at completion. These are fees paid by the newco to the fund and are usually expressed as a percentage of the amount invested. As fee set-off has become ingrained in fund LPAs, arrangement fees have, anecdotally, started to reduce in frequency, but we have no academic peer-reviewed evidence to support this assertion.

Since Newco is a new company, it has no cash to pay any fee. Essentially in the diagram in Figure 4.14 the fund lends £100m and immediately takes back, say, £3m. Therefore, why don't the investors simply invest £97m and not charge the fee? (The same applies to banks and lending.)

There are a number of explanations with different implications.

The first is that investors make more money if they lend the cash to pay fees by increasing the loan stock. They receive the fee at completion and get the loan repaid later. Even if they increase the permanent equity by the fee amount (and so are not paid twice) the investors want the fund to receive income and are happy to provide capital to pay for the income up front. The alternative would be to accrue the fee and pay it out of earnings in the future.

Secondly the fund is constrained by the availability of good opportunities and wishes to deploy capital. It deploys more capital as it charges fees but with no risk, since the fee simply flows back to the fund.

Thirdly the set-off arrangements at the fund level mean that charging fees enables the investors to set off the fee against the fund management fees that would have been due. The LPs roll the fee into the capital drawdown and do not have to budget for the fund management fees. It also flatters the publicly reported fund management fees, which appear to be lower than they actually are because the set-off is not reported separately.

Finally, the fee is accounted for as revenue in the accounts of the fund. This means that if the fund manager shares in the fee, the profits of the fund management business are increased and this is attributable to the partners of the fund management business, not the fund. It can appropriate fees from one party to another.

Monitoring Fees and Other Fees Paid to the Private Equity Fund Manager

In addition to arrangement fees payable at completion, funds usually charge monitoring or non-executive director fees that are paid to the fund manager and shared with investors in accordance with the LPA, sometimes 80/20 between the investors and the manager mimicking the carried interest calculation, sometimes 100 per cent set off against management fees. In the past these fees went to the fund manager, not the fund, and provided a source of income and profit that was not aligned with the investors or the company. This has been largely stopped on both sides of the Atlantic, but can still happen.

More difficult to manage are fees paid by investee companies to associates or other divisions of a fund manager as we discussed in Chapter 2.

Third-Party Costs

The fund will incur a wide array of costs in making each investment. These are passed on to Newco, which pays them. The array of potential fees includes:

- due diligence (financial, legal, market, environmental, etc.)
- transaction costs (corporate finance, legal, tax, etc)

Paying fees on behalf of others can create tax inefficiencies. If you pass on a cost for a service that you received to someone who did not benefit from the service, VAT is not always recoverable. The fees may also not be deductible against corporation tax because they may be incurred before Newco existed or was conducting any trade. This therefore needs careful specialist advice to avoid creating costs that cannot be relieved against future profits.

Closing Remarks

In this chapter we have walked through the deal process and looked in some detail at the key items that are specific to a private equity investment.

Our discussion and description have been necessarily detailed. In the next chapter we turn our attention to the finances and the financial instruments that are used to engineer the transaction.

5

Financial Markets, Financial Instruments, and Financial Engineering

In this chapter we turn our attention to finance and some of the fundamental, unchanging building blocks of a leveraged deal. We look at debt and equity and examine the hybrid mix that characterizes private equity investments.

We start with debt and the debt markets. Most of the innovation and change since the financial crisis has been seen in the debt markets. We take another deep dive, this time into a leverage finance debt contract to show the fine detail that is involved in each deal. Finally, we turn to equity and look at how shares are priced and used to incentivise behaviours.

Senior Debt and Mezzanine

What is Debt?

It is worth pausing to look at this seemingly trivial question. Debt is a contractual obligation to pay an amount to a lender on given dates. The cost of debt is interest. Interest is usually (but not, as we shall see, always) allowed to be deducted from profit before calculating a company's corporation tax liability.

Debt may be secured or unsecured. If it is secured, then if a borrower does not pay an amount due the lender will have the right to seize certain assets. If the security is a fixed charge the assets will be identified; if it is a floating charge the security will include assets that change from time to time.

Unsecured lenders have no preferential right to seize assets and these loans are inherently riskier than secured loans. For example, credit card debts are unsecured and therefore incur interest at much higher rates than, say, secured mortgages.

What Are Senior Debt, Junior Debt, and Subordinated Debt?

We can think of the creditors of any business as being in a queue for cash they are owed. Those at the front of the queue have priority over those at the back. Therefore priority or seniority is the position in the queue.

Senior debt is the name given to the debt that has priority over all other debt when it comes to receiving interest, capital repayments, or the proceeds from asset sales in insolvency. This seniority gives lenders the ability to heavily influence the negotiations if borrowers are unable to service their debts.

Private Equity Demystified: An explanatory guide. Fourth Edition. John Gilligan and Mike Wright, Oxford University Press (2020).
© John Gilligan & Mike Wright. DOI: 10.1093/oso/9780198866961.003.0005

Loans that rank after the senior debt are classified as junior debt, and those that rank last (but still have some claim to any residual assets) are subordinated debt.

Most companies with multiple lenders will have priority arrangements between the lenders. These may be documented by formal contracts known as inter-creditor agreements or be structurally enforced, as we discuss later.

Banks and Other Lenders

What Role Do Lenders Play in Private Equity?

Banks and other lenders provide the debt in buyouts; this debt may take many forms and be provided by many different market participants, including one or more of commercial banks, debt funds, investment banks, dedicated mezzanine providers, hedge funds or similar specialist funds, or the public markets via high-yield bonds.

What Is Leveraged Finance?

As we have seen a number of times, terminology is often woefully imprecise in corporate finance. 'Leveraged finance' is yet another term that can carry many subtly different meanings.

In general, the term suggests that a business is using more debt than it has to. There is no hard and fast definition of what is or is not leveraged lending. In one sense all lending is leveraged, as the use of any debt magnifies the returns (both positive and negative) when compared to financing with only permanent equity.

However, the industry generally defines leveraged lending with reference to either:

- the post-transaction debt to total assets ratio (the 'gearing ratio'); or
- the ratio of EBITDA to total debt (the EBITDA multiple, which is now also confusingly called the 'leverage ratio').

Where total debt is more than about 50 per cent of total assets or borrowings exceed around $3 \times$ EBITDA, most banks would define and manage the relationship as a leveraged finance loan.

What Is a High Yield Bond?

Other definitions might include the credit rating of a traded bond or the margin on a particular loan.

In investment banks, leveraged finance groups are involved in the underwriting and provision of publicly traded and syndicated loans that are at a higher yield (interest rate) than investment-grade bonds.

Investment-grade bonds are bonds that have been rated as low risk by a recognized rating agency, usually one of Standard & Poor's, Moody's, or Fitch IBCA. These are

Table 5.1. Bond ratings by rating agency

Agency		Standard & Poor's	Moody's	Fitch IBCA
Investment		AAA	Aaa	AAA
Grade Loans		AA+	Aa1	AA+
		AA	Aa2	AA
		AA−	Aa3	AA−
		A+	A1	A+
		A	A2	A
		A−	A3	A−
Leveraged		BBB+	Baa1	BBB+
Loans		BBB	Baa2	BBB
		BBB−	Baa3	BBB−
		BB+	Ba1	BB+
	Junk	BB	Ba2	BB
	Bonds	BB−	Ba3	BB−
		B+	B1	B+
		B	B2	B
		B−	B3	B−
		CCC+	Caa1	CCC+
		CCC	Caa2	CCC
		CCC−	Caa3	CCC−
		CC	Ca	CC
		C	C	C
		D		D

commercial operations that independently rate bonds into one of a series of grades ranging from AAA to C or D (depending on the agency).

What Are Junk Bonds?

Junk bonds are a subset of leveraged loans that have ratings below BB+/Ba1. We identify them separately in Table 5.1. They are the riskiest loans, either because they have become riskier since they were issued or, increasingly, because they were issued in the knowledge that they offer a higher risk/return than other debt.

The development of the sub-investment-grade market in the 1980s in the US and 1990s in Europe was a driver in the emergence of large buyout funds.

What Is the Difference between a Bilateral Loan, a Syndicated Loan and a Bond?

A syndicated loan is broadly defined as a loan made by more than one lender to a single borrower using the same terms and conditions and the same documentation. A syndicated loan becomes a bond when it is quoted and traded on a recognized public market (Figure 5.1).

Despite the fact that the usual definition of 'syndicated loans' encompasses quoted and unquoted loans, in common usage the term is generally reserved for the unquoted element of the market.

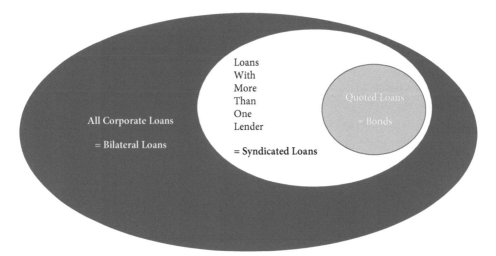

Figure 5.1. The markets for debt

Bilateral loans have only two counter parties—the borrower and the lender.

By number there are far more bilateral loans than syndicated loans or bonds. By value this reverses in Western economies.

Quoted bonds are traded in liquid markets. They therefore tend to be standardized. Nobody wants to read every suite of bond documentation before trading. They tend to have the same term and are structured to avoid and discourage early repayment. If a borrower wants to repay early there will be a punitive charge known as a **call premium**. This is a penalty paid for changing the repayment dates. Bonds therefore offer less flexibility than unquoted debt but may offer better pricing terms.

The process to raise bonds is also materially different to that used in banks and funds. It is more analogous to an IPO, when a company floats shares, than a traditional bilateral debt raising.

How Are Leveraged Loans/Junk Bonds Linked to Private Equity?

In the 1980s academic and commercial research discovered an anomaly in the quoted bond markets. If the markets were functioning efficiently, the returns on a portfolio of bonds would generally reflect both the underlying risk and rewards of holding the assets. Studies found that buying bonds that had become distressed, and therefore had fallen in value, yielded higher returns than buying investment-grade bonds. This led to the new phenomenon of new issue, sub-investment-grade bonds. The idea was that if buying loans that were sub-investment-grade due to trading difficulties at the borrower gave returns higher than the overall market, new loans that were designed to be financially riskier, but to solid companies, ought to have similar characteristics.

This market was created and led by Drexel Burnham Lambert, a now-defunct American Investment bank. Its founder Michael Milken was jailed for insider trading in the early

1990s, but the innovations that he was instrumental in creating in what is now called the leveraged finance market persisted.

The availability of junk-bond financing enabled the funds that had been pursuing leveraged buyouts to dramatically increase the size of transaction that they were able to contemplate. This fuelled the 1980s buyout boom culminating in the iconic $20bn RJR Nabisco buyout of 1988 and the book *Barbarians at the Gate*.[1]

In Europe the market developed differently. The European LBO market was originally dominated by commercial and retail banks. Their business model was to originate loans and then syndicate them to other market participants. The European high-yield bond market grew in the late 1990s and 2000s.

What Are the Sources of Leveraged Finance?

Prior to the global financial crisis, there were essentially two channels delivering leveraged finance in Europe and three in the US. Today the US and non-US markets have begun to converge, and (while they retain legal and commercial distinctions) they are more similar than they have been at any other time.

Pre Global Financial Crisis Europe

Prior to the global financial crisis, Europe was characterized by banks leading syndicates that underwrote and then distributed the debt in buyouts (see Figure 5.2). In small deals there might just be one bank but, as the transaction size grew, there could be multiple banks (Figure 5.3). The key participants were large deposit-taking banks (RBS, HSBC, Barclays, Lloyds, HBOS) and their business model was based upon winning mandates to lend to corporate clients.

They would compete fiercely to win the role of lead arranger in a transaction and then seek to sell a large portion of the loans in a syndication. If the sale was to be after the deal completed, they would underwrite the whole debt package. If it was too large to underwrite, they would build a syndicate of banks to jointly underwrite the deal and the syndicate would sell down the loans after completion. The buyers of the loans were other banks and financial institutions.

A new participant during this phase of the market's development were CLOs and CDOs focused purely on the leveraged loan markets. We describe these below.

Larger transactions could be funded using the emerging Eurobond markets. These mirrored the quoted markets in US High Yield (or junk bonds) but were less developed and therefore less able to be used for large bond issues. The largest issue achieved prior to the crisis was the *circa* £9bn Boots plc High Yield offer.

---

[1] Burrough, Bryan (1990), *Barbarians At the Gate: The Fall of RJR Nabisco* (New York: Harper & Row).

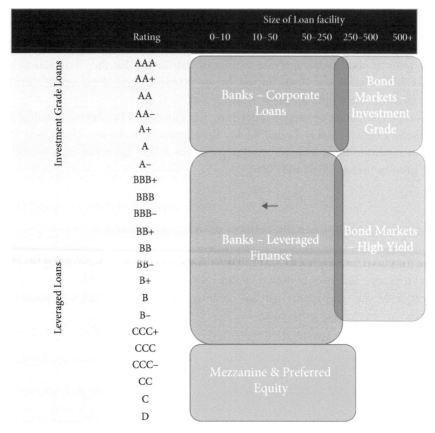

Figure 5.2. Pre-GFC structure of European Leveraged Debt Market

Source: Authors' analysis

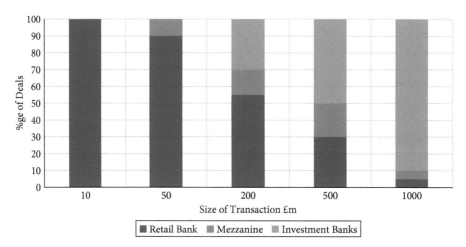

Figure 5.3. Illustrative debt sources in leveraged finance by deal size: pre-crisis

Source: Authors' analysis

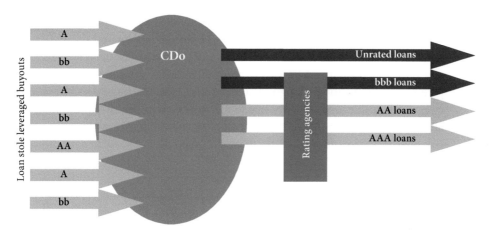

Figure 5.4. Schematic of a CDO/CLO

What Are Collateralized Debt Obligations (CDOs), Collateralized Loan Obligations (CLOs), and Structured Investment Vehicles (SIVs)?

Collateralized debt obligations (CDOs) and collateralized loan obligations (CLOs), together with structured investment vehicles (SIVs), are important fund structures (Figure 5.4). CDOs have existed for many years as vehicles to enable banks to sell loan obligations, thereby increasing capital efficiency and returns on capital, but grew in significance dramatically in the late 2000s.

For simplicity we ignore the terminological differences between CDO and CLO and concentrate on the economics of the transaction rather than the assets or management style of the fund. The SIV is simply the legal entity that takes in loans and assets which are blended together to create the CDOs.

There are basically two forms of CDO:

- **balance sheet deals:** these have existed for many years and involve a bank selling a portion of its loan portfolio to a SIV that pays for the assets from the receipts of a bond issue, or a series of contracts to transfer the default risk to other investors, usually by a credit default swap (an insurance policy against non-repayment). These deals are usually constructed to allow a bank to manage its regulated capital base efficiently;
- **arbitrage deals:** these structures attempt to capture the difference between the yield of an underlying asset and the cost of the bonds issued by the SIV to acquire the assets (or the price paid for the asset). Broadly there are two forms.
  ○ The first involves a trading strategy where the SIV actively trades bonds to generate a return. These types of vehicle were heavily involved in the sub-prime lending market and are the focus of much public discussion.
  ○ The second are cash-flow deals. These are most relevant in the LBO syndication market. In these transactions, the SIV participates in the debt syndication. It builds a portfolio of loans financed by its own equity and bridge finance from its bankers. Once the portfolio is large enough it will issue a series of bonds backed by the loans. The senior bonds are rated by a credit rating agency and are ranked first.

These are bought by investors in the bond market. Rated mezzanine bonds are also issued that rank after the senior bonds. These have a higher interest rate but carry more risk and are sold to investors seeking higher yield assets, often hedge funds and alternative asset investors. Finally, any profit or loss on the underlying assets is paid to unrated bonds ranking last. These bonds have returns and risks that are comparable with equity. They are sold to investors seeking equity returns and usually held by the SIV manager. This process of so-called 'slicing and dicing' enables risk to be dispersed throughout the market. It also makes it exceptionally difficult to know exactly where risk resides.

CDO managers earn returns in the same way as private equity fund managers; they receive fees and a carried interest. Indeed a number of CDO funds are sponsored and managed by teams affiliated with private equity fund managers and are invested in by them.

Pre Global Financial Crisis North America

In the US the banking system was structured fundamentally differently to the London market. The large deposit-taking banks were not the leaders of the leveraged buyout market. The market developed along a different path driven by different pools of capital.

The US has always had a large corporate bond market. Whereas European companies borrowed largely from banks, North American companies issued bonds to financial institutions and the public.

The Global Financial Crisis in a Nutshell

Thousands of bottles of ink have been spilled on the causes of, and blame to attribute for, the 2008 global financial crisis. We will be as brief and non-judgemental as possible. We are only interested in casting some light on why the crisis led to sharp changes in the private equity market and, more importantly, private debt markets.

The crisis was a liquidity crisis caused by widespread multi-dimensional information asymmetries. Decoding that phrase, it was the result of a lack of clarity about what risks were in the banking system and who was exposed to the risks. When nobody knew who was likely to be at risk of failure due to a lack of reliable information, banks and financial institutions stopped lending to each other. This was the 'credit crunch'.

Banks lending long-term loans need to have access to short-term facilities to make various payments on a day-to-day basis. If they can't do this, they are insolvent and confidence in them rapidly evaporates, so the banks fail. They usually borrow from each other and from companies and pension funds with excess cash to meet these obligations in the overnight markets. These loans crucially are unsecured loans and therefore are wholly reliant on the creditworthiness of the counterparty.

When the overnight markets are lacking funds, the central banks provide short-term facilities as a so-called lender of last resort to certain deposit-taking banks. When the markets froze due to fear of widespread unknown risks, central banks were called upon by most eligible financial institutions with a short-term funding requirement. This resulted in a potentially huge increase in the size of the balance sheets of central banks and the need for governments to decide whether to allow the system to fail—which would have meant millions of depositors and customers losing their access to banking—or to rescue the banks.

The governments and the regulations generally took the view that any banks or institutions that were holding assets of private individuals, or who were providing vital transactional services to individuals and companies, had to be saved or taken over. There were some institutions that did not have individual customers and were predominantly financial market participants. These were not rescued, often because there was no legal way to save them.[2] So it was that Bear Sterns, Merrill Lynch, JP Morgan, and Lehman Brothers either failed or were taken over, whereas AIG and RBS were rescued.

Post Financial Crisis Europe

Since the crisis the leveraged finance market has completely restructured, and a raft of new products and participants has entered (Figure 5.5). The driver of this has been both economic and regulatory. As a result, the structure of a typical buyout has changed since the crisis (see Figure 5.6).

As described in Chapter 1, following the financial crisis banks had to reduce their indebtedness and increase their assets. They did this in a number of ways.

Shrinking Banks' Balance Sheets

First, on the asset side of the balance sheet, they did a series of equity issues to raise new permanent capital. These ranged from the emergency rescues by governments of organizations like RBS in the UK or AIG in the US, through private off-market transactions such as the Qatar/Barclays transaction and the Berkshire Hathaway/Goldman Sachs transaction in the US. Essentially, ignoring the specifics of each deal, the economics are the same: put more permanent or long-term capital into the balance sheet of banks to reduce risk.

Secondly, banks reduced their new lending to less than they were due to be repaid from existing outstanding loans. This has two effects:

(1) it obviously reduces the total amount of assets outstanding in the form of loans to customers;

(2) it changes the cash flow of the bank from a net outflow to a net inflow. This enables the bank to start to work on the liability side of its balance sheet and pay down its own debt. This is what is known as shrinking the bank's balance sheet. Both its assets and its liabilities are reduced as the loan book shrinks and cash is used to reduce its liabilities.

---

[2] 'Ben S. Bernanke, Timothy F. Geithner, and Henry M. Paulson, Jr (2019), *Firefighting: The financial crisis and its lessons* (New York, Penguin).

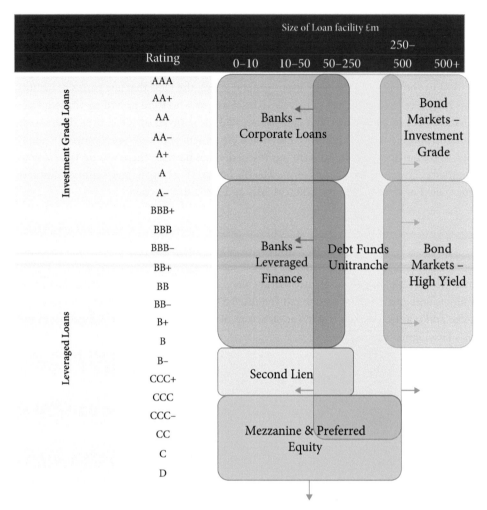

Figure 5.5. Post-crisis European debt markets

Source: Authors' analysis

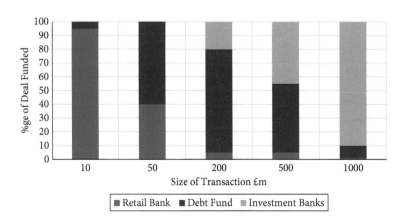

Figure 5.6. Illustrative debt sources in leveraged finance by deal size: post-crisis

Source: Authors' analysis

Table 5.2. Mid-market leveraged loan terms pre- and post-crisis

	Immediately pre-crisis	Immediately post-crisis
Term Loan A		
Length of Loan	7 years	5 years
Repayment	Equal instalments	Equal instalments
Margin	2.25%–2.50% + 3 month LIBOR	4.00% + 3 month LIBOR
Term Loan B		
Length of loan	8 years	5 years
Repayment	Single payment in year 8	Single payment in year 5
Margin	2.75%–3.00% + 3 month LIBOR	5.00% + 3 month LIBOR
Arrangement fees	1.0%–1.5%	3.0%–4.0%

Source: Authors' analysis

How Did Loan Pricing and Costs of Borrowing Change after the Crisis?

In addition to managing their balance sheets and cash flows, banks sharply raised their interest margins and fees. They dramatically put up prices.

A broad comparison on 'vanilla' loan products pre- and post-crisis might have looked something like Table 5.2.

You can argue about the exact margins and repayment schedules, but these are broadly representative of what we saw during and after the global financial crisis.

The bank would also have required the borrower to hedge part of the loan and have various so-called ancillary facilities with the lead arranger. (We discuss these facilities below.)

It is important to notice that these are margins over three-month LIBOR. One of the other results of the government response to the financial crisis was to dramatically reduce interest rates and hence LIBOR fell sharply. Therefore, the overall cost to borrowers fell after the crisis from 7.0–10.0 per cent to around 5.0–6.0 per cent at the same time as banks' fees and lending margins rose (Figure 5.7).

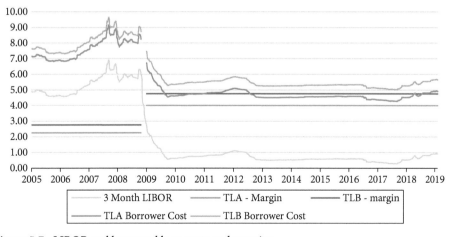

Figure 5.7. LIBOR and leveraged loan costs and margins

What Are the Effects of Basel II/III?

Among many other things, these recommendations on banking laws and regulations set out agreed practice for the capital structure of a regulated bank's balance sheet. The idea is that banks that are responsible for systemically important services, like clearing and holding customer deposits, must hold an adequate amount of capital in the right form to protect them from another credit crunch. Holding large amounts of redundant cash is very inefficient, for both the bank and the wider economy. However, as we learned in the credit crunch, banks do need to hold a certain amount of assets in a form that can be quickly turned into cash and to have liabilities that can be quickly restructured.

The asset side of the balance sheet is dealt with by requiring banks to hold what is called tier one capital. This is equity capital plus the present value of certain specific easily realizable assets. The regulations specify precisely what assets can be included in tier one. One way to increase tier one capital is to hold cash balances. Tier one capital is expensive to a bank in terms of opportunity cost for liquid assets and in terms of cost of capital for permanent equity.

After the crisis the regulations were changed to require banks to hold more tier one capital against loans with a term or average life over five years. This meant that the traditional 7year/8year TLA/TLB leveraged loan package required more expensive tier one capital. This reduced the return on capital on loans over six years to below the levels that bank could earn elsewhere. They therefore reduced the standard leveraged loan term to five years and less.

The shortening in the term and average life of the loans being made post crisis was a direct response to changes set out in the Basel II/III banking regulatory environment.

How Does Shortening the Loan Impact a Deal?

The effect of lowering the length of the loan is, all other things being equal, to reduce the amount of the loan that can be repaid out of the cashflows of the business: the business will earn less in five years than it would in seven years, so it cannot repay as much.

Therefore, either the total amount of the whole loan must decrease, or more of the borrowings will need to be in the Term Loan B element that is repaid in a single repayment at the end of the loan.

The secondary effect of Basle II/III was therefore to put pressure to reduce the total amount of debt lent and simultaneously to push debt from the A loan to the B loan. If the mix of TLA/TLB changes the overall interest cost will rise marginally.

What Impacts Did Basel II Have on the Debt Market?

As we have seen, post crisis the leveraged finance market was very profitable for the banks who were able to participate and who lent at higher margins and fees for a shorter loan duration. The impact of shortening term is lower debt levels. There was therefore a void in the market created for greater quantities of longer-term debt. This void has been filled by debt funds that are based on the US banking model. Their business model is sharply

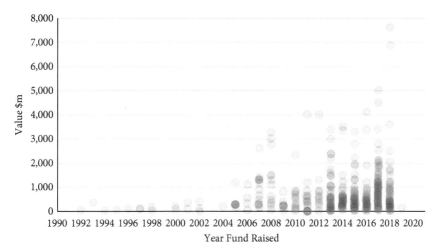

Figure 5.8. Debt fund raised by value of fund and vintage
Source: Authors' analysis of Preqin data

different to the banks. They base their business on the provision of longer-term loans to the leveraged finance market.

The market has expanded both in terms of the number of providers and the size of the funds being raised. From being a small niche investment strategy prior to the crisis, it has grown to become a major provider of funds to both buyouts and to corporates generally (see Figure 5.5).

What Are Debt Funds?

With all the usual caveats on the variability of terminology in finance, you can think of debt funds as being similar in structure to private equity funds but with some fundamental structural differences that are similar to those seen in CDO/CLOs.

First debt funds obviously invest in debt, not equity. They replace or supplement banks and high-yield bonds in a deal structure. They are becoming more standardized, but when they first emerged they were often pulling together various separate pools of capital to create a blended debt product.

They therefore operate both as originators of loans, making investments in debt, and as sophisticated managers of various pools of capital which are blended together into a single tranche of debt, commonly called **unitranche**. A tranche is from the French meaning 'slice', as in slice of cake, so uni-tranche is a single slice. It is the name given to a single slice of debt that includes what would have been classed as both senior and junior debt. It is lent as a single financial instrument with one set of pricing and terms.

We expand greatly on this definition and compare debt structures and products later.

How Are Debt Funds Rewarded?

Debt funds get rewarded in a subtly different way to private equity funds. You will recall from our earlier discussion on fees and carried interest that the base model in PE was a

Table 5.3. Comparison of private equity and debt fund terms

	Debt fund	PE fund
Fund investment terms		
Investment period	3/4 years	5/6 years
Total life of fund	5/6 years	10+2
Fees	Up to 1.0 per cent of invested capital	Up to 2.0 per cent of committed capital
Carried interest	10 per cent	20 per cent
Hurdle rate IRR	5.5 per cent	From 8.0 per cent down

10+2 (years invested) fund paying 2/20 (2 per cent fee, 20 per cent carried interest). In debt funds the metrics are often different, as shown in Table 5.3.

Note that debt funds get paid lower fees and that these fees are paid based on invested capital, not committed capital. You don't get paid for managing undrawn dry powder in the debt fund market.

Carried interest is also lower in debt funds. The amount of carried interest is also usually around half the amount paid to equity funds. This is even more challenging when you consider that debt funds have fixed upside. They cannot get a 'big win' to compensate for poor performance in other investments in the way that an equity fund can.

Leverage in Debt Funds

There is also another major difference in debt fund structures: debt funds are leveraged, meaning that they borrow in tranches within the fund, including a fixed tranche from a bank or banks. This is similar to the CDO/CLO structure we discussed earlier, except that the debt usually comes directly from institutional investors, not via a bond market rated issuance.

They need to do this as it is impossible to lend at 7–8 per cent and have an unlevered return of 10 per cent to trigger carried interest payments unless there are significant fees and early prepayment charges that are triggered.

The amount of and source of leverage varies by fund and investment strategy. Most is provided by banks and insurance companies, but there are also instances of debt funds lending to other debt funds. This is reminiscent of CLOs securitizing CLO debt prior to the financial crisis, but is on a much smaller scale.

We can see the returns on debt funds over time within the data collected by Preqin (Figure 5.9).

The latest funds (from the last three years) will generally show lower performance due to low levels of investment, early repayment, and immaturity of the assets when compared to funds that are at the end or out of the investment period. Nevertheless, Figure 5.9 shows both the large increase in the number of funds crowding into the market in the last six to seven years and an apparent compression of reported returns as measured by simple money multiple (TVPI).

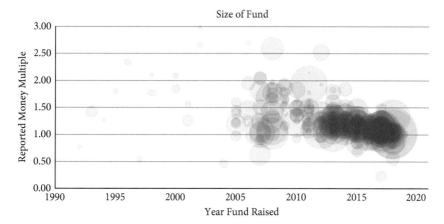

Figure 5.9. Senior debt and unitranche funds 1990–2019 at 30 September 2019 (bubble is proportionate to size of fund)

Source: Authors' analysis of Preqin data

What Are the Risks of Leveraged Lending?

There are generally six recognized risks in leveraged (or indeed any other) lending:

(1) Credit risk arises in any loan and represents the risk to capital and income of the lender due to the risk of the borrower's inability to pay. This includes the underwriter's risk prior to the syndication.

(2) Liquidity risk arises when a bank mismatches the term of its assets and liabilities. Where it has short-term borrowings supporting long-term loans a liquidity crisis can cause a bank to collapse.

(3) Price risk arises in underwritten syndications because the terms to the borrower are often agreed prior to syndication. Where the market assesses the risks to be different to the underwritten assessment of the lead bank, the price paid for any particular bond may fall and the underwriter may incur a loss.

(4) Reputational risks are the effect of adverse public perception on the prospects of an institution. In leveraged finance this includes the particular reputational damage that can occur when complex structures are put in place that are perceived to be designed to avoid moral obligations, such as the creation of offshore special purpose vehicles, characterized (often inaccurately) as tax avoidance schemes.

(5) Strategic risks include an organization's ability to manage its exposure to the particular market and the changes within the market that it operates. This might include, for example, having an organization structure that effectively monitors and reports on a loan portfolio to enable decisions to be made in a timely and informed manner.

(6) Compliance risks arise when new and innovative financial products are developed that have not previously been specifically considered by the regulator of a market. The issuer of any syndication will take responsibility for the legality of the transactions that are being completed. They have a risk that any syndicate participant will pursue them for damages in the event that an arrangement is misrepresented or is illegal.

In the credit crunch many institutions experienced a variety of these risks.

Debt and Debt Capacity

Having looked at the market we now examine the basic principles of structuring of debt and leveraged finance.

In simple terms, lenders look at two aspects of the business:

(1) Flow: How much cashflow is available from time to time to pay interest and repay the loans?
(2) Stock: If the company were to default on the loan, how much would the bank recover on a distressed sale of the business or its total stock of assets?

How Much Debt? Cash Flow Lending

Cash flow is the lifeblood of leveraged transactions and at the due diligence stage of the investment cycle an enormous amount of analysis and technology is applied in assessing what the range of probable cash flows of the target business are likely to be.

The amount of debt that a business can support falls as the interest rate rises. At low interest rates a business can either reduce its interest payments or keep its interest payments constant by borrowing more. Similarly, the amount that can be borrowed against a given cash flow increases as the term of the loan increases. You can borrow more if you pay it back more slowly.

Figure 5.10 illustrates the relationship between the interest rate, the term of the loan in years, and the amount that can be borrowed on an amortizing, or repayment, loan.

For example, a 0 per cent interest loan repaid in equal instalments over eight years can be afforded at multiples up to eight times the risk-free cash flow of the borrower.

The same loan at an interest rate of 10 per cent can only be afforded at multiples of up to 5.33 times the same cash flow. Therefore, the amount of debt that a business can support is inversely related to the interest rate and directly related to the term of the loan.

As we pointed out above, the amount that can be borrowed is also a direct function of the assessment of the risks, by which we often mean the volatility, of the projected cash flows.

A private equity fund will seek to maximize the term of the loan and minimize the interest rate subject to its appetite for financial risk. Conversely, banks will seek to maximize the interest rate while matching the term of the loan to the demands of the syndication market and their own loan portfolio. These are both ultimately driven by the term and rates seen in the bond markets. A debt fund mimics the bond market more directly. They do not usually seek repayment of the principal until the end of the loan life. High-yield bonds are heavily standardized to allow trading and are usually repaid in year 5 in a single instalment.

The private equity market takes advantage of the periodic availability of cheap credit emanating from the global bond markets. We can think of private equity funds as consumers of debt that is produced by the banks, debt funds, and bond markets in response to

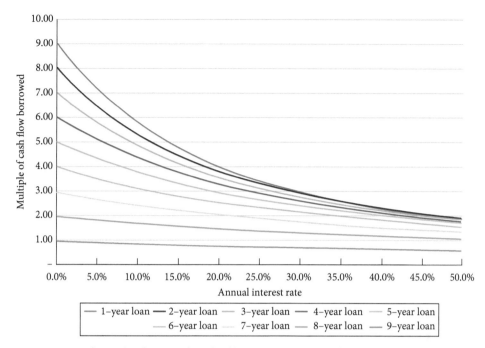

Figure 5.10. Relationship between length of loan, interest rate, and multiple of free cash flow
Source: The authors

investor demand for interest-bearing assets. Private equity is largely a taker of terms in the debt markets, not a dictator of them, but this is changing. When credit has been easier to access there has been a surge in the size of facilities that are written and a consequent growth in the size of buyouts being observed. PE funds are also more aggressively seeking both low-cost and bespoke terms in the leverage finance market.

How Much Debt? Security and Cost of Funds

The security available to a lender varies significantly from one situation to the next. At a simple level a lender might look at the total assets (value) of a company and assess a loan-to-value ratio, in much the same way as a freehold property lender will when lending a mortgage. Of course, in reality a more sophisticated approach is applied and each major item in the company's balance sheet should be assessed to establish the security value.

Each line of the balance sheet's assets will be looked at to ascertain the probable security value if a company becomes troubled. One common hierarchy of assets is illustrated in Figure 5.11.

Type of Assets

If we compare two situations with the same total assets and the same loan-to-value assumptions but a different make-up of the asset base, it can be illustrated how risk varies between different industries (Table 5.4).

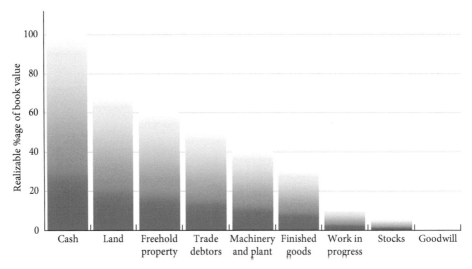

Figure 5.11. Illustrative security value of a failing company's assets

Source: The authors

Table 5.4. Stylized comparison of security in a retailer and a manufacturer

		Manufacturer		Retailer	
Type of asset	Realizable value	Net book value	Security	Net book value	Security
Cash	100%	–	–	–	–
Land	70%	–	–	–	–
Freehold property	60%	150	90	–	–
Trade debtors	50%	20	10	–	–
Machinery and plant	40%	50	20	–	–
Finished goods	30%	10	3	250	75
Work in progress	10%	10	1	–	–
Stocks	5%	10	1	–	–
Goodwill	0%	50	–	50	–
Total		300	125	300	75
Total security/total assets		42%		25%	

Source: The authors

Despite having assets with the same net book value from an accounting perspective, the security values are materially different. This reflects the different loan-to-value ratios applied to each class of assets and the difference in the asset base of the different businesses.

Generally, the more assets that are available in the higher loan-to-value categories, the more secure any loans will be. As the loans are more secure, the risk is lower to the banks providing the loans and therefore the cost to the borrower should be lower. As the cost is lower, the amount that can be serviced by any given level of projected cash flows is higher. This was a significant factor in the second buyout boom. High property prices gave the impression of high levels of security. This increased the amount of low-cost debt available which in turn allowed the total amount of debt to increase.

As the analysis above suggests, when buyouts began to emerge in the 1980s, they were originally focused on businesses with strong asset backing and predictable cash flows that enabled banks to lend with high levels of confidence and relatively low risk.

High and seasonal security variations may create potentially perverse incentives for banks. Where a business is struggling but a bank has full enforceable security, a banker may be disinclined to lend further. They have the option to call the loan in the knowledge that they will recover all their outstanding debt. For example, as we discussed, in retailers who have significant dependence on Christmas trading the cash balance of the company will often be maximized on Christmas Eve. For this reason, it is not uncommon for retailers to fail close to this Christmas cash maximum.

Asset-Based Lenders (ABL)

A common form of non-amortizing debt is invoice discounting. Invoice discounting pre-pays a proportion of outstanding debtors early and thereby creates a one-off reduction in working capital. Thereafter the rate of drawdown or repayment will be determined by the periodic increases and decreases in the debtor book. The risk is that when a business has a fall in sales, and therefore a fall in debtors, the facility will start to require repayment.

Discounting of debtors can be matched with asset finance for other assets such as plant and machinery or vehicles. Again, the idea is to trade cash today for the costs of repaying the lease in the future. ABL is limited to the value of the assets being discounted. New technology and financial technology companies have significantly increased the ceiling value of an ABL facility, but it generally remains the case that ABL is only used in smaller deals.

What Security Will Any Lenders Have?

As discussed above, the ratio of realizable assets to total borrowings is an indication of bank security.

This ratio requires judgement on both the value of the target company's assets and how readily realizable they would be in a forced sale. It is an approximate measure of the total amount of security available to the lender in the event of default on the loans. This is relevant to both the amount of debt lent and the pricing of that debt.

Bankers will typically price debt in layers. The first layer will be the most secure, with a first charge over the assets of the borrower, and therefore will be regarded as carrying the lowest risk and be priced accordingly.

Why Do You Sometimes See Two (or More) Newcos?

A bank can obtain its priority either contractually or structurally. In a contractual subordination there is an agreement between the various lenders regarding who is repaid in what order and what rights the banks have if plans go awry. This is the inter-creditor

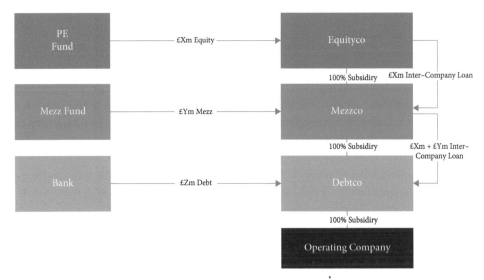

Figure 5.12. Structural subordination
Source: The authors

agreement. An alternative is to create structural subordination by using a cascade of new-cos, as in Figure 5.12.

In the event of the business underperforming, Debtco defaults on its loan to Mezzco, which becomes insolvent. Its directors have to appoint an insolvency practitioner. Mezzco's only assets are its shares in Debtco. These are, in an insolvency, worthless as the banks rank ahead of the shareholders in Debtco. The banks can therefore take 100 per cent control of the target and eliminate Equityco and Mezzco, in an efficient manner.

A further possible reason for a cascade of newcos is to create structures that are tax efficient in multinational and international businesses. This is discussed below.

Can Newco Repay the Borrowings?

Debt is repaid from cash flow, which consists of three elements:

Cash flow =
Post-tax profits/(loss)
± capital efficiency changes
± changes in external finance.

As leveraged deals are about structuring the external finance, the appropriate cash flows to analyse are operating cash flows before funding (and tax).

Operating cash flows =
EBITDA
± change in working capital
– capital expenditure
+ proceeds from sale of fixed assets at NBV

Box 5.1 Findings: What Do Secured Creditors Recover? The Academic Evidence

---

US buyouts that defaulted on their loans in the 1980s generally had positive operating margins at the time of default and, from pre-buyout to distress resolution, experienced a marginally positive change in market- or industry-adjusted value (Appendix 13). In UK buyouts that defaulted, secured creditors recovered on average 62 per cent of their investment. In comparison with evidence from a more general population of small firms, MBOs experience fewer going-concern realizations in receivership (30 per cent), make a lower average repayment to secured creditors, and make fewer 100 per cent repayments to these creditors. These results appear to contrast with expectations that the covenants accompanying high leverage in buyouts will signal distress sooner than in firms funded more by equity. That these MBOs entered formal insolvency procedures despite the presence of specialized lender monitoring suggests that these are cases that will have been the ones considered most difficult to reorganize. UK evidence on failed buyouts shows that coordination problems among multiple lenders do not create inefficiencies resulting in significantly lower secured creditor recovery rates. However, when there are multiple secured lenders, the senior secured lender gains at the expense of other secured creditors as the lender first registering the charge over assets obtains priority. Recovery rates for junior creditors are lower for private equity backed buyouts. Private equity backed firms in distress are more likely to survive as an independent reorganized company.

---

where EBITDA is earnings (profits) before interest, tax, depreciation, and amortization.

Growing businesses usually (but not always) require more working capital and capital expenditure to finance growth. Operating cash flow is therefore usually less than EBITDA in a steadily growing business. The ratio of operating cashflow to EBITDA is the **cash conversion ratio**.

The ability of Newco to repay borrowings is usually reflected largely in the ratio of EBITDA to total borrowings, having regard for cash conversion.

This ratio measures, approximately, the amount of ongoing cash flow available to pay interest (and to make loan repayments on the appointed dates).

Tax will be recalculated on the target company's projected profits based on the new capital structure (i.e. after allowable interest deductions).

Depreciation and amortization are excluded because these are non-cash items and have no impact on cash flow. However, any cash required to fund future capital investment will be taken into account in the new capital structure.

The EBITDA ratio has, on average, been rising over the recent past and, as noted above, concerns have been expressed about the prudence of certain leveraged structures with perceived high debt ratios. However, it is important to note that the ratio does not tell the whole story. For example, in businesses that have completed a major investment programme and have no further significant capital expenditure (capex) requirements in the immediate foreseeable future, a higher EBITDA multiple will be more tolerable than in companies with major future capex needs.

Generally, the more volatile and uncertain the earnings of the target, the lower the EBITDA multiple should be, and vice versa.

What Are the Potential Sources of Cash Flow to Repay Borrowings?

Companies generate trading cash flows from only three sources:

(1) increasing post-tax profits;
(2) reducing working capital;
(3) selling assets.

All other cash inflows come from the shareholders or external lenders.
Leveraged transactions focus on each source of cash flow and how they interact.

Increasing Post-Tax Profits

Increasing profitability can be achieved in five ways, only four of which impact cash flow:

(1) increase gross margins;
(2) increase volumes or sales;
(3) reduce overheads;
(4) reduce the tax charge;
(5) change accounting policies or the way they are applied.

The first three of these will flow from strategic and tactical decisions made by management and will involve management skill and hard work by all employees in a business. Such actions are not specific to private equity investment, and therefore they are not discussed further here. They are however absolutely at the centre of any investment and banking decision, and are in many ways the core skill set of any manager and investor.

The tax charge is dealt with in a detailed worked example in Chapter 6.

The appropriate application of accounting policies is a matter for review by the auditors of the business. Note that EBITDA is a key metric in many deals. EBITDA is not a defined term in accounting regulations and is prone to adjustment and definitional differences. Caution is therefore needed when looking at EBITDA in any environment. We discuss this below.

Reducing Working Capital

The amount of cash tied up in a business as working capital is broadly determined by the relative speed of being paid by customers compared to the speed at which suppliers are paid.

All private equity investors will look very closely at the working capital of the business. Many will have an explicit plan to reduce the amount of working capital by reducing stocks, or paying suppliers later, or speeding up customer collections, or a combination of all of these. From the perspective of the company, this is unequivocally a positive thing to do; it represents a step change in the efficiency of the business.

From the perspective of the overall economy, if all that happens is that the reduction in working capital in a company creates an equal and opposite increase in the working capital of its suppliers and customers, then there is unlikely to be a gain in efficiency in the supply chain. However, if the pressure to reduce working capital flows up and down the supply chain, it is a net gain in economic efficiency: the product or service is being produced using less valuable capital.

Irrespective of the overall effect on the economy, it is one significant way in which leverage creates the imperative to maximize cash flow.

Fixed Assets: To Own or Lease?

Virtually all businesses have a mix of owned and leased assets. The decision to own or lease will be based on attitudes to risk and the strategic importance of owning an asset. In leveraged buyouts the ownership of all material assets will be reviewed.

Assets that have no productive worth should always be sold. Other assets need to be reviewed in the context both of business efficiency and the security underlying the debt structure. Banks will usually wish to negotiate that some or all of the proceeds from any asset sales are used to repay borrowings, or they may want a block on asset sales that are not in the agreed business plan.

The decision therefore becomes one of owning a fixed asset or selling it. Often, where the asset is a property, the decision will be taken to sell and lease back the building. It is important to emphasize that selling any particular asset may increase overall economic efficiency, if it can be put to better use under a different owner, especially if the current owner is not using it to its full potential.

Since January 2019 the international accounting standard IFRS16 has changed the accounting for leases. Briefly, the new standard requires most leases to be shown as liabilities in the company's balance sheet.[3] It also changes the way that EBITDA is calculated. This is technical and outside of our scope.

EBITDA Multiples

Institutions use EBITDA (earnings (profits) before interest, tax, depreciation, and amortization) as a proxy for cash flow and express leverage, in EBITDA multiples.

It is vital to understand that EBITDA is a crude **measure** of leverage, **NOT** the determinant of the amount that can be borrowed. Since

$$\text{pre-tax and funding cash flow} = \text{EBITDA} - \text{working capital changes} - \text{capex},$$

in a hypothetical, stable business with no ongoing needs for increased capital (i.e. capex = depreciation) and no need to grow short-term working capital, and no fixed assets to sell at cost, pre-tax and funding cash flow will equal EBITDA.

If we define growth capital as the cash needed to fund new capex and working capital, EBITDA provides measure of cash flow excluding any requirements for growth capital.

---

[3] See: https://www.icaew.com/technical/financial-reporting/ifrs/ifrs-standards/ifrs-16-leases.

EBITDA Multiples: 3, 5, 7

Very crudely leverage loans are those where the ratio of debt to EBITDA exceeds 3.00. We might ask ourselves why this number was originally chosen.

As we discussed when talking about banks' capital requirements for leveraged loans, these are typically five to seven years in term, for reasons of capital adequacy (you may recall that the regulations about this changed after the financial crisis, to increase the amount of capital required for longer-term loans). Therefore, $3 \times$ EBITDA can be roughly thought of as using around three-fifths to three-sevenths (43 per cent to 60 per cent) of cash from profitable trading to pay back debt capital. The simple model in Table 5.5 enables us to look at this more closely.

As the table shows, a $3 \times$ EBITDA loan of 5 years at 5 per cent interest rate requires 75 per cent of the annual EBITDA (before any growth).

A $7 \times$ EBITDA loan on the same terms requires 175 per cent of the annual EBITDA. The latter is only affordable if capital efficiencies release cash flow.

We can sensitize the analysis to look at (i) different interest rates (Table 5.6) and (ii) different loan terms(Table 5.7). Again, we see the general principle that higher interest rates and shorter-term loans strain cash flow. You can ease the strain by either reducing the cost of the loan or by extending its term.

We can also see from the sensitivity analysis that $3 \times$ EBITDA can be serviced at interest rates as high as 10 per cent as long as the term exceeds four years.

Table 5.5. An example of EBITDA multiples

Company		A	B	C
EBITDA ($/£m)		100	100	100
EBITDA x	Multiple x	3	5	7
Total debt		300	500	700
Term of loan (years)		5	5	5
Annual capital repayment ($/£m)		60	100	140
Interest rate		5%	5%	5%
First year interest ($/£m)		15	25	35
Year 1 debt repayments ($/£m)		75	125	175
(= annual capital repayment + first year interest)				
% EBITDA		75%	125%	175%

Table 5.6. Sensitivity to interest rate, given 5-year term

Interest rate	$3 \times$ EBITDA	$5 \times$ EBITDA	$7 \times$ EBITDA
0.0%	60%	100%	140%
2.0%	66%	110%	154%
4.0%	72%	120%	168%
6.0%	78%	130%	182%
8.0%	84%	140%	196%
10.0%	90%	150%	210%

Table 5.7. Sensitivity to loan term, given 5 per cent interest rate

Term in years	3 × EBITDA	5 × EBITDA	7 × EBITDA
3	115%	192%	268%
4	90%	150%	210%
5	75%	125%	175%
6	65%	108%	152%
7	58%	96%	135%

At 5 × EBITDA, 96 per cent of the cash flow from EBITDA is used in year one to service 7 year debt at 5% interest cost.

At multiples over 5, cash becomes strained in year one. This simple analysis points to the simplest *rules of thumb* in leveraged loans:

Medium leverage:	3 × EBITDA	Leveraged loans
Higher leverage:	5 × EBITDA	Stretched leverage loans
Exceptional leverage:	7 × EBITDA	Super-stretched loans.

Adjusted EBITDA: Run Rate

Note that EBITDA is not a defined term in accounting regulations. It is open to manipulation and there is much debate about its use in financial market reporting and transactions.

One way to ease the strain is to achieve growth in cash flows. Debt providers are reluctant to lend against speculative growth. Therefore the more certain growth is, the more likely it is that a bank will lend a higher multiple of historic EBITDA.

There are occasions when EBITDA growth can be nearly certain. If a business is adding new customers on long-term contracts with predictable cash flows, at any particular point in time it may have 100 per cent visibility of the increase in profit that will accrue from those new contracts over the coming year.

Let us imagine a business that started the year with 1m customers paying £22 per month and an EBITDA margin of 25 per cent (Table 5.8). For simplicity we will assume no

Table 5.8. Run rate EBITDA in a contracting business: assumptions

Year	1	2
Trading assumptions		
Opening customers (000)	1,000	1,500
New customers (000)	500	750
Closing customers (000)	1,500	2,250
Growth rate	50%	50%
Revenue per customer (£/$)	22	22
EBITDA profit margin	25%	25%
Lending assumption		
Structuring EBITDA ×	5.00	

Table 5.9. Run rate EBITDA in a contracting business: annual results

Year	1	2
Annual Reported Results		
Average no of customers (000)	1,250	1,875
Annual Revenue (£m)	27,500	41,250
Costs (£m)	−6,875	−10,313
EBITDA (£m)	20,625	30,938

customers leave, so there is no churn rate. This is great business. It has high margins and high growth, so it should be able to borrow a high multiple of EBITDA.

The annual report would show revenue and profits for the year. If we assume new customers join evenly throughout the year, we can easily calculate the average number of customers and hence the annual profits and revenues (Table 5.9).

An astute borrower would point out that even without winning any new customers, the reported EBITDA understated the business's real current profitability. The new customers from last year are contracted for this year, so their contribution is already in the bank (so to speak!). We should therefore be able to borrow based on our run rate EBITDA, not our reported annual EBITDA for the prior year (Table 5.10).

If the banks accept the argument, and in our simple example it is valid, they will lend based on the run-rate EBITDA. If they use the same multiple the debt will increase by 17 per cent, from £103,125m to £123,750m (Table 5.11).

Note that if an analyst looks at this company after the deal and calculates the EBITDA/debt ratio based on the reported numbers, they will see that the lenders lent 6.0 times the historic reported EBITDA. The run rate is not reported, so the analyst will probably not be aware of the lower run-rate EBITDA multiple.

This has significant implications if the market is being driven by reported norms. If the market rate is reported as 6 × EBITDA for this type of credit profile, there will be pressure to increase the amount of lending as the market has anchored on an incorrectly calculated structuring debt multiple.

Table 5.10. Run rate EBITDA in a contracting business

Year	1	2
Run rate results		
Closing no. of customers (000)	1,500	2,250
Run rate revenues (£m)	33,000	49,500
Run rate costs (£m)	−8,250	−12,375
Run rate EBITDA (£m)	24,750	37,125
Increase in gross profit and EBITDA (£m)	4,125	6,188
Increase in structuring EBITDA (%)	20%	20%

Table 5.11. Run rate EBITDA in a contracting business: Lending impact

Lending capacity	
Debt multiple on reported results (£m)	**103,125**
Historic ×	5.00
Projected ×	3.33
Debt on adjusted results (£m)	**123,750**
Increase in debt (£m)	20,625
Increase in debt (%)	17%
Run rate debt multiple on **run rate** results	
Historic ×	5.00
Projected ×	3.33
Run rate Debt Multiple on **reported** results	
Historic EBITDA ×	6.00
Projected EBITDA ×	4.00

Adjusted EBITDA: Cost Add-Backs

As businesses grow, they often incur costs ahead of growth, both investment in capital and increased overheads.

Investment: investment in capital does not impact EBITDA, but it does reduce cash flow available for debt service by increasing the amount of working capital or increasing capex—This is negative in most (but not all) growing businesses.

Using EBITDA as the leverage multiple therefore eliminates the effects of investment from the calculation, leaving that cash requirement to be separately considered in designing the funding package.

Overheads: increases in costs that affect the profit and loss account do reduce reported EBITDA. Therefore, there is a tension between investing ahead of growth to ease financial strain and generate equity upside and using a historic measure of profitability (EBITDA) to assess the level of leverage.

To ease this tension, it has become common for banks to agree to adjustments to the way that costs are included in EBITDA when calculating structuring EBITDA.

Typically, non-recurring costs are excluded. The idea of exceptional costs has largely been removed from global accounting standards. This notion brings them back when calculating EBITDA.

These might include one-off costs such as restructuring, new systems implementation, M&A fees and similar non-trading items, payments made to the shareholders as fees or expenses that can easily be stopped if the business needs to preserve cash, and so on.

The risk is that in creating a long list of add-backs, the lender and borrower simply ignore the fact that some random costs occur in most years and adding them all back is equivalent to assuming a perfectly stable world, which history suggests is a bold assumption.

EBITDA and Liquidity

It should be clear from this discussion of adjusted EBITDA that there are perfectly legitimate reasons to make the adjustment and also temptations to massage the number to increase the amount of debt available to the business.

The danger of adjusted EBITDA lies in two areas:

(1) it encourages gaming the negotiation between the company, sponsor, and the lenders. It can transfer risk to a debt provider that ought more reasonably to lie with an equity provider;

(2) it distorts data and makes opaque the data required to create and maintain liquidity in the bond markets and syndications market. The data is distorted by overstating debt multiples, encouraging market norms to be accepted at higher levels than is actually the case. This encourages over-lending.

The lack of visibility of the EBITDA definition outside the public markets means that there is a significant data point within the syndication market that is both undefined in principle and is also routinely adjusted in bespoke ways in the loan documentation. This means that if confidence in the leveraged loan market is shaken, you are faced with a trading decision with incomplete information and uncertainty. That is a recipe for a market to fail due to the lemons problem caused by information asymmetry described by Akerlof.

How Did Banks Increase the Levels of Borrowing in Buyouts? Capital Holidays and Bullet Loans

Lenders competed to win the lead arranger mandates both by minimizing the price and by attempting to maximize the quantity of debt available. As explained above, in a normal loan paying interest and repaying capital in cash each year, the amount of debt can be increased by either extending the term or reducing the cost.

To increase the amount of debt available beyond what can be funded on an ongoing basis from cash flows, debt structures routinely include a second tranche with a so-called 'bullet repayment'. Tranches are usually identified by letters: tranche A, tranche B, etc, where each layer is usually senior to the next, so that tranche A takes priority over tranche B and so on (Figure 5.13).

Prior to the credit crunch, tranche A loans were typically seven-year amortizing loans. Amortizing is the term for a loan that repays capital according to some pre-agreed schedule, in the same way as a repayment mortgage does.

Capital holidays are periods when interest only is paid. Figure 5.14 illustrates the impact that using a variety of capital holidays has on the cash requirement of any loan.

A bullet loan (typically a tranche B) is the special case of a loan with a full capital holiday that repays the capital in a single repayment at the end of the loan. It is analogous to an interest-only mortgage. Because the capital is not repaid until the end of the loan period, cash is preserved in the business over the life of the loan, as long as either the cash retained in the business generates sufficient cash to meet the bullet repayment or the business is able to amplifies the tranche B loan at maturity. The use of a bullet loan increases gearing and therefore equity returns.

Prior to the credit crunch a typical leveraged loan package might consist of a variation around the 'standard' leveraged loan package:

(1) two-thirds seven-year 'A' senior amortizing loan: a loan repaid in instalments over seven years;

(2) one-third eight-year 'B' senior bullet loan: a loan paying interest only until the capital is repaid in one instalment (a bullet repayment) in eight years.

Types of Debt Instrument – 'Tranches'

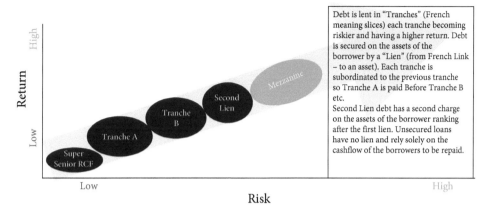

Figure 5.13. Debt tranches

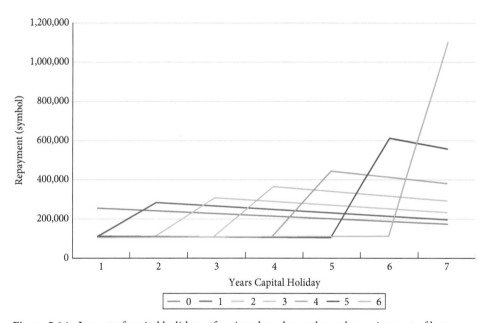

Figure 5.14. Impact of capital holidays of various lengths on the cash requirement of loans
Source: The authors

Average Life, Contribution, and Debt Capacity

In general, the cash flow requirements of any loan can be sculpted to fit the projected cash flows of a business by using a series of tranches with different capital holiday periods. The key to establishing the risks of any debt structure created is to understand fully the underlying cash dynamics of the business being lent to (i.e. how vulnerable and volatile the cash flows are).

One way to distil the risks of a loan are to calculate how long the lender will be exposed to risk. To do this you can calculate the average life of any loan, by multiplying each capital repayment by the time in years that it is planned to be lent and dividing the total by the

Table 5.12. Calculation of average life of a loan

Year	Calculation		1	2	3	4	5	6	Total
(Amount of loan A is £100m; term of loan B is 5 years)									
Opening Balance	A	£m	100	80	60	40	20	0	100
Repayment	A/B = C	£m	−20	−20	−20	−20	−20	0	−100
Closing Balance		£m	80	60	40	20	0	0	0
Year x repayment	C	£m	20	40	60	80	100	0	300
Opening Balance	A	£m							100
Average life	C/A	Years							**3.00**
Margin	D	%ge							4.5%
Contribution	A*D*(C/A)									13.50

original amount lent. It sounds complex when written in either English or as an equation, but is actually quite straightforward to do, as Table 5.12 shows.

So:

- a five-year loan with equal annual instalments has an average life of 3 years (if the repayment is made at the end of each year) and 2.5 years (i.e. half the term) if the repayments are made in the middle of the year;
- a five-year loan with a single bullet repayment in year 5 has an average life of five years (equal to its term).

The longer the average life, the longer the risk exposure and therefore the higher the margin the lender will want to charge. So, Term Loan A (which is steadily repaid) has an average of around half its term, and Term Loan B (which is a bullet loan) has an average life equal to its term. The overall package will have an average life of the weighted average of the two.

The risk of a loan therefore relates to both its security and its average life.[4]

Contribution is a crude measure of the profitability of a loan (without adjusting for the time value of money):

- Contribution = Loan margin x average life

Contribution therefore rises as average life increases. For example, for a 5 year £100m loan at a margin of 4.5 per cent with repayments at the year end:

- Contribution with equal repayments: 4.5 per cent × 3 years × £100m = £13.5m
- Contribution of a Bullet Loan: 4.5 per cent × 5 years × £100m = £22.5m

How Do Lenders Increase the Levels of Borrowings in Buyouts? Payment-in-Kind Debt (PIK) and Deep Discounted Securities (DDSs)

Another way to increase the amount of debt capacity in a business is to roll up the interest rather than pay it in cash. This has an impact on cash, profitability, and taxation.

---

[4] Technically we ought to discuss duration of loans, which is the average life adjusted for the cost of capital. The higher the cost of capital the greater the difference between the duration and the average life, but this is beyond an explanatory guide.

Table 5.13. Effect of PIK roll-up on capital value

Effect of PIK interest on redemption value					
Interest rate	8.00%				
Year	1	2	3	4	5
Opening balance (£/$)	100.0	108.0	116.6	126.0	136.0
PIK interest (£/$)	8.0	8.6	9.3	10.1	10.9
Closing balance (£/$)	108.0	116.6	126.0	136.0	146.9
Closing balance/initial investment	1.08	1.17	1.26	1.36	1.47

Payment in kind (PIK) debt is a form of loan that does not receive cash interest. Instead it receives more of the same type of loan. At maturity (or on sale or flotation if earlier) the total amount of the original loan plus the PIK notes issued in lieu of interest is repaid.

This enables the company to borrow without having the burden of a cash repayment of interest until the end of the loan. Many equity-release mortgages operate on this basis (plus having a share in any property value increase).

There is a great deal of empirical evidence to show that even experts routinely underestimate the effects of compounding interest. We discuss how this impacts management equity later in this chapter. The effect of compounding is illustrated in Table 5.13.

For the lender, the attraction is that PIK loans pay higher nominal interest rates than normal cash interest loans. This was especially attractive when investors were seeking higher-yield investments prior to the credit crunch.

Box 5.2 Findings: Where Do Buyouts Get the Cash to Pay Down the Debt? The Academic Evidence

Research on US buyouts during the 1980s indicates substantial average improvements in profitability and cash flow measures over the interval between one year prior to the transaction and two or three years subsequent to it (Appendix 14).

UK evidence from the 1980s also indicates that the vast majority of buyouts show clear improvements in profitability and working capital management. These buyouts generated significantly higher increases in return on assets than comparable firms that did not experience an MBO over a period from two to five years after buyout. Financial ratio analysis of medium-sized MBOs in the Netherlands showed that they had significantly better ratios than the average financial ratios of the industries in which they were involved in terms of cash flow, sales, and return on investment. In France, MBOs outperform comparable firms in the same industry both before and after the buyout. However, the performance of French MBO firms declines after the transaction is consummated, especially in former family businesses. More recent US and UK evidence from P2Ps finds significant increases in liquidity but not profitability. Recent UK evidence from other vendor sources provides mixed evidence regarding post-buyout return on assets but demonstrates that divisional buyouts in particular show significant improvements in efficiency. Intensity of private equity firm involvement is associated with higher levels of profitability.

A similar result is achieved if interest is 'rolled up' and repaid at the end of the loan. The only economic difference between PIK and a roll-up is that interest may accrue more rapidly on PIK debt if there is no 'interest-on-interest' on the roll-up.

Deep Discounted Securities (DDS)

A similar cash flow profile can be generated by using a discounted bond or loan, a so-called deep discounted security or DDS. These were common in the 1980s and 1990s but fell out of favour as tax regulation was tightened up and PIK offered more flexibility. A lender invests in a DDS at a value below its final redemption value (see Table 5.14).

Table 5.14. Mechanics of a deep discounted security (DDS)

Deep discounted security	
Investment in year 0 (£/$)	68.00
Redemption value in year 5 (£/$)	100.00
No of years	5.00
Yield to maturity (%)	8.02%
Discount (%)	−32%

These are essentially the two ways of achieving the same thing: charging interest but not paying until a later date.

What Is Mezzanine?

Mezzanine finance comes in many forms. The common features of all mezzanine instruments and products are that they offer a risk/return profile that lies above that of debt and below that of equity. It used to be provided by banks, but is now generally provided by specialist debt and mezzanine funds, if it is available at all.

Mezzanine is used to increase the financial leverage of transactions where the lead bankers have no appetite to lend further senior debt but there is still more capacity for long-term borrowings. This may happen for a number of reasons. It might be that the security provided by the assets of the company is fully utilized to support the senior debt package, but the cash flows will support further borrowings. A banker (or other lender) will therefore wish to receive a higher yield on the instrument that has no underlying asset cover.

Another example could be where there are large forecast cash flows contingent on executing a particular part of the business plan: for example, reducing excess stocks or selling excess assets or non-core companies in a group. In these circumstances, the lenders may take the view that they will lend against these future lumpy cash flows, but require an adequate return to reflect their risk. This is may be achieved by attaching warrants (options) to the mezzanine loan which enable the lender to share in the equity value of the business at exit.

Unitranche Debt – One Slice Covering All

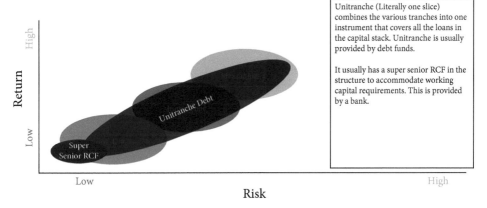

Unitranche (Literally one slice) combines the various tranches into one instrument that covers all the loans in the capital stack. Unitranche is usually provided by debt funds.

It usually has a super senior RCF in the structure to accommodate working capital requirements. This is provided by a bank.

Figure 5.15. Unitranche debt

Mezzanine therefore typically uses capital holidays and contingent repayments but charges a premium for the risk associated with the deferrals of repayment.

What Are the Advantages and Disadvantages of Unitranche?

The use of mezzanine has declined sharply over the past decade and has been largely displaced by the use of unitranche debt (Figure 5.15). Indeed, many of the earliest unitranche providers were originally mezzanine funds pre-crisis.

The key features of unitranche include:

No repayment: As we discussed earlier, the big change in the global debt market—but especially in Europe—has been the growth in a new category of lender, the debt fund. Debt funds lend bullet loans, not amortizing loans, because their ultimate investors are seeking a long-term yield. Unitranche requires no amortization and releases cash to be invested in the business rather than repaying the debt. Think of it as an interest-only mortgage.

No cash sweep: As the funders do not want to be repaid early there are no cash sweeps in unitranche. This makes the product suitable for acquisitive growth strategies.

Greater debt: Unitranche provides a single loan that incorporates debt and mezzanine in a single financial product. Unitranche originally emerged from mezzanine funds that entered the senior debt market due to the reduction in supply from the clearing banks and increase in margins that were therefore available. It therefore offers more debt than a bank's leverage finance unit would be prepared to lend. The amount varies, but as a rough rule of thumb a unitranche facility might have around a $1–2 \times$ EBITDA increase in debt.

Simplified structure: Unitranche simplifies the documentation of buyouts as all the senior facilities are provided under a single agreement with one set of terms. The need for separate inter-creditor agreements or newcos to accommodate senior lenders and mezzanine lenders is eliminated.

Higher cost: Unitranche is priced at a single blended rate across the whole facility. It is therefore more expensive than senior debt. Furthermore, because unitranche lenders do not want the capital returned early, there are much more severe penalties for early repayment.

Lower flexibility: The inability to repay without paying significant early repayment costs is particularly relevant to private equity as the investment is always predicated on a sale. There is therefore a tension between the costs of early repayment and the returns that can be achieved in a rapidly realized successful investment. These are mitigated in many deals by having reducing early repayment costs after years two/three. We have also seen transactions where unitranche has been rolled over in deals where realizations have been unexpectedly early in an investment's life.

Unitranche: Pricing the Last Slice

When comparing the cost of the increased debt of a unitranche facility to a more conventional senior debt facility with an amortizing A loan and a bullet B loan, you need to calculate the cost of the implicit final tranche of the debt in the larger facility.

Demonstrating by example: consider a $/£1,050m LBO (Table 5.15).

The unitranche facility in the example is 7 × EBITDA whereas a conventional structure only offers 5 × EBITDA. Everything else is the same, except that the amount of equity obviously reduces when you use more debt.

We have assumed that the required rate of return for the PE fund is 20 per cent and calculated the weighted average cost of capital (WACC) of both structures (Table 5.16). The WACC is reduced by using unitranche because you replace equity with debt. There is of course a corresponding increase in interest to be paid that increases the interest

Table 5.15. The transaction structure

Funding required	Senior (£m)	Unitranche (£m)
Acquire equity	400	400
Refinance existing net debt	600	600
Costs	50	50
	1,050	1,050
Structuring EBITDA	100	100
Purchase EBITDA ×	10	

Funded by	Senior		Unitranche	
Debt		500		700
Debt EBITDA ×	5 × EBITDA		7 × EBITDA	
Equity (£m)		550		350
Total (£m)		1,050		1,050

Table 5.16. Senior debt vs unitranche debt

Cost of capital	Senior	Unitranche
Cost of senior debt		
TLA (% of total debt)	60%	
Libor	0.96%	
Margin	3.50%	
Total	4.46%	
TLB (% of total debt)	40%	
Libor	0.96%	
Margin	4.50%	
Total	5.46%	
Term loan blended year 1		
Libor	0.96%	0.96%
Margin	3.90%	7.50%
Total	4.86%	8.46%
Cost of equity	20%	20%
Weighted average cost of capital		
Cost of equity	20%	20%
Debt	4.86%	8.46%
Equity (£m)	550	350
Debt (£m)	500	700
Total (£m)	1,050	1,050
Cost of equity (£m)	110	70
Cost of debt (£m)	24	59
Total (£m)	134	129
Weighted average cost of capital	12.79%	12.31%

cost (and risk). However, as the unitranche facility is non-amortizing, the cash cost of servicing debt in the early years of the scheme will actually be lower using the non-amortizing unitranche debt. We have kicked the increased risk further down the road, not eliminated it.

We can now calculate the cost of the increased lending in the unitranche facility by subtracting the senior debt from the unitranche and recalculating the cost of the implicit final tranche (Table 5.17).

The cost of the final tranche in this scheme is 12.6 per cent, made up of the increased interest margin paid on the senior element and the full margin on the 'stretch tranche'.

We can sensitize the scheme to examine how the implicit cost of funding the final tranche varies according to the amount of extra debt, by varying the EBITDA × multiple and the cost of the unitranche facility as in Table 5.18.

The table illustrates that the cost of the final tranche of the unitranche structure can be anywhere between 4.3 per cent and 42.6 per cent (i.e a debt return through to a high equity return).

This demonstrates why it is certainly NOT the case that private equity funds will always maximize debt in any investment. A PE fund manager may well decide that the

Table 5.17. Cost of 'final tranche' of unitranche

Incremental cost of unitranche	
Senior debt (£m)	500
Incremental debt (£m)	200
Total unitranche (£m)	700
Senior debt blended cost (%)	4.86%
Actual unitranche cost (£m)	59.2
Cost of senior debt (£m)	– 34.0
Incremental cost of final tranche (£m)	25.2
Amount of incremental debt (£m)	200
Incremental cost in interest (£m)	25.2
Incremental debt/incremental cost (%)	12.60%

implicit return on the stretch tranche is attractive to them. If they did, they might choose to use the smaller senior facility and invest more themselves in the deal by using more loanstock from the PE fund. This gives the fund lower financial risk, as it holds the increased debt itself. In the jargon, the PE fund will 'keep the ball' longer if, for whatever reason, the value of the business were to fall below the equity value required in the uni-tranche structure.

As senior debt generally can be repaid early with low cost, the option to refinance later using unitranche and repaying the extra loan stock will still be available if the markets are unchanged and the business performs to plan.

Table 5.18. Sensitivity of cost of final tranche to amount lent and cost of unitranche

		Unitranche EBITDA multiple					
	12.6%	6	6.25	6.5	6.75	7	7.25
Unitranche	5.5%	9.6%	8.0%	6.9%	6.2%	5.6%	5.2%
Margin %	6.0%	12.6%	10.5%	9.1%	8.1%	7.4%	6.8%
	6.5%	15.6%	13.0%	11.3%	10.0%	9.1%	8.4%
	7.0%	18.6%	15.5%	13.4%	12.0%	10.9%	10.0%
	7.5%	21.6%	18.0%	15.6%	13.9%	12.6%	11.6%
	8.0%	24.6%	20.5%	17.8%	15.8%	14.4%	13.2%
	8.5%	27.6%	23.0%	19.9%	17.7%	16.1%	14.8%
	9.0%	30.6%	25.5%	22.1%	19.7%	17.9%	16.4%
	9.5%	33.6%	28.0%	24.3%	21.6%	19.6%	18.0%
	10.0%	36.6%	30.5%	26.4%	23.5%	21.4%	19.7%
	10.5%	39.6%	33.0%	28.6%	25.5%	23.1%	21.3%
	11.0%	42.6%	35.5%	30.8%	27.4%	24.9%	22.9%

Small increases in a facility at high margins can be very expensive. Once the cost of incremental debt starts to materially exceed the fund's hurdle rate of return for carried interest (typically, you will recall, not more than 8.0 per cent), it becomes increasingly attractive to the PE fund to deploy more equity and use the cheaper lower level of debt and have less risk early in the investment life.

A Deeper Dive into a Leveraged Finance Contract

In this section we take a short but deep dive into the structure and terms of a standard LMA leveraged finance contract to give a sense of the size and complexity of the contract and the negotiations surrounding it. This is important to understand when considering the trading of loans in any secondary market or syndication. Each loan will be individually tailored from this basic 350+ page template (or its North American LSTA equivalent).

Structure and Contents of LMA Standard Leveraged Loan

At the end of 2018 a standard LMA leveraged finance template was 351 pages long and had twelve sections, forty-eight clauses and nineteen potential attached schedules. This is of course a template, not a contract, so there are sections where the final contract will remove options that are not relevant to the specific deal, and there may be non-standard terms that require adding to the template. Nevertheless, the growth of this template, year-on-year, reflects both the inevitable snowball effect of any contract's evolution and a maturing of the market to establish emerging norms that can be incorporated into the standard template (Table 5.19).

Looked at in more detail, the structure and logic of the agreement becomes clearer.

Section 1: Definitions and Interpretation defines terms used throughout the contract.

Section 2: The Facilities sets out why the loan is being made and the broad form of loan structure.

Section 3: Utilization sets out the rules about when the loan can be used.

Section 4: Repayment, Prepayment, and Cancellation contains the rules about when the loan can be repaid.

Section 5: Costs of Utilization is where the total direct costs of the loan are found (i.e. the interest rate and fees).

Section 6: Additional Payment Obligations continues with the costs of the facility by giving the rules on when indirect costs can be charged to the borrowers by the lenders.

Section 7: Guarantee is a technical section where all the lenders agree to guarantee each other's obligations so that the borrower only has to deal with one source of funds.

Table 5.19. High-level structure of the LMA leveraged loan contract

Section heading	Number of pages
Definitions and Interpretation	55
The Facilities	9
Utilization	33
Repayment, Prepayment, and Cancellation	21
Costs of Utilization	13
Additional Payment Obligations	20
Guarantee	4
Representations, Undertakings, and Events of Default	53
Changes to the Parties	20
The Finance Parties	15
Administration	37
Governing Law and Enforcement	3
Schedules	68
Grand total	351

Section 8: Representations, Undertakings, and Events of Default contains both the rules that govern default of the agreement and the information that has been relied on and is required to be provided by the borrower to the lenders.

Section 9: Changes to the Parties covers the rules about changes to the lenders or borrowers. It is where the rules of syndication and trading the loan with other parties will be found and where the effect of an insolvency of a lender (as opposed to the borrower) is dealt with. It is indicative of the changing world that prior to the global financial crisis there were usually no agreed LMA standard mechanisms to deal with the failure of the lender.

Section 10: The Finance Parties covers the organizational structures that enable the borrower and each of the lenders to administer the loan agreement. The standard structure involves an agent who coordinates the information flows from the borrower to all the lenders. There is then an issuing bank who act as the coordinating bank for cash advances and repayments. The idea is to make the mechanics of the syndicate as easy as possible for the borrower.

Section 11: Administration lays out the mechanics of all aspects of administration ranging from how a drawdown notice is made by the borrower, to how information is circulated to lenders, to what happens when a default occurs.

Section 12 is a technical section stating under which country's legal code the contract will be enforced.

The Schedules are generally either lists of parties to the original contract and their roles, or examples of the types of documents and forms that are to be used to administer the agreement. For example, there will be an example drawdown notice, the form of a letter of credit, and various other forms and notifications that might be required to do some function in the main loan agreement.

Who Writes the Standard Loan Documents?

The quoted bond markets work based on broadly standardized terms to enable efficient trading. You should not have to scrutinize every clause of a quoted investment grade bond contract because it will follow the market standards.

One of the changes that seemed to have taken root over the decade or more that we have been writing together about the private equity market was the move towards more standardized contracts that are used in the unquoted debt markets. In the UK, Europe, and elsewhere in the EMEA the documentation provided by the Loan Market Association (LMA) is currently the most widely used set. In the US and the rest of the Americas the documentation is managed by the Loan Syndication and Trading Association (LSTA), in the Asia–Pacific region there is an Asia Pacific Loan Market Association (APLMA) and in Africa each country or area has its own so-called African single jurisdiction (ASJ) having membership of the LMA. There is increasing cooperation between these bodies to create standardization.

Why Were the Loan Documents Standardized and Who Benefited?

Having a wide range of standard contractual terms makes syndication of loans much easier and cheaper. If you know that all contracts are derived from a standard set of terms that are acceptable to any major bank, all you need to do to evaluate the contract is check the deviation from the standard terms and look at the commercial terms that are not set out in the standards. To facilitate the creation of a more efficient syndications market, these organizations were therefore created by the banks to agree a widely accepted suite of contractual terms in a range of commercial matters that arise in all debt agreements.

In some areas the standard documents scope out the range of possible options for a term; in others there is an agreed set of terms that are known as either the 'boilerplate' or 'LMA standard' terms.

Who Are the Parties to the Contract?

Clearly the borrower and lenders are party to the agreement.

The borrower will usually include the actual legal company borrowing and all of its subsidiaries and parent companies. The definition of 'borrower' will try and capture all legal entities in the group of companies both currently and in the future.

The Lenders will be a group of financial institutions making the loans. An **original lender** is a lender known at the time the deal completes, but not all of the institutions who ultimately become lenders will be known at the time the loans are made. Some of the lenders will take on the risk of the loans at completion with the intention of selling them to other institutions after the deal completes. These **lead arrangers** will be known and named and they will underwrite the whole amount of the debt needed to complete the deal. There

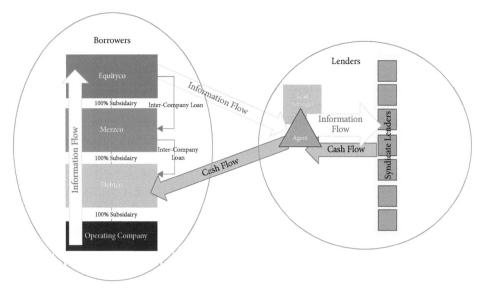

Figure 5.16. Role of the agent in a syndicated loan

may be one or more lead arrangers depending on the size of the transaction. These are usually banks and debt funds in smaller deals or investment banks in larger deals.

The lenders will charge an **arrangement fee** to the borrower based on the amount of the loans arranged. The lead arrangers will also charge an **underwrite fee** based on the amount and time that they are expecting to hold the whole of the loan.

There may be **other counterparties** to any loan agreement. These will include:

An **agent**, mandated to act on behalf of all the various lending parties to the contract in certain circumstances. This is an important co-ordinating role that defines who is responsible for administering the collection of lenders at any particular time (see Figure 5.16).

There will usually be a **security agent** or **trustee**, tasked with holding all of the legal documentation regarding the security held by the lenders. This will vary depending on whether the loans are structurally or contractually subordinated.

There may also be **hedge counterparties**, who are the institutions that are on the opposite side of any hedging arrangements, such as currency or interest rate swaps.

The lenders and various agents are collectively known as the **finance parties**, and you will see this term scattered throughout any debt contract. It essentially is the collective noun for the group of institutions with which the borrower is contracted in the loan agreement.

Ancillary Lenders and Facilities: What is a Letter of Credit?

Letters of credit, or LCs, are facilities that bridge international credit risks and facilitate trade across borders. If two companies wish to trade internationally there is a potentially large information asymmetry between them regarding each other's credit risk. Their bankers in contrast have a clearer view of both the credit risk of their customer and the credit

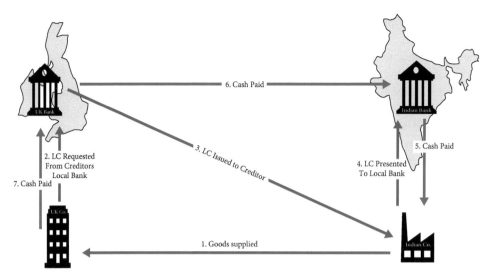

6. Cash Paid

5. Cash Paid

3. LC Issued to Creditor

2. LC Requested
From Creditors
Local Bank
7. Cash Paid

4. LC Presented
To Local Bank

1. Goods supplied

UK Bank

Indian Bank

UK Co.

Indian Co.

Figure 5.17. Diagram summarizing the operation of a letter of credit

risk of the other banks. Therefore the bank of the purchasers, who are familiar with the credit profile of the counter party bank and their own customer, can issue Letters of Credit backed by their own credit rating to seller who will present it to their own bank who will pay the amount owed.

Figure 5.17 illustrates the sequence of transactions.

Ancillary Lenders and Facilities: What is an RCF?

There will almost always be some form of **revolving committed facility** (RCF). This is a working capital facility that can be drawn and repaid over the life of the agreement. It can be thought of as being like an overdraft facility, except that it is committed for the life of the whole loan package. Overdrafts are facilities that are 'at call', meaning that the bank can cancel them at their discretion at any time that they see fit.

If the lenders are not clearing banks, they will not usually have the ability to provide these facilities. Debt funds will therefore require a clearing bank to provide this facility. These are typically called **ancillary lenders** and are included within **ancillary facilities**.

A **clearing bank** is a bank connected to the system to clear funds in a particular currency or market. In the US this includes the Federal Reserve automated clearing system and the private automated payments system. In the UK at the time of writing there are eleven members of the cheque and credit clearing system (representing nine banking groups) and in Europe there are various clearing systems for the EU area and other currencies. Without being diverted into a discussion about clearing systems, we make the essential point that any company will need to have direct access to the relevant clearing systems, often via some ancillary lender. The providers of these ancillary facilities will require security for their loans. This is usually in the form of a **super senior facility** which will place these lenders at the front of the queue if a company becomes insolvent.

What Is a Clean-Down Clause and Why are They Used?

The super senior revolving credit facility providers are lending solely to provide liquidity to the company over the course of its periodic, short-term working capital cycle. They will not want to allow the borrower to draw down funds from the revolving credit facility to pay the interest or principal of any of the other longer-term loan facilities. If the borrower uses the short-term facility to repay long-term debt, there is a potentially dangerous mismatch between the term of the borrower's assets and term of its liabilities. Remember that it is a core idea of corporate finance that you match the term of your assets and your liabilities: nobody should ever buy a house using an overdraft, or an ice cream using a five-year term loan.

To protect themselves the RCF lenders may insert a **clean-down** clause. This clause requires the borrower to have a period of some length (ranging from a few days in a given period upwards) when the RCF is not drawn at all. The idea is that if a company cannot clean down its short-term borrowing facility from time to time, there is an embedded element of long-term borrowing in the debt. An analogy in personal borrowing might be a situation where a person could never pay off their credit card bill without borrowing from someone else.

Clean-down also has implications for the amount of tier one capital that needs to be provided by the banks extending the RCF. It therefore impacts both risk and the cost of providing the facility.

What Is a Cash Sweep and Where Is It Used?

A **cash sweep** requires that the borrower use all cash above a certain limit to reduce borrowings. The idea is that excess cash is not held on the balance sheet of the borrower but is swept away to reduce borrowings and hence lenders' risk.

Cash sweeps are a mechanism that requires the borrower to use any excess cash to repay debt early. The mechanics can be intricate because it is not easy to decide when cash should be swept due to seasonality and capex requirements, nor is it as obvious as it seems to define what cash actually is (is it cash in a bank account or the cash-book balance on a particular day? Does it include short-term liquid assets and if not, how do you stop an astute finance director from sweeping cash into short term investments on the cash sweep day?)

Setting aside these details for the sake of clarity, the basic principle is that the lender has a call option on any cash over and above an agreed limit. That cash will be used to reduce the debt outstanding.

The bank will usually want to reduce the lowest priced tranche first, leaving the more expensive tranche outstanding. This reduces average life but still receives the higher margin.

The borrower will prefer to pay back the more expensive tranche. This reduces average life and margin. A pro rata reduction is a common compromise that leaves average life and margins intact.

Cash sweeps were the norm in the US and common in the UK for many years. They are predicated on the assumption that the lender wishes to reduce risk quickly. This is not the case for many non-bank lenders. As we saw, debt funds are paid fees only for cash 'in the ground' (i.e. lent). If they are repaid early this reduces and their fees are reduced accordingly. Therefore, a major contrast between debt funds and banks is the lack of cash sweeps in debt fund deals.

What Are Incremental Loans and Accordion Facilities?

Whereas the cash sweep and clean-down clauses aim to reduce the risks of the lender by accelerating the repayment of loans, the opposite is achieved by the creation of **incremental facilities**, also known as **accordion facilities**. An accordion facility is the option, but not the obligation, for the borrower to extend the facilities or to add to the facilities without having to negotiate a new contract from the lenders. The name derives from the metaphor of an accordion as an instrument that can be stretched.

The term 'accordion facility' is loose and has no generally accepted definition. It can be thought of as a generalization of a variety of committed but undrawn facilities that have always been part of a loan negotiation. For example, an acquisitive company may have an **acquisition facility**, one that requires the borrower to use the funds to acquire other businesses. Similarly, a **capex facility** is a facility to borrow only to invest in new fixed assets. A business that is growing rapidly will probably have an **undrawn working capital line** that grows as the business grows. Each of these are incremental facilities that may now be captured under the term 'accordion'.

The matters that will need to be negotiated at the time the accordion is established will include all the same items as any tranche of the loan agreement.

For example, a simple incremental facility might add a further $m to tranche A repayable pro rata (in proportion to) the current outstanding amount.

Conversely the accordion might be added to the most expensive tranche or spread across the whole facility equally. From an economic theory perspective, the accordion can be seen as a transfer of risk from the borrower to the lender. This is because the lender agrees terms for a future loan without having the benefit of the information they would have had if they had waited until the loan was needed. This should be reflected in a higher borrowing cost.

MFN, Right To Participate, and Sunset Clauses

The incremental facilities clause may not even have detailed terms. It may simply be the option for a lender to have a preferential sight of any future lending opportunity and to lend as part of any syndicate providing the new loans, via a right to participate clause. If it is, this will have a date when it ends, a **sunset clause**, and may have a right to match or beat any other lenders offer, via a **most favoured nation** (MFN) clause.

What Is the Structure of an Accordion Facility?

As we know, in all things to do with a negotiated transaction, it depends.

The borrower will usually argue that the accordion should be considered as a re-borrowing of debt already repaid, and therefore should be a redraw of tranche A first. This minimizes the cost of the incremental facility. The lenders will take the opposite view that any increase in borrowings should be at the highest rate of interest. In general the key questions will be the effect of the incremental facility on the average life of the facility, the margin of the loan, and the security of both the tranche the accordion is added to and the overall package.

In the absence of any particular negotiated position, you will generally see structures that broadly protect the banks from increases in the average life and lenders from increases in aggregate yield of the overall term debt package.

The accordion will attract a commitment fee payable by the borrower to the potential lender.

How Does an Accordion Facility Work in Practice?

Again, we are dealing in generalities when the specifics may vary, but a typical process will go something like this. The borrower writes to the agent saying they wish to drawdown £/$ million. The proposed terms of the new loan tranche will be in the request from the borrower.

The agent has the job of co-ordinating the lenders to see which ones wish to participate in the accordion tranche. Lenders usually (but not always) have the option, but not the obligation, to participate. They can decide not to lend. However, if they don't lend, they will have to refund the commitment fees that they have already been paid. This is bad news to bankers as they are targeted on fee income in their reward packages. We can therefore assume that any banker is usually positively incentivised to participate in the accordion tranche.

Each lender will have an entitlement to their share of the new loan. If others do not take up their share, the agent will offer this unallocated portion to those who do want to lend. It is of course possible that there is a shortfall after the unallocated portion has been offered to the existing lenders.

If this happens the agent may, after consulting with the borrower about the reasons for the shortfall, approach new lenders to top up the facility. The advantage to the borrower with this system is that it sharply reduces the administration required within the business's finance function. The agent takes on many of the market making roles that a finance director would usually manage with their advisers in a traditional debt raising.

Essentially the agent is building a syndicate for the new tranche and receiving a fee for doing so.

When Did Accordions Start Being Used?

Accordions emerged around 2009/10 and were sufficiently common that the LMA standard template swiftly incorporated them. As we describe above, they can be viewed in two ways: as an exercise of the power of the borrower to negotiate more certainty of future debt, or as a mutually cost-reducing way to set out the broader intentions of the borrower and the commitment of the lender to support them.

The question of whether or not accordions represent a material risk transfer from the borrower to the lender depends entirely on the specific detailed terms agreed. If a facility is a hard commitment to lend in the future subject only to minimal conditions (not in default on other loans, for example), it is a transfer of uncertainty and risk from the borrower to the lender.

If it just an option to review future lending opportunities with no commitment to lend, there is no risk increase to the lender.

The Risks of Leverage: Financial Covenants and Events of Default

To recap, a loan is a contractual obligation to repay interest and capital on pre-agreed dates. If the business performance deviates negatively from the business plan around which a debt package has been tailored, the debt structure will be put under pressure. A key part of tailoring the package is to 'stress-test' the scenarios in which the debt structure might become overly burdensome for the company.

Incurrence Covenants and Maintenance Covenants

As part of the debt package, the lender will agree a set of covenants that have to be periodically met (Figure 5.18).

These covenants can be simply that on a particular day the interest and capital due are paid. These are incurrence covenants found in all term loan agreements.

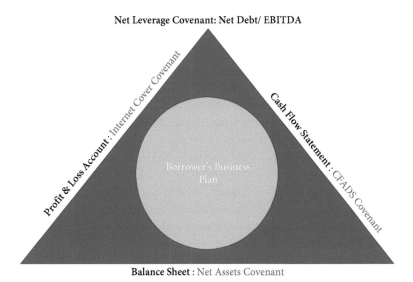

Figure 5.18. Schematic illustrating banking covenants
Source: The authors

In leveraged loans it is market practice to also see maintenance covenants that are a series of tests measuring the underlying business performance to establish whether or not the business plan that formed the basis of the debt structure is being met. They operate as both early warning devices to the bank of problems with a customer and, if the problems are serious, as powerful tools in the renegotiation of a company's capital structure.

Each set of covenants is individually negotiated for each transaction, but there are basic principles common to most.

One-to-One Cash Cover Covenant

As a general rule, banks will not lend money for the purpose of repaying their own, or others', borrowings: companies usually cannot repay term loans using an overdraft facility, for example. Therefore, there is usually a covenant that states that the borrowing company must be able to pay interest and capital out of cash generated by trading. This is the one-to-one cash cover covenant.

Leverage Covenant

In the past decade EBITDA has moved to the centre of the language of finance. The leverage covenant reflects the central place of this metric in modern leveraged finance and private equity. There will be a minimum level of EBITDA to net debt in most leveraged finance contracts with covenants. This may increase as times passes.

Net Assets Covenant

Banks also wish to preserve the asset base of the company that provides their security. They will therefore generally seek to impose a covenant stating that the net assets of the business must be greater than an agreed amount based upon the business plan. This is the net assets covenant.

Interest Cover Covenant

The bank will wish to see that interest is being paid out of profitable trading, not out of capital. They will therefore specify a ratio of interest to pre-interest profit that must be met. This is the interest cover covenant.

A breach of the interest covenant arises due to falling profits (as opposed to cash flow) or increasing interest rates.

The purpose of the various covenants is to monitor cash generation, profitability, and the asset base of a company against the business plan on an ongoing basis and to provide lenders with early warning signals if things go wrong.

Covenant Headroom

Each covenant will be set based on historic and forecast performance of the business. There will be headroom above the planned level of the ratio (i.e. an amount by which the ratio must be exceeded). This is usually in the range of 20 per cent to 40 per cent. Generally, high headroom favours borrowers, low headroom favours lenders.

An Event of Default and Corporate Failure

Failure to meet one or more of the covenants is an event of default which gives the banks the right to either increase the cost of the debt or potentially demand immediate repayment of their loans. It is relatively rare for a bank to seek to recover all the loans as soon as an event of default occurs. Typically they will seek to renegotiate the entire debt package on new terms that reflect what they see as the new circumstances of the business. This might, for example, mean rescheduling the loans to reduce the repayment in each year but charging a higher interest rate (and fees) for doing so. When a restructuring cannot be negotiated, a company may be sold or forced into administration, receivership, or liquidation when the assets of the company are realized to repay the debt.

What is Cov-Lite Lending?

From the borrower's perspective maintenance covenants offer no protections. They may encourage helpful communication with the lenders, but if breached, they simply transfer powers to the lenders. The equity sponsors will therefore want to negotiate either high headroom in a covenant or, preferably, eliminate the covenant entirely. If maintenance covenants are removed, the loan becomes a **cov-lite** loan.

In the high yield bond markets this has a particular definition, but more generally a loan is thought of as cov-lite if it has no, or materially weakened, maintenance covenants.

Cov-lite emerges when the supply of debt is high and the power to negotiate rises for the borrower. LBO funds have been particularly adept at negotiating cov-lite schemes, working continually to control risk and to stay in the driving seat for as long as possible in all scenarios. The effect of this on the risk to lenders has a been a topic of debate among regulators and commentators on many occasions.

How Can the Risks of Leverage be Mitigated?

As illustrated above, banking risk is generally caused by a combination of declining trading performance relative to the business plan and/or interest rate risk.

The risk of declining trading performance is anticipated when the business plan is finalized at the time of the transaction, and the most effective way to mitigate this type of risk is therefore to plan prudently.

However, as we shall see when we examine the equity structuring dynamics below, there are also strong incentives for management to produce an optimistic plan to increase the projected value of the equity and therefore their share of that equity. Furthermore, private equity funders will get higher debt and/or cheaper offers if more positive plans are used by the bankers to the transaction. Untangling the outcome of these powerful but contradictory incentives is a key feature of good due diligence.

Box 5.3 Findings: Does Higher Leverage Lead to Increased Likelihood of Failure? The Academic Evidence

---

There is some indication of a higher level of failure for those deals completed during boom years, especially during the first wave of the late 1980s. However, as a general point, the attention given to the claimed dangers of high capital leverage in the debate about private equity is quite misplaced since deals can sustain high capital leverage if they have high and stable interest cover which enables them to service the debt. Studies of larger US buyouts and UK research provide strong evidence that higher amounts of debt are associated with an increased probability of failure or the need for a restructuring to take place (Appendix 13).

   Higher turnover per employee and the reduction of employment on buyout is negatively associated with failure; this suggests the importance of measures taken to restructure an underperforming company early in the buyout life-cycle.

   P2Ps that subsequently enter receivership have higher initial default probability and distance to default than P2Ps that exited through IPO, trade sale, or secondary buyout, or that had no exit.

   Recent evidence comprising the population of private firms in the UK finds that after taking into account a large range of financial and non-financial factors, companies with higher leverage, whether a buyout or not, are significantly more likely to fail. Controlling for other factors including leverage, buyouts have a higher failure rate than non-buyouts with MBIs having a higher failure rate than MBOs, which in turn have a higher failure rate than PE-backed buyouts. However, MBOs and PE-backed deals completed post-2003, and the introduction of the Enterprise Act 2002 which changed the corporate bankruptcy regime in the UK, are not riskier than the population of non-buyout private firms if these other factors are controlled for.

Interest rate risk can be managed by borrowing at long-term fixed rates. This is expensive as the cost of fixed-rate loans is higher than variable rate loans to reflect the fact that the lender takes on the interest rate risk of the borrower.

   A variety of techniques exist to reduce, but not wholly eliminate, interest rate risk by hedging the interest rate on the loans. These include a variety of financial products including:

- swaps: the borrower of a fixed-rate loan swaps their interest rate exposure with another borrower who has a variable rate loan and pays them a fee to transfer the risk. These are arranged by a bank which will charge a fee for arranging the swap;
- caps: the borrower agrees a limit with the bank on their interest rate exposure. Up to the cap, the borrower still incurs the risk; above the cap the bank takes on the risk. This limits the risk to a known maximum over the term of the cap;
- collars: to reduce the cost of hedging the interest rate risk, a borrower may agree to both a cap with the bank and a collar below which any fall in interest rates will be to the benefit of the lenders not the borrowers. This effectively limits the interest rate to a maximum and minimum over the life of the arrangement.

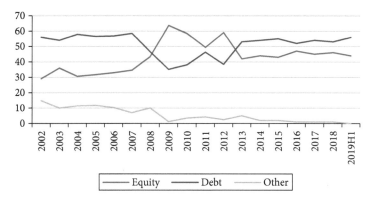

Figure 5.19. European deal structures (deals €100m or more, per cent)
Source: CMBOR/Equistone/Investec

Debt: Equity Ratio and the Equity Cushion

The lenders and banks will expect to see an appropriate sharing of risk in a financial package. The ratio of total bank debt to equity invested is an approximate measure of this risk. Since the detailed structure of the loan package in any particular transaction is not usually publicly available at the time of a transaction, the ratio of total debt to total equity is used by many commentators as a measure of the aggregate financial risk in the buyout market.

As discussed, and illustrated earlier, the amount of debt usually rises as interest rates fall (and vice versa) (see Figure 5.19).

Did the Largest Leveraged Buyouts Fail during the Recession?

Some transactions will have met plan and prospered despite the recession, whereas others will have underperformed. Of the ten largest receiverships of private equity-backed buyouts in the UK, five occurred in 2008 and the first half of 2009 (Table 5.20). However, to date, the only £1bn private equity-backed buyout to have gone into receivership in the UK is McCarthy & Stone. It needs to be borne in mind that many companies that have no contact with private equity have also filed for protection from their creditors. However, an increasing number of debt-for-equity swaps have been introduced to avoid highly geared companies entering receivership.

What are Propco/Opco Structures? A Special Case

In the early years of the buyout market most investors would not invest in businesses that generated most of their returns from property investment or development. The precise boundary of what constituted a property-based business was never entirely clear, but in the early 1990s following the collapse in UK property prices, a wave of innovative transactions involving properties were completed. The earliest transactions involved

Table 5.20. Largest UK private equity-backed receiverships

Buyout	Buyout year	Deal value (£m)	Receivership year
McCarthy & Stone (Mother Bidco)	2006	1,105.3	2009
BPC and Watmoughs/Polestar	1998	737.5	2008
Magnet	1989	630.7	1992
Orchid Pubs	2006	571	2008
Lowndes Queensway	1988	446.8	1990
Greycoat/G2 Estates	1999	282.5	2004
XL Leisure/Excel Airways	2006	225	2008
First Leisure (Nightclubs)/Whizalpha	2000	210.5	2004
Automotive Product Group	1995	181.2	2006
Finelist/Europe Auto Distribution	2000	159.2	2000
Landhurst	1990	157	1992
International Leisure Group	1987	155	1991
The Sweater Shop	1995	150	1998
Lambert Fenchurch/HLF Insurance/Heath	1999	130.9	2003
Tempo/KF Group	1999	130	2001
Ethel Austin	2004	122.5	2008
Hollis	1988	119.8	1991
Yardley (Old Bond Street Corporation)	1990	110	1998
Response Group	1988	102.8	1990
ESM/Wafer-Fab	1999	100	2002

Source: CMBOR/Investec/Equistone Partners Europe

companies operating pubs, following changes brought about by the competition authority's investigation into the pub and brewery industry.

The target company's balance sheet was carefully dissected into a company that owned properties and a company that operated businesses in the properties. A lease was then put in place between the two companies. The property company (propco) was structured and financed to appeal to investors seeking property exposure, and the operating company (opco) was separately financed (Figure 5.20). The structure capitalized on the different

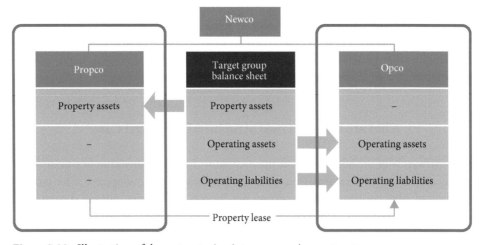

Figure 5.20. Illustration of the restructuring into a propco/opco structure

---

Box 5.4 Findings: What Are the Effects of Buyouts on Productivity and Efficiency? The Academic Evidence

---

US plant level data shows that MBO plants had higher total factor productivity (TFP) than representative establishments in the same industry before they changed owners (Appendix 15). MBO plants experienced significant improvements in TFP after the MBO, which could not be attributed to reductions in R&D, wages, capital investment, or layoffs of shop floor/blue-collar personnel.

More recent US evidence shows that private equity-backed firms increase productivity post-transaction by more than control group firms and that this increase is in large part due to more effective management and private equity being more likely to lead to closure of underperforming establishments.

UK evidence based on company-level data shows significant improvements in efficiency for up to four years post-buyout compared to non-buyout firms, although the main effect appears to be in the first two years. Divisional buyouts show higher efficiency improvements than private and secondary buyouts and more experienced private equity firms have a greater impact on post-buyout efficiency.

Data for approximately 36,000 UK manufacturing establishments, of which some 5,000 were buyouts, shows that MBO establishments were less productive than comparable plants before the transfer of ownership but experienced a substantial increase in productivity after buyout. These improvements appear to be due to measures undertaken by new owners or managers to reduce the labour intensity of production, through the outsourcing of intermediate goods and materials.

---

appetites for risk in property investors and non-property investors. Effectively the companies sold and leased back property assets with investment companies owned by their own shareholders.

The structures enabled the group to access separate pools of investment for property assets and to isolate property assets from trading companies at the low point of the property market. As with many innovations seen in private equity, there was nothing particularly new in the ideas behind the structures. The real innovation was the creation of a market for finance to efficiently fund this type of structure.

Once these structures had been created and perfected, markets rapidly utilized the precedent in an array of different situations. It is a general characteristic of the private equity industry that it is an early adopter of many financial innovations that were actually created elsewhere, such as securitization, propco/opco, CDOs, and others.

The Risks of Propco/Opco Structures

Propco/opco structures are appropriate for businesses with significant freehold property assets and predictable revenues to service the lease terms. The economics are in principle no different to those of a retailer who leases shops. Most leases are in a relatively standard form.

Box 5.5 Findings: To What Extent Do Private Equity Deals Involve Strategies to Grow the Business? The Academic Evidence

---

Buyouts are associated with refocusing the strategic activities of the firm, especially for deals involving listed corporations (Appendix 16). Divestment activity by buyouts appears to be greater than for comparable non-buyouts. However, US, UK, and Dutch evidence from the 1980s shows that buyouts are followed by significant increases in new product development and other aspects of corporate activity such as engaging in entrepreneurial ventures, technological alliances, increased R&D, and patent citations. Private equity firms also contribute to the development of improved management processes and management control systems that facilitate strategic change in different types of buyouts. Private equity funders contribute to keeping added-value strategies on track, assisting in new ventures and broadening market focus, and in having the knowledge to be able to assess investment in product development. Majority PE-backed buyouts significantly increase entrepreneurial management practices, but increased debt negatively affects entrepreneurial management. More recent evidence shows that higher levels of private equity firm experience and intensity of involvement are associated with higher levels of growth, especially in divisional buyouts.

This enables the investment market to be efficient, which helps to reduce the cost of the lease to the lessor. A standard UK institutional lease would:

- be FRI (full, repair, and insure). This means that the lessor has to deliver the property back in the same state it was taken on in. Any shortfall needs to be made up by a dilapidations payment;
- have upwards-only rent review clauses, meaning that rents never go down. Often there is a clause stating that the periodic increase will be the higher of an independent reviewer's estimate or RPI (inflation).

In the case of Southern Cross Group, a large retirement and care home group, the company was reorganized into a propco/opco structure. The propcos were owned by institutional property investors on institutional, FRI, upwards-only leases. The opco was floated on the London Stock Exchange providing an exit for its private equity owners.

Following flotation the group came under intense fee pressure from, among others, public authorities who were paying for the care of many of Southern Cross's residents. The combination of falling fees and upwards-only rents led Southern Cross to become insolvent and the company failed. The assets were taken over by a variety of alternative providers and none of the residents was made homeless. Nevertheless, the example was a stark reminder that leases are, in all economic characteristics, obligations that have to be met or the business will lose the premises concerned and in all likelihood fail. International financial reporting standards have since changed the way companies account for most leases to treat them as a form of debt.

Asset stripping as seen in the late 1960s, involved buying a company, selling all its assets, and keeping the proceeds. The company would then probably be liquidated, and the

---

Box 5.6 Findings: Do Private Equity Deals and Buyouts Have Adverse Effects on Investment and R&D? The Academic Evidence

US evidence from the 1980s strongly supports the view that capital investment falls immediately following the LBO as a result of the increased leverage (Appendix 16). The evidence on UK MBOs from the 1980s indicates that asset sales are offset by new capital investment, particularly in plant and equipment. The effect of buyouts on R&D is less clear, although on balance US evidence suggests that there is a reduction. However, as many LBOs are in low R&D industries, the overall effect may be insubstantial. There is evidence from buyouts that do have R&D needs that this expenditure is used more effectively, and that Private Equity buyouts result in increased patent citations and more focused patent portfolios.

---

creditors left unpaid. This is a criminal offence in the UK and virtually every other country. It is illegal to purchase a business with the intention of selling its assets and leaving its creditors (including its employees and pensioners) unpaid.

To prevent asset stripping, prior to October 2008 it was illegal for a private company to give financial assistance for the purchase of its own shares unless it went through a process (established in the Companies Act 1981) commonly known as the 'whitewash' procedure.

Financial assistance arises in leveraged buyouts when banks, or other lenders, take security on the assets of the target company. The banks would not lend without the security given by the company being acquired. The acquired company is therefore assisting in the raising of the finance to complete the acquisition.

In a whitewash, the directors of the target company at the date of the transaction gave a statutory declaration that at the time this was given, the company would continue to be a going concern. 'Going concern' in this context is usually taken to mean it is reasonably expected that it would be able to pay all of its current and future creditors for at least the next year. It was a criminal offence to give a statutory declaration knowing it to be false.

The whitewash procedure was only available to private limited companies, not public limited companies.

Under the Companies Act 2006, the prohibition on financial assistance by private companies was removed with effect from October 2008, but it remains in place for public companies.

What Protection Exists for Publicly Quoted Companies?

In a public-to-private transaction, the public limited company, or plc, must be converted into a private limited company prior to giving financial assistance. This can only happen after a company is delisted from the stock exchange. Banks therefore cannot perfect their security in a UK P2P until after the company has delisted and been converted to a private limited company.

To delist and convert from a plc to private limited company requires the consent of a majority (75 per cent of all votes) at an extraordinary general meeting. However, a private

> ### Box 5.7 Findings: To What Extent Is Replacement of Management Important? The Academic Evidence
>
> Recent US evidence indicates that half of CEOs in private equity-backed buyouts are replaced within two years. Unlike public companies, boards in PE-backed buyouts are likely to replace entrenched CEOs and are more likely to replace CEOs if pre-buyout return on assets is low (Appendix 16). Larger deals' outperformance is often associated with significant replacement of CEOs and CFOs, either at the time of the deal or afterwards, and the leveraging of external support.

equity fund will want to acquire 100 per cent of the shares of the target company, which it can do under the Companies Act once 90 per cent of shareholders (by value) have accepted the offer, since the remainder of the shares are then capable of being compulsorily acquired (or 'squeezed out'). Alternatively, a court sanctioned scheme of arrangement may be used as a mechanism to secure 100 per cent control subject to a vote of qualifying shareholders being supported by a 75 per cent majority by value and 50 per cent majority by number.

For this reason, leveraged offers for public companies are often conditional upon achieving at least 75 per cent acceptances and may even require 90 per cent acceptance.

The delisting and conversion into a private limited company may be some weeks after the offer has been completed. In the intervening period the bank will be at risk due to the imperfection of the security. It is expensive (and often impossible) to syndicate debt prior to perfecting security. This process therefore extends the period that banks are at risk. Typically, there are penalty clauses in the debt package that are triggered if security is not perfected within a given period after completion.

The costs of undertaking a P2P that fails to be completed can be high. Obtaining irrevocable commitments to support the bid from key shareholders can alleviate some of the uncertainties associated with the bid process. The announcement of substantial irrevocable commitments may make other potential bidders less likely to enter the contest with an alternative bid. If they do, a competing bid will have to be made within twenty-one days of the posting of the offer documents to avoid the irrevocable commitments becoming binding offer acceptances. It may, however, be difficult for an alternative buyer to complete due diligence within the required time.

Existing shareholders may have the incentive to give irrevocable commitments to encourage other shareholders to accept the offer. However, they may be able to negotiate conditions that enable them to sell their shares to a new bidder offering a higher price (so-called 'soft' commitments). Irrevocable undertakings may therefore, in fact, be revocable.

Institutional and Management Equity

The process of structuring a debt package is the first step in constructing a financeable offer.

In the second step, there are three questions at the centre of the process:

(1) What is the appropriate amount of equity to raise to fund the bid and the future needs of the company?
(2) How much equity should be put aside to recruit or retain and then motivate a management team and any other key personnel to execute the business plan that underpins the financing structure?
(3) How much equity do the banks expect to see invested?

How Much Institutional Equity?

To understand the structuring of an equity investment we need to understand the interaction between pricing a transaction, financial risk, and equity returns.

Internal Rates of Return and Short-Termism

Private equity funds have rules of thumb regarding acceptable rates of return. To a degree these vary over time as inflation and returns on alternative assets vary. However, due in part to the long-term nature of the funds' commitments, the correlation with the returns of alternative asset classes is very low. An equity IRR of 20 per cent is a commonly heard yardstick (it used to be higher).

Returns have historically generally been measured and talked about as internal rates of return (IRRs). As we discussed at length in Chapter 3, an IRR is the annualized return on an investment. As illustrated in Table 5.21 (where we have highlighted the area of targeted market norms) and Figure 5.21, IRRs are very sensitive to time.

When investments are rapidly turned, IRRs tend to be higher, but when investments are held longer, other things being equal, IRRs tend to a lower stable long-term rate.

It is a fact that maximizing IRRs does not necessarily maximize the return from an investment portfolio. If, for example, the alternative investments available to the partners in a particular fund have lower projected returns than the assets that they currently hold, returns are maximized by holding the current investment, even if the IRR declines as a

Table 5.21. IRRs at varying exit years and varying exit multiples of original investment

		Years invested								
		2	3	4	5	6	7	8	9	10
Money multiple	1.0	0%	0%	0%	0%	0%	0%	0%	0%	0%
	1.5	50%	22%	14%	11%	8%	7%	6%	5%	5%
	2.0	100%	41%	26%	19%	15%	12%	10%	9%	8%
	2.5	150%	58%	36%	26%	20%	16%	14%	12%	11%
	3.0	200%	73%	44%	32%	25%	20%	17%	15%	13%
	3.5	250%	87%	52%	37%	28%	23%	20%	17%	15%
	4.0	300%	100%	59%	41%	32%	26%	22%	19%	17%

Source: The authors

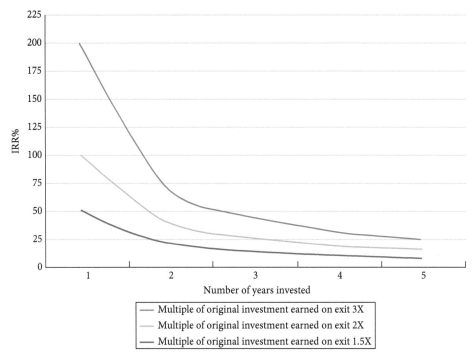

Figure 5.21. Sensitivity of IRR to time at various money multiples of investment
Source: The authors

result. In general, maximizing the net present value of a portfolio is not the same as maximizing the IRR of each individual investment.

The impact of using IRR as a measure is therefore to give undue weight to the speed with which returns are realized and may *in extremis* result in severely sub-optimal allocation of resources. In reaction to this and, cynics have argued, the general fall in returns seen in funds, the private equity industry also increasingly uses a cruder measure of 'cash-on-cash' or 'money on invested capital' (MOIC). This is analogous to the value per £1 (TVPI) invested that we discussed when talking about valuation in Chapter 3. Returns of two to three times the original investment are often quoted as targets in buyouts, but any investment that doubles in a reasonable time will probably have a broadly satisfactory return.

Over the years the target rate of return in a 'vanilla' buyout has been falling due to increased competition from new entrants to the private equity market as well as reflecting the sustained period of lower interest rates and lower inflation. The rule of thumb is currently 'double your money in four years' and as shown in Table 5.21 and Table 5.22 equates to an IRR of 20 per cent. Trebling the value of an investment in six years also equates to an IRR of 20 per cent. Twenty years ago those norms were 25 per cent IRR by doubling/trebling money in three and five years respectively.

The analysis above ignores the effect of both fees and yields on returns. In general, an IRR can be approximately decomposed into two elements:

$$IRR = (\text{to a first approximation}) \, \text{yield to maturity} + \text{annual capital growth}$$

Table 5.22. Multiple of money at varying IRRs and years of exit

		IRR of investment							
		5.0%	10.0%	15.0%	20.0%	25.0%	30.0%	35.0%	40.0%
Years invested	1	1.05	1.10	1.15	1.20	1.25	1.30	1.35	1.40
	2	1.10	1.21	1.32	1.44	1.56	1.69	1.82	1.96
	3	1.16	1.33	1.52	1.73	1.95	2.20	2.46	2.74
	4	1.22	1.46	1.75	2.07	2.44	2.86	3.32	3.84
	5	1.28	1.61	2.01	2.49	3.05	3.71	4.48	5.38
	6	1.34	1.77	2.31	2.99	3.81	4.83	6.05	7.53
	7	1.41	1.95	2.66	3.58	4.77	6.27	8.17	10.54
	8	1.48	2.14	3.06	4.30	5.96	8.16	11.03	14.76
	9	1.55	2.36	3.52	5.16	7.45	10.60	14.89	20.66
	10	1.63	2.59	4.05	6.19	9.31	13.79	20.11	28.93

Source: The authors

Thus, if an investment yields 10 per cent (on cost) per annum and grows in value by 15 per cent (compound) per annum, the IRR will be around 25 per cent.

Continuing yield is clearly more certain than unrealized capital gain. Private equity funds will therefore seek to maximize their yield, consistent with the banking structure and investment plans of the business.

Where a cash yield cannot be paid, private equity funds specify a preferred yield on their equity that is accrued but not paid until exit. This effectively guarantees a certain annual return to the PE fund ahead of management. Where the yield is greater than the annual growth in capital value, this mechanism will appropriate capital from management to the PE fund. Management and their advisers need to be very wary of structures that have a high yield accruing.

In the UK and Europe this is usually achieved by using a PIK loan as part of the equity structure. In the US and North America a rolled-up preferred dividend or liquidation preference is used to achieve the same result. We explain these more fully later in this chapter, in the section on Institutional and Management Equity.

While a high yield may appropriate value, a continuing yield also reduces the required capital gain to generate the target IRR which may be to the advantage of management.

It is somewhat paradoxical that the impact of fees on returns is not treated consistently when calculating IRRs. From the perspective of the borrower a fee can be regarded as no different to an advanced payment of interest. Therefore, all fees should be included in the calculation of the cost of funds. Private equity funds, however, generally exclude arrangement and monitoring fees received from the company when calculating their returns in their own models. In part this reflects the different treatment of fee income in different funds that we discussed earlier.

Arguably the most appropriate forward-looking measure should be to calculate present values using the hurdle rate of return of the fund for the carried interest calculation. Maximizing this value would achieve maximized profit over the life of the fund and the personal rewards of the general partners and staff in the carried interest scheme.

A private equity fund manager will therefore have to form a view as to what a reasonable rate of return for a particular investment will be relative to the industry norm of aiming to achieve 20 per cent IRR or above in successful investments. An acceptable rate of return will reflect the private equity manager's view of the risks, both company specific and of the overall sector and the economy.

How Much Equity Do Management Get in a Buyout?

We look at the detail of management stakes in Chapter 6, but there are two principal limits on how much equity management get in a buyout structure:

- the residual claimant: the maximum a management team can get is what is left after all the other providers of finance have received their returns; and
- the motivational minimum: there will also be a minimum required in order to retain and incentivise management to deliver the business plan and hence generate the returns of all parties to the transaction.

In most buyouts where management do not hold equity prior to the transaction, the amount of money they have to invest rarely has a significant influence on the amount of equity they receive. In many buyouts, management are required to invest what is often called **hurt money**—i.e. money that is material in the context of the individual's wealth. Although in recent years the traditional rule of thumb has begun to break down, it used to be the case that the senior manager in a team might be expected to invest in the region of the greater of one year's gross salary or a third of their net wealth in a typical buyout (whichever was greater). This is now highly negotiable.

In transactions where management have a significant equity stake pre-buyout, the position is different. The key is again to understand the impact on incentives and alignment of interests. The private equity firm will not wish to see substantial 'cash out' for the manager/ shareholders who are key to the ongoing achievement of the investment thesis. They will argue that this reduction in cash at risk reduces the incentives of the management team to maximize value growth.

Conversely management will often argue that taking 'money off the table' reduces their personal risk, allowing them to pursue a higher risk/higher reward strategy with their remaining wealth to the mutual benefit of themselves and the new investors.

It has become something of an industry standard in Europe for management teams to reinvest around 50 per cent of any proceeds they receive in a transaction, but this is, as usual, negotiable depending on the particular individual circumstances.

What Is the Equity Illusion?

Management teams need to understand the effect of financial engineering on the amount of money they may receive at exit. In particular they need to be acutely aware of what we term the 'equity illusion'.

We coined the term 'equity illusion' to reflect the fact that management teams who focus only on maximizing their ordinary equity percentage are often creating dramatically sub-optimal incentives. Furthermore, as management teams have become takers of terms offered by private equity houses in competitive auctions, there is a material risk that the terms offered appear to create alignment, but when properly analysed are in fact creating illusions. This is unresearched and unreported in academic work.

In a typical quoted company senior board members and managers often receive options to buy equity in the future. There is academic research that shows that in US quoted companies CEOs may receive around 3–5 per cent of the company. The researchers then point out that management teams in PE-backed buyouts receive on average about 7.5–10 per cent of the equity in the business. This comparison is however fundamentally flawed. It is an example of the equity illusion.

In a quoted company there is only third-party debt (and perhaps rarely some preference shares) that has to be repaid before the equity shares the excess (if there is any). In a buyout there are both third party debt and PE-owned loans that roll up interest during the investment (or rolled up dividends and/or liquidation preference in the US model). If we compare the effects of these different structures on two otherwise identical companies (and ignore transaction costs) as in Table 5.23, we can easily see that the equity is not equivalent and is not always, in a meaningful sense, higher in an LBO.

If we compare the equity profit to management at different assumed five-year exit enterprise values we see one fundamental difference: options have no downside and the returns on sweet equity (the equity allocated to management in a management buyout) have to exceed the cost of the private equity loan stock before they have value, thereafter they are amplified by leverage (see Figure 5.22).

All other things equal, the management team in an LBO will be worse off at negative or low increases in enterprise value than the holders of options in quoted companies because:

(1) they pay for their equity at completion, whereas option holders can avoid paying by letting them lapse; and
(2) the PE fund loanstock accumulates interest that appropriates value to the PE fund investors before the management are paid their equity share.

Table 5.23. Comparison of equivalent companies with either an option for 3.0 per cent of the equity over the base cost or 7.5 per cent of the geared equity in an LBO of the same business

		Public company option		LBO sweet equity	
		Year 0	Year 5	Year 0	Year 5
Enterprise value		100.0	200.0	100.0	200.0
Third-party debt		50.0	0.0	50.0	0.0
Private equity PIK debt		0.0	0.0	45.0	79.3
PE PIK debt interest	12.00%				
Equity value		50.0	200.0	5.0	120.7
Assumed exit year	5				
Management equity %		3.00%	3.00%	7.50%	7.50%
Equity value			6.0		9.1
Option strike price		1.5	1.5		0.0
Cost of equity				0.4	0.4
Management proceeds		0.0	4.5	0.4	8.7

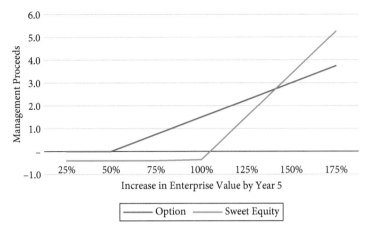

Figure 5.22. Comparison of the equity value received by managers in the scenario above at various enterprise values exiting in year 5

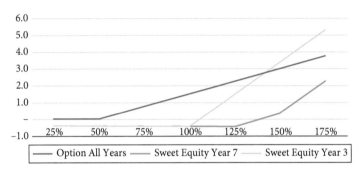

Figure 5.23. Effect on cash profit to management of exit in different years if loanstock interest is rolling up vs a public company option scheme in an equivalent company

This has a further implication to management. The longer they wait to exit, the more value will be rolled up into the PE loan notes and the less will be accruing to them. Again, comparing the same like-for-like scenarios but flexing the number of years until exit is achieved, gives the landscape of returns shown in Figure 5.23.

The longer it takes to exit, the harder it becomes to generate equity value that exceeds the comparable option scheme. If the exit takes over seven years, it becomes increasingly difficult to exceed break-even.

This is important in a cyclical economy. If the valuation of businesses moves cyclically then it is possible that a combination of delayed execution of the business plan and a downturn in the valuation cycle will leave management with little or no equity value. This creates acute misalignment in LBOs that have long lifetimes and that do not deliver a sharp value increase.

The two analyses show that it is not the equity percentage that determines how much you receive as a management team, but the overall equity structure.

To drive home the point we show how the amount received by management in an exit in year 5 of the same business varies with the loanstock interest rate (Figure 5.24).

The higher the interest rate on the loanstock, the less management receive, and because the loan interest compounds annually this situation gets progressively worse as time passes.

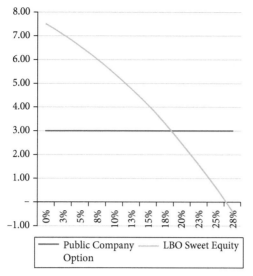

Figure 5.24. Effect of loanstock interest rates on management equity profit in an LBO vs options in an equivalent public company (assuming exit in year 5 as above and an Exit EV of 150)

In general, if the loan stock interest on PIK debt is greater than the rate of increase in enterprise value, eventually the ordinary equity/common stock, including the management's equity, will become worthless. Similar arithmetic applies to US-style equity structures with liquidation preference and rolled-up preferred dividends, although the lack of compounding reduces the effect. The length of time it takes for the compounding of interest to start to eat into the management equity value depends on two things:

(1) the initial proportion of PE equity in deal with a preferred PIK return. The higher the proportion, the greater the compounding effect; and
(2) the difference between the PIK rate and the compound growth in enterprise value. The more the PIK interest exceeds the enterprise value CAGR (compound annual growth rate) the faster the equity will become worthless.

In the limit, if the deal is 100 per cent funded by private equity loan stock and that loanstock accrues interest at a faster rate than the enterprise value increases, management will never receive any return on their investment, even if they own 100 per cent of the ordinary shares (Figure 5.25).

The equity illusion incentivises management to increase bank borrowing as long as the bank or fund debt is cheaper than the equity loanstock or preferred ordinary shares.

Therefore, if you are negotiating on behalf of the management team you should concentrate on both maximizing the equity percentage and minimizing the loanstock interest rate/preferred dividends; conversely PE funds will seek to have high loanstock interest both to protect downside scenarios and to strongly focus on rapid implementation of a plan that creates high growth in enterprise value (see Table 5.24 and Figure 5.25).

In general, the equity package needs to be aligned with the business strategy. A strategy based on a rapid repositioning or turnaround realized via a quick exit might have a higher

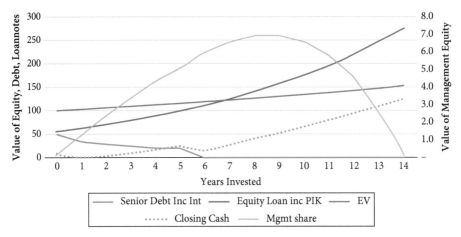

Figure 5.25. Management equity is materially impacted by the financial engineering in complex ways

Table 5.24. Trade-off in management equity value between equity percentage and PIK loan note interest (year 5)

		Management Equity %ge				
		10%	15%	20%	25%	30%
	8%	3.69	5.53	7.38	9.22	11.07
	9%	3.30	4.95	6.60	8.25	9.90
Loanstock PIK Yield	10%	2.89	4.34	5.79	7.23	8.68
	11%	2.47	3.71	4.94	6.18	7.42
	12%	2.04	3.05	4.07	5.09	6.11
	13%	1.58	2.38	3.17	3.96	4.75
	14%	1.12	1.67	2.23	279	3.35
	15%	0.63	0.95	1.26	1.58	1.89

yielding PIK note, and a higher management equity stake, than a more organic strategy with a planned longer hold period.

Problems arise when the original equity structure turns out to have been built on incorrect assumptions. If the performance is simply much worse than originally planned, it may be wholly equitable that management have no value in their equity. However, if the strategy changes from, say, rapid buy and build to a slower organic approach, the misalignment can arise in ways that require a restructuring. These negotiations are very difficult to win for management after the initial deal is done. Most power in these matters passes formally to the institutional investors.

In successful investments management will almost always be important in managing and maximizing the value in any exit. This provides an appropriate point to renegotiate to eliminate any misalignment that has occurred.

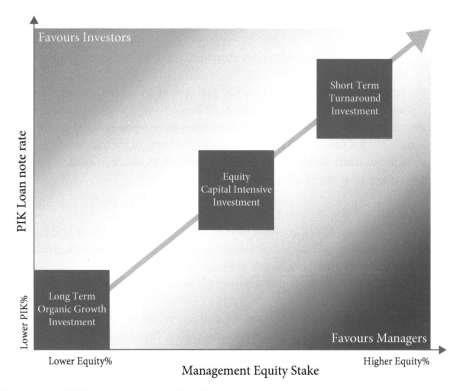

Figure 5.26. PIK interest/equity trade-off

What Is Rolling Over an Investment?

When we discussed the key terms in an equity investment, we briefly described the roll-over of equity by a vendor. If the business is a founder-owned business (or an existing PE-backed company with manager shareholders), the sale may be a partial sale to a new investor with the founders 'rolling over' some of their proceeds into the new company. Economically you can think of this as simply selling for cash then instantaneously buying an investment in the newco with some portion of the proceeds. There are knotty tax issues (which we deal with in the section on taxation) that mean that in reality the vendor sells for a mixture of cash, shares in Newco, and loan-notes issued by Newco. The mechanics work as follows.

Let us imagine a transaction of £100m where the private equity investor wishes to have the vendors remain as co-investors on the same terms for £20m to create a meaningful alignment of interests. The economics are relatively straightforward and we can summarize them in a simple step by step description:

(1) The investors invest £100m in the Newco group (£20m subscribed in shares in Topco and £80m lent to Finco).
(2) They push the £10m cash from the share subscription into Finco by making a £20m inter-company loan. The end result is that Topco owns Finco and Finco has £100m in cash.
(3) Finco then uses the £100m in cash to buy the target company from the vendor.

(4) The vendor receives £100m.

(5) The vendor:

    a) uses £2m of the proceeds to buy shares off the PE Fund equating to 20 per cent of Topco, and

    b) lends the Newco group £18m (20 per cent of £90m) of the debt from the investors, giving a total investment of £20m.

(6) Newco group uses the vendor's cash from the loan to repay £18m of the investors' loans. (The PE fund could just sell £18m of the loans to the vendors, but usually there are different rights attached to each loan, so it's easier to create a new loan and repay part of the existing one.)

The end result is shown in Table 5.25.

At the end the private equity investors own 80 per cent of the new group and have lent it £72m and the vendors own 20 per cent of the group and have lent it £18m. There is an inter-company loan of £20m from Newco to Finco.

Two particular issues arise with this sequence of transactions:

(1) *Sequential transactions and drawdown and repayment of private equity funds.* In theory there are a series of transactions happening. Investors buy shares and make loans that are subsequently repaid. No investor would want to draw down funds

Table 5.25. Management equity is materially impacted by the financial engineering in complex ways

Version One: The Economics £m	PE Fund	TopCo	Finco	Vendor
Investment In Newco				
PE Fund Buys £10m Shares	−10	10		
PE Lends £90m to Finco	−90		90	
Topco Lends Finco £10m		−10	10	
Acquisition of Target				
Finco Buys Target From Vendor for £100m			−100	100
Reinvestment by Vendor				
Vendor Buys 20% of Shares In Topco From PE for £2m	2			−2
Vendor Lends Finco £18m (20% of £90m)			18	−18
Finco Repays £18m of PE Loan	18		−18	
Final Cash Position	−80	0	0	80
Resulting Structure	PE Fund	TopCo	Finco	Vendor
Topco Shares	−8	10	0	−2
Finco Loans	−72	−10	100	−18
Total	−80	0	100	−20
Cash flow	−80	0	0	80

Table 5.26. PIK interest/equity tradeoff

Version Two: Rollover £m	PE Fund	TopCo	Finco	Vendor
Investment In Newco				
PE Fund Buys £8m Shares	−8	8		
PE Lends £72m to Finco	−72		72	
Topco Lends Finco £10m		−8	8	
Acquisition of Target				
Finco Buys Target From				
Vendor for £80m Cash			−80	80
Finco issues 2m Shares to Vendor		2		−2
Finco Issues £18m Loannote to vendor			18	−18
Final Position	−80	2	18	60
Resulting Structure	**PE Fund**	**TopCo**	**Finco**	**Vendor**
Shares	−8	10	0	−2
Loans	−72	−8	98	−18
Total	−80	2	98	−20

that are going to be immediately repaid. Therefore, in practice you would simply make all these transactions happen at the same time and transfer the net proceeds rather than doing them sequentially as described. Nevertheless, if the contracts say that the sequence described is what happened, then the contracts are the deal. The contracts are what a court will look at if there is any dispute in the future. There is a risk that the separation of each step disguises the reality of the deal.

(2) *Taxation and rollover relief.* The tax issues in this series are intricate. When the vendor sells for £100m they will make a loss or a gain. If it is a gain, that gain is liable to capital gains tax. The vendor therefore would receive less cash than £100m after tax. However, if the vendor had only sold 80 per cent of the shares in the target, rather than 100 per cent, there would have been no gain (or loss) on the 20 per cent they did not sell. It has therefore been (successfully) argued that if you look at the substance of the transaction, the vendor is really selling 80 per cent of their shareholding and rolling the remaining 20 per cent over into the new structure.

Therefore 80 per cent of the cost of the shares the vendor held should be deducted to calculate the gain on the 80 per cent received in cash. The remaining 20 per cent of the cost should be a carried forward at the existing base cost of the new investment in the Newco group and taxed only when it turns into cash.

To achieve this in the UK the tax Advisers will usually write to the tax authorities asking them to agree that the structure is a commercial arrangement and is therefore eligible for so-called roll-over relief.

To eliminate all of these sequencing issues (but still requiring clearance by the tax authorities) the deal is tweaked so that rather than receiving cash and reinvesting, or not selling 20 per cent and rearranging the capital structure, the Newco group pays the vendor the value of £100m in a mixture of £80m cash, £2m shares in Topco, and £18m loan-notes from Finco.

The issue of loan notes is equivalent to issuing free bonds. The company receives no money from the vendors but agrees to pay them £18m plus interest on certain dates in the

Table 5.27. European divestment numbers by type of exit

Positive Ratchet	Shares	Equity %	Negative Ratchet	Shares	Equity %
No of Shares Pre-Ratchet			No of Shares Pre-Ratchet		
Management	1,500	15.0%	Management	2,125	20.0%
PE Fund	8,500	85.0%	PE Fund	8,500	85.0%
Total	10,000	100.0%	Total	10,625	100.0%
Ratchet Shares Issued*	625	5.0%	Ratchet Shares Deferred#	−625	−5.0%
Post Ratchet Equity Stakes			Post Ratchet Equity Stakes		
Management	2,125	20.00%	Management	1,500	15.00%
PE Fund	8,500	80.00%	PE Fund	8,500	85.00%
Total	10,625	100.00%	Total	10,000	100.00%

* New shares issued and Treated as an option in UK tax law   #converted in to worthless deferred shares

future. The terms of these loan notes will be negotiated between the PE fund managers and the vendors. This is illustrated in Table 5.26.

A Note on Equity Ratchets

Where agreement cannot be reached between the private equity fund manager and management on a simple equity split, a performance ratchet may be put in place. A ratchet is a mechanism that varies the equity share of management depending on the achievement of certain objectives, typically driven by exit valuation or the IRR of the PE fund on exit. There are two types of ratchet (see Table 5.27 for examples):

- positive ratchets increase the equity stake of the management team if certain things are achieved; and
- negative ratchets reduce the equity stake of the management team if certain things are *not* achieved.

Behavioural economics suggest that in general 'carrots beat sticks' when you want to motivate people to do something. Therefore, positive ratchets ('carrots') are strongly commercially preferred.

Taxation of ratchets is complicated and needs careful consideration in structuring any agreement. Broadly in the UK a positive ratchet has been seen by the tax authorities as the granting of an option to purchase equity at below market value contingent on achieving some goal. This option has value and that value is a taxable benefit if it is associated with an individual's employment. This tax is payable whether or not the option ever gets exercised.

Therefore, in general, the taxation position in the UK leans towards negative ratchets. Negative ratchets operate by selling or giving away shares (or more usually converting into worthless deferred shares) and therefore there is no taxable benefit to the employee if the ratchet does not operate.

There is therefore a tension between the commercial and the tax imperatives. Commercially you wish to create a positive incentive, but from a tax perspective this creates additional cash costs for the management.

In general ratchets are messy, complicated, and costly to administer. This, coupled with the reduction in the management team's power to negotiate the deal with the private equity house directly in any auction process, has seen a decline in the use of ratchets.

Refinancing and Exits

Types of Exit

All private equity transactions are structured with an exit in mind—it is the defining feature of the investment strategy. Historically there were three exit routes:

- trade sale: sale of the business to a corporate acquirer;
- flotation on a stock market;
- receivership and liquidation.

This publication does not explain these types of exit as they are well understood. However, new routes to exit include:

- secondary buyout/sale to another private equity fund;
- leveraged recapitalization/repayment of loans and preference shares; and
- secondary market transactions including the sale of portfolios of investments to other financial institutions.

These are discussed in more detail below.

Not all exits crystallize increases in value; some investments are written off or down. We aggregate insolvencies with the forced takeover of companies by their banks as 'creditor exits' in the data below. The idea is to capture 'bad losers' where the equity is worthless, not the specific route whereby that worthlessness is crystallized.

What Has Been the Pattern of Exits from Private Equity Deals?

The number of enterprises globally owned by private equity funds has risen continuously over the past thirty years. Simultaneously the number of quoted companies has fallen on the major stock markets in the world. As shown in Figure 5.27, the period from 1995 to 2013 in Europe was marked by a general decline in the number of private equity deals that floated on a stock market (IPO). Against the backdrop of the rapidly rising number of PE-owned companies this fall is even more marked.

There has been a notable growth in the number of large secondary buyouts, providing liquidity for the buyout market at a time when alternative exit routes have been difficult or rejected. These deals may be leading to the prolongation of disintermediation from public markets. This may maintain the positive benefits of private equity governance and incentives as a longer-term organizational form. Such transactions raise important and challenging unresolved issues relating to performance evaluation. In particular, if the original private equity financiers were effective, how likely is it that further performance gains can be achieved? Increasing evidence is becoming available on the performance of secondary buyouts, with the balance of evidence indicating that returns are below those for primary buyouts (see below).

Secondary Buyouts and New Principal Agent Issues

In the early years of the buyout market it was rare for a private equity fund to be prepared to buy a business from another private equity fund. This changed in the 1990s and it is now common, accounting for about a third of larger buyout exits (Figures 5.28 and 5.29). Despite a fall in secondary buyouts in the dislocation that followed the banking crisis, the numbers of secondary deals have been rising again and 25 per cent–30 per cent of all buyouts are now transactions between private equity houses. There has also been a convergence in the value of primary and secondary deals. In 2013, the value of secondary deals completed in Europe exceeded for the first time that for primary deals. This has raised a number of issues regarding 'churn' in the private equity market.

Where a fund is approaching the end of its agreed life and has yet to exit an investment, a fund manager may face an unusual set of incentives. If the fund is extended to maximize the value of the last investment(s) there are penalties for the fund manager. Therefore, it may be more rewarding to the manager to sell the asset for whatever value can be achieved today, rather than attempt to maximize the value in the longer run. In this sense there is an apparent anomaly in Private Equity fund structures: the longer an investment has been held in a fund, the more likely it is that the Private Equity fund manager is incentivised to act based on short-term considerations.

The most liquid acquirers of corporate assets are often other Private Equity funds. Therefore, a fund seeking a quick exit will very probably approach, among others, Private Equity funds. One way to mitigate the potential forgoing of value in such a transaction might be for the vendor Private Equity fund managers to co-invest in the business alongside the new Private Equity fund and do this from another fund under their management. This could trigger the carry in the old fund and carry forward the asset in the new fund at the value established by a third-party purchaser.

Furthermore, funds that are underinvested and are approaching the end of the investment period have strong incentives to invest or lose access to the committed capital. Research suggests that secondary acquisitions late in the life of a fund have lower returns than would be normally expected. This phenomenon has become known as 'late fund stuffing'.

As the market has evolved, investors in Private Equity funds have had to be careful to ensure that the incentives of the fund manager and the investors in each and every fund are tightly aligned. Ultimately the constraint on fund managers is reputational: in the long run, investors will not support fund managers that abuse their relationships.

What Is a Leveraged Recapitalization?

As with secondary buyouts, the market in leveraged recapitalizations (or 'recaps') has become more active in recent years. A recap involves the investee company re-borrowing

---

Box 5.8 Findings: To What Extent Are Managerial Equity, Leverage, and Private Equity Board Involvement Responsible for Performance Changes? The Academic Evidence

---

Early studies show that management team shareholding size had by far the larger impact on relative performance compared to leverage in both US and UK MBOs (Appendix 17). More recent studies suggest a weaker or negative relationship. Private equity firms create active boards involving high levels of PE firm interaction with executives during the initial typically 100-day value creation plan. Private equity firm board representation and involvement partly depends on style but is higher when there is CEO turnover and in deals that take longer to exit. Private equity boards lead strategy through intense engagement with top management, whereas PLC boards accompany the strategy of top management.

Active monitoring and involvement by Private Equity firms is also an important contributor to improved performance. In particular, previous experience and industry specialization (but not buyout stage specialization) of private equity firms adds significantly to increases in operating profitability of PE-backed buyouts over the first three buyout years. More experienced private equity firms help build better businesses as their deep experience in making buyout deals helps them take the right decisions during the deal and after the acquisition. A clear strategic focus on specific target industries enables these private equity firms to build up and leverage expertise. Early and honest communication of what the buyout means for the company and its employees, including targets, risks, and rewards, is important in creating the motivation necessary to meet ambitious business plans. A strong and trust-based relationship between company management and private equity investors is the basis for value added involvement in strategic and operational decisions.

Board size and director sector experience are positively associated with growth, while director age and the number of directorships held are negatively associated with growth.

---

debt previously repaid and/or increasing borrowings (usually due to increased performance since the original buyout) from the wider banking industry. These new borrowings are used to repay and/or restructure the loan elements of the original financing structure, sometimes including the private equity investment in loan stock and/or preference shares (and sometimes paying a dividend).

The return will generally take the form of a repayment of loan stock and/or a dividend. The capital repayment can be tax free (as there is no profit or loss) and an individual receiving the dividend currently pays tax at 25 per cent.

There is little academic research regarding the effect of recaps on investment performance. Recaps arise for one, or a combination, of three reasons:

- re-borrowing debt that has previously been repaid;
- increasing the amount of debt because the performance of the business has improved;
- increasing the amount of debt because the banks are prepared to lend more debt at the same performance level.

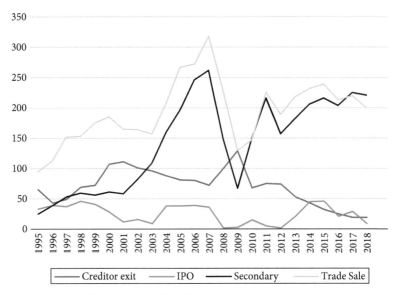

Figure 5.27. European divestment numbers by type of exit

Source: CMBOR/Equistone/Investec

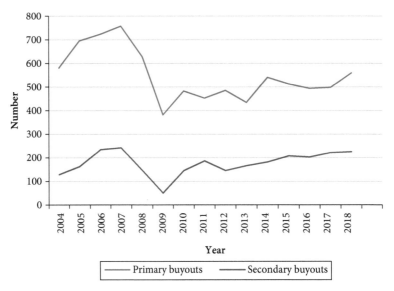

Figure 5.28. European primary and secondary buyouts by number

Source: CMBOR/Equistone/Investec

During the credit boom and more recently, the appetite of debt funds and banks to lend has been exceptionally high. This has resulted in a sharp increase in leveraged recaps.

To the extent that a business is able to replace more expensive capital with less expensive senior debt, these transactions can be seen as enhancing efficiency. The corollary is that financial risk to the business increases with the level of senior debt.

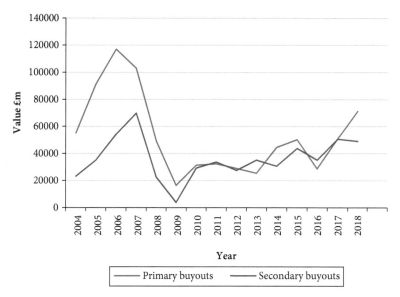

Figure 5.29. European primary and secondary buyouts by value
Source: CMBOR/Equistone/Investec

The impact on a fund's performance is to accelerate cash returned from any investment, thus increasing the IRR of the fund. However, this increase comes at the cost of reinstating or increasing financial risk in the portfolio.

The maximum amount that can be repaid without a capital profit being created will generally be the amount of the investment at cost (plus any PIK interest—see Chapter 4). To the extent that there is greater borrowing capacity a dividend may be paid. This dividend will be equal to the excess of new borrowings over the cost of the investment. This raises complex tax issues as the dividend will be received as income, not capital gain.

There is therefore a series of trade-offs to be calculated. How much borrowing is it prudent to have? What is the impact on fund returns and risks? What is the tax implication of receiving dividends rather than capital proceeds or gains?

Finally, management's position requires consideration. To the extent that they receive no benefit from a recap, management's risk is increased with no reward. This needs careful and considered negotiation before any deal is structured.

Dividends can only be paid out of retained profits or other distributable reserves. This should cap the total amount that can be extracted from a business. This is the case in most jurisdictions. In some jurisdictions however, dividends can also be paid out of new capital, including new loan capital. One of the incentives that attracts PE-owned companies to these jurisdictions is this ability to pay dividends in excess of retained profits.

Distress and Restructuring

What happens when businesses do not achieve the plans upon which the investment structure was based? There are many books written on this subject so we will be brief. We will describe the high-level mechanisms that are put in place in many private equity

---

Box 5.9 Findings: What Are the Drivers and Impact of Secondary Buyouts? The Academic Evidence

---

US evidence indicates that firms are more likely to exit through secondary buyouts when the equity market is 'cold', the debt market condition is favourable, and the sellers face a high demand for liquidity, with the last being the strongest reason (Appendix 18). Secondary buyouts appear to have been priced higher than first-time buyouts due to favourable debt market conditions. Performance declines in the primary buyout before a secondary buyout takes place and primary buyouts exiting as a secondary buyout generate lower internal rates of return on average than other forms of exit. The longer a firm has been held in the portfolio of the private equity firm, the more likely it is to exit as a secondary buyout. The systematic studies now emerging show evidence on average of a deterioration in long-run returns following secondary buyouts. UK evidence shows that secondary buyouts on average perform worse than primary buyouts in terms of profitability, productivity levels and growth, sales growth, and internal rate of return. Secondary buyouts also have lower efficiency than buyouts of private firms or divisional buyouts. The positive effects of secondary buyouts on firms' operating cash flows seem to be achieved through expansions, not by running the firms more efficiently. However, secondary buyouts between specialized private equity firms perform better than those conducted between other private equity firms.

---

structures to anticipate and deal with distressed situations, and then highlight the tools and typical negotiating positions of the various parties.

Distress is the symptom; the cause is failure to meet the business plan projections. In this section we draw a distinction between 'financial distress' and 'operating distress' which we explain below.

What Are the Types of Company Distress?

The finances of a business are more complicated than, but in principle no different to, the finances of a household. Distress arises because of three interconnected but separate outcomes:

- **operating distress** occurs when cashflows from day-to-day operation before financing are negative. This is due to loss making trading activities, absorbing working capital or investing in projects that do not generate cash. In household terms you spend more than you earn before finance costs. Unless rectified, operating distress leads inevitably to insolvency;
- **financial distress** is a special case of operating distress. It occurs when a company generates positive cashflows in its day-to-day operations, but they are insufficient to service the cash requirements of its funding structure. In household terms, you have borrowed more than you can afford to repay;
- **insolvency** occurs in two scenarios:

(1) The first is when its liabilities are greater than its assets. This is technical insolvency.

(2) The second and more pressing case is when a company cannot pay its debts as they fall due to be paid. This is a liquidity crisis. Using debt increases the amount of legal claims on the assts and cashflows of a business. Therefore, using debt increases the probability of insolvency.

There is a legal obligation on directors of all companies not to trade if a business is, or may reasonably be expected to become, insolvent.

Recalling the definitions of enterprise value and equity value, operating distress is the process that results in the enterprise value falling to zero. Where companies have significant borrowings, enterprise value may be positive but less than the value of the total borrowings. Financial distress is therefore when equity value is (or will become) zero or negative.

What Are the Early Signs of Financial Distress?

Earlier we described the structure of banks' financial covenants and how they interact to provide an early warning system of impending financial problems. Within a company, the first signs of distress are therefore often either a reduction of headroom against a covenant or a breach of a particular covenant or series of covenants.

Where loans are cov-lite, this early warning mechanism may be non-existent or impaired in its operation.

One particular form of weakened covenant loan emerged in the past ten years or so. These loans contain covenants but also have a so-called 'equity cure provision'.

What Is Equity Cure?

Equity cure is the name given to the right of a shareholder to address a covenant breach by injecting further equity capital into a business. For example, we discussed earlier the importance of the one-to-one cash covenant. This covenant ensures that a business does not create new borrowings in order to pay its existing funders. If a company breaches the one-to-one cash covenant it must either renegotiate with its banks to increase borrowings or renegotiate with all of its funders to delay payments due on the overall financing package. As a covenant breach may be an event of default (which allows a bank to seek repayment of all their loans and/or charge penalty interest) the bank will have significant power to determine the outcome of those negotiations.

Equity cure allows the shareholders to pre-empt that negotiation by having the right (but not the obligation) to invest money that will address the covenant breach, typically prior to, but sometimes immediately after, it occurs. The equity injection 'cures' the covenant breach and immunizes the penalties that would have been available to the lenders had the covenant been breached.

In effect the parties have pre-agreed a process to address financial distress.

Box 5.10 Findings: Do Private Equity Deals Involve the Short-Term 'Flipping' of Assets? The Academic Evidence

---

When we return to the question of short-termism, it is at the company level that we need to focus the analysis. The academic evidence (Appendix 10) suggests that there is a wide variation in the length of time any investment is held. There is no evidence that the industry systematically seeks to 'flip' investments in a short time period. Evidence from the 1980s in both the US and UK shows that some buyouts are exited in a relatively short period of time, while others remain with the buyout structure for periods in excess of five years. On average, larger deals exit significantly sooner than small deals. During the second private equity wave, there were very short periods to exit of some private equity deals, but this is neither new nor surprising and most are held in portfolios much longer. Some deals fail soon after completion while others may be turned around quite quickly and receive unsolicited bids by trade buyers. Over time, the average time to exit is increasing (Figure 5.30): the most common timing of exit for those deals that have exited since 2000 is in the range of 5–6 years.

What Is Financial Restructuring?

Financial restructuring is the renegotiation of a company's financial structure to allow it to alleviate financial distress. It consists of changing the financing structure of a company's balance sheet to increase the possibility of generating positive cash flows. In many ways the questions being asked in a restructuring are exactly the same as those being asked in structuring the original buyout: 'How much debt can prudently be borrowed?' 'How much equity does a company need?' 'Are the returns on the equity requirement satisfactory?'

However, the difference in the scenario lies in the dynamics of the negotiation.

Restructuring is a process of renegotiation, not recalculation, and the relative strengths of the negotiating positions are as significant as the financial arithmetic.

In a new investment each financier must compete to win the mandate to finance the investment opportunity within the constraint of an acceptable price demanded by the vendor. In a restructuring, in the absence of the option of selling their investment or simply getting another institution to refinance the position, the incumbent financiers must decide whether to invest further new money and how to reprice the existing investment to take account of the changed risks and rewards. They must therefore negotiate among themselves regarding the new financial structure that will enable the business to continue to pursue its strategic goals or agree to a process of corporate failure.

When Is Financial Restructuring Possible?

Broadly speaking, restructuring is possible when a company has a positive enterprise value but a negative (or falling) equity value—i.e. it is in financial distress but not in irreversible operating distress.

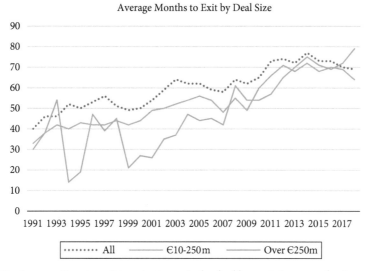

Figure 5.30. Average time to exit in private equity backed buyouts by year of exit

Prior to any investment much effort and resource is put into examining the range of possible outcomes in any investment (see the section on sensitivity analysis in Chapter 6). Similarly, much due diligence is undertaken to attempt to verify the assumptions that underlie the business plan. However, no matter how much due diligence and sensitivity analysis is undertaken, a judgement on the likely variance around the company's base plan may turn out to be incorrect.

Financial structures are engineered with an often implicit assumption about the range of possible future environments that they will have to withstand. If the world turns out to be more hostile, the structures will not operate efficiently. In general, there is a trade-off between flexibility (which is the ability to withstand volatility) and cost.

Typically distress arises from one or a combination of three reasons:

- the company's internal inability to achieve its objectives;
- the external market for the company's goods and services changes; or
- the external market for finance changes.

Similarly, problems may manifest themselves along the spectrum between two extremes:

- failure to achieve a given target (i.e. 'missing a target'); or
- a delay in the rate of progress towards achieving a target (i.e. 'being too slow').

Irrespective of which source of distress is manifested, the first step in addressing the problem is to prudently reassess the business plan of the company and the available resources, including management resources.

Box 5.11 Findings: What Is the Extent of Asset Sales and Refinancing? The Academic Evidence

US evidence from the 1980s suggests that larger buyouts involving P2Ps engage in substantial divestment of assets (Appendix11) to an extent significantly greater than for buyouts of divisions. The extent of asset sales among UK buyouts completed in the 1980s was much less than in the US. It should be noted that buyouts divesting assets may also have been making acquisitions. Partial sales peaked in Europe at 163 in 2005 and at €12 billion in 2006, but then fell sharply from 2008 until recovery in value in 2012. In 2013 there were only 65 partial sales for a total value of €9.3 billion. European refinancings also peaked in the boom years of 2005–7 at around 130 per year, with a high of €46.5 billion in 2007. Numbers then fell to below 100 per year before recovering sharply in 2013 at 125 for a total value of €41.6 billion.

What Is a Valuation Break Point?

We have seen that a business's capital structure is built up layer by layer with each layer having a priority in the queue to get paid. The senior lenders are at the front of the queue and the common equity at the back, with various others slotted in between.

When a company is assessed as being in distress it is important to understand the value of the enterprise and where in the queue of creditors is the break between those who will get paid, and those who will not.

In the UK the queue in a formal insolvency looks something like this (although there are consultations under way to make some changes to it to allow recovery of more tax in insolvency):

(1) secured creditors with a fixed charge (after costs of realization)—usually banks and other lenders;
(2) Insolvency practitioners' fees and expenses;
(3) Preferential unsecured creditors:
   a. Ordinary: certain employee pay and holiday pay;
   b. Secondary: deposits received from customers etc.;
(4) prescribed part creditors: an amount is set aside in UK law for the non-preferential unsecured creditors that ranks ahead of the secured creditors with a floating charge. This is a small amount, currently calculated as 50 per cent of the first £10k and 20 per cent of the next £3m up to a maximum of £600k;
(5) Secured creditors with a floating charge: a floating charge is a charge over current assets (stock, WIP, debtors) and ranks after the items above. You will normally see lenders taking a fixed and a floating charge on all unencumbered assets of the borrower in any buyout;
(6) non-preferential unsecured creditors: all the creditors of the business who have no charge and no legal preference;
(7) shareholders: the residual amount after all the creditors are paid.

Box 5.12 Findings: Do the Effects of Private Equity Continue after Exit? The Academic Evidence

---

An important unresolved question is whether the claimed benefits of private equity deals are sustained once the buyout structure ends (Appendix 12). US evidence is that while leverage and management equity fall when buyouts return to market (reverse buyouts), they remain high relative to comparable listed corporations that have not undergone a buyout. Pre-IPO, the accounting performance of buyouts is significantly higher than the median for the respective sectors. Following the IPO, accounting and share price performance are above the firms' sector and stock market benchmarks for three to five years, but decline during this period. This change is positively related to changes in insider ownership but not to leverage. Those PE-backed MBOs in the UK that do IPO tend to do so earlier than their non-PE-backed counterparts. There is some evidence that they are more underpriced than MBOs without private equity backing, but not that they perform better than their non-PE-backed counterparts in the long run. Private-to-public MBOs backed by more active private equity firms in the UK tend to exit earlier and these MBOs performed better than those backed by less experienced PE funds.

For example, consider a business worth £250m with the creditors assumed in Table 5.28.

If there is insufficient to pay any part of the amount owed to any particular class of creditors, the last in the queue will receive X pence/cents in the pound/dollar.

In the example, if the value fell below £175m the junior loans would not recover all their value in an insolvency. Any class of creditors after the break point are 'out of the money' and will recover nothing. Where this break point falls in the capital stack will determine which investors will lose money in an insolvency (see Figure 5.31). This will change their incentives in any restructuring discussions.

Within any class of creditors there can be further seniority (i.e. a queue within the queue). It is important to understand that other rights may temper the simple 'break point' analysis materially in the real world.

What Is a 'Haircut' and Who Bears It?

When a company fails to generate sufficient cash to service its trading liabilities it is in danger of being insolvent. Trading insolvency can only be rectified by rescheduling a company's liabilities or by injecting new cash into the business. Generally, banks will not lend money to rectify cash flow problems that arise from trading difficulties unless they can be persuaded that the shortfall has arisen because of a timing delay that will be rapidly rectified. Banks will normally expect the equity investors to make good any shortfall in operating cash flows by injecting new equity.

However, in many situations the complex interaction of incentives and threats results in a sharing of the cost of any shortfall thus decreasing their return. Those bearing these

Table 5.28. Illustrative claims in an insolvency

Creditor		Claim £	Cumulative value
1 Fixed charge creditors			
Super senior loans	RCF	10	10
Senior loans	TLA	100	110
	TLB	50	160
Junior loans	TLC	50	210
2 Insolvency fees etc.		1	211
3 Preferential unsecured creditors			
a Ordinary		2	213
b Secondary		1	214
4 Prescribed part creditors		1	215
5 Secured creditors with a floating charge		-	215
6 Non-preferential unsecured creditors		20	235
7 Shareholders: residual claim		15	250
Enterprise value		250	

costs are said to have 'taken a haircut'. The haircut is the sharing of the pain of the break point between creditors.

What Powers Does a Secured Lender Have?

In general, since banks have security over the assets of the company, nothing can be done to restructure a company with borrowings without agreeing the restructuring with the banks. They therefore hold an extremely strong negotiating position in any restructuring.

However, banks do not have the resources to actively manage the companies that have borrowed, and they must therefore accommodate the reasonable aspirations and motivations of management who will manage the company out of distress.

Furthermore, as banks have traditionally been reliant on private equity firms for new transactions, the broader commercial interrelationships must also be borne in mind by any bank during any restructuring.

There are a number of alternatives open to a bank with security.

Receivership

A secured lender whose loan is in default can seek to recover their debt by selling the assets over which they have security in a receivership. It is extremely rare that equity holders receive anything in a receivership. This is therefore the end of an attempt to restructure and effectively represents the failure of the business. The threat of receivership is, in most circumstances, more powerful than the actual receivership.

The banks' decision leading to the appointment of a receiver will be driven by their perceptions of the prospects for the business and their assessment of the amount of their lending that is at risk if a receiver is appointed.

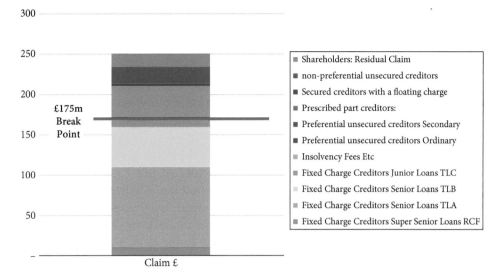

Figure 5.31. Break point at £175m enterprise value

Enforce Priorities

The layering of debt, mezzanine, and equity was illustrated earlier. The agreements between the parties will contain provisions to ensure that if the lenders with the highest priority over the company's cash resources (the senior secured lenders) are not receiving either their interest or capital repayments, then the lenders and investors that have lower priorities (or are 'subordinated' to them) will also not be paid. Thus the financial pain of underperformance falls first upon the holders of financial instruments with the lowest priority.

However, as we have seen, in many buyouts yield is rolled up and capital repayments on the least secure redeemable instruments (unsecured loans and redeemable preference shares) are made in a single bullet repayment after all the debt has been repaid. Therefore, there is no cash cost to the equity holders until the repayments are due. This leaves management in a position where the cost of the capital structure is increasing with no compensatory increase in their projected rewards. At some point the incentive of management will fall below the minimum necessary to retain and/or motivate them. In this scenario the equity illusion is stripped away and management are highly motivated to initiate a restructuring. The private equity investor continues to roll up yield throughout the negotiations, albeit that the yield may be written off as part of the restructuring.

Increased Cost of Funds

Where companies breach agreements, banks will always seek to increase the cost of funds to compensate for the increased risk. However, financial distress is characterized by an inability to service a capital structure and therefore increased interest costs may make the overall company situation more perilous.

What Tools Are Available to Restructure a Balance Sheet?

In Figure 5.32 we illustrate the various options that are available to restructure a balance sheet that has too much debt. In practice these are the limits of what could be achieved; and most reconstructions would use a hybrid solution incorporating elements of each approach, depending upon how the parties to the restructuring discussions judge the individual circumstances and prospects of the company and, equally importantly, the balance of power within the negotiations.

Reschedule and Reprice the Existing Debt ('Amend and Extend')
If a lender believes that a solution can be found, it is possible to alleviate the cash burden of the higher cost of funds by rescheduling debt repayments. However, increasing the term of a loan further lengthens the duration of the risk that the lender is exposed to and the banks will therefore seek further compensation either in the form of fees or increased margins (or both). This repricing may include a so-called 'equity kicker'. This is a mechanism (typically warrants or options to purchase equity) that allows the loans to earn a return reflecting the increased risks of the structure. Essentially a part of the debt package is repriced as a mezzanine risk.

Inject New Equity ('Equity Cure')
It is unlikely that a private equity fund would simply invest new equity to reduce debt as illustrated, but if there is a plan that justifies new equity, or the banks require an increase in equity to continue to support the business, then this may be required. Recall that equity cure is simply a pre-agreed injection of new equity that enables a rapid restructuring to occur.

Debt for Equity Swap and 'Loan-to-Own'
Where the bank perceives the risks that it is taking are closer to those of an equity investor than a bank, it is common to reschedule and reprice debt to include the conversion of a portion of the debt into equity. This will dilute the equity holding of the existing shareholders, including management, and the impact on incentives requires careful consideration. The pricing of the equity will need to reflect the changed circumstances of the company. Ultimately, a bank may take control of the equity in the company, with the private equity fund being completely removed from the ownership of business. The bank moves from being a lender to being a shareholder: so-called 'loan-to-own'.

Write Off a Portion of the Loans
If a company simply has too much debt then at some point this will have to be recognized. In the traditional banking model where loans were held by the arranging banks and a few syndicate banks, the company and equity investors could negotiate with the banks to write off a portion of the debt as part of an overall restructuring. This will normally be accompanied by an injection of new equity or other such contribution from the other funders.

Summary
Any restructuring is a negotiation in which the debt holders have a strong influence. It will typically involve a series of questions, starting with the assessment of the prospects of the

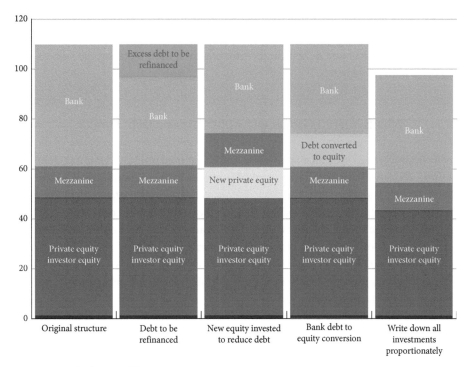

Figure 5.32. The limits of the most common restructuring options

business in its changed circumstances. The parties to the restructuring will negotiate with each other to redistribute the changed risks and seek to receive an appropriate reward in the riskier environment.

The Paradox of Syndication: The Differences in Restructuring Publicly Traded Debt

As the banking model has changed to include the issuing of more publicly quoted bonds in support of buyouts, the number of participants in a restructuring has multiplied. Since any restructuring is a process of negotiation and creation of a revised consensus, often against a severe time constraint, the proliferation of holders of debt in buyouts makes any restructuring significantly harder to achieve. Even where there are designated syndicate leaders who represent and negotiate on behalf of all bond holders, they must influence the broad church of the syndicate members. This often slows and complicates any renegotiation.

It is widely accepted that the growth in the issuance of publicly traded debt in larger buyouts has made restructuring slower and more difficult to achieve.

Therefore, in widely syndicated transactions, especially those involving publicly traded debt, negotiating any form of restructuring can be significantly more time-consuming and problematic. This has resulted in a paradoxical situation: wide syndication of debt is used as a risk mitigation mechanism for the lenders, who reduce their exposure to any one company, and borrowers, who reduce dependence on a single borrower. However, when the risks that are being mitigated start to crystallize, wide syndication makes timely response to those risks more difficult and costly, which in itself increases the risks to both the lender and the borrower.

Why Is There a Growing Use of Distressed Debt Funds?

There have always been specialist investment funds that only invest in distressed debt (and sometimes distressed publicly traded equity). In some cases these funds are based on a trading strategy that argues that the debt is undervalued. In others they adopt an 'active value' model whereby the fund actively engages in the negotiations to restructure the company. Following the credit crunch many private equity funds have either launched distressed debt funds or are actively evaluating the possibility of doing so, and in particular have sought to acquire the debt that supported their own original buyouts, either through direct purchases of the debt or by setting up specialist distressed debt funds exclusively targeting underperforming loans.

The growth of traded buyout bonds has also resulted in the emergence of new mechanisms to reduce debt for individual companies. In particular it has become possible for companies to buy back publicly traded debt at values below par using free cash and/or an equity injection. For example, Alliance Boots, the largest ever UK buyout, reported that it had repurchased £468m of its debt at prices below 70p in the pound financed by a mixture of cash generated by the business and £60m of new shares issued to the investors.

What Are Credit Default Swaps? A Perverse Set of Incentives

Credit default swaps (CDS) are a form of hedging instrument. They allow a lender to swap their risk of default with another party. They are often described as a form of insurance that will pay out if the original borrower defaults on the loan agreement. However, despite being described as a form of insurance, there are significant differences in both the operation and regulation of a CDS. As with most financial terminology, the term 'CDS' covers an array of different contractual arrangements and each situation is potentially different.

A CDS is actually closer to a third-party guarantee of a loan agreement than a hedge policy. The guarantor receives a guarantee fee and underwrites the default risk, but is not regulated, financed, or accounted for like an insurance company.

One of the important differences between CDS and insurance for the restructuring market is the fact that CDS are tradable securities. In a genuine insurance contract the insured must be able to show a loss to receive a payout. With CDS, institutions can trade their positions with those who have no risk of loss. In effect it allows institutions to hedge against losses that they will not incur.

This creates the opportunity to acquire CDS cover and to frustrate the restructuring of otherwise viable companies. For example, any holder of a loan benefiting from a credit default swap with a strong counterparty may have more incentive to seek the default on the loan it holds than to agree to a restructuring that may require debt holders to take a haircut. To complicate matters further, a restructuring itself may be defined in the CDS as an event of default.

As noted earlier, restructurings are often time-critical, and a failure to achieve a restructuring may result in the evaporation of confidence in an organization, making a previously viable company fail. The existence of CDS positions has created concerns that the time taken to negotiate with those who hold these guaranteed positions may stop otherwise agreed restructurings. There may be many market participants who have a perverse incentive to seek a bankruptcy rather than rescue a business, whether it is viable or not.

Equity Investors: The Impact of Distress

The first impact of financial distress should be recognized in the valuation of the investment within the fund.

The second impact of falling valuations is to reduce the pro-forma returns of the fund (i.e. the returns to date based on current valuations). This will make any contemporaneous fund-raising, which will be based among other things on the latest fund returns, proportionately more difficult.

It should also be appreciated that falling investment valuations reduce the prospective value, or increase the risks to the value, of any carried interest. Where an investment is a material part of the fund's portfolio value this can be a severe impact on the ability to recruit and retain key people, especially readily marketable non-partners who will see their share of any carried interest reduce.

There is therefore a strong set of incentives to restructure any investment to recover value both in the short and longer term.

Equity Investors: What Are the Options?

As active investors, private equity funds have the contractual ability to make changes to the company that bankers generally do not have. Banks may have strong negotiating positions as a result of their security arrangements and the threat of receivership, but the private equity investors have contractual levers that are readily available to effect rapid change in management and/or strategy.

In any restructuring, it is universally recognized that something must change. Businesses that are failing to perform to plan stretch their funding packages, and if the underperformance is outside the tolerances of the scheme design then either the capital structure must be changed to fit the company, or vice versa, or a combination of the two.

Change the Company
Changing the company may mean the same people adopting a new strategy, but it also often means changing elements of the management team. Private equity funds will actively replace management team members, including chief executives, finance directors/CFOs and chairmen, and replace them with people who are believed to have turnaround expertise.

This process has created an entirely new market in professional company doctors whose careers are a series of either part-time non-executive roles or full-time turnaround roles for PE-backed companies. Incentivising the new management and realigning the incentives of any existing management is a key part of any restructuring proposition.

Similarly, they will use external consultants and advisers to evaluate the options going forward. The investment agreement will allow the costs of these external analyses to be charged to the company rather than being borne by the fund or the manager.

Change the Finance Structure: Inject New Equity

If a business simply has too much debt, it may be reasonable to inject new equity and restructure the banks' debt. Since the existing equity structure will have been predicated on a required return (and an assumption of risk) there will need to be at least one of the following:

- an increase in the equity stake of the investors, or equivalently a reduction in management's equity;
- an increase in the preferred yield of the investment; or
- an increase in the expected value of the business at exit.

The first two will, other things being equal, reduce the return to management and may create significant disincentive effects that need to be managed. The latter is unlikely to be a key driver due to the dynamics of the negotiation. It is difficult to argue successfully that the terminal value of a company in distress has increased since the original investment.

Purchase the Debt

Debt purchase is now common. This reflects two unrelated facts: first, there is more publicly traded LBO debt in larger buyouts; secondly the unrelated change in strategy away from LBOs by banks previously active in the buyout market has led to an increase in the activities of private debt funds, some of which are managed by the same managers as PE funds. We discuss this more fully in Chapter 6. Debt repurchases can be achieved in two different ways: either the company can use its own resources to buy in and cancel debt, or the investors, through a separate fund, can buy debt. When debt is bought by the company and cancelled the full costs and benefits of purchasing the debt accrue to the company and all of its shareholders.

In the case of a separate fund purchase the costs and benefits are more complicated. Purchasing debt at the fund level can be preferable to injecting new equity into the company to purchase the debt. The private equity fund gains access to the security of the existing senior debt, becoming part of the banking syndicate. They can therefore influence the behaviour of the debt syndicate directly. They will of course also benefit from any uplift in the value of the debt acquired. However, unless the debt is cancelled or restructured, no benefit accrues to the company.

There are, therefore, potentially significant conflicts of interest where investors in an equity fund become investors in a distressed debt fund designed to acquire debt in existing equity investments. The control of this type of potential conflict is a matter for the fund agreement.

Reprice the Equity

Irrespective of how the restructuring is undertaken, it would normally be expected that the equity would be repriced using the tools noted above—i.e. a higher equity stake or a higher preferred yield.

What Is the Position of Management in a Restructuring?

We have explained above that in any restructuring the bank will almost always have very significant influence over the outcome. Furthermore, if the private equity investor is to invest further equity this will generally have a higher cost than the existing equity, either in yield or equity percentage or both.

We have also explained earlier that management's equity stake is determined as either the residual amount available after the private equity fund has achieved a satisfactory return or as the minimum necessary to retain and motivate key people.

Furthermore, we have argued that to change the company it is often necessary to change the management team or its strategy.

In these circumstances management's negotiating position is apparently weak. However, the commercial position depends upon whether or not the individuals concerned are part of the plan to turn the business around or if they are going to leave the company as part of the restructuring.

If management are to stay (or, in the case of new management, join) the position is essentially a repetition of the position at the date of the original investment, adjusted for the new risks. Given the equity return requirements outlined above it is not uncommon to see extremely high risk/reward structures in rescues, often with very aggressive ratchets to strongly reward recovery and generation of value.

If management are to leave, there will almost always be a 'good leaver/bad leaver' clause in the original shareholders' agreement that will come into play. We described these in Chapter 4.

6

A Detailed Worked Example
of a Leveraged Buyout

This section presents a necessarily detailed, but fictional, worked example of a transaction structure. It is intended to illustrate a financial structure and explain both the logic of the tailoring of the financial package and the complicated tax impacts of financial engineering. Our intention is to give an insight into the questions being asked and the analyses undertaken prior to and during an investment.

Each edition we consider updating this section to reflect changing market conditions and accounting regulations, but each time we return to it we are struck by the fact that whilst the prices and ratios change, the logic stays the same. We have therefore not changed the example materially. In consequence we need to add some important caveats:

Accounting: Our intention in the example is to show what is actually going on in a transaction and how the finance is tailored to the cash flow needs of the business. In doing so we consciously ignore how the accounting for various matters (typically fees, goodwill and leases) would be treated under current (or indeed past) accounting standards in any particular location. We are seeking to shed light on the mechanics and logic of the construction of a deal, not to accurately reflect the accounting for that deal.

Pricing: As we have discussed, the pricing of any instrument or company varies over time. We do not purport to show current pricing in any market for any financial instrument. In particular we do not reflect the use or high yield or unitranche.

Taxation: Tax rates and taxes vary annually. The trend is towards globally lower corporation taxes. As the arguments do not rest on tax rates, we have not attempted to stay up to date with the rates in our fictionalized example.

Again, our intention is to display the thought processes, not a 'model answer' to any particular question.

Operating Profit Projections

The operating projections of the target company are summarized in Table 6.1 and Figure 6.1.

The fictional business plan of a company is being evaluated by a private equity investor and bankers. The actual figures represent the performance in the year prior to the proposed investment. The subsequent years are forecasts. The business is being evaluated as a turnaround investment requiring changes in strategy to reposition the business.

Private Equity Demystified: An explanatory guide. Fourth Edition. John Gilligan and Mike Wright, Oxford University Press (2020).
© John Gilligan & Mike Wright. DOI: 10.1093/oso/9780198866961.003.0006

Table 6.1. Operating profit projections

Sales fall due to increased pricing and stock clearances at lower prices

Gross margins rise after stock clearances due to increased pricing

Lease chrges arise from the sale and leaseback of properties

Operating projections	Actual £000s	Year 1 £000s	Year 2 £000s	Year 3 £000s
Turnover	167,250	158,888	163,654	168,5641
Cost of goods	(91,988)	(87,388)	(83,464)	(85,968)
Gross margin	75,263	71,499	80,191	82,596
Overheads	(62,500)	(60,938)	(61,547)	(63,393)
Lease costs		(400)	(800)	(800)
EBITDA	12,763	10,162	170,844	18,403
Depreciation	(5,000)	(4,167)	(2,639)	(2,616)
Restructuring costs	0	(3,500)	0	0
EBIT	7,762	2,495	15,205	15,787
Growth in turnover		*–5.0%*	*3.0%*	*3.0%*
Gross margin	*45.0%*	*45.0%*	*49.0%*	*49.0%*
Overhead inflation		*–2.5%*	*1.0%*	*3.0%*
EBITDA %	*7.6%*	*6.4%*	*10.9%*	*10.9%*
EBIT %	*4.6%*	*1.6%*	*9.3%*	*9.4%*

Restructuring costs of £3.5m reduce overheads by £1.6m per annum

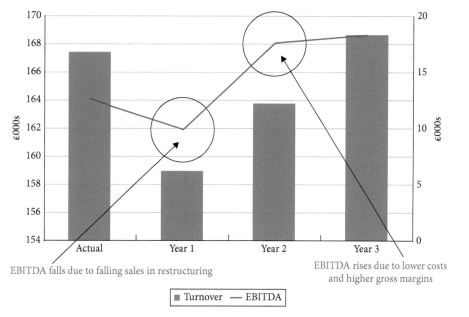

EBITDA falls due to falling sales in restructuring

EBITDA rises due to lower costs and higher gross margins

■ Turnover — EBITDA

Figure 6.1. Actual and forecast sales and profit

The cash flows of the business reflect one-off costs and gains, followed by the ongoing cash generation of the restructured business. The one-off costs and gains are:

- the restructuring of overheads;
- the inflow from the sale and leaseback of £10m of freehold properties; and
- material changes in the working capital profile of the business.

The ongoing changes include both the resulting changes in margins and the costs associated with the new lease arrangements put in place as part of the sale and leaseback.

A Note on Valuations

Note that in this example any valuation completed at the end of year 2 based upon an earnings multiple or net assets would result in a reduction in the investment's value. This is clearly a planned consequence of the investment strategy. In consequence, despite the valuation discussion above, this investment could be argued to be carried at cost. The example highlights the difficulties that mechanistic valuations can create.

Cash Flow Projections

The illustration is based upon a number of structural and strategic changes to the business acquired that are commonly seen in private equity transactions, including the following:

- **Asset disposals:** the plan assumes a sale and leaseback of £10m of assets during the first year after the transaction. This creates a new lease charge in the profit and loss account as well as a cash inflow from the sale. Note that the depreciation charge falls in year 2 because of the sale of assets.
- **Overhead reduction:** there is a planned reduction of overhead costs by £1.6m (−2.5 per cent) in year 1. It is assumed that the restructuring costs will be £3.5m in year 1. The reduction might be achieved by simple cost cutting but might also involve staff redundancies.
- **Price increases:** the plan projects an increase in gross margins from 45 per cent to 49 per cent by increasing prices. This price rise is projected to result in a 5 per cent fall in sales in year 1. Year 1 also includes a stock clearance sale that temporarily holds gross margin at 45 per cent by changing the mix of products sold.
- **Increased investment:** to achieve efficiency gains, a one-off increase in capital expenditure of £2.5m is included to update the assets of the business.
- **Working capital improvement:** the amount of working capital in the business is also forecast to reduce in year 1, generating a positive cashflow. This reflects a step change in the rate at which debtors are collected and creditors are paid and the stock clearance noted above.

Thereafter, both costs and revenues are forecast to grow at 3.0 per cent per annum and working capital grows proportionate to sales growth (see Table 6.2 and Figure 6.2).

Table 6.2. Actual and forecast operating cash flows

£000	Actual	Year 1	Year 2	Year 3
EBITA	7,762	2,495	15,205	15,787
Ongoing capex	(2,000)	(2,500)	(2,500)	(2,500)
One-off capex	–	(2,500)	–	–
Depreciation	5,000	4,167	2,639	2,616
Working capital	(500)	3,262	(292)	(301)
Operating cash flow	10,263	4,924	15,052	15,602
Proceeds of sale of fixed assets	0	10,000	0	0
Cash flow after sale of fixed assets	10,263	14,924	15,052	15,602

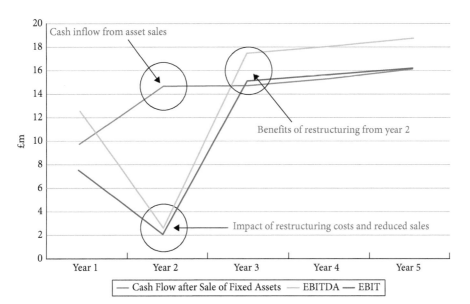

Figure 6.2. EBITDA and operating cash flows

A Profit Bridge

A common analysis undertaken in most major restructurings is to construct what is known as a profit bridge. This seeks to isolate the impact of each of the various actions on overall profitability. It always needs to be appreciated that the arithmetic presentation necessarily disguises the interaction of the various factors; for example, restructurings impact morale which may impact the motivation and productivity of the people of a business in complex and unpredictable ways. No profit bridge can illustrate these interconnections.

While recognizing its limitations, it is very commonly used by financial analysts, investors and accountants.

The profit bridge (Table 6.3 and Figure 6.3) highlights the salient features of this investment proposal. The business is restructured to achieve higher gross margins. Thereafter it grows at a broadly inflationary rate. This is important in structuring the investment since the vast majority of value will be created by the implementation of the plan in the early years of the investment. Thereafter, unless a new strategy is put in place that will accelerate growth in profitability, value accrues more slowly.

Table 6.3. Profit bridges

£000	Year 1	Year 2	Year 3	
Incr/(Decr) in slaes	(3,763)	2,145	2,406	
Incr/(Decr) in gross margins	0	6,546	(0)	Step change in profit is driven by higher gross margins
Incr/(Decr) in overhead inc. leases	1,163	(1,009)	(1,846)	
Incr/(Decr) in EBITDA	(2,601)	7,682	559	
(Incr)/Decr in depreciation	883	1,528	23	One-off restructuring costs
(Incr)/Decr in exceptional costs	(3,500)	3,500	0	
(Incr)/Decr in EBIT	(5,267)	12,710	582	
Opening EBITDA	12,763	10,162	17,844	
Incr/(Decr) in EBITDA	(2,601)	7,582	559	
Closing	10,162	17,844	18,403	

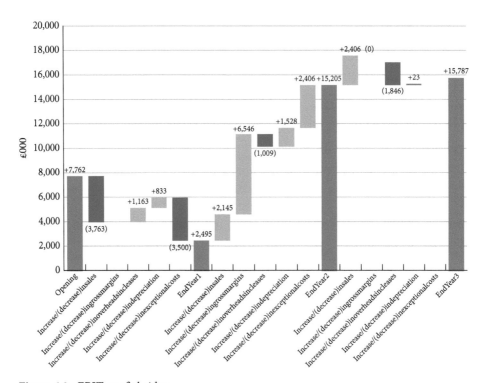

Figure 6.3. EBIT: profit bridge

Table 6.4. Funding requirement

Requirements	£000	
Purchase of 100% of shares	90,000	← Equity value or market capitalization
Refinance 100% existing debt	10,000	
Enterprise value	100,000	← Enterprise value
Periodic working capital	2,500	
Stamp duty @ 0.5%	450	← 0.5% of the price paid
Transaction fees inc. VAT	5,550	
Total requirement	108,500	
Enterprise value	100,000	
Current EBIT	7,762	
EV/EBIT	12.9	
Equivalent P/E ratio	17.9	

Funding Requirement

The task for investors is to structure an investment proposal against these projections (and the sensitivities) and offer an assumed purchase price (enterprise value) of £100m to the shareholders, representing a ratio of enterprise value/EBIT of 12.9 times (Table 6.4). The purchaser must also allow headroom within the structure so that the company can fund ongoing periodic working capital requirements (overdrafts, letters of credit, hedging, etc.) and pay the costs of the funders and advisers. Furthermore, if UK shares are acquired, stamp duty may be payable at 0.5 per cent of the value of the offer.

What Are the Transaction Fees and Expenses?

Transactions costs are a significant element in the funding requirement. These fall into a number of categories.

Transaction Taxes

Any acquisition potentially creates a number of taxes that have to be paid at completion. In the UK the most common of these is stamp duty, which is a tax payable on share purchases at 0.5 per cent (subject to certain exemptions and reliefs).

In addition to stamp duty there is VAT payable on many of the advisory fees, some recoverable, some not, that are discussed below.

Investors' and Lenders' Fees

Arrangement fees: all lenders and investors generally charge fees as upfront payments when they invest. As discussed earlier these fees may result in changes in incentives and risk/reward profiles.

Monitoring fees: many lenders and investors charge further ongoing fees to recover the costs of their ongoing monitoring of any investment or loans.

Underwriting fees: where a lender or investor is prepared to temporarily take on the full amount of the loans and/or investment prior to a later syndication, this underwriter will charge an underwriter's fee.

From the perspective of the borrower all of these fees are simply costs of doing the transaction, and in assessing the overall cost of funding the transaction should be treated in the same way as interest or any other costs. The key difference is that interest costs are ongoing costs post transaction completion that are funded by cash flow, whereas arrangement/underwriting fees are upfront day one costs which are funded by equity.

Advisers' Fees

We saw in Chapter 5 that there are a number of legal and financial advisers in any transaction. Each will require payment from the acquirer or vendor. The acquirer's costs will be recharged to the newco set up to make the acquisition.

What Are Contingent Fee Arrangements?

Contingent fees are fees that are only payable on the successful conclusion of a transaction. They transfer the risks (and rewards) of providing a particular service from the private equity funder of a transaction to their advisers. They also reduce the fixed costs of the users of advisers, but increase their variable costs.

Where the advisers are retained to advise whether or not to pursue a particular investment, contingent fees create conflicts of interest for the advisers: the adviser has no incentive to advise against doing any particular deal, but strong incentives to promote a transaction. The constraint on promoting poor transactions is twofold. Firstly, there is a direct liability issue for poor advice. The limit of the liability of advisers who give poor advice is defined in the terms of their engagement with their client. Secondly, there is the impact of reputational risk on the ability of an organization to generate new business.

Over the years there has been a great deal of discussion between the professionals providing services and banks and private equity houses regarding contingency and the amount and form of the liabilities of advisers. In the UK, the Financial Reporting Council, ICAEW, and other professional bodies place limits on the services that may be provided on a contingent basis.[1]

A Funding Structure

The funding structure needs to accommodate:

---

[1] See APB Ethical Standard 5 (revised), *Non-Audit Services Provided To Audited Entities* (April 2008) and *Ethical Standards for Reporting Accountants* (October 2006), published by the Financial Reporting Council.

(1) the purchase price of the shares;
(2) the treatment of the expected proceeds from the planned sale of assets, which will enable some of the loans to be repaid early;
(3) working capital requirements; and
(4) fees and other costs associated with the transaction.

A wide array of potential funding solutions could be constructed. The version presented here (Figure 6.4 and Table 6.5) is illustrative only.

Around 44 per cent of all funding in the example comes from the private equity investors. The same amount (including working capital facilities) comes from secured banking, and the balance (12 per cent) is in the form of mezzanine finance, which would probably be provided by a specialist mezzanine fund.

In Chapter 5, we explained how the layers of finance are structured to take account of the available security and cash flows. Using these methods and analytical techniques, a detailed structure of the transaction is given below. It is important to understand that there may be a number of different capital structures that are appropriate to the business and that there is no one right answer to this type of analysis. There is an intimate relationship between the capital structure chosen and, for example, the future strategy of the business, as well as the expectations of the parties to the deal regarding the future volatility and growth in the external market and the appetite of all parties for risk.

Figure 6.5 shows the progression from the funding requirement to the detailed financial structure and finally the share:loan split. The graphic illustrates how risk is allocated between banks, mezzanine providers, and equity investors, but nevertheless most of the invested monies are in loans, not shares.

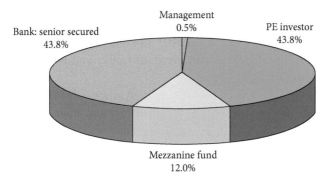

Figure 6.4. Sources of funds

Table 6.5. Sources of funding

Funding structure	£000	%
Management	500	0.5
Private equity investor	47,500	43.8
Mezzanine	13,000	12.0
Bank	47,500	43.8
Total	108,500	100.0

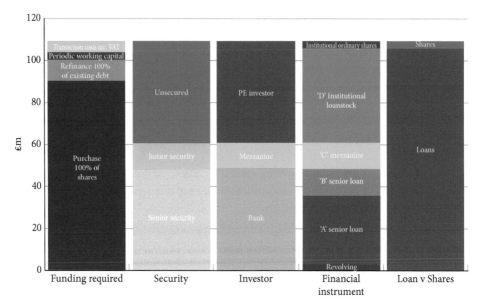

Figure 6.5. The funding package is analysed by funding requirement, security available, source of funds, detailed financial instrument and type of financial instrument

Note that revolving credit is often undrawn capital at closing but can be partly drawn to pay fees or as part of the closing working capital adjustment.

The overall structure contains seven different layers of finance (see Table 6.6) as explained below.

The banking and mezzanine package (including the working capital facility) provides 55.8 per cent of the total funding package and consists of four layers.

(1) A revolving facility to fund periodic working capital movements during the trading year. This is in effect an overdraft facility and is secured alongside the senior loans.

(2) 'A' senior loan: a loan at an interest rate a margin above LIBOR (see glossary), generally with a flat repayment profile repaid in equal annual instalments. In this example there is a significant cash inflow from asset disposals which will be used to repay part of the 'A' loan in year 2. This payment is calculated using a so-called 'cash sweep' mechanism whereby all operating cash flow in the particular period is applied to repaying the loan.

(3) 'B' senior loan: this is a loan that is repaid after the 'A' loan at a higher margin above LIBOR to reflect its longer term. For security purposes it ranks alongside the 'A' senior loan. Typically this would have been a 'bullet loan' (i.e. repayable in a single instalment after the 'A' Loan) but in this example it starts to be repaid after year 3 reflecting the early repayment of part of the 'A' loan.

(4) 'C' mezzanine loan: a long-term loan ranking after the 'A' and 'B' senior loans for security purposes, and repayable after the senior debt has been repaid. To reflect the increased risk of this loan, the interest rate is higher and the loan also has an equity warrant entitling the mezzanine providers to subscribe for 2 per cent of the equity of the group.

Table 6.6. Illustrative financing structure

Funding structure	£000	% of funding	% of equity
Management	500	0.5	17.5%
Private equity investor			
Institutional ordinary sahres	2,300		80.5%
'D' institutional loanstock	45,200		
	47,500	43.8	
Mezzanine	13,000	12.0	2.0%
Bank acquisition finance			
'A' senior loan	32,000		
'B' senior loan	13,000		
	45,000	41.5	
Acquisition price + costs	106,000		
Periodic working capital	2,500	2.3	
Total funding	108,500	100.0	100.0%

Management 'hurt money' has no impact on equity percentage

Private equity invests in a mix of shares and loans

Mezzanine generates returns from both yield and capital gain using warrants

Bank invets in layers of debt

The Private Equity fund provides funding in two layers.

(5) 'D' PIK institutional loanstock: this loan ranks after the senior debt and mezzanine, is unsecured and therefore carries significant risk. The loan is a PIK loan which, as explained in Chapter 3, rolls up its interest by issuing further loan notes rather than paying interest in cash.

(6) Institutional 'A' preferred ordinary shares: these shares will have preferential rights when compared to the other ordinary shares invested in by management.

As we illustrated in Chapter 3, the private equity fund is seeking to maximize the blended return on their total investment in the scheme. The relative cost of each layer provided by the private equity fund is therefore less significant than the blended cost of the layers taken together.

As noted above, the management provide a nominal investment which is not significant in the total funding structure, but represents the 'hurt money' commitment of the key people that the private equity investor wishes to incentivise. This is provided as:

(7) Ordinary shares: these have none of the preferred rights of the 'A' ordinary shares other than to share in capital gains.

The Impact of Leverage on Profits and Cash

The proposed funding structure is overlaid on the operating projections in Table 6.7 showing the projected profit and loss (P&L) account after funding costs.

Table 6.7. Summary of projected profit and loss after funding

Summary of projected consolidated profit and loss accounts	Actual £000	Year 1** £000	Year 2 £000	Year 3 £000	Year 4 £000
Turnover	167,250	158,888	163,654	168,564	173,621
EBITA	7,762	2,495	15,205	15,787	16,383
Goodwill amortization		(3,148)	(3,148)	(3,148)	(3,148)
EBIT	7,762	(652)	12,057	12,640	13,245
Interest					
'A' senior		(1,440)	(1,200)	(763)	(572)
'B' senior		(715)	(715)	(715)	(715)
'C' mezzanine		(1,560)	(1,755)	(1,755)	(1,755)
'D' institutional loanstock		(4,520)	(4,972)	(5,469)	(6,016)
Overdraft/cash on deposit		117	17	25	(35)
	(800)	(8,118)	(8,625)	(8,677)	4,203
Profit before tax	6,962	(8,770)	3,432	3,962	4,203
Tax	(1,950)	(1,750)	(3,371)	(3,751)	(4,039)
Deferred tax		(298)	(355)	(263)	(194)
Retained profit	5,013	(10,818)	(294)	(51)	(31)

PIK interest rolled up

Note: all costs are treated as being recognized at completion. This would not normally be the case. Costs of issuing debt instruments are accounted for under IAS39 and costs of issuing equity instruments are accounted for under IAS32. All other costs associated with the acquisition must be expensed; and all transaction fees have been omitted from the analysis.

The business thus projects a fall in net profit before tax from £6,962k profit before tax in the year prior to the transaction to a (£14,770k) loss in year 1. However, this apparent reversal of performance reflects both the accounting treatment of goodwill, transaction fees, and costs and interest charges (both paid in cash and rolled up) which are summarized in Figure 6.6 and Table 6.7.

The actual cash interest paid in each year is lower than the interest charge shown in the profit and loss account (Figure 6.7 and Table 6.8). The interest rolled up preserves the cashflows of the business and mitigates the financial risks of the highly geared structure to the company during the roll-up period.

The PIK interest increases as interest-on-interest is charged.

The cash flows of the business are therefore materially different to the reported profits, as shown in Figure 6.8 and Table 6.9.

Despite recording an accounting loss the business still has an increased liability to corporation tax. (This is explained in detail in Table 6.13.)

In Chapter 5, the basic banking financial covenants were explained and described. Figure 6.9 shows the projected values of three key ratios: cash generation to total debt service (cash cover) and two calculations of interest cover, one based on the charge in the profit and loss account, the other reflecting the actual interest payment made. Note that

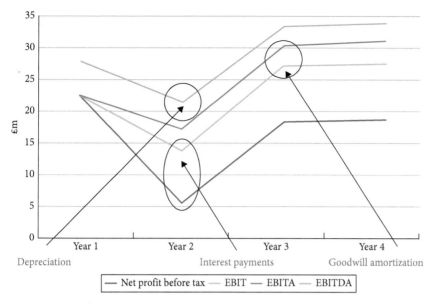

Figure 6.6. Profit: EBITDA, EBIT, NPBT

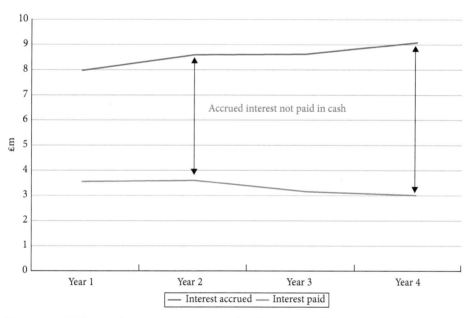

Figure 6.7. Difference between interest accrued and interest paid

the definition used is adjusted to add back budgeted restructuring costs. It is not uncommon for the bank and company/private equity investors to negotiate the exact definition of each covenant, as well as the level at which it is set, so that it is tailored precisely to the individual assumptions that underlie the transaction.

The ratio of total debt service to cash flow is analogous to the ratio of salary to total mortgage repayment in a house purchase: it measures the ability to service the loan.

Table 6.8. Reconciliation of interest charges

	Actual (£000)	Year 1 (£000)	Year 2 (£000)	Year 3 (£000)	Year 4 (£000)
Profit and loss charge	(800)	(8,118)	(8,622)	(8,694)	(9,077)
Interest rolled up and not paid	0	4,250	4,972	5,469	6,016
Interest paid	(800)	(3,598)	(3,650)	(3,225)	(3,060)

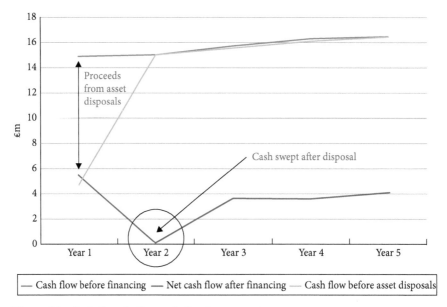

Figure 6.8. Cash flows before and after finance costs

Similarly the ratio of tangible assets (i.e. excluding goodwill) to secured borrowings is analogous to loan-to-value ratios in a mortgage. It is summarized in Figure 6.10, showing each loan layered on the next separately. The bank 'A' and 'B' senior loans become progressively less risky as they are repaid.

These projected values of the various financial ratios would form the basis of the negotiation around setting the levels of the financial covenants in the banking agreements. Typically one might expect to set covenants with headroom of 20–50 per cent before a breach would occur, depending on the particular ratio and the dynamics of the business.

Restructured Balance Sheet

The output of the financial engineering process is a restructured balance sheet that is tailored to accommodate the plan of the business. The forecast balance sheet of the business is shown in Table 6.10. The rolled up PIK interest has been shown as an increase in the loanstock.

The presentation of the company's balance sheet shows net assets as negative at completion. An alternative presentation commonly used in the management accounts of PE-backed companies shows the loanstock as if it were equity as shown in Table 6.11.

Table 6.9. Summary of cash flows after funding

Summary of projected cash flows	Actual £000	Year 1 £000	Year 2 £000	Year 3 £000	Year 4 £000
EBITA	7,762	2,495	15,205	15,787	16,383
Capex	(2,000)	(5,000)	(2,500)	(2,500)	(2,500)
Depreciation	5,000	4,167	2,639	2,616	2,596
Working capital	500	3,262	(292)	(301)	(310)
Proceeds of slae of fixed assets	0	10,000	0	0	0
Operating cash flow	10,262	14,924	15,052	15,602	16,169
Interest	(800)	(3,598)	(3,650)	(3,225)	(3,060)
	9,462	11,326	11,401	12,378	13,109
Tax	(1,950)	(490)	(1,321)	(3,250)	(3,957)
Draw down/ (repayment) of debt					
'A' senior	–	(5,333)	(9,715)	(4,238)	(4,238)
'B' senior	–	0	0	(1,096)	(1,096)
'C' mezzanine	–	0	0	0	0
'D' institutional loanstock – PIK	–	0	0	0	0
Net inflow/(outflow)	7,512	5,503	365	3,794	3,818
Opening cash/ (overdraft)	(17,512)	0	5,503	5,867	9,662
Closing cash/ (overdraft)	(10,000)	5,503	5,867	9,662	13,480

Proceeds from asset sale used to repay
'A' senior loan using a cash sweep mechanism

The business is acquired cash free/debt free therefore the borrowings are refinanced and the group has zero opening cash

This presentation is justified because while the loan stock in isolation is a debt-like instrument, it is in fact part of the overall equity investment and has equity-like risks.

The presentation highlights a fundamental feature of many Private Equity-backed transactions: the net assets of the business attributable to the equity holders remain broadly constant in the medium term as profits are used to service the funding structure put in place to acquire the business. In a quoted company context this would be conceptually equivalent to distributing all profits as dividends at the year end.

PIK Loanstock: Return of the 'Equity Illusion'?

The representation of the balance sheet in Table 6.12 highlights a feature that has become increasingly common over the past decade: the growth in net assets is almost entirely paid to the holders of the PIK loan note, typically the private equity investor.

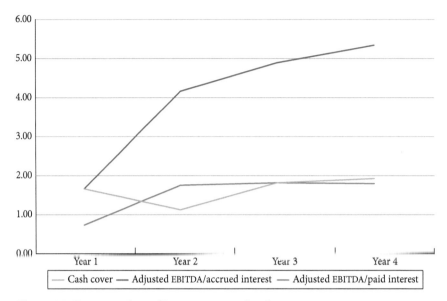

Figure 6.9. Forecast values of interest cover and cash cover

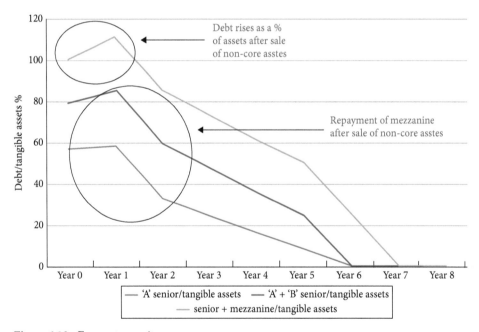

Figure 6.10. Forecast security cover

In this type of structure the management only benefit from a high equity percentage if the business can grow more rapidly than the PIK debt accrues interest. When businesses cease to grow, value flows from the ordinary shareholders (i.e. management) to the loan-stock holders (the private equity investors) due to the rolling-up interest-on-interest. This may be a deliberate trigger mechanism designed to force the earliest consideration of an exit, but in practice it can erode the managers' incentives significantly if it is, or is perceived to be, inequitable.

Table 6.10. Summary of projected balance sheets

£000	Opening	Year 1	Year 2	Year 3	Year 4
Fixed assets					
Goodwill	62,950	59,503	56,055	52,608	49,160
Tangible fixed asstes	25,000	15,833	15,964	15,579	15,482
	87,950	75,336	71,749	68,187	64,642
Working capital					
Stocks	15,000	13,815	14,229	14,656	15,096
Trade debtors	20,000	18,565	19,122	19,695	20,286
Other current asstes	2,500	2,375	2,446	2,520	2,595
Creditors	(22,500)	(22,246)	(22,913)	(23,600)	(24,308)
Other creditors	(2,000)	(2,771)	(2,854)	(1,939)	(3,028)
	13,000	9,738	10,030	10,332	10,641
Other creditors					
Corporation tax	(490)	0	(440)	(937)	(1,007)
Deferred tax	(460)	(758)	(1,113)	(1,376)	(1,571)
	(950)	(758)	(1,553)	(2,313)	(2,578)
Closing cash/ (overdraft)	(10,000)	5,503	5,687	9,662	13,480
	(32,000)				
'A' senior	(32,000)	(26,667)	(16,951)	(12,714)	(8,476)
'B' senior	(13,000)	(13,000)	(13,000)	(11,905)	(10,809)
'C' mezzanine	(13,000)	(13,000)	(13,000)	(13,000)	(13,000)
'D' institutional loanstock – PIK	(45,200)	(49,720)	(54,692)	(16,161)	(66,177)
Cash/overdraft	0	5,503	5,867	9,662	13,480
	(103,200)	(96,884)	(91,776)	(88,117)	(84,982)
Net assets	(3,200)	(12,568)	(11,550)	(11,913)	(12,276)
Ordinary shares	2,800	2,800	2,800	2,800	2,800
Reserves	(6,000)	(15,368)	(14,350)	(14,713)	(15,076)
	(3,200)	(12,568)	(11,550)	(11,913)	(12,276)

Sale of £10m property

Impact of feels paid at completion

Impact of rolling uo interest on PIK debt

This issue may also arise in secondary buyouts and recapitalizations where management roll over their original equity stake into a higher equity stake in the business, but a layer of high-cost PIK debt ranks ahead of that new equity. Integrated finance structures where one institution provides all the layers of capital are often characterized by high yield to the institution and higher equity stake to the management team. The structure increases the risks and rewards of the management while protecting the institutional investor against some of the risks of the investment.

Table 6.11. Alternative balance sheet presentation

	Opening (£000)	Year 1 (£000)	Year 2 (£000)	Year 3 (£000)	Year 4 (£000)
Net assets per the accounts	(3,200)	(12,568)	(11,550)	(11,913)	(12,276)
'D' institutional loanstock	45,200	49,720	54,692	60,161	66,177
Net assets attributable to shareholders	42,000	37,152	43,142	48,249	53,902

Table 6.12. PIK debt and the equity illusion

Alternative presentation of balance sheet	Opening (£000)	Year 1 (£000)	Year 2 (£000)	Year 3 (£000)	Year 4 (£000)
Net assets per the accounts	(3,200)	(12,568)	(11,550)	(11,913)	(12,276)
'D' institutional loanstock	45,200	49,720	54,692	60,161	66,177
Net assets attributable to shareholders	42,000	37,152	43,142	48,249	53,902
Increase/(decrease) in net assets		(4,848)	5,991	5,106	5,653
(Increase) in accrued value of 'D' loanstock		(4,520)	(4,972)	(5,469)	(6,015)
% of value accruing to loanstock		N/A	83%	107%	106%

When managers have a high-equity percentage but a low share in the growth of the value of the business, we call the situation the 'equity illusion'.

Taxation: How Much Tax Is Paid by a Private Equity-Backed Company?

It is of the utmost importance for any commentator or analyst to clearly understand that there is almost always a difference between the profits reported in a company's audited accounts and the profits calculated for taxation purposes. Failure to understand this results in misconceptions in the public understanding of how businesses are taxed and incentivised to act by the taxation system.

In the example, the profit for tax purposes is materially different from the pre-tax profit recorded in the accounts (see Table 6.13 and Figure 6.11), and this is explained in detail below.

Table 6.13. Restatement of profit for tax purposes

Tax computations	Notes	Year 1 (£000)	Year 2 (£000)	Year 3 (£000)	Year 4 (£000)
Net profit before tax		(8,770)	3,432	3,962	4,203
Depreciation	1	4,167	2,639	2,616	2,596
Writing down allowances	2	(4,375)	(3,906)	(3,555)	(3,291)
Disallowable interest	3	6,080	6,727	7,224	7,771
Disallowable fees		6,000			
Goodwill amortization	4	3,148	3,148	3,148	3,148
Taxable profit/(loss)		6,249	12,039	13,395	14,427
Tax rate	*	28.0%	28.0%	28.0%	28.0%
Tax payable	5	1,750	3,371	3,751	4,039

* Assumption: a main rate of corporation tax of 28 per cent has been used for the purpose of the case study. Actual rates can be found at www.hmrc.gov.uk.

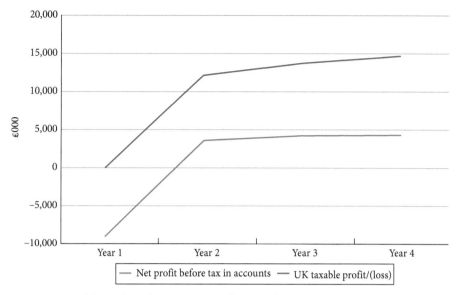

Figure 6.11. Taxable profit and accounting profit are different

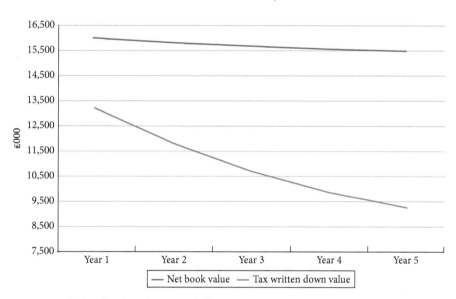

Figure 6.12. The book value of assets is different to the tax written-down value because of accelerated capital allowances

Notes 1 and 2: Depreciation and Capital Allowance

Depreciation is calculated differently for accounting and tax purposes. Typically, capital investment is allowed to be deducted more rapidly for corporation tax purposes than it is depreciated in a company's accounts, thus creating a positive tax incentive to invest in qualifying assets. This accelerated depreciation is achieved by adding back depreciation and replacing it with writing down or accelerated capital allowances (Figure 6.12).

This is common to all companies. The timing difference between recognizing depreciation and writing down allowances may give rise to a deferred tax asset/liability. This lies outside the scope of this discussion, but reflects future tax charges that have been deferred, not current ones.

Note 3: Interest Accrued but not Paid

Interest is generally allowed to be deducted when it is accrued in the company's accounts, but there are a number of regulations that are designed to prevent the artificial creation of timing differences between when interest is paid and when it is accrued. As the interest on the PIK debt is not paid within a year of the date that it is accrued, in this example it is assumed that it would not be allowed to be deducted for tax purposes.

Thin Capitalization and the Arm's-Length Test

In tax terms a UK company may be said to be thinly capitalized when it has excessive debt in relation to its arm's-length borrowing capacity, leading to the possibility of excessive interest deductions. Since March 2005, interest on loans from connected parties that are not on arm's-length commercial terms is not allowed to be deducted for corporation tax.

In some countries there is a strict limit imposed which defines the amount of debt on which interest is allowed to be deducted against corporation tax. In the UK, HMRC often uses rules of thumb relating to debt/equity and interest cover, but there is no strictly defined limit.

The main development in private equity business taxation since the last edition was published is the introduction of base erosion and profit shifting and the fixed-ratio rule, generally limiting tax-deductible interest to 30 per cent of EBITDA.

In this example, the debt capacity of the business is fully utilized to support the funding from the bank and mezzanine provider. It is therefore assumed that no third-party bank would provide the loanstock on the terms provided by the private equity investor and thus it is assumed that the interest would not be allowed to be deducted.

It is important for commentators and analysts to understand that the rules on interest deductibility have changed significantly to reduce the deductibility of interest in most leveraged buyouts.

Note 4: Goodwill Deductibility

In Chapter 3 we explained that goodwill is the difference between the acquisition cost of a business and its net asset value. The calculation of the value of goodwill in the worked example is illustrated in Table 6.14 and Figure 6.13.

In this example, the goodwill is written down in twenty equal annual instalments of £3.1m. When qualifying assets are acquired rather than shares, some or all of the goodwill may be deductible against corporation tax. However, when shares are acquired, goodwill amortization is not allowed to be deducted against corporation tax and is added back to calculate the tax charge.

Note that if a company's goodwill is impaired, a company will report a loss in the year equal to the reduction in the value of the goodwill. A distressed company may therefore report both reduced trading profits and a significant increase in losses due to the one-off impairment in goodwill. This one-off impairment charge has no impact on taxation.

Table 6.14. Calculation of goodwill

	£000
Purchase of 100% of shares	90,000
Net assets acquired	(27,050)
Goodwill	62,950

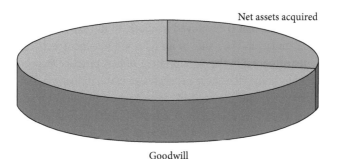

Net assets acquired

Goodwill

Figure 6.13. Representation of goodwill

Note 5: Overseas Profit and Double Taxation

Where profits have been earned and taxed in another country, there are treaties between countries that are designed to avoid the same income being taxed a second time.

For most companies, the payment of corporation tax is due nine calendar months and one day after the end of the accounting period. Large companies must pay their tax by quarterly instalments. The first of these is due six months and thirteen days from the start of the accounting period. Therefore, three payments are made before or immediately after the accounting year end and one three months later.

When shares are acquired the purchaser is responsible for the payment of tax relating to the prior year, but in most cases the acquisition price is adjusted to reflect this.

Summary of Company Corporation Tax

The detailed worked example is intended to illustrate a number of important facts about the taxation of UK corporations, including buyouts:

- writing off goodwill may materially reduce reported profits/increase reported losses, but does not reduce corporation tax where shares are being acquired;
- not all interest in leveraged buyouts is deductible against corporation tax, only arm's-length interest is deductible;
- as a result of these disallowances, even companies reporting a pre-tax loss may nevertheless still pay significant UK corporation tax;
- corporation tax paid by a company may be materially different to the tax liability recorded in its profit and loss account (this difference is disclosed in the notes to the audited accounts of all larger companies);
- when a strategy is implemented that improves profitability, generally more corporation tax will be paid, even in highly leveraged structures.

To appreciate fully the impact on UK tax revenues it is necessary to track the cash paid to advisers and bankers by the new company. The strength of the UK banking and professional services industry in private equity makes it likely, but not certain, that a high proportion of the tax revenues is generated by interest and fees.

What Is Investment Due Diligence?

Due diligence is the process that is employed to check, to the extent that it is possible, that the assumptions that underpin the value of an offer are not incorrect. The private equity industry has been instrumental in the development of best practice in pre-acquisition due diligence. It is argued by some that these processes gave the industry a material advantage in the overall market for corporate control. The focus of pre-deal investigations on the cash flows of the target not only underpins a valuation, but also enables the private equity fund to avoid many expensive investment mistakes by withdrawing from deals that are not viable.

Due diligence will cover all material relationships, contracts, and assets of the target company using a combination of legal, accounting, market, insurance, environmental, and any other specialist advisers.

Typically, full due diligence will take not less than three or four weeks to complete and will be a condition of any initial offer a private equity fund makes.

The outputs of the due diligence process are extensive, and have often enabled private equity purchasers to use their enhanced knowledge to negotiate from a position of strength after the completion of diligence. This may have contributed to the reputation of private equity buyers for 'chipping' the agreed price prior to completion.

What Is Vendor Due Diligence (VDD) and How Does It Impact Risks and Rewards?

As discussed earlier, to address the problems that can arise if due diligence is performed by the acquirer it became increasingly common for vendors to commission due diligence on behalf of the purchasers: so-called 'vendor due diligence'.

Vendor due diligence is provided and addressed to the purchaser by the authors once a headline transaction is agreed, but the initial scope of the review is set by the vendor who has the opportunity to review the reports before the purchaser does. Arguably, this reduces the risk of diligence-backed price chips close to completion. Furthermore, as it can be completed prior to agreeing a deal, it enables the process to be streamlined by several weeks. The counterargument is that any purchaser will wish to choose their own advisers and the terms on which they are working, which may not be those that would have been chosen by the potential purchaser.

The use of vendor due diligence increased as market activity increased. When transaction activity is low, it is widely expected to decrease as funders of acquirers, particularly banks, wish to use their own advisers rather than have them imposed by the vendors. This seems to be consistent with a view that vendor due diligence transfers risk to the purchaser or, equivalently, captures a greater share of the rewards of a transaction for the vendor rather than the purchaser.

Sensitivity Analysis

Sensitivity analysis is often completed by the providers of due diligence services, but it is strictly not a diligence activity as it relates to the impact of changing assumptions rather than the evaluation of the realism of those assumptions.

Prior to any transaction, a wide array of sensitivity analyses will be undertaken on the financial projections to ensure that the financing structure is robust to all reasonable outcomes. Sensitivities in the particular example above might include:

- failure to achieve, or a delay in, the planned asset sales at the assumed price;
- delay or failure to reduce overheads or greater costs of restructuring;
- greater sales loss due to increased prices, or failure to achieve higher pricing resulting in failure to achieve enhanced gross profit margins;
- delay in, or failure to achieve, improved working capital management;
- a combination of any or all of the above timing differences and changes in outcome.

An alternative approach is to test the financing package by finding the limits at which the business is unable to service its capital structure. For instance, one might analyse by how much sales can reduce before the banking covenants are breached or, conversely, by how much sales can grow within the working capital facilities of the structure.

It can be seen that even in this relatively simple stylized model, there are a wide variety of potential outcomes against which a financial structure needs to be stress tested. This process entails a great deal of analysis by the various advisers to the transaction (for example accountants, industry consultants, and market researchers) and the outputs of the analyses will form a key part of the negotiation between the private equity investors, the management, and the bankers.

If the due diligence process results in the private equity investor having to make material changes to the assumed risks and returns there may be a renegotiation with the vendor. This may result in:

- a simple price reduction;
- deferring payment, possibly contingent upon achieving a certain outcome (e.g. winning a particular revenue stream or selling a particular asset);
- the vendor co-investing alongside the funders to reduce the funding requirement and to share a portion of the risk identified;
- a failure to complete the transaction.

Exits and Returns

In this final section, we illustrate the combined effects of financial engineering and value creation on the returns to the various participants in the transaction.

There are three questions to address.

(1) How much is the enterprise value changed by the trading improvements within the company?

Table 6.15. The equity waterfall: enterprise value and equity value at exit

Exit value	Year 1 £000	Year 2 £000	Year 3 £000	Year 4 £000	Year 5 £000
EBITA	5,995	15,205	15,787	16,383	16,399
Notional tax charge	(1,679)	(4,257)	(4,420)	(4,588)	(4,592)
	4,317	10,947	11,367	11,795	11,807
P/E ratio	12.00	12.00	12.00	12.00	12.00
Gross capitalization	51,799	131,369	136,402	141,546	141,684
Less:					
'A' senior	(26,667)	(16,951)	(12,714)	(8,476)	(4,238)
'B' senior	(13,000)	(13,000)	(11,905)	(10,809)	(9,714)
'C' mezzanine	(13,000)	(13,000)	(13,000)	(13,000)	(13,000)
'D' institutional loanstock – PIK	(49,720)	(54,692)	(60,161)	(66,177)	(72,795)
Cash/(overdraft)	4,190	2,908	6,313	10,165	14,360
Net debt	(98,196)	(94,736)	(91,467)	(88,297)	(85,387)
Net equity value	(46,398)	36,633	44,935	53,248	56,298
Equity value as % of enterprise value	na	28%	33%	38%	40%

Note PIK roll-up increase value

Some models deduct exit fees and costs

Adding back restructuring cocts

Assumed to be lower than entry P/E ratio for prudence

(2) How much is the enterprise value changed by market conditions outside the company?

(3) How is the value apportioned between the various participants in the transaction?

Table 6.15 shows the projected value of the business each year on the assumption that it was sold on a debt free/cash free basis at a value calculated using a P/E ratio of 12 (i.e. 12 times forecast EBITA less a full tax charge).

The equity value initially reduces sharply then is projected to rise due to operational improvements. Thereafter equity value grows slowly and is due primarily to the accumulation of cash surpluses and debt repayment (Table 6.16).

As we have emphasized throughout the analysis, it is the blended return on the total amount invested that concerns the private equity fund, not the return on the equity

Table 6.16. Allocation of net equity value

Split of proceeds	% equity value	Year 1 (£000)	Year 2 (£000)	Year 3 (£000)	Year 4 (£000)	Year 5 (£000)
Management	17.5	0	6,411	7,864	9,318	9,852
Private equity investor	80.5	0	29,490	36,173	42,865	45,320
'C' mezzanine	2.0	0	733	899	1,065	1,126
Equity value	100	0	36,633	44,935	53,248	56,298
Management percentage of enterprise value	n/a		4.9%	5.8%	6.6%	7.0%

element of their investment. The effect on incremental value growth of the total investment including the PIK loanstock is summarized below.

It can be seen that the absolute value and the proportion of value that accrues to the
private equity fund increases over time due to a combination of the effects of increasing
enterprise value, de-leveraging by repaying bank debt, and the effect of the PIK roll-up on
loanstock values.

The increase in value can be analysed further to isolate the impact of operational performance improvements and the impact of the financial engineering.

The analysis in Table 6.18 shows that by year 3, approximately three-quarters of the
increase in value is attributable to an increase in enterprise value and one-quarter to the
effects of financial engineering. This is despite assuming a reduction in the exit EBITDA
multiple when compared to the acquisition price. There are further analyses that can be
undertaken to more fully understand the interconnection of operating performance,
external market conditions, and financial engineering, but these are outside the scope of
this book.

You will recall that earlier we pointed out that EBITDA does not cause value—it is
simply a shorthand measure that we use to talk about value. It is therefore misleading
to attribute changes in equity value to backward-looking EBITDA multiples (or

Table 6.17. Projected share of exit enterprise value by investor

Split of proceeds	Year 1 (£000)	Year 2 (£000)	Year 3 (£000)	Year 4 (£000)	Year 5 (£000)
Net debt including mezzanine warrant	48,476 (94%)	40,776 (31%)	32,204 (24%)	23,185 (16%)	13,717 (10%)
Private equity investor	3,322 (6%)	84,182 (64%)	96,334 (71%)	109,042 (77%)	118,115 (83%)
Management	0 (0%)	6,411 (5%)	7,864 (6%)	9,318 (7%)	9,852 (7%)
Total value	51,799 (100%)	131,369 (100%)	136,402 (100%)	141,546 (100%)	141,684 (100%)

Table 6.18. Reconciliation of the cumulative effects of operating performance and financial
engineering on projected equity value at exit in years 2 and 3

	Year 2 £000	Year 3 £000
Change of multiple	5,469	6,356
Change in EBITDA	25,900	30,046
Change in enterprise value	31,369	36,046
Change in net debt	8,464	11,733
Change in equity value	39,833	48,135
% due to operating performance	79%	76%
% due to financial engineering	21%	24%
Total	100%	100%

The majority of return comes from efficiency
improvements not financial engineering

Table 6.19. Split of proceeds on exit

Split of proceeds	Year 1 £000	Year 2 £000	Year 3 £000	Year 4 £000	Year 5 £000
Net debt including mezzanine warrant	48,476	40,776	32,204	23,185	13,717
Private equity investor	3,322	84,182	96,334	109,042	118,115
Management	0	6,411	7,864	9,318	9,852
Total value	51,799	131,369	136,402	141,546	141,684
Debt	94%	31%	24%	16%	10%
Private equity investor	4,190	2,908	6,313	10,165	14,360
Management	0%	5%	6%	7%	7%
	100%	100%	100%	100%	100%

The initial decrease in enterprise value falls on the equity and loan stock

forward-looking ones). Nevertheless, this analysis is very widely done and is routinely produced by advisers and funds.

Table 6.19 summarizes the projected capital returns to each party at the end of each of the first five years. At the end of year 1, management's equity has nil value, but by the end of year 2 it has accrued value. However, achievement of the forecasts thereafter does not significantly enhance their equity value. This is due to the fact that almost all the projected value increase after the bank has been serviced is appropriated by the loanstock interest roll up. This position will either encourage management to exit after the achievement of the turnaround, or create the incentives to take the business forward with a strategy that continues to generate above normal value, perhaps by acquisition or by new product development.

Whichever route is chosen, the objective of the capital structure is to create the circumstances that will encourage both the creation and the realization of value in the business with an acceptable level of risk.

The project rates of return to the various participants based upon an exit in year 3 on a P/E ratio of 12 are summarized in Table 6.20. The higher returns are correlated to the higher risks that each participant takes.

The final table (Table 6.21) shows the sensitivity of the returns to the private equity investor in this particular example to achievement of exit in a timely manner and

Table 6.20. Projected returns (IRRs) by participant (exit year 3, P/E = 12)

Projected rates of return	%
Senior debt	4.9
Mezzanine	16.2
Private equity investment	25.4
Management	150.5
Weighted cost of capital	15.5

Table 6.21. Private equity investor blended returns—sensitized by year of exit and exit P/E ratio

IRR sensitivities Years of exit	Exit private equity ratio		
	10.00	12.00	14.00
Exit in year 3		25.4%	33.3%
Exit in year 4	16.2%	22.3%	27.6%
Exit in year 5	15.0%	19.3%	23.1%

Investment 'base case' forecast returns

highlights the performance against a target rate of return of 25 per cent. Exit at a lower price or after a longer time period will have a significant impact on returns.

Closing Remarks

In this section we have described in some detail the process and logic of a particular fictional (but nevertheless realistic) leveraged buyout. We have attempted to illustrate the way that each of the financial parties to the transaction layers their investment and how the risk and returns increase as each layer is structured.

We have briefly discussed how due diligence is used to verify the assumptions behind the plan and how sensitivity analysis is used to stress test the financial structure.

We have provided a detailed example showing why loss-making private equity backed companies nevertheless often pay corporation tax. We highlight the fact that contrary to some less well-informed commentaries, interest on buyout debt is not all tax deductible, and the rules on tax deductibility have significantly tightened, mainly prior to the more recent interest in private equity.

7

The Private Equity Critics
and the Research

In this final chapter we draw together the major criticisms levelled at the private equity sector. We clarify some misrepresentations and myths, in the light of experience over the evolution of the market and the weight of systematic evidence summarized in this book. We then look at areas which, in our opinion, are under-researched.

We need to distinguish between analysis at the fund level and at the level of the underlying individual investments. The majority of studies in the finance literature are at the fund level and discuss private equity as an investment strategy. Analysis at the investment level is often done by case study, which always risks creating general conclusions from specific examples.

The non-financial academic literature has more investment-level analysis both from a quantitative and a qualitative perspective.

At the Level of Individual Investments

The Industry is Short-Termist and Results in Underinvestment and Value Extraction

One major strand of the critique of private equity is that it is short-termist and does not build long-term value.

It is claimed that private equity is about cutting jobs, stripping assets, derecognizing unions, and exiting the business in a short time horizon. This, it is claimed, is value extraction, not value creation.

There is now a very significant body of systematic evidence available—and summarized here—which shows that this view is very simplistic and cannot be applied to the majority of private equity strategies. Private equity deals are varied and heterogeneous in terms of their strategies and timescales. In Figure 7.1 we try to simplify this variety of contrasting timescales and strategies.

Some investments do involve one-off 'shock therapy' (Quadrant 4) to increase prices, reduce costs, and improve capital intensity. We need to emphasize that shock therapy can be a necessary alternative to acute and chronic underperformance. This is consistent with the principal–agent hypothesis in academic research. It may involve the reversal of value-destroying behaviour in order to improve efficiency over a short time period. This type of shock therapy was probably more typical of the first wave of PE-backed buyouts in the 1980s. In these types of transaction, the management of the company are supported by the

Private Equity Demystified: An explanatory guide. Fourth Edition. John Gilligan and Mike Wright, Oxford University Press (2020).
© John Gilligan & Mike Wright. DOI: 10.1093/oso/9780198866961.003.0007

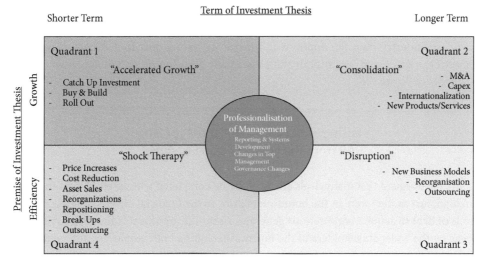

Figure 7.1. Buyout types, strategy, and timescale
Source: The authors

PE firm in introducing financial and governance processes that eliminate waste and improve efficiency.

A second category of transaction is a longer-term strategic repositioning (Quadrant 3). We might characterize these as transactions where a company needs to take a step back to take two steps forward. This is notoriously difficult to achieve as a quoted company, or as part of a quoted company, where stable earnings growth is highly valued. These situations often involve initial falls in employment and radical cost reduction in failing business lines, alongside investment in the streams that will support future growth. The idea is to rebuild the base for a more stable business over the longer term that can recover employment and profitability and return to a more stable earnings pattern.

The two other categories of transaction involve growth strategies, rather than cost cutting and reconstruction. Where businesses have been capital-constrained by their owners, a PE-backed buyout may provide the opportunity for catch-up investment or M&A that generates a step change in the business in relatively short order (Quadrant 1) (accelerated growth).

Finally, some investments are made based on longer-term growth strategies (Quadrant 2) either by sector or internationally. These may be buy and build strategies, or longer-term growth that is at the limit of the traditional 10+2 fund.

An individual investment might incorporate many or indeed all of these strategies at once.

At the centre of all of these strategies is the core idea of improving management and management systems to generate information and control that facilitates the decisions required to increase future cash flows that are the source of shareholder value.

When looked at through this lens private equity is not an investment strategy, it is a collection of strategies with a common theme of seeking to use professionalization of business management and an efficient financing structure to create and realize capital appreciation.

The critics focus on the unpleasant and damaging consequences on individuals of the efficiency strategies, but rarely comment on the employment effects of the growth strategies. The industry does the opposite and hence we have a polarized 'debate' about the impact of private equity, with both sides essentially focusing on only one or two of the quadrants of Figure 7.1.

Is There Excessive Debt and Are Gains
All from the Use of Cheap Leverage?

Critics have argued that many deals are again being completed with levels of debt that are too high, just as they were in the boom years prior to the financial crisis. Using 'excessive' levels of debt to acquire corporations generates risks. The argument is that these risks are borne by the wider stakeholders of the business including both employees and creditors. Neither of these groups benefit from the increased rewards that this risk generates.

Recent evidence has broadly confirmed that the private equity industry is a taker of increased availability of leverage, not a generator of the supply of debt. Leverage rises when credit is more freely available and falls, even for the most established private equity funds, when credit tightens.

We have seen that attribution is controversial. However, the published attribution studies show that while some gains derive from the leverage in private equity deals, the largest proportion comes from fundamental improvements to the business. It is not clear whether this reflects good stock picking (i.e. the extent to which Private Equity firms are good at selecting good deals) or good operational management post transaction (i.e. whether they add value once they have made an investment). The most recent industry research seems to show that operational improvements account for less than the inflation in overall asset prices caused by the low interest rate environment of the last decade in the West.

The evidence on growth vs efficiency is not conclusive. More data and analysis at the investment level is needed to have any clear idea if there is a difference in the overall performance of any strategy.

Looking at the risk element in the equation, our review of the evidence indicates that after taking other factors into account, PE-backed firms are not significantly more likely to enter formal bankruptcy proceedings (administration) than non-PE-backed companies.

Recent evidence based on the population of UK limited companies has also found that during the period 2008–11, and taking into account firm-specific, industry, and macro-economic factors, PE-backed buyouts reported significantly higher profitability and cumulative average growth rates than non-PE-backed private companies. These findings suggest that PE-backed firms' underlying performance held up better during the recession following the financial crash than did that for non-PE-backed private companies. This result has been independently replicated on both sides of the Atlantic.

Is Private Equity about Majority Acquisitions
of Large Listed Corporations?

While majority acquisitions by private equity firms of listed corporations tend to attract considerable media (and research) attention, these deals are only part of the private equity market. In the boom period of 1999–2003 they accounted on average for under about 5 per cent of deal numbers and less than a quarter of deal value across Europe. Even after something of a resurgence from 2017, in 2018 these P2Ps accounted for 2 per cent of deal numbers and almost 16 per cent of total deal value in Europe.

In contrast, the largest single source of deal numbers across Europe has traditionally involved buyouts of private/family firms, followed by divestments and secondary buyouts. The largest single source of deal value has traditionally been divestments by domestic or foreign corporations, though in recent years secondary buyouts have taken the top position.

The extent of majority private equity stakes was once very much a function of the size of the deal, with larger deals having majority equity stakes held by PE firms. Today majority private equity ownership is becoming the norm even in smaller deals.

What Happened to 'The Wall of Debt' and Is There a New One?

Many commentators forecast that the debt raised by buyouts in the boom years would precipitate a secondary crisis when it came to be refinanced. This so-called 'wall of debt' to be refinanced was effectively dealt with by the market and did not cause the predicted problems. Low interest rates and 'pretend and extend', whereby loans are rolled over despite being behind the original plan, went a long way to alleviating and pushing the supposed problem into the future.

An increasing appetite by banks, bond holders, and debt funds to grow their business lending books again has led to an increase in debt availability. Debt funds do not generally lend amortizing loans: their core product is a unitranche loan with a bullet repayment. Furthermore, cov-lite (which we explained in Chapter 5) also re-emerged. There is therefore still a 'wall of debt' to repay or refinance. We would caution that if this trend were to continue, problems may be created for the future.

Is there a Lack of Consultation in Private Equity Owned Firms?

Concerns about lack of consultation with workers relates to periods both prior to and after a private equity acquisition. This criticism gets caught up with the TUPE issue we discussed earlier. Because private equity usually involves both a transaction and a change or refocusing of strategy, there are huge changes in the business, both real and perceived. It may well be good commercial practice to consult with some wider stakeholder groups about these changes, but there is no reason to believe that consulting in and of itself is socially desirable or effective and therefore should be a requirement. It is clear that a change of ownership necessarily entails uncertain times for many people. There is no evidence that we are aware of that the cohort of companies owned by private equity consult more or less than any other business in a similar change of ownership.

Furthermore, we are not aware of any evidence-based consensus that such a consultative process is correlated with the economic and social outcomes of any investment or group of investments.

If we take the consensus from the evidence bases on corporate mergers and acquisitions (M&A) and private equity, we arrive at a very different conclusion. It is widely believed that M&A by corporates tends to be unsuccessful in generating shareholder value. It is also, less strongly, believed that private equity has generated returns higher than those of quoted companies. Therefore, the question for research is not whether PE-style transactions should change their management approach; rather it is why are corporations worse at mergers and acquisitions than private equity investors?

Is There Tax Avoidance and Why Are Tax Havens Used?

There are two threads to these criticisms. The first revolves around the deductibility of interest paid on loans borrowed to fund buyouts. While the position varies from country to country, the general position is similar. Whereas in the past most interest was deductible, for many years in most countries this has no longer been the case. All tax authorities acted to stop abuse by using excessive levels of debt. The critics who raise this argument are often apparently unaware that authorities acted to deal with the issue many years ago.

The second, more general criticism is that both investee companies and the private funds themselves adopt artificial and convoluted structures to reduce tax in ways that are legal but not available to others, and therefore unfairly favour private equity. This is wrong in detail. Many of the apparently artificial structures have nothing to do with tax. They are designed within the confines of countries' laws to manage liabilities as well as taxation.

There are no particular arrangements available to private equity funds that are not also available to others. Therefore, the debate about offshore and international taxation is a manifestation of a more general debate, outside the scope of this commentary, about the taxation of corporations and individuals generally.

Our only observation is that the critics do not seem to be arguing that any laws are being broken. They appear to be arguing that the laws are wrong or wrongly interpreted. That is surely a matter for politicians and legislators. Businesses are not responsible for the regulatory framework, nor should they be.

Is there a Misalignment of Incentives?

Not all of the critics are ideologically opposed to the industry. Criticisms concerning misalignment of incentives have arisen from among those actively involved in private equity. The central assumption of private equity is that shareholders' interests should be the primary concern of the management of any company. While it may sound controversial to some, this is simply a restatement of the basic responsibilities of any director of a 'for profit' limited company. The shareholders own the business and management are duty bound to act in the interests of the shareholders, subject to the constraint that they must not trade insolvently and must observe the various rights of employees, customers, and other groups. There are those who believe that businesses should have wider objectives—indeed in the UK these are entrenched in statute. But there are no significant differences between PE and non-PE businesses in those respects.

Equity illusion. As we described, management of portfolio companies may suffer from 'equity illusion'. They may hold a significant proportion of the equity of the business (a large 'equity percentage'). However, they may have so much investment ranking ahead of them that has to be repaid before any value is shared by the equity that they cannot realistically accrue any value in their apparent equity stake. In this scenario, management are no longer aligned with the private equity sponsors. This misalignment arises where investors take a priority yield that may effectively appropriate equity value to the private equity fund.

Time value of money. Management teams are typically interested in the absolute amount of capital gain whereas private equity funds may target a return on their investment. This can create differences in exit strategy between shareholders and managers due to the time value of money. Fund lifetimes and the mechanics of carried interest may also create differences in the exit preferences between investors and management.

Funding acquisitions. Acquisitions often require further equity funding. Where this dilutes management equity or puts instruments that have a priority return to equity into the capital structure, incentives may change.

Credit default swaps. Hedging techniques have created potentially perverse incentives for purchasers or holders of debt in distressed companies. Where loans are publicly traded, purchasers of loans that are 'guaranteed' using credit default swaps may be incentivised to bring about a loan default rather than avoid one. They may therefore be incentivised to induce failure.

At the Fund Level

Conflicts of Interest and Value Extraction

At the fund level there are criticisms of the potential conflicts of interest that arise when funds have strong control of the underlying investee companies and low controls on their actions from their limited partners. The argument is simple and logical. Private equity funds control the companies they acquire. Due to the partnership structures used in funds to limit investors' liability, the fund managers are not controlled in a similar way by those investors. LPs simply cannot have any management controls without risking losing limited liability. This creates the possibility that fund managers can operate in a 'black box' and extract value from investments in a way that benefits their business interests, not their investors. This is not a theoretical risk. It has been found to have happened in high-profile funds in a number of countries. Significant fines have been paid as a result.

It is argued that reputational risk will limit these behaviours. LPs will not invest in funds that they think will abuse their relationships. This is logical but is not supported by any comprehensive research we know of. In part this is because there is very poor data on private equity fund failure. It takes many years to unwind a dying portfolio and the research on the secondary market in zombie funds is very thin indeed.

Historical Performance is Misrepresented

We have already described at some length the issue around performance measurement at the fund level. Surprisingly little is published about performance at the individual investment level.

The data that exists is reasonably clear. Gross performance has exceeded most alternatives that investors might have invested in, but that comes with a significant lack of liquidity that carries risks. Performance after fees is obviously lower and the trend seems to be that it is falling and compressing. Both the average fund performance and the variance of returns seem to be falling. However, private equity funds are hard to assess as they are investing, and therefore all analysis is always incomplete.

IRR is a poor measure of performance and is widely abused in marketing materials. It is however deeply embedded in the private equity discourse, not least because carried interest is usually paid after achieving a hurdle expressed as an IRR.

The appropriate yardstick for any individual potential investor is their opportunity cost, measured by comparing what they would have earned had they not invested in private equity. This results in an array of public market equivalent indices. The data on these is still poor, but the published research still shows PME outperformance in the past. There is a debate about which index to use that highlights the real underlying issue: investment decisions cannot be distilled into single figures, no matter how compelling the narrative that the index creates.

Valuation of Unrealized Investments Is Manipulated

Private equity managers are fund managers who seek to raise a series of funds. Due to the long-term nature of the funds and the unquoted nature of the investments made, the ultimate returns on any fund are not known until the fund is fully realized. This will become clear long after the usual six-year investment horizon. Therefore, the valuation of the unrealized investments in any existing fund will be an important influence on the decision of existing and new investors looking to invest in any new fund a manger is raising. There is therefore a material incentive to flatter the returns of unrealized fund investments when fund raising. There is some evidence that this occurs but other evidence to suggest that valuations are excessively prudent when compared to realized exits.

In a small minority of funds fees are paid on the value of assets, not their cost, giving another incentive to overvalue.

Most funds will have their valuations audited, but it is the responsibility of the directors, not the auditors, to value the assets. More work needs to be done.

Fund Level Fees Are Excessive

Investors in private equity have been vocal in their concern that the original tightly aligned model of the industry has been materially weakened as funds have become larger and managers have become multi-fund managers. Whereas a small PE fund relies heavily on sharing in capital gains to generate wealth for its partners, large multi-fund managers may be more motivated by the fees generated than the outcomes achieved. Fees have become larger as funds have grown, and the excess of fees over fund costs has grown in absolute terms, providing a higher guaranteed income to the manager and, therefore, higher profit to its partners.

Therefore, there is an incentive to maximize the fund size (consistent with the investment opportunities for the fund) in order to increase the management fee income. Critics have argued that as fund size has grown, the funds' costs have grown less rapidly and therefore the profit from fee income has become more material. It is argued that this income, which is effectively guaranteed, has created a misalignment between the partners in private equity funds and their investors. In essence a new principal–agent problem is said to have been created by the high levels of guaranteed income from fees. There is some evidence that is consistent with this criticism.

Transaction Fees

These fees which are payable by investee companies to the fund ('arrangement fees'), as opposed to fees payable to transaction advisers, represent inefficiency in the private equity market. Investors' money is invested into a transaction and immediately repaid to the fund managers and/or the fund. Increasingly investors are putting pressure on fund managers to direct these fees to the fund, not the fund manager. This is in effect a subset of the more general criticism of the 'black box' relationship between fund managers and their investee companies.

Is There Sufficient Permanent Capital in Private Equity Funds?

There were concerns regarding the minimum regulatory capital requirement of fund structures. These were largely misplaced as industry norms for ten-year commitments ensured funds were 100 per cent equity backed. The concern was more appropriate for non-private equity funds, and indeed once clarity over the difference in fund structures was understood, the regulators incorporated changes to acknowledge the differences between most private equity funds and, say, hedge funds. It was a good example of a problem that seems to have abated: journalists and commentators now rarely conflate private equity and hedge funds. They are totally different ways of generating returns. They are no more alike than swimming and skating are similar ways of making a journey across water: liquidity makes all the difference!

Does Private Equity Create Systemic Risk?

A long-standing criticism dating back to the first private equity wave in the 1980s is that the higher leverage in PE deals was likely to have adverse systemic implications. The traditional private equity fund structure operated to limit systemic risk by offering long-term, illiquid, unleveraged investment assets to investors with large diversified portfolios. The private equity industry did generate increased demand for debt during the second PE wave. However, the contribution of industry to the market failures seen in 2007–8 arose through failures in the associated acquisition finance banking market, not within the private equity fund structures.

Pressure to increase leverage within funds and to provide liquidity to investors has, as we predicted in the third edition of this guide, led to geared private equity funds.

The use of subscription lines and NAV loans does increase risk in the fund. However, LPs did not have to cash collateralize their commitments and could raise leverage against their holdings in any fund in the past. Therefore, the growth of fund level debt only increases risks if it increases the total amount of debt in the system. This is monitored by central banks and regulators but is very difficult to accurately track.

Do Debt Funds Increase Risks?

The emergence of debt funds that are leveraged, have no amortization requirements, and will lend blended mezzanine and senior debt is a new phenomenon that is almost wholly unresearched.

On the one hand the reduction of lending by systemically important banks to private equity should assuage the critics. On the other the investors in debt funds include institutional investors some of which are systemically important, such as pension funds and insurance companies.

The concern is that this lending is outside the banking regulations that constrain deposit-taking banks. Until interest rates rise, liquidity is disrupted and/or recession comes, there is no data to illuminate this debate beyond speculation and projection.

Is There a Culture of Secrecy?

There are concerns about a lack of public information on the funds and their investors. If private equity funds intended to be secretive, they have been very poor at achieving it. The number of papers on private equity in academia goes back to the early 1980s and continues to grow.

Similarly, the public commercial data sources are extensive and growing. The level of interest has tracked the growth of the industry, just as it would in any similar growth area with reported high returns. Doubtless some organizations and individuals have raised their profiles and with it that of the industry in general. However, it is our contention that private equity was not secretive but simply not forthcoming with information to a largely uninterested public. This was not due to any strategy to avoid openness, but rather due to the absence of any communication strategy at all with the wider public. In an industry that has grown from a few small transactions in the 1980s to many global fund managers in less than forty years, it is not surprising that an information void appeared. This void is being filled rapidly both by regulatory data disclosure requirements and commercial organizations and research groups, but still exists.

Is there Overpayment of Executives?

There are widespread criticisms of the compensation of partners and staff of the funds. The criticism is that people are paid too much and that it cannot reflect the real economic worth of those individuals. There are two separate issues to consider in this criticism. Firstly, there is the return to the founders of the private equity companies. This reflects the reward for establishing and building major global financial institutions in less than a generation. Second, and unrelated, is the return to those who joined the firms when they were established and successful.

Is There a Misalignment of Incentives?

At the fund level, there are a number of other circumstances where the interests of the various parties in a leveraged transaction may not be aligned.

Zombie funds. As funds have started to 'fail', the incentives of the various parties have diverged, and some perverse incentives have emerged. Where a manager will not be able to raise a new fund and the investments will not generate carried interest, the motivation of the manager can be to do as little as possible for as long as possible, to keep earning fees.

Late fund stuffing. As funds approach the end of their investment period, there is a strong incentive to invest committed capital. Finishing one fund accelerates the raising of new funds and incremental management fees for successful managers.

It is also particularly intense where the fund is poorly performing or the likelihood of raising a new fund is low. If a fund is not performing the manager might as well take on a riskier project in the hope that it will turn the overall portfolio performance around. There is research to suggest that secondary transactions completed late in the investment life of funds show significantly lower returns than the overall population of PE-backed investments. This would be consistent with the 'late stuffing' conjecture.

Do the Conclusions to be Reached about Private Equity Depend on the Evidence Base?

What becomes clear from our review of the claims and counterclaims about private equity is that it is critical to be careful about the evidence base being used. The evidence base may be flawed or may apply to only a particular part of the PE market.

The use of specific cases to draw general conclusions about the effects of private equity on employment and employee relations is self-evidently discredited. Further, some of the cases either did not demonstrate the problem being claimed, took a short-term perspective, or had little to do with mainstream private equity. In some cases, it is unclear what would have happened in the absence of the buyout, such as whether the business would have survived at all. It is particularly important to develop qualitative studies that take account of all relevant perspectives rather relying only on a managerial, private equity firm, employee, or trade union perspective. Not only may management and unions have differing perspectives, but employees may also have different perspectives from their erstwhile union representatives.

With respect to more quantitative analyses, problems have arisen because in many jurisdictions performance data are not readily available for private companies. Where such data are used, they may be biased. Much of the US data refer to higher performing companies coming to market, and hence are disclosing data on their performance as a private firm in the flotation prospectus. Other sources relate to the larger end of the market which uses public debt and therefore produces bond prospectuses.

Because of the difficulties in obtaining data on the performance of PE funds and portfolio companies, many studies have made use of proprietary databases. While these do provide rich access to data otherwise unavailable, it became clear that some of these were flawed, for example in terms of measures used and whether or not data have been updated. This is an important issue because the impact is not simply a question of minor differences in the same direction of findings but directionally in terms of whether PE funds have under- or over-performed. The leading commercial databases, such as Preqin and Pitchbook, continue to invest to improve data accuracy and completeness. They are in fact major sources of information on the size of the missing data problem.

Some other quantitative studies have sought to draw general conclusions about the performance of PE-backed portfolio companies when they are only referring to a part of the private equity market, such as larger deals or majority PE-owned MBI/IBOs.

For the future, studies can do more to be clear about the limitations and boundaries of their datasets. Replication studies can also help build up a reliable picture. However, questions remain if significant parts of the market are still systematically omitted. In general, there is a greater need for representative studies covering the whole PE-backed buyout population that allows comparison with non-PE-backed companies after controlling for other factors as far as possible. Compared to the US, for example, the UK offers an important context where such studies are feasible, since accounting data are available on private companies generally and non-PE-backed buyouts can be identified.

What Are the Areas for Further Research?

Despite the extensive body of systematic evidence now available, further areas for research remain. The following represent a non-exhaustive list of areas warranting further examination:

Performance and Returns

Almost all work on fund performance could be replicated at the investment level to understand returns at a more granular level.

The effects of changing fund structures, especially leverage in funds, on returns are not currently captured in the literature, nor is the growth of co-investing.

What are the relative performance effects of buyouts involving private equity firms that are more or less actively involved in their portfolio firms?

What are the relative contributions of different forms of innovation versus cost restructurings to growth and returns in PE-backed buyouts?

How do buyouts funded by mainstream private equity firms differ from those funded by non-mainstream private equity firms in terms of their characteristics, performance, and survival?

How do private equity firms' exit routes evolve over the economic life-cycle? To what extent and how are private equity firms shifting their attention to forms of primary buyouts in the light of evidence regarding the performance effects of secondary buyouts?

There is no research to date on the performance of the large debt funds that have emerged.

Is there a limit to the private equity ownership market and could it displace public markets? Is it realistic and possible that the future will have a majority of public companies who are quoted fund managers of privately owned trading businesses?

Deal Structures

What are the drivers and impacts of deal financing by new types of funders, including co-fundings between different types of funders?

There is very little research of any kind on debt funds and their spread across the market.

How does the industry respond to changes in the global tax regime? How agile are private equity funds when the regulators act to change the rules?

Governance

What are the most effective portfolio company board compositions in terms of the expertise of executive and non-executive directors for different types of private equity buyout? Size and diversity issues are also poorly researched in private equity.

What have been the effects on employee relations and human resource management in PE-backed buyouts during and subsequent to the recession? In what types of cases have the impacts been positive and which have they been negative? To what extent are any effects down to the PE-backed buyout or to other factors? How has training provision changed for different groups of workers and managers following a buyout?

What are the relative contributions of different forms of innovation versus cost restructurings to growth and returns in private equity backed buyouts?

While we know there is extensive senior management turnover on buyout, we lack systematic evidence on the process of selecting a skill and cognitive balance of the senior team, integration with other senior management members, and success of replacement members.

Process

To what extent do private equity firms learn from their experience over time to enhance the effectiveness of their involvement in portfolio firms? To what extent and how do private equity firms adapt their investment approaches in the light of outturns from existing portfolio firms while they are in the process of still investing current funds?

How does the process of information acquisition and analysis differ between private equity funds and acquisitive corporates? Does the PE process really reduce risk and generate returns?

New Markets

How does private equity enter new markets and what constrains investors from supporting new regional funds?

Many firms have all the characteristics of funded deals but appear reluctant to pursue growth. How can funders, advisers, governmental agencies, etc. encourage them to grow, as a contribution to addressing national and regional growth shortcomings?

To what extent are there gaps to fund buyout opportunities in particular regions and countries? What are the roles of cross-regional funding and government incentives in addressing such gaps?

What role can private equity have in developing economies? How can the model operate where there are poor insolvency laws restricting the attraction of being a debt provider and poor capital markets limiting access to equity and exit opportunities?

Secondary Markets: Debt and Equity

What are the outcomes from secondary fund purchases at both the fund and underlying portfolio company levels? How do these outcomes compare with those associated with primary funds?

There is almost no research that examines how liquidity grows in these opaque markets and what necessary conditions there are to enable the creation of these new markets.

Political Environment

To what extent is political and economic turbulence—such as Brexit and its (eventual) aftermath; populism of the left and right, etc.—presenting new conditions for the private equity market in terms of both opportunities and threats relating to deal sourcing, deal funding, and returns?

Information

Is it what you know, or who you know, that drives investment success? Is our conjecture that private equity should be analysed as an information/liquidity trade-off supported by the data?

Addendum: Covid-19 Crisis

To help write this addendum I asked Jim Strang, Chair and Managing Director of EMEA for Hamilton Lane, to collaborate. I should make clear that Jim is not responsible for any of the main text that precedes this addendum.

Introduction

Mike Wright and I finished writing the fourth edition of *Private Equity Demystified* shortly before Mike's untimely death in November 2019. His death and the academic publishing cycle meant that the final drafts were submitted to OUP in February 2020, weeks before the world changed due to the Covid-19 global pandemic.

In this edition we have been at pains to stress both the mechanics of private equity and, much more importantly, why those mechanisms exist and what problems they seek to solve. We looked through the market at each level of analysis and briefly highlighted concerns, tactics, and potential future strategies.

Our conclusions were based on a sense that we were at the top of the economic cycle and that the real test of the evolving private equity model would come in the next downturn. We had no inkling that the test was on the horizon and that it would be borne by a virus.

Jim Strang and I are writing this addendum in mid-April 2020 without being able to meet, and that, in and of itself, is data that points to the enormous disruption the market faces. One of the key new risks that none of us has ever encountered before is the inability to meet face to face. No investor or lender in private equity has ever done deals without meeting any of the other parties to that deal in person. It remains to be seen how this entirely novel feature affects the ability to react to the crisis.

The Level of the Individual Investment

To state the obvious, an unexpected exogenous shock of the type brought by Covid-19 is a severe test for any business. Private equity uses leverage and leverage amplifies outcomes. Capital structures are tailored to each investment and are designed with some degree of tolerance to unexpected outcomes, but none will have anticipated this.

Businesses fail due to acute cash shortages (often preceded by chronic lack of profitability). The response of any business in a crisis is therefore to focus on the preservation of cash flow. As we have said, cash can only come from three sources: profits after tax, capital reduction, or external parties.

Profitability

In the first instance companies do all that they can to optimize profitability. Clearly that means seeking to drive revenues as far as practicable. This is something private equity is increasingly good at, having developed a set of muscles for this topic since the last global financial crisis. Obviously, businesses will also require to optimize their costs as best they can. The external perspective brought by private equity helps here, with the aim being to trim the fat—but not the muscle and certainly not the bone. In the Covid world, governments have provided an unprecedented level of support to businesses, and the people that work within them, to support companies through the worst of the storm. Governments have already indicated that taxation will be deferred to ease cash flows for many businesses. This includes both the effect on cash of not collecting corporation taxes, as well as the working capital effect of delaying collection of sales taxes and employment taxes.

Capital Reduction

This requires either the sale of fixed assets or a reduction in working capital.

Selling fixed assets in a falling market is difficult and time-consuming for many asset classes and causes fire sale losses. Also, stating the obvious, selling fixed assets reduces the productive capacity of the business permanently—which is no-one's goal.

Reducing working capital is a zero-sum game in the overall economy (unless there are material supply chain inefficiencies). We expect there to be an immediate and severe increase in pressure on the terms of trade. Accelerating payments owed by debtors will be difficult for most businesses. All businesses, whether PE-backed or otherwise, will look at delaying or avoiding payments to their creditors, including governments via the tax system. In addition to supplies needed for the business's normal trade, creditors typically include property (either through leases or rents) and services. These are already under severe pressure. Many companies use credit insurance to help them manage what would otherwise be the onerous requirement to fully fund their debtor balances. Thus the current crisis will require those relatively few firms that provide credit insurance be given sufficient support to allow them to maintain the terms so badly needed by their clients.

Where services are provided via a subscription, it is more difficult to defer payment and still be confident that the services will be available. We therefore expect property and physical asset leasing to bear the brunt of delayed payments. This will necessarily impact private equity real estate funds. The least affected may be mission-critical subscription services, such as software.

Management and the Equity Illusion

The one certainty of the crisis is that the timescales assumed in designing the incentive structures of management will turn out to have been wrong. The implications are subtle. Private equity investments involve both third-party leverage and leverage in the equity.

As we discussed in the section on the equity illusion, the longer it takes to achieve an exit, the more preferred interest on PE loanstock (or preferred dividends on preferred equity) will eat into the value of the ordinary shares or common stock. Therefore, to the extent that the crisis extends the hold period for investments, the management teams running the businesses are losing out. It is especially problematic because the fixed yields that are rolling up come against a backdrop of a looming deep recession. It will be very hard for managers to find ways to grow more rapidly than the yield is rolling up, so equity values for managers may fall, even if enterprise values do not. In such cases the alignment between the management team and the equity sponsor breaks down, exposing the equity sponsor to considerable downside risk that the management simply looks out for its own self-interest.

External Funders

Once the investee company has implemented all cash savings from within its operations, new cash can only come from the existing shareholders, new shareholders, lenders, or government. This can come from new capital inflows or stopping capital outflows.

The delay in repayments of financial capital provided by lenders and investors has implications for them that we discuss below.

Businesses with undrawn facilities have often drawn them down to maximize the availability of cash and eliminate the risk that facilities are cancelled. This reflects the lessons learned in the last crisis when banks started to fail and undrawn facilities were cancelled at the earliest opportunity to reduce lenders' exposures. In this crisis there is no sense yet of a 'banking' crisis, but companies and their private equity owners have erred on the side of caution and drawn down the facilities.

Leveraged businesses have additional costs in interest payments that can be stopped. The shareholders of a business must weigh up the likelihood that a lender who stops receiving payments will seek to recover their debts via a formal insolvency.

Governments around the world are tweaking the insolvency process to attempt to enable lenders and borrowers to work through the crisis. They are also providing guarantees and loan facilities to try to increase the available liquidity to all companies. There is much debate about whether this ought to be available to private equity backed companies.

Those arguing against the availability of loans to PE-backed businesses argue that the shareholders, the private equity funds, have access to liquidity through their undrawn committed capital or 'dry powder'. It is argued that investee companies are in some sense part of a group with the PE fund as the parent company and that the businesses should look to the parent to fund them. This repeats two errors of analysis. First, PE funds are investment vehicles to allow collective investment, not conglomerates. The owners of the businesses are not the fund, they are the LPs. The fund is just a wrapper to allow collective investment. Secondly, the line of arguing implicitly assumes that one particular type of ownership structure, private equity, can be separately identified and excluded from the general support of all other businesses: it cannot.

In summary, at the level of the investment, as for any company in a crisis, cash is king.

Moral Hazard and Rescue Funding

An argument that has reappeared since the start of the crisis is the effect of so-called moral hazard on long-term incentives. Essentially the argument is that if highly leveraged businesses (of any kind, not just PE-backed) can expect to be rescued by the state in a crisis, they benefit from an implicit guarantee. This will substantially weaken or remove the market constraint on lenders to avoid over-lending, because they can ignore the risk of material market-wide shocks. This is by implication important to private equity because, as we saw in the chapter on debt, PE firms are takers of debt when it is loosely available. This is a somewhat philosophical argument about incentives. At the firm or fund level such philosophic thoughts are rarely discussed. Funds and businesses will take tactical advantage of any port in a storm, but it is big stretch to make that a general argument about an industry.

More prosaically, if we look at the various schemes that have been created we see there are practical limitations on their use to try to limit abuse. In the US there is a limit on the total leverage of 6x EBITDA, in the UK the business must demonstrate viability to the satisfaction of a third party bank, and there are other carefully, if quickly, designed criteria to attempt to stop abuse.

At a social level, the question seems somewhat more straightforward: if there is a social benefit to rescuing businesses in a crisis, why wouldn't that social purpose exist for PE-backed companies that have been shown in numerous academic studies to be more efficient and productive than the overall business community? Whatever the reason for this productivity, excluding these businesses from the rescue schemes needs a strong rationale. We have not to date heard a compelling one.

The Lenders

In the main text we described how the debt market had changed, particularly in Europe, since the global financial crisis. Not wishing to become repetitive, the key difference is the emergence of debt funds to replace banks and the growth in unitranche to replace amortizing loans. We have also seen the return of cov-lite lending both in the bond markets and from funds and banks.

These changes combine to reduce the immediate threat to businesses unless they are approaching the redemption date on a unitranche facility. Debt has become slightly shorter in duration since the crisis, but nevertheless, it is not likely that the need to repay debt will cause a general increase in failures in the short term.

The evidence from the last crisis was independently examined in the US and UK and those studies showed that failures were lower in PE-backed companies, even adjusting for various other factors. The evidence suggested that PE-backed businesses were more robust than others. A second harsh test is upon us.

The wall of debt in leveraged finance (Figure Add.1) is larger than at the time of the last crisis, but similar in duration. Again, that wall was efficiently repaid, refinanced, and traded away.

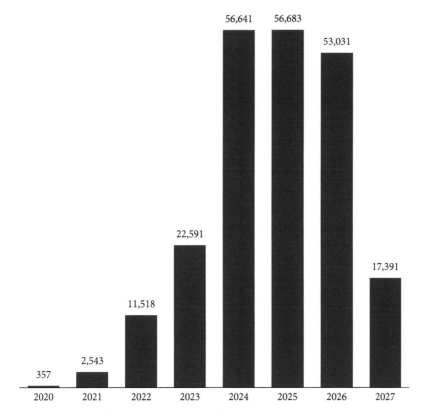

Figure Add.1. Leveraged Finance Maturity Wall at May 2020
Source: S&P

The level of arrears in loan books of lenders is not yet being reported but we expect it to rise sharply as companies choose to stop paying lenders through the shutdown. To the lender a build-up of arrears of capital and interest creates two decision points:

(1) The lender must decide whether to impair the value of the asset in its own books. To a regulated bank, this increases the amount of tier one capital required in the lender's balance sheet and therefore reduces the return on capital of the lenders by both the numerator (reduced interests received) and the denominator (increased amount of capital used).

(2) The lender must decide if and how to use its powers to recover its capital. As shown in the main body of this book, most debt funds are less than ten years old. Few have built work-out or so-called 'special situations' teams. They therefore must choose to build workout teams, use external advisers, or sell the loans in the secondary markets. Debt advisers will be busy.

Large funds and banks have the resources and reputational requirement to manage non-performing loans in-house.

Facing this environment, on the one hand a lender may choose to try to sell loans in the secondary market at a discount rather than working through the problems. On the other hand, this crystallizes the loss and, in a fund, reduces fund fees (which are calculated on the value of assets under management).

We expect there will be an uptick in secondary loan transactions, but the incentives are not such that this will happen sharply in any but the most acute cases. Nevertheless, we do expect that a lack of new deal flow, coupled with impaired portfolios of loans, will probably result in consolidation in the small debt fund market.

An unknown is the effect that non-standard terms will have on the secondary markets and bond markets. As loans have become bespoke—that is, having their own unique terms—the amount of information asymmetry in the secondary markets has increased. Pricing those variations can be slow and costly, or in the limit, impossible. If there is a wholesale move to reduce the holdings of leveraged loans, this lack of standardization may cause issues with the liquidity of that market. Governments have moved quickly to act as purchasers in these markets, thereby maintaining liquidity. We may see pressure to return to more standardized terms like those developed by the LMA and LSTA.

One thing that seems highly likely is a return of private equity funds buying back non-performing debt in their investments. This is the equivalent of investing new equity with a preferred return equal to the discount paid. GPs will be scanning their portfolios for opportunities to buy.

PE Funds

Historically crises have had two effects on private equity: deals done before the crisis tended to have lower returns; deals done in, and after, the crisis did better. A counter-cyclical narrative has grown up around private equity. We look at this shortly.

Traditionally PE funds have been bankrupt remote. They had no creditors that were not matched to their debtors, so could not become insolvent. Failing ones just withered away. Today there is debt in funds from both subscription lines and NAV loans.

Subscription lines are matched to a guarantee from an LP, so do not create significant bankruptcy risk. A defaulting LP would be highly unlikely, as we discuss later.

NAV loans are more nuanced. They rely on the value of the underlying, unrealized assets for security, and this brings us to the issue of valuations.

Valuation

In simple terms, values are usually calculated by multiplying an appropriate profit metric by a factor that reflects some combination of traded comparables and relevant M&A transactions. Such a process lends itself to a highly subjective outcome. New investments in the same company can be thought of as comparable transactions for these purposes. This is of course only a proxy for the real value of an asset, which is solely determined by the expected value of its future cash flows and the cost of capital to the potential purchaser.

Thus, valuations are uniquely challenging at this time. What is the most appropriate period to consider as regards profitability? Historic, LTM, something else? Also, how should the large and ever growing number of adjustments to profitability be accounted for from a valuation perspective? Then what multiple to use? What is the relevant peer set?

What should be in the basket, and what not? There is no one correct answer. Best in class GPs rely on transparency and consistency of approach to help validate these inherently uncertain values. GPs thus must be thoughtful in how they derive valuations in times of such extreme uncertainty, and LPs must understand that valuations are as much art as science.

This brings us to the effects on LPs.

LPs

Existing Investments

Of course, if the LPs all intend to hold the fund to maturity this valuation issue is of no great importance. The ultimate returns will be what they are, and this was very largely the position in 2008. However, since then the secondary market in LP positions has grown dramatically. Many investors' strategies are based on being able to dip in and out of positions depending on their individual needs. All these trades have traditionally been articulated based on discounts and premia to net assets.

Just as EBITDA multiples are not causes of value, but measures, so NAV discounts do not cause portfolio values, they just express them. However, the valuation challenges alluded to above will certainly disrupt 'normal operations' in the secondary market until some semblance of normality returns to markets. The large established participants will probably prosper as they have the resources and processes to evaluate these potential trades. Either way, LPs should expect secondary trades to be much more protracted and discounts to NAV to be less reliable guides to fundamental value. In the limit the secondary market could sharply contract or even temporarily freeze.

New Investments

The market for new funds raising will of course be disrupted by the crisis. LPs will be examining their programmes trying to understand valuations, liquidity needs, and any changes to investment strategy that the crisis will determine. Furthermore, as the deal markets slow, so will fundraising. There's no need to raise a new fund if you are still investing the old one! Most likely the market sees a short-term hiatus where the most proven and experienced GPs are able to raise funds, while those not so fortunate find conditions harder, at least until markets stabilize.

There are potential knotty issues for funds that were fund raising before the crisis broke but had not reached a final close. First the timetable will have lengthened. Second, there are scenarios where a fund has reached a first close, started investing, and must perform a valuation of the new investments before the final close. There could be a material write-down of the assets. Traditionally private equity has been viewed as a long-term investment and the true-up mechanism would have ignored temporary valuation movements (in either direction). Potential new investors in funds that have not reached final close may not be as keen to buy into losses as they might have been in the past.

Returns

There are many ways of examining returns. The most popular, IRR, is not a perfect metric and is distorted by the effects of time and compounding. TVPI mixes cash and valuation, and DPI, while cash based, ignores residual values and timing. The effects of the crisis will be to slow the emergence and realization of most winners and eliminate some. It may create some new successes, but we have no particular insights to know where they are.

The delay will reduce IRRs. Revaluations will reduce TVPI in the short term. The end of dividend recaps will delay DPI, but overall we cannot be sure whether investments will recover lost value. Historically, new deals that emerge from a crisis have been priced at levels that resulted in strong returns, but each crisis has hit an increasingly mature private equity industry, so the past is not a solid guide to the future.

LP Defaults

There has already been an increase in the discussion of potential LP defaults. As we saw in the main body of the text, this is both poorly documented and vanishingly rare because the consequences are financially and reputationally disastrous.

In the last crisis LPs and GPs cooperated to avoid defaults, and this will happen again. The methods included suspending new investments, extending the fund life, allowing greater recycling of funds received by the fund, and some wholesale restructuring of funds with new economic terms, usually resulting in lower fees if the GP initiated the process. The availability of NAV loans and preferred equity adds a new alternative that was not available in the GFC. For new investments, funds also have the cushion of subscription lines for short- to medium-term needs, and LPs could use their private equity interests to secure debt in an 'NAV loan type' arrangement outside the fund.

The secondary market provides an avenue to exit private equity, but as we have said, this market is unlikely to be as liquid in the short term as it has been.

Overall, it seems very unlikely that there will be LP defaults on any material scale.

Closing Remarks

Uncertainty is a theme throughout this book. This addendum was written against a background of great uncertainty. In a crisis it is tempting to see only the storm. During the dot-com crisis a partner at a fund remarked that 'the thing about mass hysteria is that we've probably all got it to some extent'. Nevertheless, each crisis has tested the private equity model and each one to date has ended with the industry stronger and larger than it was before the storm broke. We expect the new debt market participants to feel the brunt of the storm, but the overall industry to emerge intact.

Largest UK Buyouts to Mid 2019

Company name	Deal year	Deal source	Activity	Value (£m)
Alliance Boots	2007	Public to private	Retail and distribution	11100
MEPC/Leconport	2000	Public to private	Real estate	3488
Travelport Worldwide Ltd	2019	Public to private	Internet technology	3460
Acromas Holdings/Saga and AA	2007	Secondary buyout	Business services, leasing	3350
EMI Group (Maltby)	2007	Public to private	Media	3223
Paysafe	2017	Public to private	Banking, insurance, and finance	2960
Tomkins/Gates Global	2010	Public to private	Other manufacturing	2890
Spirit Amber/S & N Retail	2003	Local divestment	Hotels, catering, and leisure	2510
CPA Global	2017	Secondary buyout	Business services, leasing	2400
Zoopla/ZPG plc	2018	Public to private	Internet technology	2224
Somerfield/Gateway	1989	Public to private	Retail distribution and repair	2157
Yell Group	2001	Local divestment	Business services, leasing	2140
Worldpay/Global Merchant Services	2010	Local divestment	Banking, insurance, and finance	2025
Unique Pub & Voyager Pub/ The Pub Estate/Unique Pub Company	2002	Secondary buyout	Hotels, catering, and leisure	2013
Ascential/Top Right Group/EMAP	2008	Public to private	Media	2000
New Look	2015	Secondary buyout	Retail distribution and repair	1900
Meridien Hotels/Grand Hotels	2001	Local divestment	Hotels, catering, and leisure	1900
Expro International Group	2008	Public to private	Business services, leasing	1806
Punch Taverns	2017	Public to private	Hotels, catering, and leisure	1776
The Automobile Association/AA	2004	Local divestment	Business services, leasing	1750

Continued

Company name	Deal year	Deal source	Activity	Value (£m)
Debenhams (Baroness Retail)	2003	Public to private	Retail distribution and repair	1720
FNZ	2018	Secondary buyout	Computer: software	1650
Whitbread Pubs/Laurel Pub Company	2001	Local divestment	Hotels, catering, and leisure	1630
Warner Chilcott plc (Waren Acquisition)	2005	Public to private	Medical: pharmaceutical	1614
United Biscuits	2006	Secondary buyout	Food	1600
RAC	2016	Secondary buyout	Business services, leasing	1570
Iceland Foods	2012	Insolvency	Retail distribution and repair	1450
Spire Healthcare/BUPA Hospitals	2007	Local divestment	Medical: healthcare	1440
Avecia	1999	Local divestment	Chemicals and m-m-f	1362
Parkdean Resorts	2017	Secondary buyout	Hotels, catering, and leisure	1350
Saga Group	2004	Secondary buyout	Hotels, catering, and leisure	1350
United Biscuits/Finalrealm	2000	Public to private	Food	1300
Brakes Group	2007	Secondary buyout	Food	1300
Virgin Active	2015	Secondary buyout	Hotels, catering, and leisure	1300
Misys	2012	Public to private	Computer: software	1270
NDS Group	2009	Public to private	Computer: software	1248
Gala Clubs/Gala Coral	2003	Secondary buyout	Hotels, catering, and leisure	1240
Biffa plc (Wasteacquisitionco)	2008	Public to private	Business services, leasing	1231
Esure Group plc	2018	Public to private	Banking, insurance, and finance	1207
Laird plc	2018	Public to private	Electrical engineering and electronics	1200
SSP/Select Service Partners and Creative Host Services	2006	Local divestment	Hotels, catering, and leisure	1200
General Healthcare (BMI Healthcare/Partnerships in Care/ BMI Health Services)	2000	Secondary buyout	Medical: healthcare	1200
Iglo Group/Birds Eye Iglo Group	2006	Local divestment	Food	1154
Rank Hovis McDougall/RHM	2000	Local divestment	Food	1140
Caudwell Holdings/Phones 4u and Lifestyle Services	2006	Private	Retail distribution and repair	1112
McCarthy & Stone (Mother Bidco)	2006	Public to private	Real estate	1105
Foodvest/Findus	2008	Secondary buyout	Food	1100
Wood Mackenzie	2012	Secondary buyout	Business services, leasing	1100

ERM Group/Environmental Resources Management	2015	Secondary buyout	Business services, leasing	1092
Somerfield (Violet Acquisitions)	2005	Public to private	Retail distribution and repair	1082
TI Automotive/TI Group	2001	Local divestment	Vehicles and shipbuilding	1073
Travelex	2005	Secondary buyout	Banking, insurance, and finance	1055
Countrywide (Castle Bidco)	2007	Public to private	Real estate	1054
Iris Software Group	2018	Secondary buyout	Computer: software	1000
Civica	2017	Secondary buyout	Computer: software	1000
Calvin Capital (Evergreen Bidco)	2017	Local divestment	Wholesale distribution	1000
NewDay	2017	Secondary buyout	Banking, insurance, and finance	1000
Argus Media Ltd	2016	Private	Media	1000
RAC	2011	Local divestment	Business services, leasing	1000

Sources: CMBOR; Investec; Equistone Partners Europe

Largest UK LBO Failures to Mid 2019

Company name	PE backed	Deal year	Deal source	Original deal value (£m)	Exit year
McCarthy & Stone	Yes	2006	Public to private	1105	2009
Four Seasons Health Care	Yes	2012	Local divestment	825	2019
BPC and Watmoughs/Polestar	Yes	1998	Secondary buyout	738	2008
Phones 4u	Yes	2011	Secondary buyout	677	2014
Magnet	Yes	1989	Public to private	631	1992
Orchid Pubs	Yes	2006	Local divestment	571	2008
Unipoly	Yes	1997	Local divestment	515	2008
Saville Gordon Estates (Chambercroft)/Industrious	Yes	2002	Public to private	498	2009
IMO Car Wash	Yes	2006	Secondary buyout	450	2009
Lowndes Queensway	Yes	1988	Public buy-in	447	1991
Peacock Group (Henson No 1)	Yes	2006	Public to private	404	2012
British Steel/Tata Steel Long Products Europe	Yes	2016	Foreign divestment	400	2019
Kingfisher/Woolworth Hldg	Yes	1982	Public buy-in	310	2008
Republic/Teen Topco	Yes	2010	Secondary buyout	300	2013
Greycoat/G2 Estates	Yes	1999	Public to private	283	2004
Castlebeck Care (Castle Holdings)	Yes	2006	Secondary buyout	255	2013
Drive Assist UK	Yes	2007	Secondary buyout	250	2012
XL Leisure/Excel Airways	No	2006	Local divestment	225	2008
Dreams	Yes	2008	Private	225	2013
Focus DIY Group	Yes	2007	Secondary buyout	225	2011
Paramount Hotels/Dawnay Shore Hotels	Yes	2004	Secondary buyout	215	2014
First Leisure (Nightclubs)/Whizalpha	Yes	2000	Local divestment	211	2004
Parabis Law/Plexus Law/Cogent Law	Yes	2012	Private	200	2015
Europackaging Holdings	Yes	2006	Private	190	2009
Automotive Product Group	Yes	1995	Local divestment	181	2006
Tattershall Castle Group/TCG Pubs	Yes	2005	Local divestment	177	2015
Orchard Care Homes	No	2007	Local divestment	175	2018
Covenant Healthcare (Transform/Abbey/Churchills)	Yes	2005	Secondary buyout	170	2010
Palmer & Harvey/P&H Group	No	2008	Secondary buyout	165	2017

Finelist/Europe Auto Distribution	Yes	2000	Public to private	159	2000
Jarvis Hotels (Kayterm)	Yes	2004	Public to private	159	2011
Landhurst	Yes	1990	Local divestment	157	1992
International Leisure Group	Yes	1987	Public to private	155	1991
London & Henley	Yes	1998	Secondary buyout	150	2008
The Sweater Shop	Yes	1995	Private	150	1998
Everest (Ever 1951)	Yes	2007	Secondary buyout	150	2012
Poundworld Retail	Yes	2015	Private	150	2018
DAMtel Ltd	Yes	2015	Private	149	2016
Premier Bathrooms	Yes	2007	Private	142	2017
Gaucho Grill	Yes	2016	Secondary buyout	131	2018
Lambert Fenchurch/HLF Insurance/Heath	Yes	1999	Public to private	131	2003
2e2	Yes	2006	Secondary buyout	130	2013
Tempo/KF Group	Yes	1999	Private	130	2001
Upperpoint Distribution	Yes	2005	Secondary buyout	128	2012
Viasystems/Forward Group plc	Yes	1997	Public to private	127	2002
Ethel Austin	Yes	2004	Secondary buyout	123	2008
Bezier Holdings	Yes	2011	Secondary buyout	120	2013
Hollis/Oval (387)	Yes	1988	Local divestment	120	1991
Betterware	Yes	1998	Public to private	116	2012
Hewden Stuart	Yes	2010	Foreign divestment	110	2016
Chorion	Yes	2006	Public to private	110	2012
Yardley (Old Bond Street Corporation)	Yes	1990	Local divestment	110	1998
Reponse Group/Flairdial	Yes	1988	Local divestment	103	1989
Andrew Page	Yes	2010	Private	100	2014
La Senza	Yes	2006	Secondary buyout	100	2012
ESM/Wafer-Fab	Yes	1999	Insolvency	100	2002

Fee Offset Calculations

Assumptions	Inputs			
Fund Size (£m)	1,000			
Management Fee	2.00%			
Non-executive fee per investment (£000)	100			
No of investments	5			
Average investment size (£m)	100			
Average negotiation fee	3.00%			
Fee offset	80%			
Corporation tax (at say)	0%			

No pass through or offset	LP	Manager	Portfolio Co	Tax
Negotiation fee (£m)		15.00	−15.00	
Non-executive fees (£m)		0.50	- 0.50	
Taxable Income/(cost) (£m)	-	15.50	−15.50	
Gross management fee (£m)	−20.00	20.00		
	−20.00	35.50	−15.50	
Corporation tax (£m)				-
Total (£m)	−20.00	35.50	−15.50	-
Gross fee/income	−2.00%	2.00%		
Net fee/income	−2.00%	3.55%		
After-tax fee/income	−2.00%	3.55%		

Fees passed through 100%	LP	Manager	Portfolio Co	Tax
Negotiation fee (£m)		15.00	−15.00	
Non-executive fees (£m)		0.50	−0.50	
Fee passed through (£m)	15.50	−15.50		
Taxable income/(cost) (£m)	15.50	-	−15.50	
Gross management fee (£m)	−20.00	20.00		
Net cost(£m)	−4.50	20.00	−15.50	
Corporation tax (£m)	−			-
Total	−4.50	20.00	−15.50	-
Gross fee/income	−2.00%	2.00%		
Net fee/income	−0.45%	2.00%		
After-tax fee/income	−0.45%	2.00%		

Fees Offset 80:20	LP	Manager	Portfolio Cos	Tax
Negotiation fee (£m)		15.00	−15.00	
Non-executive fees (£m)		0.50	−0.50	
Fee income (£m)	-	15.50	−15.50	
Gross management fee (£m)	−20.00	20.00		
Fee offset (£m)	12.40	−12.40		
Taxable Income/(cost) (£m)	−7.60	23.10	−15.50	
Corporation tax (£m)				-
	−7.60	23.10	−15.50	-

Gross fee/income	−2.00%	2.00%
Net fee/income	−0.76%	2.31%
After-tax fee/income	−0.76%	2.31%

Summary fees (paid)/received before tax	Cost to LP	Fee to Gp	Portfolio Co
No pass through or offset	2.00%	3.55%	3.00%
Fees passed through 100%	0.45%	2.00%	3.00%
Fees offset 80:20	0.76%	2.31%	3.00%

Pro-Forma Term Sheet: Sale to Private Equity Fund

PROJECT []
TERM SHEET FOR THE PROPOSED SALE OF THE ENTIRE ISSUED SHARE CAPITAL
OF [TARGET COMPANY]

Definitions

Investor: [private equity investor]

Buyer: Investor (via a newly incorporated company, Newco)

Buyer's Solicitors: [Investor's solicitors]

Completion: completion of the Proposed Transaction (as defined below)

Exit: a realization by the Investor of its (direct and indirect) investment in the Target Company whether by share sale, asset sale, or liquidation

Investor Consent: consent of the Investor

Investor Loan Notes: quarterly rolled and compounding [12]% non-cash paid loan notes

Management: those members of the management team/employees who are shareholders and who will remain with or join (as applicable) the Target Group post-completion (and Manager means any one of them)

Management Loan Notes: quarterly rolled and compounding [10]% non-cash paid loan notes

Sellers: Management and [non-rolling sellers]

Sellers' Solicitors: [Management's solicitors]

Target Company: [company being acquired by Newco]

Target Group: The Target Company and its direct and indirect subsidiary undertakings (the Subsidiaries)

In this term sheet, any gender includes all genders.

Acquisition Terms

Acquisition Structure	The Sellers will sell the entire issued and to be issued share capital of the Target Company (the Sale Shares) to the Buyer at Completion (Proposed Transaction). Principal transaction documents shall comprise the Share Purchase Agreement (incorporating a tax covenant) (SPA) and the Disclosure Letter. The initial draft of the SPA shall be prepared by the Buyer's Solicitors.
Consideration and Completion Accounts	The Buyer shall acquire 100% of the Sale Shares for an enterprise value of £[] (assuming a cash free, debt free balance sheet and normal level of working capital) (Consideration). Such Consideration is to be adjusted by reference to Completion Accounts (Purchase Price).
	The target level of working capital is to be confirmed following satisfactory completion of financial due diligence.
	The Purchase Price shall be payable by the Buyer to the Sellers in cash (subject to the Management Rollover referred to below) in proportion to their respective holdings of the Sale Shares.
	The Completion Accounts shall include a calculation of Actual EBITDA as at [].

Completion	The SPA will be exchanged and completed simultaneously.
the Investor Funding and Bank Debt	the Investor's funding for the transaction will include Investor Loan Notes to be subscribed by the Investor.
SPA Warranties	Management and [non-rolling sellers] (together, the 'Warrantors') will provide the Buyer with customary contractual warranties (not representations) appropriate for the Proposed Transaction, on a several basis, and a customary tax covenant, with aggregate liability capped at an amount equal to £[] *[NB adjust Sellers' warranty and tax covenant liability downwards if warranty and indemnity insurance is to be utilized]*
	All Sellers will give title and capacity warranties, on a several basis, with liability capped at 100% of that part of the Purchase Price paid to each of them.
	Typical market standard warranty limitations will also apply. Definition of 'Disclosed' will include disclosure of dataroom.
Seller Limitations	Threshold: £[] De minimis/throw away: £[]

Equity Terms

Newco Structure and Re-Investment	Subject to finalization of tax structuring, a four Newco structure (comprising private limited companies incorporated in England and Wales) will be established with ordinary shares being issued by Topco and Loan Notes being issued by Finco.
	The Investor will subscribe for A Ordinary Shares (being the institutional strip equity) and Investor Loan Notes.
	Management will roll [50]% of the gross proceeds of sale received by each of them into B Ordinary Shares and Management Loan Notes (which shall be subscribed in the same proportions as the Investor subscribes for A Ordinary Shares and Investor Loan Notes) (Management Rollover).
	The aggregate fully diluted ordinary share capital (A Ordinary Shares and B Ordinary Shares) subscribed for on day 1 will be £[] in aggregate. The balance of the Investor and Management investment will be Loan Notes (as detailed above).
	Subject to the re-investment assumptions set out above and to re-investment and tax structuring advice, the share capital of Topco will be divided as follows:
	A Ordinary Shares to be held by the Investor.
	B Ordinary Shares to be held by Management.
	C Ordinary Shares to be allocated on Completion as Sweet Equity (defined below) and, where unallocated, will be issued to Management at Exit (see below)..
	Percentage allocations of each class of share will be confirmed by the Buyer during the process. The Investor and Management will work to ensure Management's tax position is as beneficial as possible.
Sweet Equity	Subject to finalization of tax structuring, a sweet equity pot of C Ordinary Shares representing up to [10]% of the fully diluted share capital of Topco ('Sweet Equity') is to be reserved for Management/future management and allocated: (i) as required by the CEO with Investor Consent, where allocated on Completion; and otherwise (ii) as required by the Board acting by majority with Investor Consent. Any C Ordinary Shares which remain unallocated on Exit will be issued to Management as required by the CEO with Investor Consent or otherwise in proportion to Management's then holdings of Shares.
	Management/future management will subscribe in cash for any C Ordinary Shares.

Continued

Equity Terms	
Loan Notes	Investor Loan Notes—the coupon on the Investor Loan Notes shall be [12]%. The Investor Loan Notes will also include the right for interest to be paid by way of PIK notes and the Investor Loan Notes will be capable of being listed.
	Management Loan Notes—the coupon on the Management Loan Notes shall be [10]%. Leaver loan note coupon becomes 0% upon relevant holder becoming a Very Bad Leaver.
	Minority Loan Notes—the coupon on the Minority Loan Notes shall be [10]%.
	All Loan Notes will be non-cash paid and compound (roll-up) quarterly.
	The Loan Notes shall rank *pari passu* with each other and shall be on the same economic terms (but for the coupon) and shall be treated equally in respect of any required subordination to third party debt.
	The Loan Notes shall be redeemed at par plus accrued but unpaid interest upon the earlier to occur of:
	an Exit (unless sold as part of any sale); or
	the sixth anniversary of Completion (subject to the availability of suitable refinancing).
Voting	The A Ordinary Shares, B Ordinary Shares and C Ordinary Shares shall all be voting shares and the Investor's shares will confer control. In certain circumstances shares held by Management will cease to carry votes (e.g. upon leaving or certain default events (including Material Underperformance (defined below) and breach of equity covenants set by reference to the banking covenants once agreed)).
	Material Underperformance shall be defined as underperforming in respect of the recurring revenue as set out management business plan base case by more than 25% on a consistent basis over two quarters.
Dividends	All A Ordinary Shares, B Ordinary Shares and C Ordinary Shares shall have pari passu rights as to dividends and any other distributions made by Topco.
Return of Capital	The A Ordinary Shares, B Ordinary Shares and C Ordinary Shares will rank pari passu in relation to any return of capital.
Permitted transfers	C Ordinary Shares shall be allocated at Completion to the extent that they are to be issued to existing Management. Any unallocated C Ordinary Shares to be allocated to (future) Management shall be warehoused by the Investor on Completion and will be allocated as requested by the Board acting by majority with Investor Consent. Any C Ordinary Shares which remain unallocated on Exit will be issued to Management as required by the CEO with Investor Consent or otherwise in proportion to Management's then holdings of Shares.
	If a holder of B Ordinary Shares or C Ordinary Shares is also a holder of loan notes, then any transfer of such shares will be subject to such holder transferring an equivalent proportion of their loan notes to the same transferee.
	Management will be permitted to transfer shares to family and family trusts for tax planning purposes subject always to retaining a majority of their Shares personally. Shares may be transferred to family and family trusts on death of a shareholder.
Pre-emption on new share issues	Other than Permitted Issues (see below), all issues of new equity shares will be made on a pre-emptive basis as between the Investor and Management.
	Permitted Issues will include:
	if required by the Board acting by majority with Investor Consent: an issue of C Ordinary Shares not issued on Completion up to a maximum of [10]% of the fully diluted share capital; and
	any Emergency Share Issue, on the terms and subject to the conditions set out in the Emergency Share Issue section below.
	All issues of shares or other securities will require prior Investor Consent.

Emergency Share Issue	Topco (with Investor Consent) to be able to issue shares in relation to an emergency funding situation without offering such shares to any other shareholders provided that Management shall have a "catch-up" right to subscribe at the same price as in the Emergency Share Issue for their pro-rata allocation of shares (and, where applicable, loan notes, on a 'stapled' basis) within 60 business days of the share issue, so that their equity holdings are not diluted as a result.
Drag/Tag	Drag rights to apply where the holders of more than 50% of the issued share capital of Topco wish to accept a bona fide third party offer for the acquisition of Topco provided always that during the period of three years from completion the exercise of the drag rights will also require the consent of the holders of a majority of the shares held by Management.
	Standard tag rights to apply on the proposed sale of a controlling interest in Topco (being more than 50% of the entire issued share capital) to a third party purchaser.
Exit	the Investor and the Board propose to work together to achieve an Exit (including by way of sale or listing of Topco) within an agreed period of time following Completion.
	Exit shall be controlled by the Investor but shall be discussed transparently and collaboratively throughout the investment period to ensure continued alignment of interests and strategic goals. An Exit will be subject to the Investor's investment committee approval.
	On any such Exit, incumbent management shareholders shall provide customary warranties and undertakings (in each case subject to customary limitations) and (from each incumbent management shareholder) a leakage indemnity in respect of any leakage received by him.
	The Investor shall give warranties as to title and capacity only and a leakage indemnity in relation to leakage received by it (in the event of a locked box based sale).
Compulsory Transfer Provisions	The B Ordinary Shares and C Ordinary Shares and Management Loan Notes shall be subject to Leaver provisions (see below).
	Any holder of B Ordinary Shares and C Ordinary Shares who ceases to be a director or employee of Topco (or any member of its group) (a Leaver) may be required by the Board (with Investor Consent) to transfer all of their B Ordinary Shares and C Ordinary Shares to another Manager or the Company or the Investor unless such holder leaves as a Good Leaver or Intermediate Leaver (as set out below).
Good Leaver/Bad Leaver Definitions	Good Leaver—is a Leaver, who:
	leaves due to death or permanent ill health or disability; or
	leaves in circumstances constituting wrongful dismissal or unfair dismissal; or
	is otherwise determined by the Board to be a Good Leaver.
	Intermediate Leaver—is a Leaver who:
	voluntarily terminates his employment other than where this relates to constructive dismissal; or
	is otherwise not a Good Leaver or a Very Bad Leaver.
	Bad Leaver—is a Leaver who:
	is summarily dismissed or whose employment ceases in circumstances where there are grounds for summary dismissal;
	in circumstances where having been treated as a Good Leaver, subsequently is in material breach of the restrictive covenants contained in the Investment Agreement or his respective Service Agreement;
	Very Bad Leaver—is a Leaver who commits a non-trivial crime which results in a custodial sentence or fraud.

Continued

Equity Terms	
Leaver Price	Upon his ceasing to be a director or employee:
	a Manager may be required to offer his equity (B Ordinary Shares unless he is a Good Leaver or an Intermediate Leaver, and C Ordinary Shares) for sale. Such equity shall be offered first, if so required, to the Investor and subsequently to any incoming Manager with Investor Consent; and
	the coupon on any Management Loan Notes held by such Manager shall reduce to 0% if he is a Very Bad Leaver.
	In the case of a Good Leaver:
	A Good Leaver's B Ordinary Shares shall become disenfranchised.
	The price for a Good Leaver's C Ordinary Shares shall be the higher of the original subscription price and Market Value (as defined below) of the shares.
	A Good Leaver may require some or all of its loan notes to be repaid together with the coupon accrued to such date of repayment.
	In the case of an Intermediate Leaver:
	An Intermediate Leaver's B Ordinary Shares shall become disenfranchised.
	The price for an Intermediate Leaver's C Ordinary Shares shall be determined using a vesting arrangement which will determine the percentage of C Ordinary Shares to be sold at what price based on the number of whole months the Intermediate Leaver has served from Completion until the date of leaving such that those C Ordinary Shares which have vested will be sold at the higher of the original subscription price and Market Value (as defined below) and those which have not will be sold at the lower of Market Value and the subscription price.
	In the case of a Bad Leaver:
	A Bad Leaver shall not be required to sell his B Ordinary Shares on the condition that such shares shall become disenfranchised.
	The price for a Bad Leaver's C Ordinary Shares shall be the lower of Market Value and the subscription price.
	In the case of a Very Bad Leaver:
	A Very Bad Leaver shall be required to sell both his B Ordinary Shares and C Ordinary Shares and until such time as the relevant transfer completes he shall become disenfranchised.
	The price for a Very Bad Leaver's B Ordinary Shares shall be the lower of Market Value and the subscription price.
	The price for a Very Bad Leaver's C Ordinary Shares shall be £1 in aggregate.
	Payment will be satisfied in cash on (or around) the date of leaving. Subject to the above in respect of Good Leavers, Loan Notes will be repaid at Exit.
Market Value Definition	Market value shall be the value agreed between the Board and the relevant Leaver (with Investor Consent).
	If no agreement is reached, market value shall be determined by an independent valuer in accordance with a market typical procedure to be agreed and set out in the Articles with no discount to value applied for minority stakes and as if the transaction was on an arm's length basis.
	The costs of the valuer will be borne as determined by the valuer and, if there is no determination, equally by the relevant Leaver and Topco.

Board Composition	On Completion, the Topco Board shall consist of:
	two directors appointed by Management (being the CEO and CFO);
	[two] Investor Directors;
	a non-executive director and the Chairman—both of whom shall be appointed to the Board in consultation with the CEO (who may veto up to two such proposed appointees with the third being as required by the Investor after such consultation).
	the Investor shall have the right to appoint and remove a maximum of [2] Investor Directors as it determines.
	the Investor shall also have the right to appoint Observers to the Board.
	On a stalemate, the Investor (as majority shareholder) to have a casting vote. When two Investor Directors are in post but only one Investor Director attends a meeting, that one shall have two votes at that meeting (plus a casting vote where this arises). the Investor will have board level and equity swamping rights in certain circumstances (e.g. in the case of Material Underperformance (as defined above) and breach of equity covenants).
Frequency of board meetings & quorum	There will be at least ten Board meetings in each calendar year or as determined by the Investor Directors.
	The quorum for Board meetings will be two directors, at least one of whom shall be an Investor Director (or his alternate) and one of whom shall be the CEO from time to time (or his alternate), with a provision allowing a quorum to be formed by the Investor Director where the CEO is given notice of a board meeting and fails to attend.
Information Package	Topco will be required to furnish the Investor with regular and event driven information which is customary for a private equity investment.
Reserved Matters	The Investment Agreement shall include a customary list of consent rights/matters reserved for the Investor Directors or Investors approval together with certain positive covenants around day to day running of the business.
	Standard consents/veto rights to include (without limitation):
	capex over an agreed threshold;
	approval of budgets;
	acquisitions/disposals;
	senior appointments above £60k pa;
	significant change to agreed strategy and business plan;
	entry into, or amending existing, debt facilities/security; and
	changes to managers' remuneration (including bonuses).
Investment Agreement warranties	Warranties from Management on the business plan, due diligence reports, and management questionnaires.
Limits on liability in Investment Agreement	Liability of each Manager warrantor to be capped at [1] x gross annual basic salary and be time limited to [say 18 months from investment] (subject to the usual exceptions for fraud and dishonesty).
	Threshold for claims is £[75,000] with an individual claim de minimis of £[10,000].
Equity covenants	Equity covenants will be set by reference to the bank covenants and otherwise will also include Material Underperformance as defined above. Equity covenants will be a trigger for swamping rights.

Employment Terms

Period for Restrictive Covenants	Investment Agreement and SPA: 18 months post cessation of employment. Service Agreement: 12 months post cessation of employment. Restrictive Covenants may be waived in specific instances by Investor consent.

Continued

Equity Terms	
Service Agreements	If required, new service agreements/employment contracts will be entered into by Management and "key" employees[1] with base salaries to remain static to the extent that they are in line with generally accepted market norms.
	Notice period: [6] months.
	Summary dismissal to include:
	gross misconduct;
	material and persistent underperformance; and
	material and persistent breach of only the key terms of the equity documents which are not capable of remedy.

General	
Governing law for transaction documents	England and Wales.
Jurisdiction for transaction documents	Exclusive jurisdiction of the courts of England and Wales for claims by the Buyer.
Costs	Sellers to bear their own deal costs in relation to the SPA. Bidco to bear Management's costs (including professional Advisers) in relation to the equity aspects of the transaction.
	Investor costs (including professional Advisers) to be borne by Bidco. The Investor will not charge any arrangement fee but will charge an annual monitoring fee of £[100,000] plus VAT payable by Bidco.

[1] Key employees to be confirmed following completion of due diligence

Structure of the Standard LMA Leveraged Loan Contract at 2018

Section heading and clause sub-heading	Brief description	Number of pages
Definitions and Interpretation		55
Definitions and Interpretation	Definition of key terms in the contract	55
The Facilities		9
Conditions of Utilization	The reason for the loan	4
Purpose		1
The Facilities		4
Utilization		33
Ancillary Facilities	The rules of use of the loan facility	7
Establishment of Incremental Facilities		9
Letters of Credit		7
Optional Currencies		1
Utilisation—Letters of Credit		6
Utilisation—Loans		3
Repayment, Prepayment and Cancellation		21
Illegal, Voluntary Prepayment and Cancellation	The rules governing repayment of the loans	4
Mandatory Prepayment and Cancellation		6
Repayment		8
Restrictions		3
Costs of Utilization		13
Changes to Calculation of Interest	The interest rates and fees of the loan and the dates of payment	5
Fees		3
Interest		2
Interest Periods		3
Additional Payment Obligations		20
Costs and Expenses	Other costs that the lenders can recover from the borrower	2
Increased Costs		2
Mitigation by Lenders		2
Other Indemnities		3
Tax Gross Up and Indemnities		11
Guarantee		4
Guarantee and Indemnity	The guarantee ties all syndicate members together as one	4
Representations, Undertakings and Events of Default		53
Events of Default	The rules governing when the loan is in default and becomes repayable on demand, plus the information that ahs been relied on and is required.	8
Financial Covenants		12
General Undertakings		15
Information Undertakings		7
Representations		11
Changes to the Parties		20

Continued

Section heading and clause sub-heading	Brief description	Number of pages
Changes to Lenders	The rules governing changes to the lenders or	8
Changes to Obligators	borrowers	5
Restriction on Debt Purchase Transactions i/ii		7
The Finance Parties		**15**
Conduct of Business by the Finance Parties	The rules of the lending syndicate	1
Role of the Agent, the Arranger, the Issuing Bank and Others		12
Sharing among the Finance Parties		2
Administration		**37**
Amendments and Waivers	The rules that govern how the loans are	12
Calculations and Certificates	administered by the agent and the lenders	1
Confidential Information		6
Confidentiality of Funding Rates and Reference Bank Quotations		2
Counterparts		1
Disclosure of Lender Details by Agent		2
Notices		4
Partial Invalidity		2
Payment Mechanics		5
Remedies and Waivers		1
Set-Off		1
Governing Law and Enforcement		**3**
Enforcement	The country's law that governs the contract	2
Governing Law		1
Schedules		**68**
The Original Parties	Various forms and letters that are required to	4
LMA Form of Confidentiality Undertaking	administer different situations that may arise in the future	1
Timetables		3
Form of Letter of Credit		3
Material Companies		1
Agreed Security Principles		2
Form of Increase Confirmation		4
Forms of Notifiable Debt Purchase Transaction Notice		2
Other Benchmarks		2
Form of Incremental Facility Notice		6
Form of Incremental Facility Certificate		4
Conditions Precedent		13
Request and Notices		6
Mandatory Costs Schedule		1
Form of Transfer Certificate		4
Form of Assignment Certificate		6
Form of Accession Deed		2
Form of Resignation Letter		2
Form of Compliance Certificate		2
Grand total		**351**

Summary of Academic
Research by Area of Investigation

Pre-Buyout Governance in P2Ps

Authors	Country	Nature of Transactions	Findings
Maupin (1987)	US	P2P MBOs	Ownership concentration, price/book value ratio, cash flow to net worth, cash flow to assets, P/É ratio, dividend yield and book value of assets to original costs distinguish P2Ps from comparable non-P2Ps
Singh (1990)	US	P2P MBOs, LBOs	Prior takeover attempt, cash flow to sales and net assets to receivables predict likelihood of buyout
Eddey, Lee, and Taylor (1996)	Australia	MBOs	Takeover threat strongly associated with going private
Weir, Laing, and Wright (2005a)	UK	MBO, MBIs, listed corporations	Firms going private have higher CEO ownership, higher institutional block-holder ownership, more duality of CEO and board chair but no difference in outside directors or takeover threats compared to firms remaining listed
Evans, Poa, and Rath (2005)	Australia	MBOs, acquisitions of listed corporations	Firms going private have higher liquidity, lower growth rates, lower leverage pre-buyout, and lower R&D. FCF is not significantly different. Takeover threat less likely to be associated with going private
Weir and Wright (2006)	UK	MBOs, MBIs, acquisitions of listed corporations	Firms going private have higher CEO ownership, higher institutional block-holder ownership, more duality of CEO and board chair but no difference in outside directors or takeover threats compared to firms subject to traditional takeovers
Boulton, Lehn, and Segal (2007)	US	Management and non-management led P2Ps	Firms going private underperformed but had more cash assets than industry peers, and had higher relative costs of compliance with Sarbanes–Oxley
Wright, Weir, and Burrows (2007)	UK	PTPs	Irrevocable commitments for PTPs depend on extent of takeover speculation, value of the bid and level of board shareholding, the premium offered to other shareholders and how active the PE-bidder was in this market, especially in MBOs, less so in MBIs
Andres, Betzer, and Weir (2007)	Europe	P2Ps	Companies with a high pre-LBO free float and weak monitoring by shareholders show high abnormal returns
Cornelli and Karakas (2008)	UK	All P2Ps	Decrease in board size from pre to post PTP, especially for LBOs funded by experienced PE firms

Billett, Jiang, and Lie (2008)	US	All P2Ps	FCF and undervaluation arguments stronger in first wave than second wave; firms lacking change in control protective covenants for bondholders more likely to be buyout targets in second wave
Mehran and Peristiani (2010)	US	All P2Ps	P2Ps in second wave mainly younger firms with declining analyst coverage, declining institutional ownership and low stock turnover
Bharath and Dittmar (2010)	US	All P2Ps	FCF important for first wave P2Ps; in second wave P2Ps less liquid, less financially constrained, less analyst coverage and lower institutional ownership
Fidrmuc, Palandri, Roosenboom, and van Dijk (2013)	UK	P2Ps	Management-led buyouts more likely if target undervalued, managers own large equity stakes, target opaque to outside investors, and target generates cash flows to support external financing
Harford, Stanfield, and Zhang (2019)	US	P2Ps	Managers and controlling shareholders time management buyouts (MBOs) and freezeout transactions to take advantage of industry-wide undervaluation and are announced during troughs of industry profitability

Earnings Manipulation, Earnings Quality, and Insider Information in Buyouts and Private Equity

Authors	Country	Nature of Transactions	Findings
DeAngelo (1986)	US	LBOs	No evidence of earnings manipulation
Smith (1990)	US	Abandoned and completed LBOs	No evidence to support insider information argument as positive stock price returns only occur in completed buyouts
Lee (1992)	US	Abandoned and completed LBOs	No evidence to support insider information argument as positive stock price returns only occur in completed buyouts
Degeorge and Zeckhauser (1993)	US	Reverse LBOs	Suggest, but don't test, that underperformance by reverse LBOs in first year post float may be due to performance manipulation or hidden private information
Easterwood, Singer, Seth, and Lang (1994)	US	LBOs	Pre-buyout shareholders get a higher price for their stock if outside acquirers compete for control with the proposed MBO; although suggesting some support for insider information, competing bids generally results in higher prices
Perry and Williams (1994)	US	MBOs	Downward earnings management through increases in discretionary accruals in the year preceding the public announcement of MBO bid
Holthausen and Larcker (1996)	US	Reverse LBOs	No evidence managers exploit information asymmetries in reverse LBOs at the expense of new shareholders in the offering
Chou, Gombola, and Liu (2006)	US	Reverse LBOs	Positive and significant discretionary current accruals in reverse LBO offerings
Fischer and Louis (2008)	US	MBOs	Significantly negative pre-buyout accruals in the year preceding buyout announcements; managers who depend on external funds the most report less negative accruals prior to buyout
Katz (2009)			Private firms with private equity as shareholders have higher-quality financial statements than comparable private companies without private equity investors

Beuselinck and Manigart (2007); Beuselinck, Deloof, and Manigart (2008; 2009)		PE-backed buyouts	Private firms with private equity as shareholders have higher-quality financial statements than comparable private companies without private equity investors; reporting quality is lower where private equity investors have higher ownership stakes than in companies where they have a lower equity stake
Chou, Gombola, and Liu (2010)	US	Reverse LBOs	Little evidence of upward earnings management around private equity placements; little predictive power of abnormal accruals for long-run stock performance following private equity placements
Ang, Hutton, and Majadillas (2014)	US	LBOs where management divested part of their pre-buyout holding	Positive relation between management's divestment and pre-LBO upward earnings management and stock price run-ups, more aggressive buyout negotiations, higher buyout premium, and risk-taking following the buyout
Mao and Renneboog (2015)	UK	MBOs, IBOs, non-buyouts	Strong negative earnings management via both accrual and real earnings activities in MBOs; modest negative accrual management and insignificant real earnings manipulation in IBOs; positive earnings management in non-buyout firms

Financial Returns to Private Equity and Leveraged and Management Buyouts

Authors	Country	Nature of transactions	Findings
Kaplan (1989a)	US	LBOs	Investors in post-buyout capital earn a median market-adjusted return of 37%
Ljungqvist and Richardson (2003)	US	VC and LBO funds	Mature funds started 1981–93 generate IRRs in excess of S&P 500 returns net of fees; returns robust to assumptions about timing of investment and portfolio company risk; buyout funds generally outperform venture funds, these differences partially reflecting differences in leverage used in investments; sample from one LP with disproportionate share of (larger) buyout funds
Jones and Rhodes-Kropf (2003)	US	VC and LBO funds	LBO funds have a value-weighted IRR of 4.6% and VC funds have a value weighted IRR of 19.3%, commensurate with factor risks borne by investors; considerable variation in fund returns
Cumming and Walz (2004)	US, UK, Continental Europe (39 countries)	MBO/MBI, LBO, and VC	Private Returns to Investors in Relation to Law Quality, Fund Characteristics and Corporate Governance Mechanisms
Kaplan and Schoar (2005)	US	VC and buyout funds	LBO fund returns gross of fees earn returns in excess of S&P 500 but net of fees slightly less than S&P 500; unlike mutual funds is persistence in returns among top performing funds; higher returns for funds raised in 1980s; acknowledge that average returns potentially biased as do not control for differences in market risk and possible sample selection bias towards larger and first-time funds; funds raised in boom times less likely to raise follow-on funds and thus appear to perform less well
Knigge, Nowak, and Schmidt (2006)	Multi-country	VC and buyout funds	In contrast to VC funds, the performance of buyout funds is largely driven by the experience of the fund managers regardless of market timing.
Groh and Gottschalg (2006)	US and non-US	MBOs	Risk-adjusted performance of US buyouts significantly greater than S&P index
Froud, Johal, Leaver, and Williams (2007); Froud and Williams (2007)	UK	Mid-sized and large funds	General partners in successful mid-sized funds can expect carried interest to generate £5–15 million on top of their salaries while general partners in large, successful funds can expect $50–150 million

Lerner, Schoar, and Wongsunwai (2007)	US	VC and LBO funds	Early and later stage funds have higher returns than buyout funds in funds raised 1991–98; considerable variation in returns by type of institution; presence of unsophisticated performance-insensitive LPs allows poorly performing GPs to raise new funds
Phalippou and Gottschalg (2009)	US and non-US	LBO funds	After adjusting for sample bias and overstated accounting values for non-exited investments, average fund performance changes from slight over-performance to underperformance of 3% per annum with respect to S&P 500; Gross of fees, funds outperform by 3% per annum; venture funds underperform more than buyout funds; previous past performance most important in explaining fund performance; funds raised 1980–2003
Ljungqvist, Richardson, and Wolfenzon (2007)	US	LBO funds	Established funds accelerate investments and earn higher returns when opportunities improve, competition eases and credit conditions loosen; first-time funds less sensitive to market conditions but invest in riskier deals; following periods of good performance funds become more conservative
Driessen, Lin, and Phalippou (2007)	US	VC and buyout funds	Data from 797 mature private funds over 24 years shows high market beta for venture capital funds and low beta for buyout funds, and evidence that private equity risk-adjusted returns are surprisingly low. Higher returns larger and more experienced funds mainly caused by higher risk exposures, not abnormal performance
Nikoskelainen and Wright (2007)	UK	MBOs	Private returns to investors enhanced by context-dependent corporate governance mechanisms
Metrick and Yasuda (2007)	US	VC and LBO funds	Buyout fund managers earn lower revenue per managed dollar than managers of VC funds; buyout managers have substantially higher present values for revenue per partner and revenue per professional than VC managers; buyout fund managers generate more from fees than from carried interest. Buyout managers build on prior experience by raising larger funds, which leads to significantly higher revenue per partner despite funds having lower revenue per dollar
Ernst and Young (2008)	Worldwide	Larger PE-backed buyouts	Average annual enterprise value grew significantly more than in public company equivalents, but PTPs performed less well than divisional, secondary or private buyouts

Continued

Authors	Country	Nature of transactions	Findings
Diller and Kaserer (2009)	Europe	VC and MBO Funds	Highly significant impact of total fund inflows on fund returns. Private equity funds' returns driven by GPs' skills as well as stand-alone investment risk
Maula, Nikoskelainen, and Wright (2011)	UK	MBOs	Industry growth drives exited buyout returns and is particularly high in MBOs, divisional buyouts and top-quartile deals
Lopez di Silanes, Phalippou, and Gottschalg (2011)	Worldwide	PE investments	Median investment IRR (PME) 21% (1.3), gross of fees; 1/10 investments goes bankrupt but 1/4 has an IRR above 50%; 1/8 investments held for less than 2 years, but have highest returns; scale of PE firm investors is influential: investments held at times of a high number of simultaneous investments underperform substantially, with diseconomies of scale highest for independent firms, less hierarchical firms, and those with managers of similar professional backgrounds
Stucke (2011)	US	VC and buyout funds	Previous studies' findings may be biased downwards due to data source used; severe anomalies in underlying data result from ceasing data updates. Many empirical results established using these databases may not be replicable with correct data; the claim that private equity has not outperformed public equity is unlikely to hold with true numbers
Higson and Stucke (2012)	US	Buyout funds	For almost all vintage years since 1980, US buyout funds significantly outperformed S&P 500. Liquidated funds 1980–2000 delivered excess returns 450 basis points per year. 60% of funds do better than the S&P; excess returns driven by top-decile funds; higher returns for funds set up in the first half of each of the past three decades; significant downward trend in absolute returns over all 29 vintage years; results robust to measuring excess returns via money multiples instead of IRRs
Franzoni, Nowak, and Phalippou (2012)	Worldwide	Liquidated buyout investments	The unconditional liquidity risk premium on PE is close to 3% annually and, the inclusion of this liquidity risk premium reduces alpha to zero
Chung, Sensoy, Stern, and Weisbach (2012)	International	Buyout funds	Indirect pay for performance from future fund-raising is similar to direct pay for performance from carried interest, and is stronger when managerial abilities are more scalable and weaker when current performance is less informative about ability

Kleymenova, Talmor, and Vasvari (2012)	Worldwide	Secondary buyout funds	A PE fund interest is more liquid if the fund is larger, has a buyout-focused strategy, less undrawn capital, has made fewer distributions and is managed by a manager whose funds were previously sold in the secondaries market; PE funds' liquidity improves if more non-traditional buyers, as opposed to dedicated secondary funds, provide bids and overall market conditions are favourable
Axelson, Sorensen, and Stromberg (2013)	Worldwide	Buyout deals from a large fund of funds	Gross of fee betas of 2.2–2.4 and alphas of 8.3%–8.6% annually
Castellaneta, Gottschalg, and Wright (2013)	Europe and US	PE-backed buyouts	Completeness of feedback on performance of past deals has a positive impact on the IRR of subsequent deals; this positive impact is moderated by the proportion of feedbacks on past deals showing negative returns
Valkama, Maula, Nikoskelainen, and Wright (2013)	UK	MBOs	Governance variables have limited role in driving value creation but use of a ratchet is positively related to both equity and enterprise value returns; leverage has a positive impact on median and top-quartile equity returns; returns are driven by buyout size and acquisitions made during holding period; the effect of industry growth is strong in insider-driven, divisional buyouts, and top quartile transactions
Harris, Jenkinson, Kaplan, and Stucke (2013)	US	VC and buyout funds	Significant persistence for pre–2000 funds for buyout funds and, particularly for venture funds. Post–2000, mixed evidence of persistence in buyout funds. Sorting by quartile of performance of previous funds, performance of the current fund is statistically indistinguishable regardless of quartile; performance/size relationship absent. Post–2000, performance in venture capital funds remains as persistent as pre–2000
Cornelli, Lichtner, Perembetov, Simintzi, and Vig (2013); Cornelli, Simintzi, and Vig (2016)	Worldwide	PE funds	PE firms experiencing the highest turnover between funds (or those in the top turnover tercile) outperformed those experiencing the lowest turnover (or those in the bottom turnover tercile) by 13.5 percentage points; funds that replenished with operational expertise demonstrated improved performance, especially during recessions; turnover of professionals with financial backgrounds did not impact performance; turnover of professionals with private equity experience negatively impacted performance; in the short run, performance improves when bad performers are fired, in the long run, turnover helps teams to adapt and replenish their skills in response to shifting external demand

Continued

Authors	Country	Nature of transactions	Findings
Giot, Hege, and Schwienbacher (2014)	US	Buyout and VC funds	Novice PE firms invest larger amounts in less promising LBOs than experienced peers; experienced Pes invest in bigger deals than novice PE firms after successful IPOs
Phalippou (2014)	US	Buyout funds	Adjusting for size premium as buyout funds mainly invest in small companies, average buyout fund return is in line with small-cap listed equity
Harris, Jenkinson, and Kaplan (2014)	US	VC and buyout funds	US buyout fund net of fee returns have exceeded those of public markets for most vintages since 1984 using various benchmarks (e.g. 3% per annum using S&P 500) and various data sources from multiple LPs; but some data sources biased downwards in fund returns; both absolute performance and performance relative to public markets are negatively related to aggregate capital commitment
Sensoy, Wang, and Weisbach (2014)	US	Investments by LPs in buyout and venture funds	Superior performance of endowments in 1991–8 due to greater access to top-performing VC funds; in 1999–2006 endowments do not outperform as no longer have success access nor better at making selection decisions than other types of LPs
Harford and Kolasinski (2014)			Public companies buying PE firm portfolio companies, experiencing positive abnormal returns on announcement but long-run post-transaction abnormal returns indistinguishable from zero; large portfolio company payouts to private equity have no relation to future portfolio company distress, suggesting debt investors do not suffer systematic wealth losses; inconsistent with short-termism portfolio companies invest no differently than matched public control firms, even when not profitable
Fang, Ivashina, and Lerner (2015)	Direct investments by seven large institutional investors	Direct investments by institutions in PE	Solo investments by institutions outperform co-investments; outperformance driven by deals where informational problem not severe [proximity; late stage] and in peak years; poor performance of co-investment due to selective offering by fund managers of large deals
Taussig and Delios (2015)	Emerging and developing countries	PE firms	PE firms in countries with weak contractual enforcement and foreign PE firms with experience in these countries can enforce contracts through informal local networks; performance undermined by a lack of access to local financing options resulting from weak financial development
Robinson and Sensoy (2016)	US	Buyout funds	Using data from a single LP, buyout fund returns outperform public market benchmark

Jegadeesh, Kräussl, and Pollet (2015)	International	Listed funds of funds	Market expects unlisted private equity funds to earn abnormal returns of approximately 1% per year and listed private equity funds to earn zero or marginally negative abnormal returns net of fees; both listed and unlisted private equity funds have market betas close to one; private equity fund returns are positively related to GDP growth and negatively related to the credit spread
L'Her, Stoyanova, Shaw, Scott, and Lai (2016)	International	Buyout funds	After adjusting for systematic risks of underlying companies in buyout funds, no significant outperformance of buyout fund investments versus the public market equivalent on a dollar-weighted basis
Braun, Jenkinson, and Stoff (2017)	World	Funds and deal levels	Persistence of fund managers has declined as PE has matured and become more competitive; PE largely conforms to the pattern found in most other asset classes with past performance a poor predictor of the future
Ang, Chen, Goetzmann, and Phalippou (2018)	International	LP returns	Cyclicality in private equity returns differs according to fund type; capital market segmentation contributes to private equity returns
Harris, Jenkinson, Kaplan, and Stucke (2018)	International	Funds of funds (FOF)	After accounting for fees, FOFs provide returns equal to or above public market indices for both buyout and venture capital; FOFs focusing on buyouts outperform public markets, but underperform direct fund investment strategies in buyout; FOFs in venture capital (but not in buyouts) are able to identify and access superior performing funds
Phalippou, Rauch, and Umber (2018)	International		GPs receive fee payments from companies whose boards they control. Fees do not vary with business cycles, company characteristics, or GP performance, but vary significantly across GPs and are persistent within GPs. GPs charging the least raise more capital post-financial crisis and are backed by more skilled LPs

Employment, Wage, and HRM Effects

Authors	Country	Unit of analysis	Nature of transactions	Findings
Panel A: Employment effects				
Wright and Coyne (1985)	UK	Firm	MBOs	44% of firms shed employees on buyout; 18% of pre-buyout jobs lost subsequent re-employment but below pre-MBO levels
Kaplan (1989)	US	Firm	LBOs	Small increase in employment post-buyout but falls after adjusting for industry effects
Wright, Chiplin, Thompson, and Robbie (1990a)	UK	Firm	MBOs	25% of firms shed employment on buyout
Smith (1990)	US	Firm	LBOs	Small increase in employment post-buyout but falls after adjusting for industry effects
Lichtenberg and Siegel (1990)	US	Plant	LBOs, MBOs	8.5% fall in non-production workers over 3-year period; production employment unchanged
Muscarella and Vetsuypens (1990)	US	Firm	Reverse LBOs	Median number of employees fell between LBO and IPO but those LBOs without asset divestment reported median employment growth in line with top 15% of control sample; divisional LBOs more likely to increase employment than full LBOs
Opler (1992)	US	Firm	LBOs	Small increase in employment post-buyout
Wright, Thompson, and Robbie (1992)	UK	Firm	MBOs, MBIs	Average 6.3% fall in employment on MBO but subsequent 1.9% improvement by time of study
Robbie, Wright, and Thompson (1992); Robbie and Wright (1995)	UK	Firm	MBIs	38% reduced employment

Robbie, Wright, and Ennew (1993)	UK	Firm	MBOs in receivership	Over three fifths did not effect redundancies on buyouts, a sixth made more than 20% redundant and that the median level of employment fell from 75 to 58
Amess and Wright (2007)	UK	Firm	MBOs and MBIs	Employment growth is 0.51 of a percentage point higher for MBOs after the change in ownership and 0.81 of a percentage point lower for MBIs.
Wright, Burrows, Ball, Scholes, Meuleman, and Amess (2007)	UK	Firm	MBOs, MBIs	On average, employment initially falls but then grows above pre-buyout level in MBOs; In MBIs, employment falls after buyout; majority of MBOs and MBIs experience growth in employment
Thornton (2007)	UK	Firm	MBIs, MBOs	Based on same data as Wright et al. (2007) and Amess and Wright (2007a), MBOs increased employment. MBIs tended to cut it. Remaining workers often experienced significantly less job security. Employment cuts may have been planned pre-buyout
Cressy, Munari, and Malipiero (2007)	UK	Firm	Private equity backed and non-private equity backed companies	Employment in buyouts falls relative to control group for first four years but rises in fifth; Initial rationalization creates basis for more viable job creation
Amess, Girma, and Wright (2008)	UK	Firms	LBOs, MBOs, MBIs, acquisitions, private equity and non-private equity backed	Private equity- backed LBOs have no significant effect on employment. Both non-private equity backed LBOs and acquisitions have negative employment consequences
Weir, Jones, and Wright (2015)	UK	Firms	PTPs	PE-backed deals experienced job losses in years immediately after going private but employment increased subsequently, non-PE-backed buyouts increased employment after the first year post-deal
Jelic (2008)	UK	Firms	MBOs, MBIs	More reputable PE firms associated with increases in employment in both post-buyout and post-exit phases

Continued

Authors	Country	Unit of analysis	Nature of transactions	Findings
Goergen, O'Sullivan, and Wood (2011)	UK	Firms	IBOs/MBIs of listed companies	Employment falls in the year immediately after the completion of the IBO compared with non-acquired firms; no parallel or subsequent increase in productivity or profitability
Amess and Wright (2012)	UK	Firm	MBOs, MBIs, private equity and non-private equity backed	After controlling for endogeneity in selection of buyouts, difference between employment effects of private equity versus non-private equity backed buyouts not significant
Davis, Haltiwanger, Handley, Jarmin, Lerner, and Miranda (2014)	US	Firm and establishment	Matched private equity backed and non-private equity backed firms and establishments	Employment grows more slowly in private equity cases than in control pre-buyout and declines more rapidly post-buyout but in 4–5th year employment mirrors control group; buyouts create similar amounts of jobs to control and more greenfield jobs
Goergen, O'Sullivan, and Wood (2014a, 2014b)	UK	Firm	IBOs and non-acquired firms	Significant loss in employment in IBOs in the year immediately following the acquisition, compared to control groups
Agrawal and Tambe (2016)	US	Firm	LBOs	Employment increases; post-LBO employment spells increase
Guery, Stevenot, Wood, and Brewster (2017)	France	Firm	Establishment	Foreign investors significantly more likely to induce job shedding and employment insecurity than are French investors
Faccio and Hsu (2017)	US	Firm / establishment		During period one year before to five years after buyout employment grows more in establishments controlled by politically connected PE firms than in non-politically connected PE firms.
Olsson and Tåg (2017)	Sweden	Firm	Employer-employee data in buyouts and non-buyouts	Buyouts generally do not affect unemployment incidence but it doubles for workers in less productive firms who perform routine or offshorable job tasks; job polarization much more marked among workers affected by buyouts than for the economy generally
Olsson and Tåg (2018)	Sweden	Firm	Registry data on buyouts	Domestic PE-backed buyouts increased unemployment incidence by a fifth and duration by a third; foreign-backed buyouts no effect

Panel B: Wages				
Lichtenberg and Siegel (1990)	US	Plant	MBOs, LBOs	Decline in relative compensation of non-production workers
Amess and Wright (2007)	UK	Firm	MBOs, MBIs	Average wages in both MBOs and MBIs are lower than their non-buyout industry counterparts
Wright, Burrows, Ball, Scholes, Meuleman, and Amess (2007)	UK	Firm	MBOs, MBIs	Wages grow post-buyout compared to pre-buyout year; the majority of MBOs and MBIs showed growth in wages
Amess, Girma, and Wright (2008)	UK	Firms	LBOs, MBOs, MBIs, acquisitions, private equity and non-private equity backed	Employees gain higher wages after acquisitions but lower after LBO
Davis, Haltiwanger, Handley, Jarmin, Lerner, and Miranda (2014)	US	Firm and establishment	All LBOs	Wages decline on average by 2.4%
Goergen, O'Sullivan, and Wood (2014a, 2014b)	UK	Firm	IBOs and non-acquired firms	Significantly lower wages in IBOs in the year immediately following the acquisition, compared to control groups
Agrawal and Tambe (2016)	US	Firm	LBOs	Worker employability increases especially where jobs transformed by production upgrades, so that long-run wages increase
Olsson and Tåg (2018)	Sweden	Firm	Registry data on buyouts	Domestic PE-backed buyouts lowered labour income by 7%. Foreign-backed buyouts: no effect
Panel C: HRM effects				
Wright, Coyne, and Lockley (1984)	UK	Firm	MBOs	65% of firms recognized unions before buyout, falling to 60% afterwards; 40% of firms recognized one union; 8% of firms involved wider employee share ownership after buyout
Bradley and Nejad (1989)	UK	Division	NFC MEBO	Employee share ownership had greater effect on 'cooperation' than on performance but did improved employee cost consciousness

Continued

Authors	Country	Unit of analysis	Nature of transactions	Findings
Wright, Chiplin, Thompson, and Robbie (1990a)	UK	Firm	MBOs	58% of firms recognized unions before buyout, 51% afterwards; 52% of firms recognized one union; 14.3% of firms involved wider employees in shareholding; 6% had share option scheme pre-buyout, 10.4% afterwards
Pendleton, Wilson, and Wright (1998)	UK	Firm and employees	Privatized MEBOs	Shareholding and participation in decision making associated with feelings of ownership; perceptions of employee ownership significantly associated with higher levels of commitment and satisfaction
Bacon, Wright, and Demina (2004)	UK	Firm	MBOs, MBIs	Buyouts resulted in increased employment, adoption of new reward systems and expanded employee involvement; 'insider' buyouts and growth oriented buyouts had more commitment-oriented employment policies
Bruining, Boselie, Wright, and Bacon (2005)	UK and Netherlands	Firm	MBOs	MBOs lead to increases in training and employee empowerment. These effects were stronger in the UK than in the Netherlands
Amess, Brown, and Thompson (2007)	UK	Firm	MBOs	Employees in MBO firms have more discretion over their work practices
Bacon, Wright, Demina, Bruining, and Boselie (2008)	UK, Netherlands	Firm	MBOs, MBIs, private equity and non-private equity backed	Insider buyouts show greater increase in high commitment practices; buyouts backed by private equity firms report fewer increases in high commitment management practices
Thornton (2007)	UK	Firm	MBOs, MBIs	Based on data in Wright, Burrows, et al. (2007) and Amess and Wright (2007a); in the case of MBIs, significant cuts in wages generally took place

Bacon, Wright, Scholes, and Meuleman (2009)	Pan-European	Firm	All PE-backed buyouts above €5m transaction value	Negligible changes to union recognition, membership density and attitudes to trade union membership; absence of reductions in terms and conditions subject to joint regulation; more firms report consultative committees, which are more influential on their decisions, and increased consultation over firm performance and future plans; private equity firms adapt their approaches to different social models and traditional national industrial relations differences persist
Boselie and Koene (2009)	Netherlands	Firm	Single firm PE-backed buyout negotiation	In PE-backed buyout negotiations, aloof top management can have negative effect on employee commitment and trust, exacerbating uncertainty and rendering HR-change initiatives powerless; binding effect of informal management practices undermined by financial pressures that dominated senior management decision-making; divisional HR managers focused on divisional responsibilities in context of increasingly politicised relationships between division and centre; important for top management to engage with the organization and introduce realistic people management initiatives; HR acting as a business partner with line management led to tension between corporate and divisional HR levels, limiting ability of local HR to engage with proactive corporate people management initiatives
Gospel, Pendleton, Vitols, and Wilke (2011)	UK, Germany, Spain	Firm	Case of LBOs, hedge fund and SWF investments	Employment reductions in each case, though to varying extent; few changes in work organization developments in employee voice and representation. National systems of labour regulation affect the extent to which worker representatives receive information after, though not during, the acquisition

Continued

Authors	Country	Unit of analysis	Nature of transactions	Findings
Bacon, Wright, Meuleman, and Scholes (2012)	Europe	Firm	All PE-backed buyouts above €5m transaction value	Impact of PE on high performance work practices (HPWP) affected more by length of investment relationship than by countries where PE is going to or is coming from; buyouts backed by Anglo-Saxon PE firms as likely to introduce new HPWP as those backed by non-Anglo-Saxon PE firms
Clark (2011, 2016)	UK	Firm	Single firm	Existing trade union derecognized by management with support of existing staff and replaced by a new staff association registered as an independent union
Appelbaum, Batt, and Clark (2013)	US/UK	Firm	Cases of PE-backed buyouts	PE-backed buyouts involve breach of trust and implicit contracts
Bacon, Hoque, and Wright (2019b)	UK	Matched firm, establishment, and employees	MBOs and MBIs, PE-backed or not; non-buyouts	No consistent evidence of higher job insecurity in LBOs as measured by workforce reduction practices (redundancy rates, job security/ no-compulsory redundancies policies and redundancy consultation), dismissal rates, labour use practices (non-permanent employment contracts and outsourcing), and employees' job security perceptions. Job insecurity no higher in either current or former LBOs than elsewhere and no higher in private equity-backed LBOs, management buy-ins, or high-debt LBOs, and only partial and weak evidence of higher job insecurity in short-hold LBOs; job insecurity no higher in perfect storm LBOs (PE-backed management buy-ins that are short-holds with high-debt)
Bacon, Hoque, and Wright (2019a)	UK	Matched firm, establishment and employees	MBOs and MBIs, PE-backed or not; non-buyouts	Compared to non-LBOs, job quality is no lower overall in LBOs, or in MBIs or high debt LBOs; partial evidence of lower job quality in LBOs that are quick flips, private equity (PE)-backed, and 'perfect storms' (PE-backed or management buy-in quick flips with high debt)

Effects on Debt-Holders and Taxation

Authors	Country	Nature of Transactions	Findings
Effects on debt holders			
Marais, Schipper, and Smith (1989)	US	LBOs	No evidence of wealth transfer from pre-buyout bondholders
Asquith and Wizman (1990)	US	LBOs	Small average loss of 2.8% of market value to pre-buyout bondholders. Bonds with protective covenants had a positive effect, those without experience negative reaction
Cook, Easterwood, and Martin (1992)	US	Division LBOs	Bondholders with covenants offering low protection against corporate restructuring lose some percentage of their investment
Warga and Welch (1993)	US	LBOs	Bondholders with covenants offering low protection against corporate restructuring lose some percentage of their investment
Billett, Jiang, and Lie (2008)	US	All P2Ps	Firms lacking change-in-control protective covenants for bondholders more likely to be buyout targets in second wave
Taxation effects			
Jensen, Kaplan, and Stiglin (1989)	US	LBOs	Total amount of taxes collected by government does not decrease as a result of LBOs
Kaplan (1989b)	US	LBOs	Tax savings account for small fraction of value gains in LBOs; significant correlation between estimated tax savings and buyout bid premium
Schipper and Smith (1988)	US	LBOs	Tax savings account for small fraction of value gains in LBOs; significant correlation between estimated tax savings and buyout bid premium
Muscarella and Vetsuypens (1990)	US	Reverse LBOs	Few control sample firms had lower tax rates than buyouts
Newbould, Chatfield, and Anderson (1992)	US	LBOs	LBOs would have paid significantly more tax depending on tax structure; significant proportion of premia paid on LBO appears to be caused by reduction in taxes due to additional tax shields from debt; after Tax Reform Act 1986 less than 50% of premium paid on LBO can be attributed to reduction in taxes

Continued

Authors	Country	Nature of Transactions	Findings
Renneboog, Simons, and Wright (2007)	UK	P2Ps	No significant relationship between pre-P2P tax to sales ratio and shareholder wealth gains (premia) on announcement of P2P but bidders willing to pay higher premia for firms with lower debt-to-equity ratios which proxies for the tax advantage of additional interest deductibility and for the ease of financing the takeover operation
Weir, Jones, and Wright (2015)	UK	P2Ps	Tax paid is significantly below the industry average in each year post going private but is not statistically different in the year prior to going private but lower tax may be a function of lower profitability reported post P2P rather than from the tax shield element of going private

Longevity

Authors	Country	Nature of Transactions	Findings
Kaplan (1991)	US	LBOs	Heterogeneous longevity. LBOs remain private for median 6.8 years. 56% still privately owned after year 7. LBOs funded by leading private equity firms no more likely to stay private than other buyouts; no difference in longevity of divisional or full LBOs
Wright et al. (1993)	UK, France, Sweden, Netherlands	MBOs	State of development of asset and stock markets, legal infrastructures affecting the nature of private equity firms' structures and the differing roles and objectives of management and private equity firms influence timing and nature of exits from buyouts
Wright et al. (1994)	UK	MBOs	Heterogeneity of longevity influence by managerial objectives, fund characteristics and market characteristics; larger buyouts and divisional buyouts significantly more likely to exit more quickly
Wright, Thompson, Robbie, and Wong (1995)	UK	MBOs, MBIs	Heterogeneous longevity. Greatest exit rate in years 3–5; 71% still privately owned after year 7. MBIs greater rate of exit than MBOs in short term consistent with higher failure rate of MBIs. Exit rate influenced by year of deal [economic conditions]. To achieve timely exit, private equity firms are more likely to engage in closer (hands-on) monitoring and to use exit-related equity-ratchets on management's equity stakes
Gottschalg (2007)	Worldwide	Private equity backed buyouts	Average longevity of PE investment five years; average length of PE investment compares favourably with that of blockholders in public firms
Strömberg (2008)	Worldwide	Private equity backed buyouts	58% of deals exited more than 5 years after initial transaction; exits within 2 years account for 12% and have been decreasing
Caselli, Garcia-Appendini, and Ippolito (2009)	Italy	Early and late stage private equity	Duration of investment shorter than in US and UK; exit primarily by trade sale; IRR positively related to initial undervaluation, target firm risk, PE firm experience; fund size, lock-up clauses, puttable securities and exit ratchets
Jelic (2011)	UK	PE-backed and non-PE-backed MBOs and MBIs	Average time to exit 46 months; Smaller PE-backed deals take longer to exit; PE backed MBOs exit sooner, have higher exit rates but fewer liquidations; Syndicated PE-backed MBOs exit sooner; Backing by more reputable PE firms increases likelihood of IPO exit
De Prijcker, Manigart, Maesseneire, and Wright (2013)	Europe	PE-backed buyouts	More efficient and high growth buyouts more likely to exit successfully, particularly through an IPO or secondary buyout, but not through a trade sale; having a cross-border lead private equity (PE) investor further increases the likelihood of a successful exit, especially for secondary buyouts; cross-border syndicate investors are more important in trade sale exits

Asset Sales and Disposals

Authors	Country	Nature of transactions	Findings
Bhagat, Shleifer, and Vishny (1990)	US	LBOs	43% of assets in hostile LBOs sold within three years
Muscarella and Vetsuypens (1990)	US	Reverse LBOs	43% of reverse LBOs divested or reorganised facilities; 25% made acquisitions; divestment activity greater among full LBOs
Kaplan (1991)	US	LBOs	34% of assets sold within six years of buyout
Liebeskind, Wiersema, and Hansen (1992)	US	LBOs	LBOs show significantly greater reduction in number of plants than control sample of matched public corporations and divested significantly more businesses in terms of mean employees, revenues and plants but not in terms of median revenue and plants; LBO managers downsized more lines of businesses than in the control group
Wright, Thompson, and Robbie (1992)	UK	MBOs	18% sold surplus land and buildings; 21% sold surplus equipment
Seth and Easterwood (1993)	US	Large LBOs	5/32 firms were complete bust-ups, all involving buyout (private equity) specialists; 14/32 firms refocused by divesting unrelated lines; 21/32 firms engaged in business focus by divesting related lines and 9/32 in market focus
Easterwood (1998)	US	LBOs	The average abnormal returns to publicly listed bonds of LBOs around asset sales depends on whether firm experiences financial distress; distressed firms experience negative and significant wealth effects, no distressed firms experience positive and significant returns; evidence is consistent with returns being determined by whether divestment price exceeds, equals or is below expected price for the anticipated divestment
Wright, Burrows, Ball, Scholes, Meuleman, and Amess (2007)	UK and Europe	MBOs, MBIs	Partial sales of subsidiaries or divisions of buyouts accounted for one-third of total realised in the UK in 2001 but accounted for one-quarter in 2005; number of partial sales generally ranges between 70 and 100 per annum; €9 billion was raised through partial sales in UK in 2005; in Continental Europe partial sales accounted for less than one-twentieth of total exit value in 2005
Hege, Lovo, Slovin, and Sushka (2018)	US	Divestments to PE and corporate acquirers	Corporate sellers obtain significantly greater positive excess returns in PE deals than for intercorporate asset sales; corporate seller excess returns are positively correlated with subsequent gains in asset enterprise value; only restructuring capabilities of PE (not acquisition of undervalued assets) explain the pattern of the gains generated in PE deals

Post-Exit Effects

Authors	Country	Nature of transactions	Findings
Holthausen and Larcker (1996)	US	Reverse LBOs	Leverage and management equity fall in reverse buyouts but remain high relative to comparable listed corporations that have not undergone a buyout. Pre-IPO accounting performance significantly higher than the median for the buyouts sector. Following IPO, accounting performance remains significantly above the firms' sector for four years but declines during this period. Change is positively related to changes in insider ownership but not to leverage
Bruton, Keels, and Scifres (2002)	US	Reverse LBOs	Agency cost problems did not reappear immediately following a reverse buyout but took several years to re-emerge
Jelic, Saadouni, and Wright (2005)	UK	Reverse MBOs, MBIs	Private equity backed MBOs more underpriced than MBOs without venture capital backing but perform better than their non-VC backed counterparts in the long run. Reverse MBOs backed by more reputable VCs exit earlier and perform better than those backed by less prestigious VCs
Cao and Lerner (2009)	US	Reverse LBOs	For a sample of 526 RLBOs between 1981 and 2003, three- and five-year stock performance appears to be as good as or better than other IPOs and the stock market as a whole, depending on the specification. There is evidence of a deterioration of returns over the time
Von Drathen and Faleiro (2007)	UK	LBO-backed and non-LBO backed IPOs	For a sample of 128 LBO-backed IPOs and 1,121 non-LBO backed IPOs during 1990–2006 LBO-backed IPOs outperform non-LBO backed IPOs and a stock market index; percentage of equity retained by buyout group post-offering drives out-performance
Jelic and Wright (2011)	UK	MBOs, MBIs	Improvements in employment, leverage, sales efficiency, and sales up to five years post-IPO, especially for more reputable PE firms; no significant change in employment and efficiency following non-float exit

Distress, Failure, and Recovery

Authors	Country	Nature of Transactions	Findings
Bruner and Eades (1992)	US	LBOs	Given REVCOs debt and preference dividend obligations and its context, low probability could have survived the first three years
Kaplan and Stein (1993)	US	LBOs	Overpayment major cause of distress
Wright, Wilson, Robbie, and Ennew (1996)	UK	MBOs, MBIs	Failed buyouts more likely than non-failed buyouts to be more highly leveraged, have lower liquidity ratios, be smaller and have lower labour productivity
Andrade and Kaplan (1998)	US	LBOs	Net effect of high leverage and distress creates value after adjusting for market returns
Citron, Wright, Rippington, and Ball (2003)	UK	MBOs, MBIs	Secured creditors recover on average 62% of loans in failed buyouts
Citron and Wright (2008)	UK	MBOs, MBIs	Multiple secured creditors does not lead to inefficiency in the distress process but lead secured creditors obtained significantly higher recovery rates than other secured lenders
Strömberg (2008)	Worldwide	Private equity backed buyouts	No significant relationship between bankruptcy and deal size; divisional buyouts significantly less likely to end in distress; private equity backed deals somewhat more likely to go bankrupt; no major difference in probability of bankruptcy across time periods; buyouts of distressed firms significantly more likely to fail
Chapman and Klein (2009)	US	LBOs	2.66% default rate for deals completed during 1984–2006
Kaplan and Strömberg (2009)	US	LBOs	1.2% default rate for deals completed 1970–2002
Demiroglu and James (2010)	US	PTP LBOs	Buyouts sponsored by high reputation PE firms are less likely to experience financial distress or bankruptcy ex-post
Guo, Hotchkiss, and Song (2011)	US	LBOs	3.14% default rate for deals completed during 1990–2006

Sudarsanam, Wright, and Huang (2011)	UK	PTP LBOs	PTPs significantly higher default probability than non-acquired firms that remain public; high bankruptcy risk at going private increases chance of subsequent bankruptcy; post-PTP bankruptcy likelihood less when PTP is an MBO and with independent board pre-PTP
Borell and Tykvova (2012)	Europe	LBOs, non-LBOs	PE investors select companies which are less financially constrained than comparable companies and financial constraints tighten after buyout, especially for stand-alone transactions and in times of cheap debt; PE-backed companies do not suffer from higher mortality rates, unless backed by inexperienced private equity funds
Hotchkiss, Strömberg, and Smith (2011)	US	PE backed and non-PE backed firms obtaining leveraged loan financing	50% of defaults involve PE-backed firms; PE backed firms not more likely to default than other firms with similar leverage characteristics; recovery rates for junior creditors lower for PE backed firms; PE backed firms in distress more likely to survive as an independent reorganized company
Lopez de Silanes, Phalippou, and Gottschalg (2013)	81 countries	PE-backed deals	Bankruptcy rates vary across countries: UK 9%; US 12%; Germany 13%; France 8%; Scandinavia 5%
Wilson and Wright (2013)	UK	MBOs, MBIs, private equity backed buyouts, non-buyouts	Buyouts have a higher failure rate (entering administration) than non-buyouts with MBIs having a higher failure rate than MBOs which in turn have a higher failure rate than private equity backed buyouts/buy-ins
Wright, Cressy, Wilson, and Farag (2014); Cressy and Farag (2012)	UK	PE-backed buyouts and listed corporations	Creditors of PE-backed firms recover 63% of secured debt against 30% for listed corporations
Bernstein, Lerner, and Mezzanotti (2018)	UK	PE-backed buyouts and control group	During the financial crisis PE-backed companies decreased investments less than control group peers; experienced greater equity and debt inflows, higher asset growth, and increased market share; Financially constrained companies and those with PE investors with more resources at crisis onset especially benefited

Cumulative Abnormal Returns and Premia on Public-to-Private Buyouts

Study	Country	Type of deal	Event window	CAR	Premium
DeAngelo, DeAngelo, and Rice (1984)	US	ALL	−1,0 days	22.27%	56.30%
			−10,10 days	28.05%	
Lowenstein (1985)	US	MBO	-	-	56.00%
Torabzadeh and Bertin (1987)	US	ALL	−1,0 months	18.64%	-
			−1,1 months	20.57%	
Lehn and Poulsen (1989)	US	ALL	−1,1 days	16.30%	36.10%
			−10,10 days	19.90%	
Amihud (1989)	US	MBO	−20,0 days	19.60%	42.90%
Kaplan (1989a, 1989b)	US	MBO	−40,60 days	26.00%	42.30%
Marais, Schipper, and Smith (1989)	US	ALL	0,1 days	13.00%	-
			−69,1 days	22.00%	
Asquith and Wizman (1990)	US	ALL	-	-	37.90%
Lee (1992)	US	MBO	−1,0 days	14.90%	-
			−69, 0 days	22.40%	
Lee, Rosenstein, Rangan, and Davidson (1992)	US	MBO	−1,0 days	17.84%	-
			−5,0 days	20.96%	
Frankfurter and Gunay (1992)	US	MBO	−50,50 days	27.32%	-
			−1,0 days	17.24%	
Travlos and Cornett (1993)	US	ALL	−1,0 days	16.20%	41.90%
			−10,10 days	19.24%	
Harlow and Howe (1993)	US	ALL	-	-	44.90%
Easterwood, Singer, Seth, and Lang (1994)	US	MBO	-	-	32.90%
Halpern, Kieschnick, and Rotenberg (1999)	US	ALL	-	-	n.a.
Goh, Gombola, Liu, and Chou (2002)	US	ALL	−20,1 days	21.31%	-
			0,1 days	12.68%	
Andres, Betzer, and Hoffmann (2003)	EU	ALL	−1,1 days	15.78%	-
			−15,15 days	21.89%	
Renneboog, Simons, and Wright (2007)	UK	ALL	−1,0 days	22.68%	41.00%
			−5,5 days	25.53%	
			−40,40 days	29.28%	
Andres, Betzer, and Weir (2007)	EU	ALL	−30, 30 days	24.20%	-
Oxman and Yildirim (2007)	US	ALL	-	-	29.2% (small) 33.80% (big)
Officer, Ozbas, and Sensoy (2010)	US	ALL	−1,1 days	-	-

Operating Performance Changes Post-Buyout

Authors	Country	Nature of transactions	Findings
Operating Performance			
Kaplan (1989a)	US	LBOs	Profits and cash flows increase post buyout; operating income/assets up to 36% higher for LBOs compared to industry median
Muscarella and Vetsuypens (1990)	US	Reverse LBOs	Operating income/sales increases by more than all of control sample firms; improvements in operating performance compared to control sample mainly due to cost reductions rather than revenue or asset turnover improvements
Smith (1990)	US	LBOs	Operating cash flow per employee and per dollar of operating assets improves post buyout; Working capital improves post buyout; Changes not due to lay-offs or capex, marketing, etc. expenditures; cash flow to employees 71% higher than industry median
Singh (1990)	US	Reverse LBOs	Revenue growth post buyout, working capital management and operating income better than industry comparators, especially for divisional LBOs
Opler (1992)	US	LBOs	Operating cash flow/sales ratio increased by 16.5% on average three years post buyout
Wright, Thompson, and Robbie (1992)	UK	MBOs, MBIs	68% showed improvements in profitability; 17% showed a fall; 43% reduced debt days and 31% increased creditor days
Bruining (1992)	Netherlands	MBOs	Buyouts display significantly higher than industry average cash flow and return on investment
Smart and Waldfogel (1994)	US	LBOs	Median shock effect of buyout [correcting for forecast performance] of 30% improvement in operating income/sales ratio between pre-LBO year and second post-LBO year
Chevalier (1995)	US	LBOs	Consumers may face higher prices in supermarkets subject to LBO
Wright, Wilson, and Robbie (1996)	UK	Matched MBOs and non-MBOs	Profitability higher for MBOs than comparable non-MBOs for up to 5 years
Desbrières and Schatt (2002)	France	MBOs, MBIs	Accounting performance changes depend on vendor source of deal
Cressy, Munari, and Malipero (2007)	UK	MBOs, MBIs	Operating profitability of private equity backed buyouts greater than for comparable non-buyouts by 4.5% over first three buyout years

Continued

Authors	Country	Nature of transactions	Findings
Operating Performance			
Meuleman, Amess, Wright, and Scholes (2009)	UK	Divisional, family and secondary buyouts	Higher growth in divisional buyouts
Weir, Jones, and Wright (2015)	UK	PTPs	Performance deteriorates relative to the pre-buyout situation but firms do not perform worse than firms that remain public and there some evidence that performance improves; PE-backed deals have a negative effect on profitability relative to pre-buyout; PE-backed deals performed better than the industry average; non-PE-backed buyouts expenses lower after going private and profit per employee higher, z-scores improved
Boucly, Thesmar, and Sraer (2009)	France	LBOs	Post-LBO growth in sales, assets, productivity, and jobs higher in industries that have insufficient internal capital
Gaspar (2009)	France	LBOs	LBOs exhibit significantly higher operating returns of 2–3% relative to matched control group, due to increase in gross margins, productivity gains, and improved working capital utilization
Jelic and Wright (2011)	UK	MBOs, MBIs, PE-backed	Significant improvements in output for PE-backed buyouts exiting by IPO; performance of secondary MBOs declines during first buyout but performance in second buyout stabilizes until year 3
Guo, Hotchkiss, and Song (2011)	US	P2Ps	Returns to pre- or post-buyout capital significantly positive except for firms ending in distressed restructuring. Returns to post-buyout capital greater when deal financed with a greater proportion of bank financing, or when there is more than one private equity sponsor
Wilson, Wright, Siegel, and Scholes (2012)	UK	MBOs, MBIs, PE-backed, non-PE Companies	PE backed buyouts show stronger economic performance before and during recession than comparable private and listed companies; with up to 4.8% higher ROA
Chung (2011)	UK	PE-backed buyouts and non-buyout companies	Post buyout assets, sales, employment, and capital expenditures of private targets increase while they decrease for public targets; though private equity firms select targets with growth potential, they do help target firms grow and expand post-buyout
Bernstein and Sheen (2013)	US	PE-backed restaurant establishments	Health and sanitation violations decline post PE buyout and correlate with increases in customer satisfaction and declines in menu prices and workers per outlet

Wilson and Wright (2013)	UK	PE-backed and non-PE-backed buyouts	For 1998–2011, PE-backed buyouts have significant and positive associations with cumulative average growth rates for 3 and 5 year periods; For 2008–2011, PE-backed buyouts are significant and positively associated with growth in all variables for both CAGR 3 and 5 year periods, indicating their growth has held up better than non-PE-backed private companies
Zhou, Jelic, and Wright (2014)	UK	SBOs	Strong evidence of a deterioration in long-run abnormal returns following SBO deals; SBOs also perform worse than primary buyouts in terms of profitability, labour productivity, and growth
Scellato and Ughetto (2013)	Europe	Private buyouts and non-buyouts	Positive impact of buyouts on growth of total assets and of employment in target firms in short- and mid-term
Cohn, Mills, and Towery (2014)	US	P2P and control	Evolution of return on sales, return on assets, and economic value added (EVA) relative to the control group of similar listed peers flat from two years before to three years after buyout
Ayash and Schütt (2016)	US	P2P	Adjusting measures to account for the LBO process, there is no robust evidence of post-buyout improvements in public-to-private LBOs, regardless of the time period of the study

Productivity Changes in Buyouts and Private Equity

Authors	Country	Unit of analysis	Nature of transactions	Findings
Lichtenberg and Siegel (1990)	US	Plant	Divisional and full-firm LBOs and MBOs of public and private companies	Plants involved in LBOs and MBOs are 2% more productive than comparable plants before the buyout; LBOs and especially MBO plants experience a substantial increase in productivity after a buyout to 8.3% above; employment and wages of non-production workers at plants (but not production workers) declines after an LBO or MBO; no decline in R&D investment
Amess (2002)	UK	Firm	MBOs	MBOs enhance productivity; marginal value added productivity of labour is significantly higher than in comparable non-buyouts
Amess (2003)	UK	Firm	MBOs	MBOs have higher technical efficiency 2 years pre-MBO and lower technical efficiency 3 or more years before than comparable non-buyouts; MBOs have higher technical efficiency in each of 4 years after buyout but not beyond 4 years than comparable non-buyouts
Harris, Siegel, and Wright (2005)	UK	Plant	Divisional and full-firm LBOs and MBOs of public and private companies	Plants involved in MBOs are less productive than comparable plants before the buyout; they experience a substantial increase in productivity after a buyout; plants involved in an MBO experience a substantial reduction in employment
Davis, Lerner, Haltiwanger, Miranda, and Jarmin (2009)	US	Firm/ establishment	Matched private equity backed and non-private equity backed firms and establishments	Private equity backed firms increase productivity in 2 years post transaction on average by 2% more than controls; 72% of increase due to more effective management; private equity firms more likely to close underperforming establishments, as measured by labour productivity; private equity backed firms outperformed control firms before buyout
Wilson, Wright, Siegel, and Scholes (2012)	UK	Firm	MBOs, MBIs, PE backed, non-PE Companies	PE backed buyouts show stronger economic performance before and during recession than comparable private and listed companies with up 11% productivity differential

Alperovych, Amess, and Wright (2013)	UK	Firm	PE-backed LBOs	Post-buyout efficiency increases in 3 years post-deal but mainly in first two years; divisional buyouts show higher efficiency improvements than private and secondary buyouts; there is a positive and significant effect of PE firm experience on post-buyout efficiency
Scellato and Ughetto (2013)	Europe	Firm	Private buyouts and non-buyouts	No clear short and long term pattern of productivity increase
Goergen, O'Sullivan, and Wood (2011, 2014a, 2014b)	UK	Firms	IBOs/MBIs of listed companies	Despite employment falls in the year immediately after the completion of the IBO no parallel or subsequent increase in productivity or profitability

Strategy, Investment, R&D, and Control System Changes in Buyouts

Authors	Country	Unit of analysis	Nature of transactions	Findings
Wright (1986)	UK	Firm	MBOs	Divisional MBOs reduce dependence on trading activity with former parent
Bull (1989)	US	Firm	MBOs, LBOs	Evidence of both cost reduction but greater managerial alertness to opportunities for wealth creation more important
Malone (1989)	US	Firm	Smaller LBOs	Major changes in marketing and NPD; cost control given greater importance
Kaplan (1989a)	US	Firm	LBOs	Capex falls immediately following LBO
Smith (1990)	US	Firm	LBOs	Capex and R&D fall immediately following LBO
Muscarella and Vetsuypens (1990)	US	Firm	Reverse LBOs	Capex declines compared to pre-LBO
Lichtenberg and Siegel (1990)	US	Plant	LBOs, MBOs	LBOs typically in low R&D industries. R&D fall both pre and post buyout not statistically significant; R&D fall may be accounted for by divestment of more R&D-intensive divisions
Wright, Chiplin, Thompson, and Robbie (1990b)	UK	Firm	MBOs, MBIs	Divisional buyouts reduce trading dependence on former parent by introducing new products previously prevented from doing
Wright, Thompson, and Robbie (1992)	UK	Firm	Divisional, and Full-firm MBOs of private companies	MBOs enhance new product development; 44% acquired new equipment and plant that would not otherwise have occurred
Jones (1992)	UK	Firm	MBOs	Buyouts result in better match between accounting control systems and context, with increased reliance on management control systems influenced by pressure to meet targets
Green (1992)	UK	Firm	MBOs	Buyout ownership allowed managers to perform tasks more effectively through greater independence to take decisions. Managers had sought to take entrepreneurial actions prior to buyout but had been prevented from doing so because of the constraints imposed by parent's control

Long and Ravenscraft (1993)	US	Division	LBOs and MBOs	LBOs result in a reduction in R&D expenditure but LBOs typically in low R&D industries; R&D intensive buyouts outperform non-buyout industry peers and other buyouts without R&D expenditure
Seth and Easterwood (1993)	US	Firm	LBOs	Buyouts focus strategic activities towards more related businesses
Wiersema and Liebeskind (1995)	US	Firm	Large LBOs	Large LBOs reduce lines of business and diversification
Lei and Hitt (1995)				LBOs may lead to a reduced resource base for organizational learning and technology development
Phan and Hill (1995)	US	Firm	LBOs	Buyouts focus strategic activities and reduce diversification
Zahra (1995)	US	Firm	MBOs	MBOs result in more effective use of R&D expenditure and new product development
Robbie and Wright (1995)	UK	Firm	MBIs	Ability of management to effect strategic changes adversely affected by asymmetric information, need to attend to operational problems and market timing
Bruining and Wright (2002)	Netherlands	Firm	Divisional MBOs	MBOs result in more entrepreneurial activities such as new product and market development
Bruining, Bonnet, and Wright (2004)	Netherlands	Firm	MBOs	MBOs result in introduction of more strategic control systems that allow for entrepreneurial growth
Brown, Fee, and Thomas (2007)	US	Firm	Suppliers to LBOs and leveraged recapitalizations	Suppliers to LBO firms experience significantly negative abnormal returns at announcements of downstream LBOs but no the case for leveraged recapitalizations. Suppliers who have made substantial relationship-specific investments more negatively affected. Suggests increased leverage without accompanying change in organizational form does not lead to improved bargaining power
Ernst and Young (2007)	Europe	Firms	Exited larger PE-backed buyouts	2/3 of growth in EBITDA from business expansion, with organic growth most important; acquisitions also important
Gottschalg (2007)	International	Firms	PE-backed LBOs	Pure restructuring deals less frequent than growth-oriented deals; combination of growth-oriented (acquisitions, new marketing and markets, new products, JVs, etc.) and restructuring-oriented (divestments, layoffs, cost-cutting, closure of non-core units, etc.) changes common; 43% had complete/partial replacement of management

Continued

Authors	Country	Unit of analysis	Nature of transactions	Findings
Lerner, Strömberg, and Sørensen (2008)	Worldwide	Firm	Private equity backed buyouts	Buyouts increase patent citations after private equity investment but quantity of patenting unchanged, maintain comparable levels of cutting edge research, patent portfolios become more focused after private equity investment
Acharya, Gottschalg, Hahn, and Kehoe (2009)	UK	Firms	PE-backed LBOs	Significant replacement of CEOs and CFOs either at the time of the deal or afterwards and leveraging of external support important especially related to investee out-performance
Cornelli and Karakas (2008)	UK	Firms	PE-backed PTPs (LBOs and MBOs)	High CEO and board turnover during post-PTP restructuring
Ernst and Young (2009)	UK	Firms	Larger PE-backed buyouts	Organic growth; strategic and operational improvements
Bloom, van Reenen, and Sadun (2009)	Asia, Europe, US	Firms	Private equity owned and other firms	Private equity management practices better than in other firms in terms of operational management, people based management practices and evaluation practices
Ughetto (2010)	Europe	Firm	PE-backed buyouts	An increase in patenting post buyout
Gong and Wu (2011)	US	Firm	LBO	CEO turnover rate of 51% within two years of LBO; boards replace CEOs in companies with high agency costs, low pre-LBO ROA and entrenched CEOs
Bruining, Wervaal, and Wright (2013)	Netherlands	Firms	PE and non-PE backed buyouts	Majority private equity backed buyouts significantly increase entrepreneurial management practices but increased debt negatively affects entrepreneurial management; entrepreneurial management positively affects exploration and exploitation, but the latter does not impact firm performance
Cumming and Zambelli (2011)	Italy	Firms	Private equity backed buyouts	Following legislative changes PE investors become more involved in the management and governance of the target firm by increasing ownership stake, the use of convertible debt, adopting more control rights especially right to CEO and the right to take majority board position
Chung (2011)	UK	Firms	PE-backed buyouts and non-buyout companies	Post buyout private targets make more acquisitions than public targets
Bertoni, Le Nadant, and Perdreau (2014)	UK	Firms	LBOs	LBOs do not have lower innovation and R&D than non-LBOs during the financial crisis; innovation and R&D decline in financially constrained LBOs prior to the buyout

Engel and Stiebale (2014)	UK/France	Firm	PE backed buyouts and expansion finance	In both countries, portfolio firms have higher investment levels and fewer financial constraints after expansion financing; in UK, PE-backed buyouts outperform non-private equity backed firms on both indicators
Amess, Stiebale, and Wright (2015)	UK	Firms	PE-backed buyouts	Buyouts results in a 6% increase in quality-adjusted patent stock three years after the deal, most notably in private-to-private transactions with a 14% increase in quality-adjusted patent stock
Ughetto (2016)	UK, France, Italy, Spain	Firm	Low and medium tech buyouts	Sensitivity of investments to cash flows is increased on buyout, while investment levels not affected after a buyout

Drivers of Post-Buyout Changes

Authors	Country	Nature of transactions	Findings
Malone (1989)	US	Smaller private equity backed LBOs	Management equity stake important driver of post buyout changes
Thompson, Wright, and Robbie (1992)	UK	MBOs, MBIs returning to market	Management team equity stake by far larger impact on relative performance of returns to equity investors from buyout to exit than leverage, equity ratchets, etc.
Denis (1994)	US	LBO and leveraged recapitalization	Gains in LBO greater than in leveraged recapitalization attributed to more important role of equity ownership and active investors in LBOs
Phan and Hill (1995)	US	LBOs of listed corporations	Managerial equity stakes had a much stronger effect on performance than debt levels for periods of three and five years following the buyout
Robbie and Wright (1995)	UK	Smaller MBIs	Private equity firms less closely involved; debt commitment and covenants important trigger for corrective action
Cotter and Peck (2001)	US	LBOs	Active monitoring by a buyout specialist substitutes for tighter debt terms in monitoring and motivating managers of LBOs. Buyout specialists that control a majority of the post-LBO equity use less debt in transactions. Buyout specialists that closely monitor managers through stronger representation on the board also use less debt
Cressy, Munari, and Malipero (2007)	UK	MBOs, MBIs	Industry specialization, but not buyout stage specialization, of private equity firm adds significantly to increase in operating profitability of private equity backed buyouts over first three buyout years
Cornelli and Karakas (2008)	UK	PE-backed PTPs (LBOs and MBOs)	Board representation and active involvement by private equity firms changes according to private equity firm style and anticipated challenges of the investment; Board size falls less and PE firm representation higher when is CEO turnover and for deals that take longer to exit
Acharya, Gottschalg, Hahn, and Kehoe (2009)	UK	PE-backed LBOs	High levels of PE firm interaction with executives during the initial 100-day value creation plan, creating an active board

Meuleman, Amess, Wright, and Scholes (2009)	UK	Divisional, family and secondary buyouts	Private equity firms' experience significant driver of higher growth in divisional buyouts; PE experience important influence on growth but not profitability or efficiency; intensity of PE involvement associated with higher profitability and growth; amount of management investment insignificant or negative relationship with profitability or productivity change
Acharya, Kehoe, and Reyner (2009)	UK	Board members of large PE portfolio firms and PLCs	Value creation focus of PE boards versus governance compliance and risk management focus of PLC boards. PE boards lead strategy through intense engagement with top management, PLC boards accompany strategy of top management. Almost complete alignment in objectives between executive and non-executive directors only in PE boards. PE board members receive information primarily cash-focused and intensive induction during due diligence; PLC board members collect more diverse information and undergo a more structured (formal) induction
Leslie and Oyer (2009)	US	PTPs that IPO'd	PE-owned companies use much stronger incentives for top executives and have substantially higher debt levels. Little evidence that PE-owned firms outperform public firms in profitability or operational efficiency; compensation and debt differences between PE-owned companies and public companies disappear over a very short period (one to two years) after the PE-owned firm goes public
Demiroglu and James (2010)	US	PTP LBOs	Buyouts sponsored by high reputation PEs pay narrower loan spreads, have fewer and less restrictive financial loan covenants, use less traditional bank debt, borrow more and at a lower cost from institutional loan markets, and have higher leverage; no direct effect of PE firm reputation on buyout valuations
Pe'er and Gottschalg (2011)	US	LBOs	Positive association between a more aligned institutional context (US states dominated by Republican Party) and volume of buyout activity and different measures of performance for these buyouts
Zhou, Jelic, and Wright (2014)	UK	SBOs	PE firm's reputation and change in management are important determinants of improvements in profitability and labour productivity, respectively; high debt and high percentage of management equity associated with poor performance measured by profitability and labour productivity; none of the buyout mechanisms (i.e. financial, governance, operating) generate growth during the secondary buyout phase

Continued

Authors	Country	Nature of transactions	Findings
Alperovych, Amess, and Wright (2013)	UK	PE-backed SBOs and non-SBOs	PE firm experience significantly increases efficiency post-buyout
Wilson and Wright (2013)	UK	PE-backed buyouts and non-buyouts	Extent of UK experience of PE firms is significant and positively associated with growth in value added, assets, sales, equity and employment; foreign PE firms are significant and positively associated with growth in asset and equity but significant and negatively associated with employment growth; board size and director sector experience positively associated with growth; director age and number of directorships negatively associated with growth
Scellato and Ughetto (2013)	Europe	PE-backed buyouts and non-buyouts	Generalist funds negatively and significantly impact operating profitability of PE-backed firms, turnaround specialists have a positive impact; target companies with lead investor located in the same country show relatively higher profitability performance

Secondary Buyouts

Authors	Country	Nature of Transactions	Findings
Meuleman, Amess, Wright, and Scholes (2009)	UK	Divisional, family and SBOs	Higher growth in divisional buyouts
Achleitner and Figge (2012); Achleitner, Bauer, Figge, and Lutz (2012)	Europe and North America	SBOs	No difference in performance of primary and secondary deals
Wang (2012)	UK	SBOs	The positive effects of secondary buyouts on firms' operating cash flows seem to be achieved through expansions, not by running the firms more efficiently
Alperovych, Amess, and Wright (2013)	UK	SBOs and PE-backed non-SBOs	Secondary buyouts remain below the average in terms of performance
Zhou, Jelic, and Wright (2013)	UK	SBOs and primary buyouts	Strong evidence of a deterioration in long-run abnormal returns following SBO deals; SBOs also perform worse than primary buyouts in terms of profitability, labour productivity, and growth
Arcot, Fluck, Gaspar, and Hege (2015)	US and 12 European countries	SBOs	SBOs more likely if buyer fund under pressure to invest or seller fund under pressure to exit; buyers under pressure may pay relatively more and sellers under pressure accept lower prices; sellers under pressure have more bargaining power than buyers under pressure
Jenkinson and Sousa (2015)	Europe	SBOs and primary deals	SBOs underperform compared to primary deals in terms of operating income
Bonini (2015)	Europe	SBOs and primary deals	SBOs underperform compared to primary deals in terms of operating income
Degeorge, Martin, and Phalippou (2016)	Worldwide	SBOs	SBOs underperform primary buyouts in terms of cash multiples and IRR while their risk is similar; SBOs between specialized PE firms perform better
Jelic, Zhou, and Wright (2019)	UK	SBOs	Financial (rather than operational) experience of PE directors in acquiring PE firms significantly increases post-SMBO profitability while high level business education is significantly increases post-SMBO growth; complementary expertise, provided by directors in buying and selling PE firms, plays an important role only in post-SMBO growth improvements

Glossary

1st lien, 2nd lien, etc. The order of priority in which claims on assets pledged as security are paid—1st lien is senior to 2nd lien, etc.

Absolute return The return an asset achieves over time, without comparison to the overall market, other assets, or benchmarks.

Acquisition The obtaining of control, possession, or ownership of a company.

Acting in concert Persons acting in concert are persons who, pursuant to an agreement or understanding (whether formal or informal), actively cooperate throughout the acquisition by any of them acquiring shares in a company, to obtain or consolidate control of that company.

Agency fee A fee paid to an institution for acting as agent for a syndicate of investors or lenders. Usually seen in syndicated loans.

Alternative Investment Fund Managers Directive (AIFMD) EU regulation covering private equity funds and other alternative investment funds.

Alpha A measure of performance as the excess return of an investment relative to the return of a benchmark index.

Alternative Investment Market (AIM) The London Stock Exchange's market for new, fast-growing companies. AIM offers the benefit of operating both an electronic quote and order trading facility. It commenced trading in June 1995.

Alternative investments/assets Investments covering among others Private Equity and venture capital, hedge funds, real estate, infrastructure, commodities, or collateralised debt obligations (CDOs).

Anchor LP An investor in a Private Equity/venture capital fund that commits a significant amount of the total fundraising to the fund upfront.

Arm's length The relationship between persons (whether companies or not) who deal on purely commercial terms, without the influence of other factors such as common ownership; a parent/subsidiary relationship between companies; existing family or business relationships between individuals.

Asset allocation A fund manager's allocation of his investment portfolio into various asset classes (eg, stocks, bonds, Private Equity).

Asset class A category of investment, defined by the main characteristics of risk, liquidity, and return.

Asset cover One of the indicators used by banks to calculate debt ceiling. It is the extent to which debt is secured against the company's assets. Banks apply different weighting factors to various classes of asset, depending on their liquidity and the typical reliability of the valuation.

Asset deal A sale of assets not essential for the vendor's core business.

Asset stripping Dismantling an acquired business by selling off operational and/or financial assets.

Auction A process in which an investment bank or other corporate finance adviser invites several private equity houses to look at a particular company that is for sale and to offer a bid to buy it.

Basis point (bp) One hundredth of one per cent (0.01%).

Beauty parade An accepted mechanism for an investee company to select a provider of financial and professional services. The investee normally draws up a short list of potential providers, who are then invited to pitch for the business.

BIMBO *See* **Buy-in management buyout.**

Bond A debt obligation, often secured by a mortgage on some property or asset of the issuer.

Borrowing base The amount of commitments that a subscription is secured on.

Break fee A sum agreed between the offeror and the target company to be paid to the offeror by the target only if specified events occur which prevent the offer from proceeding or if the offer fails. Also referred to as an inducement fee.

Bridge financing Financing made available to a company in the period of transition from being privately owned to being publicly quoted.

Bridge vehicle A fund raised by a GP on an interim basis, before launching a new fund. Bridge vehicles are often of a smaller size, compared to the normal fund.

Broker One who acts as an intermediary between a buyer and a seller of securities.

Business model The underlying model of a company's business operation.

Business plan A document which describes a company's management, business concept, and goals. It is a vital tool for any company seeking any type of investment funding, but is also of great value in clarifying the underlying position and realities for the management/owners themselves.

Buy-and-build strategy Active, organic growth of portfolio companies through add-on acquisitions.

Buyback A corporation's re-purchase of its own stock or bonds.

Buy-in management buyout (BIMBO) A combination of a management buy-in (MBI) and a management buyout (MBO).

Buyout A transaction in which a business, business unit, or company is acquired from the current shareholders (the vendor).

BVCA British Private Equity and Venture Capital Association https://www.bvca.co.uk/.

Call premium The amount a borrower must pay in penalties to repay a bond early. *See also* **Early repayment compensation.**

Capital gain If an asset is sold at a higher price than that at which it was bought, there is a capital gain.

Capital market A market place in which long-term capital is raised by industry and commerce, the government, and local authorities. Stock exchanges are part of capital markets.

Capital under management This is the total amount of funds available to fund managers for future investments plus the amount of funds already invested (at cost) and not yet divested.

Captive fund A fund in which the parent organisation of the management company contributes most of the capital—i.e. where the parent organisation allocates money to a captive fund from its own internal sources and reinvests realised capital gains into the fund.

Carried interest An entitlement accruing to an investment fund's management company or individual members of the fund management team. Carried interest becomes payable once the investors have achieved repayment of their original investment in the fund plus a defined hurdle rate.

Cash alternative If the offeror offers shareholders of the target company the choice between offeror securities and cash, the cash element is known as the cash alternative.

Cash flow EBITDA ± working capital movement - capital expenditure - taxation.

CDD Commercial due diligence.

CDO Collateralized debt obligation.

CDS Credit default swap.

Certain funds period When loans are not drawn down in one instalment, they may continue to be available to the borrower for the length of the certain funds period.

Chinese walls Deliberate information barriers within a large company to prevent conflict of interest between different departments.

CLO Collateralized loan obligation.

Class of securities Classes of securities are securities that share the same terms and benefits. Classes of capital stock are generally alphabetically designated (e.g. Class C Common Stock, Class A Preferred Stock, etc).

Clawback option A clawback option requires the general partners in an investment fund to return capital to the limited partners to the extent that the general partner has received more than its agreed profit split. A general partner clawback option ensures that, if an investment fund exits from strong performers early in its life and weaker performers are left at the end, the limited partners get back their capital contributions, expenses, and any preferred return promised in the partnership agreement.

Closed-end fund Fund with a fixed number of shares. These are offered during an initial subscription period. Unlike open-end mutual funds, closed-end funds do not stand ready to issue and redeem shares on a continuous basis.

Closing A closing is reached when a certain amount of money has been committed to a private equity fund. Several intermediate closings can occur before the final closing of a fund is reached.

Club deal A deal where several buyout houses pool their resources together when buying a company of significant size, which would be otherwise inaccessible for them alone, either due to the purchase price or fund investment restrictions.

Co-lead investor Investor who has contributed a similar share with the lead investor in a private equity joint venture or syndicated deal.

Collateral Assets pledged to a lender until a loan is repaid. If the borrower does not pay back the money owed, the lender has the legal right to seize the collateral and sell it to pay off the loan.

Commercial paper An unsecured obligation issued by a corporation or bank to finance its short-term credit needs (e.g. accounts receivable or inventory). Maturities typically range from 2 to 270 days.

Commitment A limited partner's obligation to provide a certain amount of capital to a private equity fund when the general partner asks for capital.

Competent authority A term used within Directives produced by the European Commission to describe a body identified by a member state of the European Union as being responsible for specified functions related to the securities market within that member state. Areas of competence include the recognition of firms permitted to offer investment services; the approval of prospectuses for public offerings; and the recognition and surveillance of stock markets. A member state may nominate different competent authorities for different areas of responsibility.

Completion The moment when legal documents are signed; normally also the moment at which funds are advanced by investors.

Compliance The process of ensuring that any other person or entity operating within the financial services industry complies at all times with the regulations currently in force. Many of these regulations are designed to protect the public from misleading claims about returns they could receive from investments, while others outlaw insider trading. Especially in the UK, regulation of the financial services industry has developed beyond recognition in recent years.

Co-invest Generally, the option to invest alongside the equity sponsor in a transaction. The term has many uses that are discussed in the main text.

Concert party Any persons or parties acting in concert (see definition of acting in concert).

Conditions precedent Certain conditions that a private equity firm may insist are satisfied before a deal is completed.

Confidentiality agreement An agreement in which an employee, customer or vendor agrees not to disclose confidential information to any third party or to use it in any context other than that of company business. Also called a non-disclosure agreement.

Conflict of interest For example, in a public-to-private transaction a potential conflict of interest invariably arises if the directors of the target company are (or will be) directors of the offeror, in which case their support for the offer gives rise to a potential conflict with the interests of the shareholders of the target company.

Connected persons Companies related by ownership or control of each other or common ownership or control by a third person or company, and individuals connected by family relationships or, in some instances, by existing business relationships (such as individuals who are partners).

Contributed capital Contributed capital represents the portion of capital that was initially raised (committed by investors) which has been drawn down in a private equity fund.

Conversion The act of exchanging one form of security or common stock equivalent for another security of the same company (e.g. preferred stock for common stock, debt securities for equity).

Convertible security A financial security (usually preferred stock or bonds) that is exchangeable for another type of security (usually ordinary shares) at a fixed price. The convertible feature is designed to enhance marketability of preferred stock as an additional incentive to investors.

Covenant-lite (Cov-lite) loan A loan with lighter or no covenants, providing the borrower more operational flexibility while limiting the lender's protection against strong changes in their financial performance.

Covenant An agreement by a company to perform or to abstain from certain activities during a certain time period. Covenants usually remain in force for the full duration of the time a private equity investor holds a stated amount of securities and may terminate on the occurrence of a certain event such as a public offering. Affirmative covenants define acts which a company must perform and may include payment of taxes, insurance, maintenance of corporate existence, etc. Negative covenants define acts which the company must not perform and can include the prohibition of mergers, sale or purchase of assets, issuing of securities, etc.

Credit spread The difference in yield between two securities that are identical (in maturity and duration) except for their credit quality. Often the credit spread is used to compare corporate bonds with government bonds.

Creditor exit A buyout which has exited due to some kind of financial failure. The equity value of the company is generally written down to zero, and the company has ceased trading.

Cumulative dividend A dividend which accumulates if not paid in the period when due and must be paid in full before other dividends are paid on the company's ordinary shares.

Cumulative preferred stock A form of preference shares which provide that, if one or more dividends is omitted, those dividends accumulate and must be paid in full before other dividends may be paid on the company's ordinary shares.

Deal flow The number of investment opportunities available to a private equity house.

Debenture An instrument securing the indebtedness of a company over its assets.

Debt fund An investment pool in which the core holdings comprise fixed income investments. On average, the fee ratios are lower than those attached to equity funds as overall management costs are lower.

Debt service Cash required in a given period to pay interest and matured principal on outstanding debt.

Debt-to-equity ratio A measure of a company's leverage, calculated by dividing long-term debt by ordinary shareholders' equity.

Defined benefit plan A pension plan that promises a specified benefit to be paid to the employee at retirement. In a defined benefit plan the company bears the risk of the pension scheme being underfunded. *See also* **Defined contribution plan.**

Defined contribution plan A pension plan that does not promise a specific amount of benefits at retirement. Both employee and employer contribute to a pension plan; the employee then has the right to the balance of the account. This balance may fluctuate over the lifetime of the pension plan. *See also* **Defined benefit plan.**

Delisting The removal of a company from a listing on an exchange.

Derivative or **derivative security** A financial instrument or security whose characteristics and value depend upon the characteristics and value of an underlying instrument or asset (typically a commodity, bond, equity, or currency). Examples include futures, options, and mortgage-backed securities.

Development capital *See* **Expansion capital.**

Dilution Occurs when an investor's percentage in a company is reduced by the issue of new securities. It may also refer to the effect on earnings per share and book value per share if convertible securities are converted or stock options are exercised.

Distribution The amount disbursed to the limited partners in a private equity fund.

Dividend cover A ratio that measures the number of times a dividend could have been paid out of the year's earnings. The higher the dividend cover, the safer the dividend.

DPI (Distribution to paid-in) Measures the cumulative distributions returned to investors (limited partners) as a proportion of the cumulative paid-in capital. DPI is net of fees and carried interest. This is also often called the 'cash-on-cash return'. This is a relative measure of the fund's 'realized' return on investment.

Drag-along rights If the venture capitalist sells their shareholding, they can require other shareholders to sell their shares to the same purchaser on the same terms.

Drawdown When investors commit themselves to back a private equity fund, all the funding may not be needed at once. Some is used and drawn down later. The amount that is drawn down is defined as contributed capital.

Due diligence For private equity professionals, due diligence can apply either narrowly to the process of verifying the data presented in a business plan/sales memorandum or broadly to complete the investigation and analytical process that precedes a commitment to invest. The purpose is to determine the attractiveness, risks, and issues regarding a transaction with a potential investee company. Due diligence should enable fund managers to realise an effective decision process and optimise the deal terms.

Early repayment compensation (ERC) The amount a borrower must pay for repaying a loan early. *See also* Call premium.

Earn-out An arrangement whereby the sellers of a business may receive additional future payments for the business, conditional to the performance of the business following the deal.

EBIT (Earnings before interest and taxes) A financial measurement often used in valuing a company (price paid expressed as a multiple of EBIT).

EBITDA (Earnings before interest, taxes, depreciation, and amortization) A financial measurement often used in valuing a company (price paid expressed as a multiple of EBITDA).

Envy ratio The ratio between the effective price paid by management and that paid by the investing institution for their respective holdings in the Newco in an MBO or MBI.

Equity contribution The percentage of total funding in a transaction that is funded by the equity sponsor's capital, whether invested as shares or loanstock.

Equity cure The option for a sponsor to invest further money that may be added back in calculating covenants to 'cure' a breach. If added back to EBITDA it is an EBITDA cure.

Equity Ownership interest in a company, represented by the shares issued to investors.

Equity illusion A high equity percentage hiding the effect of rolling up of PIK interest on the falling share of the enterprise value received by management.

Equity kicker In a mezzanine loan, equity warrants payable on exit.

Equity ratio One of the indicators used by banks to calculate debt ceiling. It consists of net equity divided by the company's total assets. Banks apply yardstick ratios for different industry sectors to arrive at a minimum level of funding that shareholders are required to contribute.

European Securities Monitoring Authority (ESMA) EU body responsible for overseeing securities regulation https://www.esma.europa.eu/.

Exercise price The price at which shares subject to a stock option may be purchased. Also known as the strike price.

Exit (Realization) Liquidation of holdings by a private equity fund. Among the various methods of exiting an investment are trade sale; sale by public offering (including IPO); write-offs; repayment of preference shares/loans; sale to another venture capitalist; sale to a financial institution.

Exit strategy A private equity house or venture capitalist's plan to end an investment, liquidate holdings and achieve maximum return.

Expansion capital Financing provided for the growth and expansion of a company. Capital may be used to finance increased production capacity; for market or product development; or to provide additional working capital. Also called **Development capital**.

FDD Financial due diligence.

Financial Conduct Authority (FCA) A UK independent non-governmental body which exercises statutory powers under the Financial Services and Markets Act 2000. The FCA is the conduct regulator for financial services firms and financial markets in the UK and the prudential regulator for many of those firms. The FCA took over these responsibilities from the Financial Services Authority in 2013.

Financial secondaries Secondary deals involving a fund's portfolio of companies that are relatively mature (five to seven years old), with some exits already realized but not all capital drawn down.

First close When raising a fund there will be one, or more closures. At first close the fund has reached its minimum size and can start investing.

Free cash flow The after-tax operating earnings of the company, plus non-cash charges (e.g. depreciation), less investment in working capital, property, plant and equipment, and other assets.

Foreign divestments A buyout from a parent company which is based in a different country—e.g. A buyout of a company with UK headquarters from a parent company in Germany.

Fund A private equity investment fund is a vehicle for enabling pooled investment by a number of investors in equity and equity-related securities of companies (investee companies). These are generally private companies whose shares are not quoted on any stock exchange. The fund can take the form either of a company or of an unincorporated arrangement such as a limited partnership.

Fund of funds A fund that takes equity positions in other funds. A fund of funds that primarily invests in new funds is a primary or primaries fund of funds. One that focuses on investing in existing funds is referred to as a secondary fund of funds.

Fund size The total amount of capital committed by the limited and general partners of a fund.

Fundraising The process in which private equity firms themselves raise money to create an investment fund. These funds are raised from private, corporate, or institutional investors, who make commitments to the fund which will be invested by the general partner.

General partner (GP) A partner in a private equity management company having unlimited personal liability for the debts and obligations of the limited partnership and the right to participate in its management.

General partner's commitment Fund managers typically invest their personal capital right alongside their investors capital, which often works to instil a higher level of confidence in the fund. The limited partners look for a meaningful general partner investment of 1% to 3% of the fund.

Goodwill The value of a business over and above its tangible assets. It includes the business's reputation and contacts.

Grandfather rights Special rights given to a limited partner to access a follow-on fund, after having been invested in the previous fund.

GMG Guideline Monitoring Group of the private equity reporting group. Set up under the Walker Guidelines to monitor large UK private equity investments.

Hedge fund An investment vehicle where managers invest in a variety of markets and securities to achieve the highest absolute return. Investments could be either made in financial markets, using stocks, bonds, commodities, currencies and derivatives, or by using advanced investment techniques such as shorting, leveraging, swaps, and arbitrage.

Hedging An investment made to offset the risk of price movements of one security by taking an opposite position in a different security, hence balancing the risk of the first investment. Examples are derivatives, such as options and futures, linked to a certain security.

High-yield bonds These play a similar role to mezzanine finance in bridging the gap between senior debt and equity. High-yield bonds are senior subordinated notes not secured against the assets of the company, and which therefore attract a higher rate of interest than senior debt.

Hurdle rate A rate of return that must be achieved before a private equity fund manager becomes entitled to carried interest payments from a fund; usually set as an IRR (internal rate of return) but related to the risk-free rate of return an investor could obtain in the same country as the fund is investing in.

Independent fund One in which the main source of fundraising is from third parties.

Inducement fee *See* **Break fee**.

Information rights A contractual right to obtain information about a company, including, for example, attending board meetings. Typically granted to private equity firms investing in privately held companies.

Insolvency (as a source of a buyout) A company which has been bought out from a company which was in receivership/administration/insolvent.

Institutional buyout (IBO) Outside financial investors (e.g. private equity houses) buy the business from the vendor. The existing management may be involved from the start and purchase a small stake. Alternatively, the investor may install its own management. Sometimes referred to as an investor-led buyout.

Institutional Limited Partners Association (ILPA) Trade body for LPs https://ilpa.org/.

Interest cover One indicator used by banks to calculate debt ceiling. It consists of EBIT divided by net interest expenses. This ratio is a measure of the company's ability to service its debt.

Invest Europe European trade body representing the venture capital and private equity industry https://www.investeurope.eu/. Formerly the European Venture Capital Association (EVCA).

IPO (Initial public offering) The sale or distribution of a company's shares to the public for the first time. An IPO of the investee company's shares is one of the ways in which a private equity fund can exit from an investment.

IRR (Internal rate of return) The IRR is the net return earned by investors (limited partners) from the fund, from inception to a stated date. The IRR is calculated as an annualized effective compounded rate of return using monthly cash flows to and from investors, together with the residual value as a terminal cash flow to investors. The IRR is therefore net—i.e. after deduction of all fees and carried interest. In cases of captive or semi-captive investment vehicles without fees or carried interest, the IRR is adjusted to create a synthetic net return using assumed fees and carried interest.

J-curve The curve generated by plotting the returns generated by a private equity fund against time (from inception to termination). The common practice of paying the management fee and start-up costs out of the first drawdowns does not produce an equivalent book value. As a result, a private equity fund will initially show a negative return. When the first realizations are made, the fund returns start to rise quite steeply. After about three to five years the interim IRR will give a reasonable indication of the definitive IRR. This period is generally shorter for buyout funds than for early stage and expansion funds.

Junk bond A bond or company debt which is rated as 'BB' or lower, indicating a higher risk of not being repaid by the company. Junk bonds are also known as 'high-yield-bonds'. Within the private equity market, junk bonds are related to buyout investments, when bonds of a transaction are rated as 'BB' or lower. *See also* **High-yield bonds**.

LBO (Leveraged buyout) A buyout in which the Newco's capital structure incorporates a level of debt, much of which is normally secured against the company's assets.

Lead investor Investor who has contributed the majority share in a private equity joint venture or syndicated deal.

Leverage ratio Either the ratio of debt to assets, or, more commonly total debt to EBITDA.

Leveraged build up (LBU) A private equity firm builds up the company it owns by acquiring smaller companies to amalgamate into the larger firm, thus increasing the total value of its investments through synergies between the acquired companies.

Leverage loan market The market in which leverage loans are syndicated by a lead bank and hence sold on to other borrowers.

Leveraged recapitalization Transaction in which a company borrows a large sum of money and distributes it to its shareholders.

LIBOR *See* London inter-bank offer rate.

LIBOR floor A minimum base rate in a loan agreement. These became common due to low and negative bank rates.

Limited partner (LP) An investor in a limited partnership (private equity fund).

Limited partnership The legal structure used by most venture and private equity funds. The partnership is usually a fixed-life investment vehicle, and consists of a general partner (the management firm, which has unlimited liability) and limited partners (the investors, who have limited liability and are not involved with the day-to-day operations). The general partner receives a management fee and a percentage of the profits. The limited partners receive income, capital gains, and tax benefits. The general partner (management firm) manages the partnership using policy laid down in a partnership agreement. The agreement also covers, terms, fees, structures, and other items agreed between the limited partners and the general partner.

Listing The quotation of shares on a recognized stock exchange.

Loan Markets Association (LMA) issues templates for standard debt documents in leverage finance outside the Americas https://www.lma.eu.com/.

Loan note A form of vendor finance or deferred payment, in which the purchaser acts as a borrower, agreeing to make payments to the holder of the transferable loan note at a specified future date.

Local Divestment A company which is bought out from a parent company based in the same country—e.g. a buyout of a company with UK headquarters from a parent company with UK headquarters.

London Inter-bank Offer Rate (LIBOR) The interest rate that the largest international banks charge each other in the London inter-bank market for loans. This is used as a basis for gauging the price of loans outside the inter-bank market. LIBOR is to be phased out and replaced by 2021.

LPA (Limited partners agreement) The contract that governs the relationship and conduct of the limited partnership set up to hold the fund and its investments.

LPAC (Limited partners advisory committee) The committee that represents the interests of LPs established in the LPA.

LSTA (Loan Syndications and Trading Association) Association issuing templates for standard debt documents in leverage finance within the Americas https://www.lsta.org/. *See also* **Loan Markets Association**.

MACC Material adverse change clause.

M&A Mergers and acquisisitions.

Management buy-in (MBI) A buyout in which external managers take over the company. Financing is provided to enable a manager or group of managers from outside the target company to buy into the company with the support of private equity investors. Where many of the non-managerial employees are included in the buyout group it is called a management/employee buyout (MEBO).

Management buyout (MBO) A buyout in which the target's management team acquires an existing product line or business from the vendor with the support of private equity investors.

Management fees Compensation received by a private equity fund's management firm. This annual management charge is equal to a certain percentage of investors' initial commitments to the fund.

Margin Spread between a base rate, historically usually three-month LIBOR, and the cost of the loan to the borrower. e.g three-month LIBOR +2.5%

Margin stepdown/margin ratchet An agreed schedule of reductions in interest margins if certain criteria (usually cash or profit targets) are met.

Market capitalization (market cap) The number of shares outstanding multiplied by the market price of the stock. Market capitalization is a common standard for describing the worth of a public company.

Marketing in Financial Instruments Directive (MiFID) EU directive governing the process of marketing financial products within the EU. Revised with effect from 2018 by MiFID II and the Markets in Financial Instruments Regulation (MiFIR).

Mezzanine finance Loan finance that is halfway between equity and secured debt, either unsecured or with junior access to security. Typically, some of the return on the instrument is deferred in the form of rolled-up payment-in-kind (PIK) interest and/or an equity kicker. A mezzanine fund is a fund focusing on mezzanine financing.

NAV loan A facility secured on the Net Asset Value (NAV) of the investments in a fund.

Net debt Short and long-term interest-bearing debt minus cash (and equivalents). The concept of net debt is the same under cash and accrual-based financial reporting. High levels of net debt impose a call on future revenue flows to service that debt.

Newco A generic term for a new company incorporated for the purpose of acquiring the target business, unit or company from the vendor in a buyout transaction.

Non-disclosure agreement *See* **Confidentiality agreement**.

Non-Executive Director (NED or NXD) A member of the board of directors of a company who has no management or executive function within the underlying company.

Offer The offer (or bid) made for the target company by the Newco offeror established by the Private Equity provider and the participating directors of the target company (those directors who are part of the management buyout team).

Open-end fund A fund which sells as many shares as investors demand.

Option A contractual right to purchase something (such as stock) at a future time or within a specified period at a specified price.

Ordinary shares (common shares/stock) Owners of ordinary shares are typically entitled to vote on the selection of directors and other important issues. They may also receive dividends on their holdings, but ordinary shares do not guarantee a return on the investment. If a company is liquidated, the owners of bonds and preferred stock are paid before the holders of ordinary shares.

Payment in kind (PIK) A feature of a security permitting the issuer to pay dividends or interest in the form of additional securities of the same class.

Permanent establishment A fixed place of business through which the business of an enterprise is wholly or partly carried on. Within private equity, permanent establishment refers to the possibility that a limited partner, either owning or having a stake in a private equity or venture capital fund in a particular country, is considered as a resident of that country and hence liable for national taxation.

Pillar one pension A public pension provided by the government.

Pillar two pension An occupational pension, provided by an employer.

PIPE Private investment in public equity.

Placement agent A person or entity acting as an agent for a private equity house in raising investment funds.

PME Public market equivalent.

Portfolio company (investee company) The company or entity into which a private equity fund invests directly.

Preference shares (preferred stock) Shares which have preference over ordinary shares, including priority in receipt of dividends and upon liquidation. In some cases these shares also have redemption rights, preferential voting rights, and rights of conversion into ordinary shares. Venture capitalists generally make investments in the form of convertible preference shares.

Price-to-earnings (P/E) ratio The market price of a company's ordinary share divided by earnings per share for a given year.

Primary loan market (syndicated loan market) Market in which a new loan is syndicated/sold. *See* Syndicated loan.

Private buyout A buyout from private or family shareholders.

Privatization A buyout of a company from government ownership.

Public buy-in A buyout of a stock market listed company with the company remaining on the stock market after the buyout.

Public offering An offering of stock to the general investing public. For a public offering, registration of prospectus material with a national competent authority is generally compulsory.

Public-to-private (P2P, PTP) A transaction involving an offer for the entire share capital of a listed target company by a new company (Newco) and the subsequent re-registration of that listed target company as a private company.

Quartile The IRR which lies a quarter from the bottom (lower quartile point) or top (upper quartile point) of the table ranking the individual fund IRRs.

Ratchet/sliding scale A bonus where capital can be reclaimed by managers of investee companies, depending on the achievement of corporate goals.

RCF (Revolving credit facility) A committed facility to fund short term periodic working capital movements.

Recapitalization/refinance Change in a company's capital structure. For example, a company may want to issue bonds to replace its preferred stock in order to save on taxes. Recapitalization can be an alternative exit strategy for venture capitalists and leveraged buyout sponsors.

Redemption Repurchase by a company of its securities from an investor.

Representations (Reps) and Warranties Declarations made by the seller of one or more target companies in relation to the financial, legal, and commercial status of the target companies, the financial instruments (to be) issued, the assets owned or used and the liabilities due, and whereby such persons represent and warrant that such declarations are true and correct as of a certain date.

Retail investor A non-institutional investor who purchases securities for their own account.

Reverse takeover The acquisition of an unlisted company by a smaller listed company, thus achieving a stock market listing 'through the back door'. The acquisition is carried out by the listed company issuing new shares in order to acquire the unlisted company. As the unlisted company is larger than the listed one, the bidder has to issue so many new shares that the owners of the unlisted company end up with a controlling stake in the listed company.

Revolving facilities A committed loan facility allowing a borrower to draw down and repay amounts (up to a limit) for short periods throughout the life of the facility. Amounts repaid can be re-borrowed, thereby combining some of the flexibility of the overdraft facility with the certainty of a term loan.

RVPI/RPI (Residual value to paid-in) The RVPI measures the value of the investors' (limited partners') interest held within the fund, relative to the cumulative paid-in capital. RVPI is net of fees and carried interest. This is a measure of the fund's 'unrealized' return on investment.

SEC Securities and Exchange Commission, the US securities exchanges regulator https://www.sec.gov/.

Secondary buyout A buyout of a company which had already undergone a buyout and is then sold directly to another buyout team or private equity company. A tertiary buyout is when this process is undertaken again, and so on for fourth and subsequent buyouts.

Secondary investment An investment where a fund buys either a portfolio of direct investments of an existing private equity fund or limited partners' positions in these funds.

Secondary loan market Market in which loans trade after their primary market syndication.

Secondary market A market or exchange in which securities are bought and sold following their initial sale. Investors in the primary market, by contrast, purchase shares directly from the issuer.

Second-round financing Most companies need more than the initial injection of capital, whether to enable them to expand into new markets, develop more production capacity, or to overcome temporary problems. There can be several rounds of financing.

Secured debt Loans secured against a company's assets.

Semi-captive fund A fund in which, although the main shareholder contributes a large part of the capital, a significant share of the capital is raised from third parties.

Senior debt A debt instrument which specifically has a higher priority for repayment than that of general unsecured creditors. Typically used for long-term financing for low-risk companies or for later-stage financing.

Share purchase agreement Agreement further to which one or more purchasers buy shares issued by one or more target companies from one or more sellers. The agreement will set out the type and amount of shares sold, the representations and warranties, the indemnification in the event of misrepresentation and may also include post-closing covenants (such as the obligation for the sellers not to compete with the purchasers).

Squeeze-out Statutory provisions entitling an offeror who has acquired the support of a certain percentage of shareholders to acquire the balance of shares in the target company.

Staple financing A pre-arranged financing package that a financial adviser or investment bank offers to the potential buyer in an auction process, when putting up a company for sale.

Structuring EBITDA The agreed definition of EBITDA used when structuring the initial investment. It may also be used to measure leverage covenants.

Subordinated debt (junior debt) Debt that ranks lower than other loans and will be paid last in case of liquidation.

Subscription agreement Agreement further to which one or more investors undertake to subscribe for shares. The agreement will set out the type and amount of instruments to be issued, the representations and warranties, the indemnification in the event of misrepresentation and may also include post-closing covenants (such as further investment obligations or restrictions on the transfer of the instruments that will be acquired).

Subscription line A working capital facility secured on the undrawn commitments of LPs.

Sweet/sweat equity Equity that is allocated to management in a management buyout.

Syndicated loan A very large loan in which a group of banks work together to provide funds for one borrower. There is usually one lead bank that takes a small percentage of the loan and syndicates the rest to other banks.

Target company The company that the offeror is considering investing in. In the context of a public-to-private deal this company will be the listed company that an offeror is considering investing in with the objective of bringing the company back into private ownership.

Tax transparency A fund structure or vehicle is tax transparent when the fund itself is not liable to taxation and the investment in an underlying company is treated as if it would be a direct investment for the initial investor (the LP), who is taxed only when the investment structure distributes its gains and revenues.

Trade sale The sale of company shares to industrial investors.

TUPE Transfer of Undertakings (Protection of Employment) Regulations 2006. UK legislation designed to protect employees interests when either assets are sold or operations are transferred by employers without selling a company's shares.

TVPI (Total value to paid-in) The sum of the DPI and the RVPI. TVPI is net of fees and carried interest.

Unitranche debt A hybrid loan structure combining senior and subordinated debt into one loan facility at a blended interest rate that falls between the rates of the two types of debt.

Unsecured debt Loans not secured against a company's assets.

Upper quartile The point at which 25% of all returns in a group are greater and 75% are lower.

VDD Vendor due diligence.

Vendor financing Can either be in the form of deferred loans from, or shares subscribed by, the vendor. The vendor may well take shares alongside the management in the new entity. This category of finance is generally used where the vendor's expectation of the value of the business is higher than that of management and the institutions backing them.

Vesting The process by which an employee is granted full ownership of conferred rights such as stock options and warrants (which then become vested rights). Rights which have not yet been vested (unvested rights) may not be sold or traded and can be forfeited.

Vintage year The year of fund formation and first drawdown of capital.

Voluntary repayment The right to repay a loan early.

Warrant Type of security usually issued together with a loan, a bond, or preferred stock. Warrants are also known as stock-purchase warrants or subscription warrants, and allow an investor to buy ordinary shares at a pre-determined price.

Warranty Statement, usually contained in a share subscription or purchase agreement, as to the existing condition of the company which, if not true, supports a legal action for compensation by way of money damages.

Weighted average cost of capital A discount rate used in valuation models reflecting the opportunity cost of all capital providers, weighted by their relative contribution to the company's total capital.

Winner's curse The tendency for the winner of a competitive process to have overpaid for an asset.

Write-down A reduction in the value of an investment.

Write-off The write-down of a portfolio company's value to zero. The value of the investment in the portfolio company is eliminated and the return to investors is zero or negative.

Write-up An increase in the value of an investment. An upward adjustment of an asset's value for accounting and reporting purposes.

Yield The rate of return on a debt instrument if the full amount of interest and principal are paid on schedule. Current yield is the interest rate as a percentage of the initial investment.

Bibliography

Acharya, V., Gottschalg, O., Hahn, M., and Kehoe, C., 2009. Corporate governance and value creation evidence from private equity. http://dx.doi.org/10.2139/ssrn.1324016.

Acharya, V., Kehoe, C., and Reyner, M., 2009. Private equity vs PLC boards: A comparison of practices and effectiveness, *Journal of Applied Corporate Finance* **21**(1): 45–56.

Achleitner, A. K. and Figge, C., 2014. Private equity lemons? Evidence on value creation in secondary buyouts, *European Financial Management* **20**: 406–33.

Achleitner, A., Bauer, O., Figge, C., and Lutz, E., 2012. Exit of last resort? Empirical evidence on the returns and drivers of secondary buyouts as private equity exit. CEFS, TUM Business School.

Agrawal, A. and Tambe P., 2016. Private equity and workers' career paths: The role of technological change, *Review of Financial Studies* **29**(9): 2455–89.

Alperovych, Y., Amess, K., and Wright, M., 2013. Private equity firm experience and buyout vendor source: What is their impact on efficiency? *European Journal of Operational Research* **228**(3): 601–11.

Andrade, G. and Kaplan, S., 1998. How costly is financial (not economic) distress? Evidence from highly leveraged transactions that became distressed, *Journal of Finance* **53**(5): 1443–93.

Amess, K., 2002. Management buyouts and firm-level productivity: Evidence from a panel of UK manufacturing firms, *Scottish Journal of Political Economy* **49**(3): 304–17.

Amess, K., 2003. The effects of management buyouts and on firm-level technical efficiency: Evidence from a panel of U.K. machinery and equipment manufacturers, *Journal of Industrial Economics* **51**(1): 35–44.

Amess, K., Brown, S., and Thompson, S. 2007. Management buyouts, supervision and employee discretion, *Scottish Journal of Political Economy* **54**(4): 447–74.

Amess, K. and Wright, M., 2007. The wage and employment effects of leveraged buyouts in the UK, *International Journal of Economics and Business* **14**(2): 179–95.

Amess, K. and Wright, M., 2012. Leveraged buyouts, private equity, and jobs, *Small Business Economics* **38**(4): 419–30.

Amess, K., Girma, S., and Wright, M., 2008. What are the wage and employment consequences of leveraged buyouts, private equity and acquisitions in the UK? CMBOR Occasional Paper.

Amess, K., Stiebale, J., and Wright, M., 2015. The impact of private equity on firms' patenting activity, *European Economic Review* **86**: 147–160.

Amihud, Y., 1989. *Leveraged Management Buyouts* (New York: DowJones–Irwin).

Andres, C., Betzer, A., and Hoffman, M., 2003, Going private via LBO—shareholder gains in the European market. University of Bonn Working Paper.

Andres, C., Betzer, A., and Weir, C., 2007. Shareholder wealth gains through better corporate governance: The case of European LBO transactions, *Financial Markets Porfolio Management* **21**: 403–24.

Ang, A., Chen, B. Goetzmann, W., and Phalippou, L., 2018. Estimating private equity returns from limited partner cash flows, *Journal of Finance* **73**: 1751–83.

Ang, J. S., Hutton, I., and Majadillas, M., 2014. Manager divestment in leveraged buyouts, *European Financial Management* **20**: 462–93.

Appelbaum, E., Batt, R., and Clark, I., 2013. Implications for employment relations research: Evidence from breach of trust and implicit contracts in private equity buyouts, *British Journal of Industrial Relations* **51**: 498–518.

Arcot, S., Fluck, Z., Gaspar, J.-M., and Hege, U., 2015. Fund managers under pressure: rationale and determinants of secondary buyouts, *Journal of Financial Economics* **115**: 102–35.

Asquith, P. and Wizman, T., 1990. Event risk, wealth redistribution and its return to existing bondholders in corporate buyouts, *Journal of Financial Economics* **27**: 195–213.

Axelson, U., Jenkinson, T., Strömberg, P., and Weisbach, M., 2007. Leverage and pricing in buyouts: An empirical analysis. Swedish Institute for Financial Research Conference on The Economics of Private Equity Market. http://dx.doi.org/10.2139/ssrn.1027127.

Axelson, U., Sorensen, M., and Stromberg, P., 2013. Alpha and beta of buyout deals. Paper presented at the Coller Institute Conference on Private Equity, London Business School.

Ayash, B., and Schütt, H., 2016. Does going private add value through operating improvements? *Journal of Corporate Finance* 40: 192–215.

Bacon, N., Wright, M., and Demina, N., 2004. Management buyouts and human resource management, *British Journal of Industrial Relations* 42(2): 325–47.

Bacon, N., Wright, M., Demina, N., Bruining, H., and Boselie, P., 2008. HRM, buyouts and private equity in the UK and the Netherlands, *Human Relations* 61: 1399–1433.

Bacon, N., Wright, M., Scholes, L., and Meuleman, M., 2009. Assessing the impact of private equity on industrial relations in Europe. CMBOR Occasional Paper.

Bacon, N., Wright, M., Meuleman, M., and Scholes, L., 2012. The impact of private equity on management practices in European buyouts: Short-termism, Anglo-Saxon or host country effects? *Industrial Relations* 51(S1): 605–26.

Bacon, N., Wright, M., Ball, R., and Meuleman, M., 2013. Private equity, HRM and employment, *Academy of Management Perspectives* 27: 7–21.

Bacon, N., Hoque, K., and Wright, M., 2019b. Is job insecurity higher in leveraged buyouts? *British Journal of Industrial Relations* 57(3): 479–512.

Bacon, N., Hoque, K., and Wright, M., 2019a. Private equity, quick flips, and perfect storms: the heterogeneous impact of leveraged buyouts on job quality. CMBOR Working Paper.

Baker, G. and Wruck, K., 1989. Organizational changes and value creation in leveraged buyouts: The case of the O.M. Scott & Sons Company, *Journal of Financial Economics* 25(2): 163–90.

Bergmann, B., Christophers, H., Huss, M., and Zimmermann, H., 2009. Listed private equity. http://dx.doi.org/10.2139/ssrn.1362390.

Bernstein, S. and Sheen, A., 2013. The operational consequences of private equity buyouts. Paper presented at the Coller Institute Conference on Private Equity, London Business School.

Bernstein, S., Lerner, J., Sorensen, M., and Strömberg, P., 2016. Private equity and industry performance, *Management Science* 63(4): 901–1269.

Bernstein, S., Lerner, J., and Mezzanotti, F., 2018. Private equity and financial fragility during the crisis, *Review of Financial Studies* 32(4): 1309–73.

Bertoni, F., Ferrer, M. A., and Martí, J., 2013. The different roles played by venture capital and private equity investors on the investment activity of their portfolio firms, *Small Business Economics* 40: 607–33.

Bertoni, F., Le Nadant, A.-L., and Perdreau, F., 2014. Innovation and R&D investments by leveraged buyout companies in times of crisis, *Economic Bulletin* 34: 856–64.

Beuselinck, C. and Manigart, S., 2007. Financial reporting quality in private equity backed companies: The impact of ownership concentration, *Small Business Economics* 29: 261–74.

Beuselinck, C., Deloof, M., and Manigart, S., 2008. Private equity investments and disclosure policy, *European Accounting Review* 17: 607–39.

Beuselinck, C., Deloof, M., and Manigart, S., 2009. Private equity involvement and earnings quality, *Journal of Business Finance and Accounting* 36: 587–615.

Bhagat, S., Shleifer, A. and Vishny, R., 1990. Hostile takeovers in the 1980s: The return to corporate specialization, *Brookings Papers on Economic Activity: Microeconomics*, 1–84.

Bharath, S. T. and Dittmar, A. K., 2010. Do firms use private equity to opt out of public markets? *Review of Financial Studies* 23(5): 1771–1818.

Billett, M. T., Jiang, Z., and Lie, E., 2008. The role of bondholder wealth expropriation in LBO transactions. Working paper.

Bloom, N., van Reenen, J., and Sadun, R., 2009. Do private equity-owned firms have better management practices? In Gurung, A. and Lerner, J. (eds), *The Global Economic Impact of Private Equity Report 2009*, Globalization of Alternative Investments Working Papers Volume 2 (New York: World Economic Forum), pp. 1–24.

Bonini, S., 2015. Secondary buyouts: operating performance and investment determinants, *Financial Management* 44: 431–70.

Borell, M. and Tykvova, T., 2012. Do private equity investors trigger financial distress in their portfolio companies? *Journal of Corporate Finance* 18: 138–50.

Boselie, P. and Koene, B., 2009. Private equity and human resource management: 'Barbarians at the gate!' HR's wake up call? *Human Relations* 63(9): 1297–1319.

Boucly, Q., Thesmar, D., and Sraer, D., 2009. Leveraged buyouts—evidence from French deals. In Gurung, A. and Lerner, J. (eds), *The Global Economic Impact of Private Equity Report 2009*, Globalization of Alternative Investments Working Papers Volume 2 (New York: World Economic Forum), pp. 47–64.

Boulton, T., Lehn, K., and Segal, S., 2007. The rise of the US private equity market. In Fuchita, Y. and Litan, R. E. (eds), *New Financial Instruments and Institutions: Opportunities and Policy Challenges* (Washington, DC: Brookings Institution Press), pp. 141–61.

Bradley, K. and Nejad, A., 1989. *Managing owners—the NFC Buyout* (Cambridge: Cambridge University Press).

Braun, R., Jenkinson, T., and Stoff, I., 2017. How persistent is private equity performance? Evidence from deal-level data, *Journal of Financial Economics* 123: 273–91.

Brown, D. T., Fee, C. E., and, Thomas, S. E., 2007. Financial leverage and bargaining power with suppliers: Evidence from leveraged buyouts. AFA 2007 Chicago Meetings Paper. http://dx.doi.org/10.2139/ssrn.813025.

Bruining, H., 1992. Performance improvement post-management buyout. Unpublished PhD dissertation, Erasmus University Rotterdam, Haveka.

Bruining, H. and Wright, M., 2002. Entrepreneurial orientation in management buyouts and the contribution of venture capital, *Venture Capital: An International Journal of Entrepreneurial Finance* 4: 147–68.

Bruining, H., Bonnet, M., and Wright, M., 2004. Management control systems and strategy change in buyouts, *Management Accounting Research* 15: 155–77.

Bruining, H., Boselie, P., Wright, M., and Bacon, N., 2005. The impact of business ownership change on employee relations: buyouts in the UK and the Netherlands, *International Journal of Human Resource Management* 16: 345–65.

Bruining, H., Wervaal, E., and Wright, M., 2013. Private equity ownership and entrepreneurial management in management buyouts, *Small Business Economics* 40(3): 591–605.

Bruner, R. and Eades, K., 1992. The crash of the Revco leveraged buyout: The hypothesis of inadequate capital, *Financial Management* 21(1): 35–49.

Bruton, G., Keels, J. K., and Scifres, R. L., 2002. Corporate restructuring and performance: An agency perspective on the complete buyout cycle, *Journal of Business Research* 55: 709–24.

Bull, I., 1989. Management performance in leveraged buyouts: An empirical analysis, *Journal of Business Venturing* 3: 263–78.

Cao, J. X. and Lerner, J., 2009. The performance of reverse leveraged buyouts, *Journal of Financial Economics* 91(2): 139–57.

Caselli, S., Gracia-Appendini, E., and Ippolito, F., 2009. Explaining returns in private equity investments. http://ssrn.com/abstract=1600227.

Castellaneta, F., Gottschalg, O., and Wright, M., 2013. The advantages of complete and negative performance feedback: Evidence from private equity backed buyouts.

Castellaneta, F., Hannus, S., and Wright, M., 2018. A framework for examining the heterogeneous opportunities of value creation in private equity buyouts, *Annals of Corporate Governance* 4(2): 87–146.

Chapman, J. L. and Klein, P. G., 2009. Value creation in middle-market buyouts: A transaction-level analysis. CORI working paper 2009-01. http://dx.doi.org/10.2139/ssrn.1372381.

Chevalier, J., 1995. Do LBO supermarkets charge more? An empirical analysis of the effects of LBOs on supermarket pricing, *Journal of Finance* 50(4): 1095–1112.

Chou, D., Gombola, M., and Liu, F., 2006. Earnings management and stock performance of reverse leveraged buyouts, *Journal of Financial and Quantitative Analysis* 41(2): 407–38.

Chou, D., Gombola, M., and Liu, F., 2010. Earnings management and long-run stock performance following private equity placements, *Review of Quantitative Finance and Accounting* 34(2): 225–45.

Chung, J. W., 2011. Leveraged buyouts of private companies. http://dx.doi.org/10.2139/ssrn.1904342.

Chung, J. W., Sensoy, B. A., Stern, L., and Weisbach, M. S., 2012. Pay for performance from future fund flows: The case of private equity, *Review of Financial Studies* 25: 3259–3304.

Citron, D., Wright, M., Rippington, F., and Ball, R., 2003. Secured creditor recovery rates from management buyouts in distress, *European Financial Management* 9: 141–62.

Citron, D. and Wright, M., 2008. Bankruptcy costs, leverage and multiple secured creditors: The case of management buy-outs, *Accounting and Business Research* 38: 71–89.

Clark, I., 2011. Private equity, union recognition and value extraction at the Automobile Association: The GMB as an emergency service? *Industrial Relations Journal* 42(1): 36–50.

Clark, I., 2016. Financialization, ownership and employee interests under private equity at the AA, part two, *Industrial Relations Journal* 47(3): 328–53.

CMBOR, 2007. Trends in management buyouts. Management Buyouts: Quarterly Review from the Centre for Management Buyout Research. CMBOR: University of Nottingham.

Cohn, J. B., Mills, L. F., and Towery, E. M., 2014. The evolution of capital structure and operating performance after leveraged buyouts: Evidence from US corporate tax returns, *Journal of Financial Economics* 111: 469–94.

Colla, P., Ippolito, F., and Wagner, H., 2012. Leverage and pricing of debt in LBOs, *Journal of Corporate Finance* 18: 124–37.

Cook, D., Easterwood, J., and Martin, J., 1992. Bondholder wealth effects of management buyouts, *Financial Management* 21(1): 102–13.

Cooper, D., 2010. *Leadership Risk: A Guide for Private Equity and Strategic Investors* (Chichester: Wiley).

Cornelli, F. and Karakas, O., 2008. Private equity and corporate governance: Do LBOs have more effective boards? In Lerner, J. and Gurung, A. (eds), *The Global Impact of Private Equity Report 2008*, Globalization of Alternative Investments Working Papers Volume 1 (New York: World Economic Forum), pp. 65–84.

Cornelli, F., Lichtner, K., Perembetov, K., Simintzi, E., and Vig, V., 2013. Team stability and performance in private equity. Coller Institute of Private Equity, London Business School.

Cornelli, F., Simintzi, E., and Vig, V., 2016. Team stability and performance: Evidence from private equity. Working paper, Coller Institute of Private Equity, London Business School.

Cotter, J. F. and Peck, S. W., 2001. The structure of debt and active equity investors: the case of the buyout specialist, *Journal of Financial Economics* 59: 101–47.

Cressy, R., and Farag, H., 2012. Do private equity-backed buyouts respond better to financial distress than PLCs? *European Journal of Finance* 18: 239–59.

Cressy, R., Malipiero, A., and Munari, F., 2007. Playing to their strengths? Evidence that specialization in the private equity industry confers competitive advantage, *Journal of Corporate Finance* 13: 647–69.

Cressy, R., Munari, F., and Malipiero, A., 2007. Creative destruction: Evidence that buyouts cut jobs to raise returns. University of Birmingham working paper.

Cumming, D., Siegel, D. S., and Wright, M., 2007. Private equity, leveraged buyouts and governance, *Journal of Corporate Finance* 13: 439–60.

Cumming, D. and Walz, U., 2004. Private equity returns and disclosure around the world. http://dx.doi.org/10.2139/ssrn.514105.

Cumming, D. J. and Zambelli, S., 2010. Illegal buyouts, *Journal of Banking and Finance* 34: 441–56.

Davis, S., Lerner, J., Haltiwanger, J., Miranda, J., and Jarmin, R., 2008. Private equity and employment. In Lerner, J. and Gurung, A.(eds), *The Global Impact of Private Equity Report 2008*, Globalization of Alternative Investments Working Papers Volume 1 (New York: World Economic Forum), pp. 43–64.

Davis, S., Lerner, J., Haltiwanger, J., Miranda, J., and Jarmin, R., 2009. Private equity, jobs and productivity. In Gurung, A. and Lerner, J. (eds), *The Global Economic Impact of Private Equity Report 2009*, Globalization of Alternative Investments Working Papers Volume 2 (New York: World Economic Forum), pp. 25–46.

Davis, S., Haltiwanger, J., Handley, K., Jarmin, R., Lerner, J., and Miranda, J., 2014. , *American Economic Review* **104**(12): 3956–90.

DeAngelo, H., DeAngelo, L., and Rice, E., 1984. Shareholder wealth and going private, *Journal of Law and Economics* **27**: 367–402.

DeAngelo, L., 1986. Accounting numbers as market valuation substitutes: A study of management buyouts of public stockholders, *Accounting Review* **61**: 400–20.

Degeorge, F., Martin, J., and Phalippou, L., 2016. On secondary buyouts, *Journal of Financial Economics* **120**: 124–45.

Degeorge, F. and Zeckhauser, R., 1993. The reverse LBO decision and firm performance: Theory and evidence, *Journal of Finance* **48**(4): 1323–48.

Demiroglu C. and James, C. M., 2010. The role of private equity group reputation in LBO financing, *Journal of Financial Economics* **96**: 306–30.

Denis, D. J., 1994. Organizational form and the consequences of highly leveraged transactions: Kroger's recapitalization and Safeway's LBO, *Journal of Financial Economics* **36**: 193–224.

De Prijcker, S., Manigart, S., Maeseneire, W., and Wright, M., 2013. Modeling IPO, trade sale and secondary buyout exits: Agency perspectives versus resource-based arguments.

Desbrières, P. and Schatt, A., 2002. The impacts of LBOs on the performance of acquired firms: The French case, *Journal of Business Finance and Accounting* **29**: 695–729.

Diller, C. and Kaserer, C., 2009. What drives private equity returns? Fund inflows, skilled GPs, and/or risk? *European Financial Management* **15**(3): 643–75.

Driessen, J., Lin, T-C., and Phalippou, L., 2012. A new method to estimate risk and return of non-traded assets from cashflows: The case of private equity funds, *Journal of Financial and Quantitative Analysis* **47**(3): 511–35.

Easterwood, J. C., 1998. Divestments and financial distress in leveraged buyouts, *Journal of Banking and Finance* **22**: 129–59.

Easterwood, J., Singer, R., Seth, A., and Lang, D., 1994. Controlling the conflict of interest in management buyouts, *Review of Economics and Statistics* **76**: 512–22.

Eddey, P., Lee, K., and Taylor, S., 1996. What motivates going private? An analysis of Australian firms, *Accounting and Finance* **36**: 31–50.

Engel, D., and Stiebale, J., 2014. Private equity, investment and financial constraints: Firm-level evidence for France and the United Kingdom, *Small Business Economics* **43**: 197–212.

Ernst and Young, 2007. How do private equity firms create value? Ernst and Young.

Ernst and Young, 2008. How do private equity firms create value? A global study of 2007 exits. Ernst and Young.

Ernst and Young, 2009. Report on performance of private equity backed companies. London: BVCA.

Evans, J., Poa, M., and Rath, S., 2005. The financial and governance characteristics of Australian companies going private, *International Journal of Business Studies* **13**: 1–24.

Faccio, M. and Hsu, H.-C., 2017. Politically connected private equity and employment, *Journal of Finance* **72**: 539–73.

Fang, L., Ivashina, V., and Lerner, J., 2015. The disintermediation of financial markets: Direct investing in private equity, *Journal of Financial Economics* **116**: 160–78.

Fidrmuc, J., Palandri, A., Roosenboom, P., and van Dijk. D. (2013). When do managers seek private equity backing in public-to-private transactions? *Review of Finance* **17**(3): 1099–1139.

Fischer, P., and Louis, H., 2008. Financial reporting and conflicting managerial incentives: The case of management buyouts, *Management Science* **54**: 1700–14.

Folkman, P., Froud, J., Johal, S., and Williams, K., 2007. Capital market intermediaries and present day capitalism, *Business History* **49**(4): 552–72.

Frankfurter, G. M. and Gunay, E., 1992. Management buyouts: The sources and sharing of wealth between insiders and outside shareholders, *Quarterly Review of Economics and Finance* **32**: 82–95.

Franzoni, F., Nowak, E., and Phalippou, L., 2012. Private equity performance and liquidity risk, *Journal of Finance* **67**(6): 2341–73.

Froud, J. and Williams, K., 2007. Private equity and the culture of value extraction. CRESC WP 31, University of Manchester.

Froud, J., Johal, S., Leaver, A., and Williams, K., 2007. Memorandum submitted to Treasury Select Committee Inquiry into Private Equity. Centre for Research on Socio Cultural Change, University of Manchester.

Gaspar, J., 2009. The performance of French LBO firms: New data and new results. ESSEC working paper.

Geranio, M. and Zanotti, G., 2010. Equity markets do not fit all: An analysis of public-to-private deals in Continental Europe, *European Financial Management*, 18(5): 867–95.

Giot, P., Hege, U., and Schwienbacher, A., 2014. Are novice private equity funds risk-takers? Evidence from a comparison with established funds, *Journal of Corporate Finance* 27: 55–71.

Goergen, M., O'Sullivan, N., and Wood, G., 2011. Private equity takeovers and employment in the UK: Some empirical evidence, *Corporate Governance: An International Review* 19(3): 259–75.

Goergen, M., O'Sullivan, N., and Wood, G., 2014a. The employment consequences of private equity acquisitions: The case of institutional buy outs, *European Economic Review* 71: 67–79.

Goergen, M., O'Sullivan, N., and Wood, G., 2014b. The consequences of private equity acquisitions for employees: New evidence on the impact on wages, employment and productivity, *Human Resource Management Journal* 24(2): 145–58.

Goh, J., Gombola, M., Liu, F. Y., and Chou, D., 2002. Going-private restructuring and earnings expectations: a test of the release of favorable information for target firms and industry rivals. Working paper.

Gong, J. and Wu, S., 2011. CEO turnover in private equity sponsored leveraged buyouts, *Corporate Governance: An International Review* 19(3): 195–209.

Gospel, H., Pendleton, A., Vitols, S., and Wilke, P., 2011. New investment funds, restructuring, and labor outcomes: A European perspective, *Corporate Governance: An International Review* 19(3): 276–89.

Gottschalg, O., 2007. Private equity and leveraged buyouts. Study IP/A/ECON/IC/2007–25, European Parliament, Policy Department: Economic and Scientific Policy.

Gottschalg, O. and Wright, M., 2008. Understanding the buyers' role in private equity returns—The influence of skills, strategy and experience. Paper presented at Strategic Management Society Conference, Cologne.

Green, S., 1992. The impact of ownership and capital structure on managerial motivation and strategy in management buyouts: A cultural analysis, *Journal of Management Studies* 29(4): 513–35.

Groh, A. and Gottschalg, O., 2006. The risk-adjusted performance of US buyouts. Working paper.

Guery, L., Stevenot, A., Wood, G., and Brewster, C., 2017. The impact of private equity on employment: The consequences of fund country of origin—New evidence from France, *Industrial Relations* 56: 723–50.

Guo, S., Hotchkiss, E., and Song, W., 2011. Do buyouts (still) create value? *Journal of Finance* 66: 479–517.

Halpern, P., Kieschnick, R., and Rotenberg, W., 1999. On the heterogeneity of leveraged going private transactions. *Review of Financial Studies* 12: 281–309.

Harford, J. and Kolasinski, A., 2014. Do private equity returns result from wealth transfers and short-termism? Evidence from a comprehensive sample of large buyouts, *Management Science* 60: 805–1081.

Harford, J., Stanfield, J., and Zhang, F., 2019. Do insiders time management buyouts and freezeouts to buy undervalued targets? *Journal of Financial Economics* 131: 206–31.

Harlow, W. V. and Howe, J. S., 1993. Leveraged buyouts and insider nontrading, *Financial Management* 22: 109–18.

Harris, R., Siegel, D. S., and Wright, M., 2005. Assessing the impact of management buyouts on economic efficiency: Plant-level evidence from the United Kingdom, *Review of Economics and Statistics* 87: 148–53.

Harris, R.S., Jenkinson, T., and Kaplan, S., 2014. Private equity performance: What do we know? *Journal of Finance* 69: 1851–82.

Harris, R. S., Jenkinson, T., Kaplan, S., and Stucke, R., 2013. Has persistence persisted in private equity? Evidence from buyout and venture capital funds. Darden Business School working paper 2304808; Fama-Miller working paper. http://dx.doi.org/10.2139/ssrn.2304808.

Harris, R., Jenkinson, T., Kaplan, S., and Stucke, R., 2018. Financial intermediation in private equity: How well do funds of funds perform? *Journal of Financial Economics* 129: 287–305.

Hege, U., Lovo, S., Slovin, M., and Sushka, M., 2018. Divisional buyouts by private equity and the market for divested assets, *Journal of Corporate Finance* 53: 21–37.

Higson, C. and Stucke, R., 2012. The performance of private equity. http://dx.doi.org/10.2139/ssrn.2009067.

Hochberg, Y. and Rauh, J., 2013. Local overweighting and underperformance: Evidence from limited partner private equity investments, *Review of Financial Studies* 26(2): 403–51.

Holthausen, D. and Larcker, D., 1996. The financial performance of reverse leverage buyouts, *Journal of Financial Economics* 42: 293–332.

Hoskisson, R., Shi, W., Yi, X., and Jin, J., 2013. The evolution and strategic positioning of private equity firms, *Academy of Management Perspectives* 27: 22–38.

Hotchkiss, E., Strömberg, P., and Smith, D., 2011. Private equity and the resolution of financial distress. http://dx.doi.org/10.2139/ssrn.1787446.

Huyghebaert, N. and Priem, R. K., 2015. How do lead financiers select their partners in buyout syndicates? Empirical results from buyout syndicates in Europe, *European Management Review* 12: 221–46.

Ick, M. M., 2006. Private equity returns: Is there really a benefit of low co-movement with public equity markets? http://dx.doi.org/10.2139/ssrn.871930.

Ivashina, V. and Kovner, A., 2011. The private equity advantage: Leveraged buyout firms and relationship banking, *Review of Financial Studies* 24: 2462–98.

Jegadeesh, N., Kräussl, R., and Pollet, J. M., 2015. Risk and expected returns of private equity investments: Evidence based on market prices, *Review of Financial Studies* 28: 3269–330.

Jelic, R., 2011. Staying power of UK buyouts, *Journal of Business Finance and Accounting* 38(7–8): 945–86.

Jelic, R., Saadouni, B., and Wright, M., 2005. Performance of private to public MBOs: The role of venture capital, *Journal of Business Finance and Accounting* 32: 643–82.

Jelic, R., Zhou, D., and Wright, M., 2019. Sustaining the buyout governance model: Inside secondary management buyout boards, *British Journal of Management* 30(1): 30–52.

Jelic, R. and Wright, M., 2011. Exits, performance, and late stage private equity: The case of UK management buyouts, *European Financial Management* 17: 560–93.

Jenkinson, T. and Stucke, R., 2011. Who benefits from the leverage in LBOs? Working paper, Oxford University.

Jenkinson, T. and Sousa, M., 2012. Keep taking the private equity medicine. Working paper, Oxford University.

Jenkinson, T. and Sousa, M., 2015. What determines the exit decision for leveraged buyouts?, *Journal of Banking and Finance* 59: 399–408.

Jensen, M. C., Kaplan, S. N., and Stiglin, L., 1989. Effects of Lbos on tax revenues of the U.S. Treasury, *Tax Notes* 42(6).

Jones, C. M. and Rhodes-Kropf, M. 2003. The price of diversifiable risk in venture capital and private equity. Working paper, Columbia University.

Jones, C. S., 1992. Accounting and organizational change: An empirical study of management buyouts, *Accounting, Organizations and Society* 17: 151–68.

Kaplan, S.N., 1989a. The effects of management buyouts on operating performance and value, *Journal of Financial Economics* 24: 217–54.

Kaplan, S. N., 1989b. Management buyouts: evidence on taxes as a source of value, *Journal of Finance* 44: 611–32.

Kaplan, S. N., 1991. The staying power of leveraged buyouts, *Journal of Financial Economics* 29: 287–313.

Kaplan, S. N. and Schoar, A., 2005. Private equity returns: persistence and capital flows, *Journal of Finance* 60: 1791–1823.

Kaplan, S. N. and Stein, J., 1993. The evolution of buyout pricing in the 1980s, *Quarterly Journal of Economics* 108: 313–57.

Kaplan, S. N. and Strömberg, P., 2009. Leveraged buyouts and private equity, *Journal of Economic Perspectives* 23: 121–46.

Katz, S., 2009. Earnings quality and ownership structure: The role of private equity sponsors, *Accounting Review* 84: 623–58.

Kieschnick, R. L., 1998. Free cash flow and stockholder gains in going private transactions revisited, *Journal of Business Finance and Accounting* 25: 187–202.

Klein, P., Chapman, J., and Mondelli, M., 2013. Private equity and entrepreneurial governance: Time for a balanced view, *Academy of Management Perspectives* 27: 39–51.

Kleymenova, A., Talmor, E., and Vasvari, F., 2012. Liquidity on the secondaries private equity market. London Business School.

Knigge, A., Nowak, E., and Schmidt, D., 2006. On the performance of private equity investments: Does market timing matter? *Journal of Financial Transformation* 16: 123–34.

Lahmann, A. D. F., Stranz, W., and Velamuri, V. K., 2017. Value creation in SME private equity buyouts, *Qualitative Research in Financial Markets* 9: 2–33.

Lee, D. S., 1992. Management buyout proposals and inside information, *Journal of Finance* 47: 1061–79.

Lee, C. I., Rosenstein, S., Rangan, N., and Davidson, W. N., III, 1992. Board composition and share-holder wealth: the case of management buyouts, *Financial Management* 21: 58–72.

Lehn, K. and Poulsen, A., 1989. Free cash flow and stockholder gains in going private transactions, *Journal of Finance* 44: 771–88.

Lei, D. and Hitt, M., 1995. Strategic restructuring and outsourcing: The effects of mergers and acquisitions and LBOs on building firms skills and capabilities, *Journal of Management* 21: 835–59.

Lerner, J., Schoar, A., and Wongsunwai, W., 2007. Smart institutions, foolish choices: The limited partner performance puzzle, *Journal of Finance* 62(2): 731–64.

Lerner, J., Strömberg, P., and Sørensen, M., 2008. Private equity and long-run investment: The case of innovation. In Lerner, J. and Gurung, A. (eds), *The Global Impact of Private Equity Report 2008*, Globalization of Alternative Investments Working Papers Volume 1 (New York: World Economic Forum), pp. 27–42.

Lerner, J., Sorensen, M., and Strömberg, P., 2011. Private equity and long-run investment: The case of innovation, *Journal of Finance* 66(2): 445–77.

Leslie, P. and Oyer, P., 2009. Do private equity firms create value? NBER working paper 14331.

L'Her, J., Stoyanova, R., Shaw, K., Scott, W., and Lai, C., 2016. A bottom-up approach to the risk-adjusted performance of the buyout fund market, *Financial Analysts Journal* 72(4): 36–48.

Liebeskind, J., Wiersema, M., and Hansen, G., 1992. LBOs, corporate restructuring and the incentive-intensity hypothesis, *Financial Management* 21(1): 73–88.

Lichtenberg, F. R. and Siegel, D. S., 1990. The effect of leveraged buyouts on productivity and related aspects of firm behavior, *Journal of Financial Economics* 27: 165–94.

Ljungqvist, A. and Richardson, M., 2003. The cash flow, return and risk characteristics of private equity. NYU finance working paper 03-001. http://dx.doi.org/10.2139/ssrn.369600.

Ljungqvist, A., Richardson, M., and Wolfenzon, D., 2007. The investment behavior of buyout funds: theory and evidence. ECGI finance working paper 174/2007.

Long, W. F. and Ravenscraft, D., 1993. LBOs, debt and R & D intensity, *Strategic Management Journal* 14(S1): 119–35.

Lopez de Silanes, F., Phalippou, L., and Gottschalg, O., 2013. Giants at the gate: On the cross-section of private equity investment returns. http://dx.doi.org/10.2139/ssrn.1363883.

Lowenstein, L., 1985. Management buyouts, *Columbia Law Review* 85: 730–84.

Malone, S., 1989. Characteristics of smaller company leveraged buyouts, *Journal of Business Venturing* 4: 345–59.

Mao, Y. and Renneboog, L., 2015. Do managers manipulate earnings prior to management buyouts? *Journal of Corporate Finance* 35: 43–61.

Marais L., Schipper, K., and Smith, A., 1989. Wealth effects of going private on senior securities, *Journal of Financial Economics* 23: 155–91.

Masulis, R., and Thomas, R. 2009, Does private equity create wealth? The effects of private equity and derivatives on corporate governance, *University of Chicago Law Review* 76: 219–60.

Maula, M., Nikoskelainen, E., and Wright, M., 2011. Macroeconomic and industry drivers of private equity buyout firm-level returns. CMBOR working paper.

Maupin, R., 1987. Financial and stock market variables as predictors of management buyouts, *Strategic Management Journal* 8: 319–27.

Meerkott, H. and Liechtenstein, H., 2008. Get ready for the private equity shake-out. Boston Consulting Group/IESE.

Mehran, H. and Peristiani, S., 2010. Financial visibility and the decision to go private, *Review of Financial Studies* 23(2): 519–47.

Metrick, A. and Yasuda, A., 2010. The economics of private equity funds, *Review of Financial Studies* 23: 2303–41.

Meuleman, M., Amess, K., Wright, M., and Scholes, L., 2009. Agency, strategic entrepreneurship and the performance of private equity backed buyouts, *Entrepreneurship Theory and Practice* 33: 213–40.

Muscarella, C. and Vetsuypens, M., 1990. Efficiency and organizational structure: a study of reverse LBOs, *Journal of Finance* 65: 1389–1413.

Narasimhan, J., Kraussl, R., and Pollet, J., 2010. Risk and expected returns on private equity investment: evidence based on market prices. Working paper.

Newbould, G., Chatfield, R., and Anderson, R., 1992. Leveraged buyouts and tax incentives, *Financial Management* 21(1): 50–7.

Nikoskelainen, E. and Wright, M., 2007. The impact of corporate governance mechanisms on value increase in leveraged buyouts, *Journal of Corporate Finance* 13(4): 511–37.

Officer, M. S., Ozbas, O., and Sensoy, B. A., 2010. Club deals in leveraged buyouts, *Journal of Financial Economics* 98: 214–40.

Olsson, M. and Tåg, J., 2018. Are foreign private equity buyouts bad for workers? *Economics Letters* 172: 1–4.

Olsson, M. and Tåg, J., 2017. Private equity, layoffs, and job polarization, *Journal of Labor Economics* 35: 697–754.

Opler, T. C., 1992. Operating performance in leveraged buyouts, *Financial Management* 21: 27–34.

Oxman, J. and Yildirim, Y., 2007. Evidence of competition in the leveraged buyout market. http://dx.doi.org/10.2139/ssrn.972060.

Pe'er, A. and Gottschalg, O., 2011. Red and blue: The relationship between the institutional context and the performance of leveraged buyout investments, *Strategic Management Journal* 32(12): 1356–67.

Pendleton, A., Wilson, N., and Wright, M., 1998. The perception and effects of share ownership: Empirical evidence from employee buyouts, *British Journal of Industrial Relations* 36: 99–124.

Perry, S. and Williams, T., 1994. Earnings management preceding management buyout offers, *Journal of Accounting and Economics* 18(2): 157–79.

Phalippou, L., 2014. Performance of buyout funds revisited? *Review of Finance* 18: 189–218.

Phalippou, L., 2011. Why is the evidence on private equity performance so confusing? http://dx.doi.org/10.2139/ssrn.1864503.

Phalippou, L. and Gottschalg, O., 2009. Performance of private equity funds: Another puzzle? *Review of Financial Studies* 22: 1747–76.

Phalippou, L., Rauch, C., and Umber, M., 2018. Private equity portfolio company fees, *Journal of Financial Economics* 129(3): 559–85.

Phan, P. and Hill, C., 1995. Organizational restructuring and economic performance in leveraged buyouts: An ex post study, *Academy of Management Journal* 38: 704–39.

Renneboog, L. D. R., Simons, T., and Wright, M., 2007. Why do public firms go private in the UK? *Journal of Corporate Finance* 13(4): 591–628.

Robbie, K. and Wright, M., 1995. Managerial and ownership succession and corporate restructuring: The case of management buy-ins, *Journal of Management Studies* 32: 527–50.

Robbie, K., Wright, M., and Thompson, S., 1992. Management buy-ins in the UK, *Omega* 20(4): 445–56.

Robbie, K., Wright, M., and Ennew, C., 1993. Management buyouts from receivership, *Omega* 21(5): 519–30.

Robinson, D. T. and Sensoy, B. A., 2016. Cyclicality, performance measurement, and cash flow liquidity in private equity, *Journal of Financial Economics* **122**(3): 521–43.

Scellato, G. and Ughetto, E., 2013. Real effects of private equity investments: Evidence from European buyouts, *Journal of Business Research* **66**: 2642–49.

Schipper, K. and Smith, A., 1988. Corporate income tax effects of management buy-outs. Working paper, University of Chicago.

Scholes, L., Wright, M., Westhead, P., Burrows, A., and Bruining, H., 2007. Information sharing, price negotiation and management buy-outs of private family-owned firms, *Small Business Economics* **29**(3): 329–49.

Sensoy, B. A., Wang, Y., and Weisbach, M. S., 2014. Limited partner performance and the maturing of the private equity industry, *Journal of Financial Economics* **112**: 320–43.

Seth, A. and Easterwood, J., 1993. Strategic redirection in large management buyouts: The evidence from post-buyout restructuring activity, *Strategic Management Journal* **14**(4): 251–73.

Singh, H. 1990. Management buyouts and shareholder value, *Strategic Management Journal* **11**: 111–29.

Slovin, M. B., Sushka, M. E., and Bendeck, Y. M., 1991. The intra-industry effects of going-private proposals, *Journal of Finance* **46**: 1537–50.

Smart, S. B. and Waldfogel, J., 1994. Measuring the effect of restructuring on corporate performance: The case of management buyouts, *Review of Economics and Statistics* **76**: 503–11.

Smith, A., 1990. Capital ownership structure and performance: The case of management buyouts, *Journal of Financial Economics* **13**: 143–65.

Sorensen, M. and Jagannathan, R., 2015. The public market equivalent and private equity performance, *Financial Analysts Journal* **71**(4): 43–50.

Sousa, M., 2011. Why do private equity firms sell to each other? Working paper, University of Oxford.

Steffen, S., Schmidt, D. M., and Szabó, F., 2009. Exit strategies of buyout investments: An empirical analysis. http://dx.doi.org/10.2139/ssrn.1101025.

Strömberg, P., 2008. The new demography of private equity. In Lerner, J. and Gurung, A. (eds), *The Global Impact of Private Equity Report 2008*, Globalization of Alternative Investments Working Papers Volume 1 (New York: World Economic Forum), pp. 3–26.

Stucke, R., 2011, Updating history, Working paper, University of Oxford.

Sudarsanam, S., Wright, M., and Huang, J., 2011. Target bankruptcy risk and its impact on going private performance and exit, *Corporate Governance: An International Review* **19**(3): 240–58.

Tåg, J., 2010. The real effects of private equity buyouts. IFN Working Paper 851. http://dx.doi.org/10.2139/ssrn.1674759.

Taussig, M., and Delios, A., 2015. Unbundling the effects of institutions on firm resources: The contingent value of being local in emerging economy private equity, *Strategic Management Journal* **36**: 1845–65.

Thompson, S., Wright, M., and Robbie, K., 1992. Management equity ownership, debt and performance: Some evidence from UK management buyouts, *Scottish Journal of Political Economy* **39**: 413–30.

Thornton, P., 2007. *Inside the Dark Box: Shedding Light on Private Equity* (London: Work Foundation).

Torabzadeh, K. M. and Bertin, W. J., 1987. Leveraged buyouts and shareholder wealth, *Journal of Financial Research* **10**: 313–19.

Travlos, N. G. and Cornett, M. M., 1993. Going private buyouts and determinants of shareholders' returns, *Journal of Accounting, Auditing and Finance* **8**: 1–25.

Ughetto, E., 2010. Assessing the contribution to innovation of private equity investors: A study on European buyouts, *Research Policy* **39**: 126–40.

Ughetto, E., 2016. Investments, financing constraints and buyouts: The effect of private equity investors on the sensitivity of investments to cash flow, *Manchester School* **84**: 25–54.

Valkama, P., Maula, M., Nikoskelainen, E., and Wright, M., 2013. Drivers of holding period firm-level returns in private equity-backed buyouts, *Journal of Banking and Finance* **37**(7): 2378–91.

Van de Gucht, L. M. and Moore, W. T., 1998. Predicting the duration and reversal probability of leveraged buyouts, *Journal of Empirical Finance* **5**: 299–315.

Von Drathen, C. and Faleiro, F., 2007. The performance of leveraged buyout-backed initial public offerings in the UK. http://dx.doi.org/10.2139/ssrn.1117185.

Wang, Y., 2012. Secondary buyouts: Why buy and at what price? *Journal of Corporate Finance* **18**: 1306–25.

Warga, A. and Welch, I., 1993. Bondholder losses in leveraged buyouts, *Review of Financial Studies* **6**(4): 959–82.

Weir, C. and Wright, M., 2006. Governance and takeovers: Are public to private transactions different from traditional acquisitions of listed corporations? *Accounting and Business Research* **36**(4): 289–308.

Weir, C., Laing, D., and Wright, M., 2005a. Incentive effects, monitoring mechanisms and the threat from the market for corporate control: An analysis of the factors affecting public to private transactions in the UK, *Journal of Business Finance and Accounting* **32**: 909–44.

Weir, C., Laing, D., and Wright, M., 2005b. Undervaluation, private information, agency costs and the decision to go private, *Applied Financial Economics* **15**: 947–61.

Weir, C., Wright, M., and Scholes, L., 2008. Public to private buyouts, distress costs and private equity, *Applied Financial Economics* **18**: 801–19.

Weir, C, Jones, P., and Wright, M., 2015. Public to private transactions, private equity and financial health in the UK: An empirical analysis of the impact of going private, *Journal of Management and Governance* **19**: 91–112.

Wiersema, M. and Liebeskind, J., 1995. The effects of leveraged buyouts on corporate growth and diversification in large firms, *Strategic Management Journal* **16**(6): 447–60.

Wilson, N. and Wright, M., 2011. Private equity, buyouts and insolvency risk, *Journal of Business Finance and Accountancy* **40**(7–8): 949–90.

Wilson, N., Wright, M., Siegel, D., and Scholes, L., 2012. Private equity portfolio company performance through the recession, *Journal of Corporate Finance* **18**: 193–205.

Wilson, N. and Wright, M., 2013. A convenient truth: Private equity and portfolio company growth. https://ssrn.com/abstract=2290983.

Wood, G. and Wright, M., 2010. Private equity and human resource management: An emerging agenda, *Human Relations* **63**(9): 1279–96.

Wright, M., 2007. Private equity and management buyouts. In Landstrom, H. (ed.), *Handbook of research on venture capital* (Cheltenham: Edward Elgar).

Wright, M. and Coyne, J., 1985. *Management Buyouts* (Beckenham: Croom Helm).

Wright, M., 1986. The make–buy decision and managing markets: The case of management buyouts, *Journal of Management Studies* **23**: 443–64.

Wright, M., 2013. Private equity: Managerial and policy implications, *Academy of Management Perspectives* **27**: 1–6.

Wright, M., Amess, K., Bacon, N., and Siegel, D., 2018. *The Routledge Companion to Management Buyouts* (London: Routledge).

Wright, M., Coyne, J., and Lockley, H., 1984. Management buyouts and trade unions: Dispelling the myths, *Industrial Relations Journal* **15**: 45–52.

Wright, M., Chiplin, B., Thompson, S., and Robbie, K., 1990a. Management buyouts, trade unions and employee ownership, *Industrial Relations Journal* **21**(2): 136–46.

Wright, M., Chiplin, B., Thompson, S., and Robbie, K., 1990b. Management buyouts and large–small firm relationships, *Management International Review* **30**: 55–72.

Wright, M., Cressy, R., Wilson, N., and Farag, H., 2014. Financial restructuring and recovery in private equity buyouts: The UK evidence, *Venture Capital: An International Journal* **6**: 109–29.

Wright, M., Robbie, K., Thompson, S., and Starkey, K., 1994. Longevity and the life cycle of MBOs, *Strategic Management Journal* **15**: 215–27.

Wright, M., Thompson, S., and Robbie, K., 1992. Venture capital and management-led leveraged buyouts: A European perspective, *Journal of Business Venturing* **7**: 47–71.

Wright, M., Thompson, S., Robbie, K., and Wong, P., 1995. Management buyouts in the short and long term, *Journal of Business Finance and Accounting* **22**: 461–82.

Wright, M., Wilson, N., Robbie, K., and Ennew, C., 1996. An analysis of failure in UK buyouts and buy-ins, *Managerial and Decision Economics* **17**: 57–70.

Wright, M., Wilson, N., and Robbie, K., 1996. The longer term effects of management-led buyouts, *Journal of Entrepreneurial and Small Business Finance* 5: 213–34.

Wright, M., Robbie, K., Romanet, Y., Thompson, S., Joachimsson, R., Bruining, H., and Herst, A., 1993. Harvesting and the longevity of management buyouts and buy-ins: A four country study, *Entrepreneurship Theory and Practice* 18: 90–109.

Wright, M., Burrows, A., Ball, R., Scholes, L., Meuleman, M., and Amess, K., 2007. The implications of alternative investment vehicles for corporate governance: A survey of empirical research. A report prepared for the Steering Group on Corporate Governance, OECD.

Wright, M., Weir, C., and Burrows, A., 2007. Irrevocable commitments, going private and private equity, *European Financial Management* 13: 757–75.

Zahra, S. A., 1995. Corporate entrepreneurship and financial performance: The case of management leveraged buyouts, *Journal of Business Venturing* 10: 225–47.

Zhou, D., Jelic, R., and Wright, M., 2014. SMBOs: buying time or improving performance? *Managerial and Decision Economics* 35: 88–102.

ICAEW connects more than 180,000 chartered accountants and students worldwide, providing this community of professionals with the power to build and sustain strong economies.

The Corporate Finance Faculty is the ICAEW's centre of professional expertise in corporate finance. It contributes to policy development and many consultations by international organisations, governments, regulators and other professional bodies.

It provides a wide range of services, information, guidance, events and media to its members, including its highly regarded magazine Corporate Financier and its popular series of best-practice guidelines.

The faculty's extensive network includes more than 80 member organisations as well as many individuals. They are drawn from major professional services groups, specialist advisory firms, companies, banks and alternative lenders, private equity, venture capital, law firms, brokers, consultants, policy-makers and academic experts. More than 40 per cent of the faculty's membership is from beyond ICAEW. The faculty also provides technical expertise for the ICAEW's Diploma in Corporate Finance.

Author Index

Subject Index